W9-CQQ-864

Adobe® Photoshop® CS2

User Guide

Adobe

© 2005 Adobe Systems Incorporated. All rights reserved.

Adobe® Photoshop® CS2 User Guide for Windows® and Macintosh

If this guide is distributed with software that includes an end user agreement, this guide, as well as the software described in it, is furnished under license and may be used or copied only in accordance with the terms of such license. Except as permitted by any such license, no part of this guide may be reproduced, stored in a retrieval system, or transmitted, in any form or by any means, electronic, mechanical, recording, or otherwise, without the prior written permission of Adobe Systems Incorporated. Please note that the content in this guide is protected under copyright law even if it is not distributed with software that includes an end user license agreement.

The content of this guide is furnished for informational use only, is subject to change without notice, and should not be construed as a commitment by Adobe Systems Incorporated. Adobe Systems Incorporated assumes no responsibility or liability for any errors or inaccuracies that may appear in the informational content contained in this guide.

Please remember that existing artwork or images that you may want to include in your project may be protected under copyright law. The unauthorized incorporation of such material into your new work could be a violation of the rights of the copyright owner. Please be sure to obtain any permission required from the copyright owner.

Any references to company names in sample templates are for demonstration purposes only and are not intended to refer to any actual organization.

Adobe, the Adobe logo, Acrobat, Acrobat Capture, Adobe Dimensions, Adobe Gamma, Adobe Premiere, After Effects, FrameMaker, GoLive, Illustrator, ImageReady, InDesign, the OpenType logo, PageMaker, Photomerge, Photoshop, PostScript, Streamline, and Version Cue are either registered trademarks or trademarks of Adobe Systems Incorporated in the United States and/or other countries.

Microsoft, OpenType, and Windows are either registered trademarks or trademarks of Microsoft Corporation in the United States and/or other countries. Apple, AppleTalk, ColorSync, LaserWriter, Mac, and Macintosh are trademarks of Apple Computer, Inc. registered in the U.S. and other countries. Kodak is a registered trademark of Eastman Kodak Company.

The Spelling portion of this product is based on Proximity Linguistic Technology. The Proximity Hyphenation System ©1989 All rights reserved Proximity Technology, Inc. Proximity and Linguibase are registered trademarks of Proximity Technology Inc. This product includes software developed by the Apache Software Foundation (www.apache.org). This product contains either BISAFE and/or TIPEM software by RSA Data Security, Inc. This product includes cryptographic software written by Eric Young (eay@cryptosoft.com). This software is based in part on the work of the Independent JPEG Group. © 1994 Hewlett Packard Company. Portions of this code are licensed from Apple Computer, Inc. under the terms of the Apple Public Source License Version 2. The source code version of the licensed code and the license are available at www.opensource.apple.com/apsl.

PANTONE® Colors displayed in the software application or in the user documentation may not match PANTONE-identified standards. Consult current PANTONE Color Publications for accurate color. PANTONE® and other Pantone, Inc. trademarks are the property of Pantone, Inc. © Pantone, Inc., 2003. Pantone, Inc. is the copyright owner of color data and/or software which are licensed to Adobe Systems Incorporated to distribute for use only in combination with Adobe Photoshop. PANTONE Color Data and/or Software shall not be copied onto another disk or into memory unless as part of the execution of Adobe Photoshop.

Notice to U.S. Government End Users: The Software and Documentation are "Commercial Items," as that term is defined at 48 C.F.R. §2.101, consisting of "Commercial Computer Software" and "Commercial Computer Software Documentation," as such terms are used in 48 C.F.R. §12.212 or 48 C.F.R. §227.7202, as applicable. Consistent with 48 C.F.R. §12.212 or 48 C.F.R. §§227.7202-1 through 227.7202-4, as applicable, the Commercial Computer Software and Commercial Computer Software Documentation are being licensed to U.S. Government end users (a) only as Commercial Items and (b) with only those rights as are granted to all other end users pursuant to the terms and conditions herein. Unpublished-rights reserved under the copyright laws of the United States. Adobe agrees to comply with all applicable equal opportunity laws including, if appropriate, the provisions of Executive Order 11246, as amended, Section 402 of the Vietnam Era Veterans Readjustment Assistance Act of 1974 (38 USC 4212), and Section 503 of the Rehabilitation Act of 1973, as amended, and the regulations at 41 CFR Parts 60-1 through 60-60, 60-250, and 60-741. The affirmative action clause and regulations contained in the preceding sentence shall be incorporated by reference.

Adobe Systems Incorporated, 345 Park Avenue, San Jose, California 95110, USA.

Part Number: 90056847 (04/05)

Contents

❷ Indicates a topic that appears only in Help

❷ Indicates a topic that appears only in Help

❷ Indicates a topic that appears only in Help

Drawing

Painting

Chapter 14: Applying filters for special effects

Type

❓ Indicates a topic that appears only in Help

Chapter 1: Getting started

Installation and registration

To install

1 Close any Adobe® applications that are open.

2 Insert the product CD into your computer's CD drive.

3 Double-click the CD icon, and then follow the on-screen instructions.

After the installation, you may be prompted to activate your copy of the product. (See `To activate' on page 1.)

For more detailed instructions about installing the product, see the How To Install file on the product CD. For instructions about uninstalling the product, see the How To Uninstall file on the product CD.

To activate

Activation is a simple, anonymous process you must complete within 30 days of installing the product. Activation allows you to continue using the product, and it helps prevent casual copying of the product onto more computers than the license agreement allows. To learn more about activation, visit the Adobe website at www.adobe.com/activation/main.html.

1 Start the product to access the Activation dialog box. (If you've just installed Adobe Creative Suite or Adobe Photoshop®, the Activation dialog box appears automatically.)

2 Follow the on-screen instructions.

Important: If you intend to install the product on a different computer, you must first transfer the activation to that computer. To transfer an activation, choose Help > Transfer Activation.

For more detailed instructions about activating the product and transferring an activation, see the How To Install file on the product CD.

To register

Register your Adobe product to receive complimentary support on installation and product defects and notifications about product updates. Registering your product also gives you access to the wealth of tips, tricks, and tutorials in Adobe Studio® and access to Adobe Studio Exchange, an online community where users download and share thousands of free actions, plug-ins, and other content for use with Adobe products. Adobe Studio is available in English, French, German, and Japanese. Find it from the home page of the Adobe website.

❖ Do one of the following:

• Install and activate the software to access the Registration dialog box, and then follow the on-screen instructions. An active Internet connection is required.

• Register at any time by choosing Help > Registration.

Adobe Help Center

About Adobe Help Center

Adobe Help Center is a free, downloadable application that includes three primary features.

Product Help Provides Help topics for Adobe Photoshop Elements and Adobe CS2 products installed on your system. (If none of these products are installed, Help topics for them aren't available.) Help topics are updated periodically and can be downloaded through Adobe Help Center preferences.

Expert Support Provides information about Adobe Expert Support plans and lets you store details about plans you've purchased. If you have an active support plan, you can also use the Expert Support section to submit web cases—questions sent to Adobe support professionals over the web. To access links in the Expert Support section, you must have an active Internet connection.

More Resources Provides easy access to the extensive resources on Adobe.com, including support pages, user forums, tips and tutorials, and training. You can also use this area to store contact information for friends, colleagues, or support professionals, or even websites you turn to for inspiration or troubleshooting information.

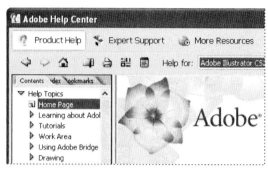

Product Help, Expert Support, and More Resources in Adobe Help Center

To check for updates

Adobe periodically provides updates to software and to topics in Adobe Help Center. You can easily obtain these updates through Adobe Help Center. An active Internet connection is required.

1 Click the Preferences button 🔲.

2 In the Preferences dialog box, click Check For Updates. If updates are available, follow the on-screen directions to download and save them.

To set Adobe Help Center preferences

1 Click the Preferences button 🔲. Set any of the following options:

Region Specifies your geographical location. Changing this option may affect which services are available to you.

Language Specifies the language in which Expert Support content is displayed.

Display Renewal Reminders For Expert Support Contracts Displays reminder screens when your Expert Support plan has almost expired. Deselect this option if you'd like to turn off these reminders.

Enable Auto Login For Web Case Submission Allows you to submit support questions over the web. This option is available only if you have an active Expert Support plan.

User Interface Language Specifies the language in which Adobe Help Center interface text is displayed.

Check For Updates Searches for new updates to software and Help topics as they become available from Adobe.

Network Administrators Displays options for network administration.

2 Click OK.

To display More Resources

The More Resources section in Adobe Help Center provides easy access to some of the content and services available from the Adobe website, including support, training, and tutorials.

❖ To display this section, click More Resources.

To add contact information in More Resources

1 Click More Resources, and then click Personal Contacts.

2 Do any of the following:

• To add a contact, click New, type the contact information you want to save, and click OK.

• To edit a contact, click a contact in the list, click Edit, make changes to the information, and click OK.

• To delete a contact, click a contact in the list, and then click Delete. To confirm the deletion, click Yes when prompted, or click No to cancel.

Using Help

Using Help

The complete documentation for using your Adobe product is available in Help, a browser-based system you can access through Adobe Help Center. Help topics are updated periodically, so you can always be sure to have the most recent information available. For more information, search for "check for updates" in Help.

Important: Adobe Help systems include all of the information in the printed user guides, plus additional information not included in print. The Resources and Extras CD included with the software also includes a PDF version of the complete Help content, optimized for printing.

Product Help section of Adobe Help Center
A. *Returns you to Help home page* **B.** *Adds bookmark for current topic* **C.** *Prints contents of right pane* **D.** *Opens Preferences dialog box* **E.** *Opens About Adobe Help Center window*

To navigate Help

❖ Do any of the following:

• To view Help for a product, choose the product name from the Help For menu. (To view only topics that apply across all Creative Suite products, choose Adobe Creative Suite.)

• To expand or collapse a section, click the blue triangle to the left of the section name.

• To display a topic , click its title.

To search Help topics

Search using words or phrases to quickly find topics. You can search Help for one product or for all Adobe products you've installed. If you find a topic that you may want to view again, bookmark it for quick retrieval.

1 In Adobe Help Center, click Product Help.

2 Type one or more words in the Search box. To search across Help for all Adobe products you have installed, click the black triangle to the left of the Search box and choose Search All Help.

Search Help for one product or for all products you've installed

3 Click Search. Topics matching the search words appear in the navigation pane.

4 To view a topic, click its title.

5 To return to the navigation pane, do one of the following:

• Click the Home button.

• Click the Back button.

• Click Next Topic or Previous Topic.

Search tips

Adobe Help search works by searching the entire Help text for topics that contain all of the words typed in the Search box. These tips can help you improve your search results in Help:

- If you search using a phrase, such as "shape tool," put quotation marks around the phrase. The search returns only those topics containing all words in the phrase.

- Make sure that the search terms are spelled correctly.

- If a search term doesn't yield results, try using a synonym, such as "web" instead of "Internet."

To print a topic from Help

1 Select the topic you want to print, and click the Print button.

2 Choose the printer you'd like to use, and then click Print.

To change the view

By default, Adobe Help Center opens in Full view. Full view gives you access to the Product Help, Expert Support, and More Resources sections. Switch to Compact view when you want to see only the selected Help topic and you want to keep the Help window on top of your product workspace.

❖ Click the view icon 🖳 to switch between Full and Compact views.

To use bookmarks

You can bookmark especially helpful topics for easy access, just as you bookmark pages in a web browser, and reread them at another time.

1 Click the Bookmarks tab in the navigation pane to view the bookmarks.

2 Do any of the following in the Bookmarks pane:

- To create a bookmark, select the topic you want to mark, and click the Bookmark button 🗐. When the Bookmark dialog box appears, type a new name in the text box if desired, and then click OK.

- To delete a bookmark, select it and click the Delete button. Click Yes to confirm the deletion.

- To rename a bookmark, select it and then click the Rename button 🗐. In the dialog box, type a new name for the bookmark and then click OK.

- To move a bookmark, select it and then click the Move Up button 🔼 or the Move Down button 🔽.

Tips and training

Learning resources

Adobe provides a wide range of resources to help you learn and use Adobe products.

- Tutorials in Help: Short step-by-step lessons through Adobe Help Center.

- Total Training Video Workshop CD: Professional training videos from experts.

- Adobe Studio: Videos, tips and tricks, and other learning material on Adobe products.

- *Adobe Creative Suite Design Guide* (Adobe Creative Suite only): A full-color printed book about using Adobe Creative Suite 2 as a complete design and publishing toolbox, including five guided projects on print, web, and mobile workflows.

- Technical information: Reference material, scripting guides, and other in-depth information.

- Other resources: Training, books, user forums, product certification, and more.

- Support: Complimentary and paid technical support options from Adobe. For more information, see the Expert Support section in Adobe Help Center.

- Extras: Downloadable content and software.

Tutorials in Help

The Help system for each Adobe CS2 product includes several step-by-step tutorials on key features and concepts. These tutorials are also available in the complete, printable, PDF version of the Help contents, included on the Resources and Extras CD.

To use these tutorials with the product, select the tutorial you want from the Contents pane in Adobe Help Center, and click the View icon to switch to Compact view. Compact view keeps the Help window on top of the application windows, regardless of what window or application is selected. Drag an edge or a corner of the Help window to resize it.

Total Training Video Workshop CD

Presented by experts in their fields, Total Training videos provide overviews, demos of key new features, and many useful tips and techniques for beginning

and advanced users. Look for accompanying step-by-step instructions to selected Total Training videos in monthly updates to Adobe Studio.

Short Total Training web videos on a variety of products and topics are also available in Adobe Studio, and complete Total Training courseware can be purchased online from the Adobe Store.

Adobe Studio

Adobe Studio provides a huge wealth of tips and tricks, tutorials, and instructional content in video, Adobe PDF, and HTML, authored by experts from Adobe and its publishing partners. You can search the entire collection or sort by product, topic, date, and type of content; new content is added monthly. Adobe Studio is available in English, French, German, and Japanese. Find it from the home page of the Adobe website.

Tips and tutorials in Adobe Studio

Technical information

The Technical information folder on the Resources and Extras CD included with your Adobe product includes several useful documents in PDF, fully searchable and optimized for printing. These documents provide conceptual and reference material on various in-depth topics, such as scripting, transparency, and high-end printing. For complete developer documentation and resources, visit the Developers area of the Adobe website at http://partners.adobe.com/public/developer/main.html. For additional backgrounders and instructional content, visit Adobe Studio.

The Resources and Extras CD also includes the entire Help content optimized for printing. Note that the Help content includes everything in the printed Adobe user guides, plus much more.

Other resources

Additional sources of information and help are available for Adobe products.

* Visit the Training area of the Adobe website for access to Adobe Press books; online, video, and instructor-led training resources; Adobe software certification programs; and more.

* Visit the Adobe user forums, where users share tips, ask questions, and find out how others are getting the most out of their software. User forums are available in English, French, German, and Japanese on the main Support page of your local Adobe website.

* Visit the Support area of the Adobe website for additional information about free and paid technical support options. Top issues are listed by product on the Adobe U.S. and Adobe Japan websites.

* Visit the Developers area of the Adobe website to find information for software and plug-in developers, including SDKs, scripting guides, and technical resources.

* Click More Resources in Adobe Help Center to access many of the resources on the Adobe website and to create your own list of frequently visited user groups and websites and valuable contacts.

* Look in Bridge Center for RSS feeds on the latest technical announcements, tutorials, and events. To access Bridge Center, select it in the Favorites panel

in Adobe Bridge. (Bridge Center is available with Adobe Creative Suite only.)

Extras

The Resources and Extras CD included with your CS2 product includes a Goodies folder that contains bonus content and files for use with your Adobe product. For more free content and add-ons, visit Adobe Studio Exchange, an online community where users download and share thousands of free actions, plug-ins, and other content for use with Adobe products. To visit Adobe Studio Exchange, go to Adobe Studio from the home page of the Adobe website.

In addition, your CS2 product includes Adobe Stock Photos, an integrated service available within Adobe Bridge that lets you search, view, try, and buy royalty-free stock photography from leading stock libraries. Because of the tight integration between Stock Photos and CS2 products, you can download images directly into your Adobe Illustrator®, Adobe InDesign®, and Adobe GoLive® projects. From Photoshop, you can open any downloaded image.

Other downloads

The Downloads area of the Adobe website includes free updates, tryouts, and other useful software. In addition, the Plug-ins section of the Adobe Store provides access to thousands of plug-ins from third-party developers, helping you automate tasks, customize workflows, create specialized professional effects, and more.

What's new

New features

Workflow improvements

Adobe Bridge Simplify file handling in Photoshop and within Adobe Creative Suite with Adobe Bridge, the next-generation file browser. Efficiently browse, tag, search, and process your images. (See `About Adobe Bridge' on page 53.)

Color management improvements Maintain common color settings throughout the Adobe Creative Suite components. Print with the simplified printing interface for color management. (See `To synchronize color settings across Adobe applications' on page 191.)

Version Cue® 2.0 Manage files and versions as a single user or in a small workgroup. Integrate with Adobe Bridge to manage files for your Photoshop and Adobe Creative Suite projects. (See `Version Cue managed projects' on page 85.)

Enhanced photo capabilities

Multi-image Camera Raw Process an entire photo shoot in a fraction of the time. With support for a comprehensive range of digital cameras, you can automatically adjust settings, convert to universal Digital Negative (DNG) format, and apply nondestructive edits to batches of images. (See `The Camera Raw plug-in' on page 145.)

High Dynamic Range (HDR) Work with images in 32-bits-per-channel, extended dynamic range. Photographers can capture the full dynamic range of a scene with multiple exposures and merge the files into a single image. (See `About High Dynamic Range images' on page 139.)

Optical lens correction Correct for lens aberrations such as barrel and pincushion distortion, chromatic aberration, and lens vignetting. Easily correct image perspective using the filter's grid. (See `The Lens Correction filter' on page 256.)

Noise reduction Reduce digital image noise, JPEG artifacts, and scanned film grain. (See `Reducing image noise' on page 258.)

Smart Sharpen filter Sharpen images with new algorithms for better edge detection and reduced sharpening halos. Control the amount of sharpening in the highlights and shadows. (See `To use the Smart Sharpen filter' on page 260.)

Spot Healing tool Quickly heal spots and blemishes without selecting source content. (See `To use the Spot Healing Brush tool' on page 273.)

One-click red-eye correction Fix red eyes with one click. Set options to adjust pupil size and darkening amount. (See `To remove red eye' on page 275.)

Blur filters Apply blur effects using new blur filters: Box Blur, Shape Blur, and Surface Blur. (See Photoshop Help.)

Productivity boosters

Customizable menus Set up and save custom menus and workspaces, highlight new or commonly used menu items, and reduce on-screen clutter for easier access to the tools you need. (See `To define a set of menus' on page 40.)

Image Processor Process a batch of files to multiple file formats. (See Photoshop Help.)

All new PDF engine Comprehensive, customizable presets and PDF 1.6/Acrobat 7.0 compatibility. (See `Saving files in Photoshop PDF format' on page 336.)

Script and action event manager Set JavaScripts and Photoshop actions to run automatically when a specified Photoshop event occurs. (See Photoshop Help.)

UI font size customization Customize the size of text in the options bar, palettes, and the Layer Style dialog box. (See `To change the font size in the work area' on page 40.)

Update Manager Automatically search for Photoshop updates.

Variables Create data-driven graphics in Photoshop as you now do in ImageReady. (See Photoshop Help.)

Video preview Display your document on a video monitor using a Firewire (IEEE1394) link. (See `To preview your document on a video monitor' on page 379.)

WYSIWYG Font menu Preview font families and font styles directly in the Font menu. (See Photoshop Help.)

Designer enhancements

Vanishing Point Paste, clone, and paint image elements that automatically match the perspective planes in an image. (See `About Vanishing Point' on page 277.)

Smart Objects Perform nondestructive transforms of embedded vector and of pixel data. Create multiple instances of embedded data and easily update all instances at once. (See `Smart Objects' on page 316.)

Multiple layer control Work with layers as objects. Select multiple layers and move, group, align, and transform them. (See `Selecting layers' on page 290 and `To group and ungroup layers' on page 291.)

Image Warp Easily create packaging mock-ups or other dimensional effects by wrapping an image around any shape or stretching, curling, and bending an image using Image Warp. (See `The Warp command' on page 269.)

Animation Create animated GIF files in Photoshop much as you create animation in ImageReady. (See Photoshop Help.)

Japanese type features Format text with new character alignment (Mojisoroe) and more Kinsoku Shori types. (See Photoshop Help.)

Smart Guides Align the content of layers as you move them using guidelines that appear only when you need them. (See `About guides and the grid' on page 36.)

Integrated Adobe Online Services Access and download professional Adobe Stock Photos and share and print online with Adobe Photoshop Services. (See `About Adobe Stock Photos' on page 75.)

What's changed

If you've worked with a previous version of Photoshop, you'll find that some things work a little differently in Photoshop CS2.

Layer grouping You can group layers using the keyboard shortcut Control+G (Windows) or Command+G (Mac OS). The shortcut for creating a clipping mask is now Control+Alt+G (Windows) or Command+Option+G (Mac OS).

Layer linking and multiple layer selection Working with multiple layers is easier now because you can select multiple layers in the Layers palette or in the document window using the Move tool. The layer linking column was removed. To link layers, select multiple layers and click the link icon at the bottom of the Layers palette. Some menu commands that work on linked layers have been changed to work on multiple layers.

To add or subtract layers from a selection in the Layers palette, Shift-click (or drag) in the document with the Move tool, with the Auto Select Layer option selected. Previously, Shift-clicking linked and unlinked layers. For more information, see `To select layers in the Layers palette' on page 291.

Merging layers To merge all visible layers into a new layer, press Alt (Windows) or Option (Mac OS) and choose Layer > Merge Visible. Previously you created a new layer and selected it before merging. To merge any two layers, select them in the Layers palette and choose Layer > Merge Layers. You can still merge two adjacent layers in the Layers palette by selecting the top layer and choosing Layer Merge Down.

Loading a selection To load a layer as a selection, Control-click (Windows) Command-click (Mac OS) the layer's thumbnail in the Layers palette. Previously you could click anywhere in the layer.

Clipping mask visibility To hide all layers except the clipping mask layer and the layer it is clipped to, Alt-click (Windows) or Option-click (Mac OS) the layer's visibility icon. Previously, Alt-clicking or Option-clicking hid all layers.

File Browser Adobe Bridge handles all the tasks that you previously did in the File Browser. Flagging is now handled by the star ratings. Files previously flagged are

now marked with one star. In Bridge, Control+D
(Windows) or Command+D (Mac OS) now duplicates an image rather than deselecting it in the
thumbnail view.

Placing a file Files that you place into Photoshop with
the Place command now become Smart Objects.

Chapter 2: Work area

Work area basics

About the Welcome window

When you launch Photoshop or ImageReady, the Welcome window automatically appears. Select the options in this window to learn about Photoshop or ImageReady by reading tutorials or by viewing a movie about new features. In Photoshop, you can also learn how to set up a color management system.

Choose Help > Welcome Screen to display the window if it's not already open.

About the work area

The Photoshop and ImageReady work area is arranged to help you focus on creating and editing images.

The work area has these components:

Menu bar Contains menus organized by tasks. For example, the Layers menu contains commands for working with layers. In Photoshop, you can customize the menu bar by showing, hiding, or adding color to menu items.

Options bar Provides options for using a tool.

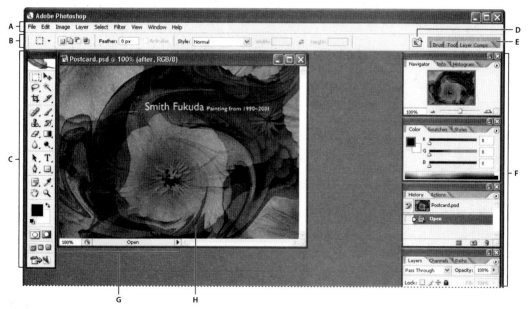

Photoshop work area
A. Menu bar B. Options bar C. Toolbox D. Go to Bridge E. Palette well F. Palettes G. Status bar H. Active image area

Toolbox Contains tools for creating and editing images.

Active image area Displays the active open file. The window containing an open file is also called the *document window*.

Palette well Helps you organize the palettes in your work area.

Palettes Help you monitor and modify images. You can customize the palette locations in the workspace. In Photoshop, you can also show, hide, or add color to items in palette menus.

In Photoshop, you can change the font size of the text in the options bar, palettes, and tool tips.

About the status bar

The status bar is located at the bottom of every document window and displays useful information—such as the current magnification and file size of the active image, and brief instructions for using the active tool. The status bar also displays Version Cue information if you have Version Cue enabled.

Note: In ImageReady, if the document window is wide enough, two image information boxes appear, enabling you to view two different information options for the image at the same time. You can also view copyright and authorship information that has been added to the file. This information includes standard file information and Digimarc watermarks. Photoshop automatically scans opened images for watermarks using the Digimarc Detect Watermark plug-in. If a watermark is detected, Photoshop displays a copyright symbol in the image window's title bar and updates the Copyright & URL area of the File Info dialog box.

To display file information in the document window

1 Click the triangle in the bottom border of the document window.

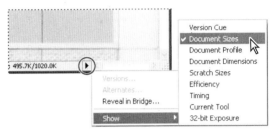

File information view options in Photoshop

2 Choose a view option from the pop-up menu:

Note: If you have Version Cue enabled, choose from the Show submenu.

Version Cue Displays the Version Cue workgroup status of your document, such as open, unmanaged, unsaved, and so forth. This option is available only if you have Version Cue enabled.

Document Sizes Information on the amount of data in the image. The number on the left represents the printing size of the image—approximately the size of the saved, flattened file in Adobe Photoshop format. The number on the right indicates the file's approximate size, including layers and channels.

Document Profile The name of the color profile used by the image.

Document Dimensions The dimensions of the image.

Scratch Sizes Information on the amount of RAM and the scratch disk used to process the image. The number on the left represents the amount of memory currently being used by the program to display all open images. The number on the right represents the total amount of RAM available for processing images.

Efficiency The percentage of time actually spent performing an operation instead of reading or writing to the scratch disk. If the value is below 100%, Photoshop is using the scratch disk and is therefore operating more slowly.

Timing The time it took to complete the last operation.

Current Tool The name of the active tool.

32-bit Exposure Option for adjusting the preview image for viewing 32-bits-per-channel high dynamic range (HDR) images on your computer monitor. The slider is available only when the document window displays an HDR image.

Click anywhere in the file information area of the status bar to see a thumbnail preview showing how your document (at its current image size) will be printed in the current page setup.

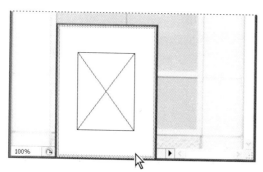

Click the file information area in the status bar to see a thumbnail preview of how the image will be printed.

For more information, see 'Version Cue managed projects' on page 85 and 'To adjust HDR image viewing' on page 143.

To display image information in ImageReady

1 Click an image information box at the bottom of the document window.

2 Select a view option:

Original/Optimized File Size The file size of the original and optimized images. The first value indicates the file size of the original image. The second value (present if the original image has been optimized) indicates the file size and file format of the optimized image based on the current settings in the Optimize palette.

Optimized Information The file format, file size, number of colors, and dither percentage of the optimized image.

Image Dimensions The pixel dimensions of the image.

Watermark Strength The strength of the Digimarc digital watermark, if present, in the optimized image.

Undo/Redo Status The number of undos and redos that are available for the image.

Original in Bytes The size, in bytes, of the original, flattened image.

Optimized in Bytes The size, in bytes, of the optimized image.

Optimized Savings The reduction percentage of the optimized image, followed by the difference in bytes between the original and optimized sizes.

Output Settings Output settings that control how HTML files are formatted, how files and slices are named, and how background images are handled when you save an optimized image.

Size/Download Time The file size of the optimized image and estimated download time using the selected modem speed.

Note: Download times may vary based on Internet traffic and modem compression schemes. The value displayed is an approximation.

For more information, see `Adding digital copyright information' on page 361.

To jump between Photoshop and ImageReady

You can easily jump between Photoshop and ImageReady to use features in both applications when preparing graphics for the web or other purposes. Jumping between the applications lets you use the full feature sets of both applications while maintaining a streamlined workflow. Files and documents updated in one application can be automatically updated in the other application. Jumping to an application eliminates the need to close the file in one application and reopen it in another.

❖ Do one of the following:

• Click the Edit In Photoshop button at the bottom of the toolbox.

• Choose File > Edit In Photoshop or File > Edit in ImageReady.

When you jump between Photoshop and ImageReady, the applications use a temp file for transferring changes.

Jumping to other applications

In addition to jumping to current versions of Photoshop, you can jump to other graphics-editing applications and HTML-editing applications from within Photoshop and ImageReady.

When you install Photoshop or ImageReady, Adobe graphics-editing and HTML-editing applications currently on your system are added to the Jump To submenu. You can add more applications, including non-Adobe applications, to the Jump To submenu.

When you jump to a graphics-editing application, the original file is opened in the destination application. When you jump to an HTML editor, the optimized file and the HTML file are saved and opened in the desti-nation application. If the image contains slices, all files for the full image are included. You can set a preference for automatically updating files when you jump to Photoshop or ImageReady after editing files in another application.

To jump to another application from ImageReady

1 Do one of the following:

• Choose File > Jump To, and choose the desired application from the submenu.

• If the desired application doesn't appear in the Jump To submenu, choose Other Graphics Editor or Other HTML Editor to specify the application.

2 If the file has been modified since the last save, choose an option in ImageReady for saving the file:

• Click Save, and save the file with its current name and location.

• Click Save As, and save the file with a new name, in a new location, or both.

To add an application to the Jump To submenu

1 Create a shortcut (Windows) or an alias (Mac OS) for the application you want to add to the menu.

2 Drag the icon for the shortcut or alias into the Jump To Graphics Editor folder or the Jump To HTML Editor folder, located in the Helpers folder inside the Photoshop program folder.

3 Restart ImageReady to view the application in the Jump To submenu.

To enable automatic file updates in ImageReady

You can set a preference to automatically update a file when returning to ImageReady from another application.

1 Do one of the following:

• (Windows) Choose Edit > Preferences > General.

• (Mac OS) ImageReady > Preferences > General.

2 Select Auto-Update Open Documents.

Palettes and menus

To use palettes

❖ Palettes help you monitor and modify your work. You can customize the default palette arrangement in the following ways:

• To hide or show all palettes, including the toolbox and options bar, press Tab. To hide or show all palettes except for the toolbox, press Shift+Tab.

• To display a palette menu, position the pointer on the triangle in the upper right corner of the palette, and press the mouse button.

• To change the size of a palette, drag any corner of the palette (Windows) or drag the size box at its lower right corner (Mac OS). Some palettes, such as the Color palette, cannot be resized by dragging.

• To collapse a group of palettes to their titles only, double-click the palette's tab, or click the Minimize button (Windows) or the Zoom box (Mac OS). You can open the palette menu even when the palette is collapsed.

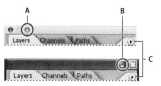

Using palettes
*A. Click to collapse or expand a Mac OS palette **B.** Click to collapse or expand a Windows palette **C.** Click to display the palette menu*

• To make a palette appear at the front of its group, click the palette's tab.

• To move an entire palette group, drag its title bar.

- To rearrange or separate a palette group, drag a palette's tab. Dragging a palette outside an existing group creates a new palette window.

- To move a palette to another group, drag the palette's tab to that group.

- To dock palettes so that they move together, drag a palette's tab to the bottom of another palette.

- To move an entire docked palette group, drag its title bar.

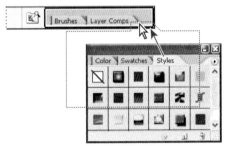

Docking a palette in the palette well

- To return palettes to their default sizes and positions, choose Window > Workspace > Reset Palette Locations (Photoshop) or Window > Workspace > Default Palette Locations (ImageReady).

- (ImageReady) To show or hide options for palettes that include hidden options (the Optimize, Layer Options, and Slice palettes), click the double triangle icon in a palette tab to cycle through palette displays, or choose Show Options or Hide Options from the palette menu.

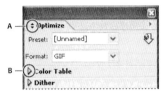

ImageReady palette
A. *Click to show options for the palette* **B.** *Click to show options for the option set*

About the palette well

The Photoshop and ImageReady options bars include a palette well that helps you organize and manage palettes. The palette well stores, or docks, palettes that you use frequently, so that you don't have to keep them open on the work area.

The palette well is available only when the screen resolution is greater than 800 pixels x 600 pixels (a setting of at least 1024 x 768 is recommended).

Click a palette's tab to use the palette in the palette well. The palette remains open until you click outside it or click the palette's tab again.

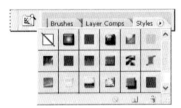

Docked palette in the palette well

To enter values in palettes, dialog boxes, and the tool options bar

❖ Do any of the following:

- Type a value in the text box, and press Enter or Return (Mac OS only).

- Drag the slider.

- (Photoshop) Move the pointer over the title of a slider or pop-up slider. When the pointer turns to a pointing finger, drag the scrubby slider to the left or right. This feature is available only for selected sliders and pop-up sliders.

- Drag the dial.

- Click the arrow buttons in the palette to increase or decrease the value.

- (Windows) Click the text box and then use the Up Arrow key and the Down Arrow key on the keyboard to increase or decrease the value.

- Select a value from the menu associated with the text box.

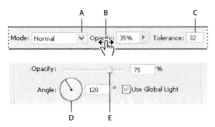

Ways to enter values
A. *Menu arrow* **B.** *Scrubby slider* **C.** *Text box* **D.** *Dial* **E.** *Slider*

For more information, see`About scrubby sliders' on page 19.

About pop-up sliders

Some palettes, dialog boxes, and options bars contain settings that use pop-up sliders (for example, the Opacity option in the Layers palette). If there is a triangle next to the text box, you can activate the pop-up slider by clicking the triangle. Position the pointer over the triangle next to the setting, hold down

the mouse button, and drag the slider or angle radius to the desired value. Click outside the slider box or press Enter to close the slider box. To cancel changes, press the Esc key.

To increase or decrease values in 10% increments when the pop-up slider box is open, hold down Shift and press the Up Arrow or Down Arrow key.

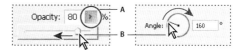

Using different kinds of pop-up sliders
A. *Click to open pop-up slider box.* **B.** *Drag slider or angle radius.*

💡 *(Photoshop) You can also "scrub" some pop-up sliders. For example, if you hold the pointer over the word "Fill" or "Opacity" in the Layers palette, the pointer changes to the Hand icon. Then you can move the pointer left or right to change the fill or opacity percentage.*

About scrubby sliders

In some palettes, dialog boxes, and options bars, you can drag scrubby sliders to change option values. Scrubby sliders are hidden until you position the pointer over the title of sliders and pop-up sliders. When the pointer changes to a pointing finger, you drag to the left or right. Holding down the Shift key while dragging accelerates the scrubbing by a factor of 10.

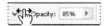

Hovering over the title of a slider or pop-up slider shows the scrubby slider

About pop-up palettes

Pop-up palettes provide easy access to available options for brushes, swatches, gradients, styles, patterns, contours, and shapes. You can customize pop-up palettes by renaming and deleting items and by loading, saving, and replacing libraries. You can also change the display of a pop-up palette to view items by their names, as thumbnail icons, or with both names and icons.

Click a tool thumbnail in the options bar to show its pop-up palette. Click an item in the pop-up palette to select it.

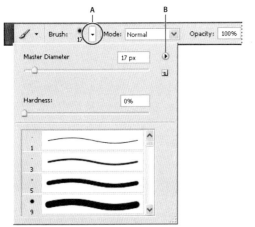

Viewing the Brush pop-up palette in the options bar
A. *Click to show the pop-up palette.* **B.** *Click to view the pop-up palette menu.*

To rename or delete an item in a pop-up palette

❖ Select an item, click the triangle in the upper right corner of the pop-up palette, and choose one of the following:

Rename Lets you enter a new name for the item.

Delete Deletes an item in the pop-up palette.

Note: You can also delete an item in a pop-up palette by holding down Alt (Windows) or Option (Mac OS) and clicking the item.

To customize the list of items in a pop-up palette

1 Click the triangle in the upper right corner of the pop-up palette to view the palette menu.

2 To return to the default library, choose the Reset command. You can either replace the current list or add the default library to the current list.

3 To load a different library, do one of the following:

- Choose the Load command to add a library to the current list. Then select the library file you want to use, and click Load.

- Choose the Replace command to replace the current list with a different library. Then select the library file you want to use, and click Load.

- Choose a library file (displayed at the bottom of the palette menu). Then click OK to replace the current list, or click Append to add the current list.

4 To save the current list as a library for later use, choose the Save command. Then enter a name for the library file, and click Save.

(Mac OS) Include the extension of the library file name so that you can easily share the libraries across operating systems. Select Append File Extension Always in the File Handling Preferences to append extensions to file names.

To change the display of items in a pop-up palette

1 Click the triangle in the upper right corner of the pop-up palette to view the palette menu.

2 Select a view option: Text Only, Small Thumbnail, Large Thumbnail, Small List, or Large List.

To display context menus

Context menus display commands relevant to the active tool, selection, or palette. They are distinct from the menus across the top of the work area.

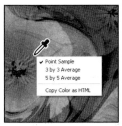

Viewing the context menu for the Eyedropper tool

1 Position the pointer over an image or palette item.

2 Right-click (Windows) or Control-click (Mac OS).

Tools

About tools and the toolbox

The first time you start the application, the toolbox appears at the left side of the screen. You can move the toolbox by dragging its title bar. You can also show or hide the toolbox by choosing Window > Tools.

Some tools in the toolbox have options that appear in the context-sensitive tool options bar. These include the tools that let you use type, select, paint, draw, sample, edit, move, annotate, and view images. Other tools in the toolbox allow you to change foreground/background colors, go to Adobe Online, work in different modes, and jump between Photoshop and ImageReady applications.

You can expand some tools to show hidden tools beneath them. A small triangle at the lower right of the tool icon signals the presence of hidden tools.

You can view information about any tool by positioning the pointer over it. The name of the tool appears in a *tool tip* below the pointer. Some tool tips contain links leading to additional information about the tool.

For more information, see each tool gallery in Photoshop Help.

To use a tool

❖ Do one of the following:

- Click a tool in the toolbox. If there is a small triangle at a tool's lower right corner, hold down the mouse button to view the hidden tools. Then click the tool you want to select.

- Press the tool's keyboard shortcut. The keyboard shortcut is displayed in its tool tip. For example, you can select the Move tool by pressing the V key.

Toolbox overview

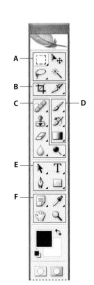

Ⓐ Selection tools

- ▪ ⬚ **Rectangular Marquee (M)**
- ○ Elliptical Marquee (M)
- Single Column Marquee (M)
- Single Row Marquee (M)
- ▪ ⊕ **Move (V)**
- ▪ ◯ **Lasso (L)**
- Polygonal Lasso (L)
- Magnetic Lasso (L)
- ▪ ✳ **Magic Wand (W)**

Ⓑ Crop and slice tools

- ▪ 🔲 **Crop (C)**
- ▪ ✂ **Slice (K)**
- Slice Select

Ⓒ Retouching tools

- ▪ ✐ **Spot Healing Brush (J)**
- Healing Brush (J)
- Patch (J)
- Red Eye (J)
- ▪ 🖉 **Clone Stamp (S)**
- Pattern Stamp (S)
- ▪ ⬛ **Eraser (E)**
- Background Eraser (E)
- Magic Eraser (E)
- ▪ ◯ **Blur (R)**
- Sharpen (R)
- Smudge (R)
- ▪ ◍ **Dodge (O)**
- Burn (O)
- Sponge (O)

Ⓓ Painting tools

- ▪ ✎ **Brush (B)**
- Pencil (B)
- Color Replacement (B)
- ▪ ✐ **History Brush (Y)**
- Art History Brush (Y)
- ▪ ▭ **Gradient (G)**
- Paint Bucket (G)

Ⓔ Drawing and type tools

- ▪ ▸ **Path Selection (A)**
- Direct Selection (A)
- ▪ ◊ **Pen (P)**
- Freeform Pen (P)
- Add Anchor Point (P)
- Delete Anchor Point (P)
- Convert Anchor Point (P)
- ▪ T **Horizontal Type (T)**
- Vertical Type (T)
- Horizontal Type Mask (T)
- Vertical Type Mask (T)
- ▪ ▭ **Rectangle (U)**
- Rounded Rectangle (U)
- Ellipse (U)
- Polygon (U)
- Line (U)
- Custom Shape (U)

Ⓕ Annotation, measuring, and navigation tools

- ▪ 📝 **Notes (N)**
- Audio Annotation (N)
- ▪ ✒ **Eyedropper (I)**
- Color Sampler (I)
- Measure (I)
- ▪ ✋ **Hand (H)**
- ▪ 🔍 **Zoom (Z)**

Ⓖ ImageReady only tools

- ▪ 🗺 **Rectangle Image Map (P)**
- Circle Image Map (P)
- Polygon Image Map (P)
- ▪ 🗺 **Image Map Select (J)**
- ▪ ▭ **Tab Rectangle (R)**
- Pill Rectangle (R)
- ▪ 🗺 **Toggle Image Map Visibility (A)**
- ▪ 🖼 **Toggle Slices Visibility (Q)**
- ▪ 🖐 **Preview Document (Y)**
- ▪ 🌐 **Preview in Browser (cmd+option+P)**

▪ Indicates default tool   * Keyboard shortcuts appear in parenthesis

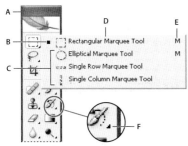

Using the selecting tools
A. *Toolbox* **B.** *Active tool* **C.** *Hidden tools* **D.** *Tool name* **E.** *Tool shortcut* **F.** *Hidden tool triangle*

Note: In ImageReady, click the downward-pointing triangle at the bottom of the hidden tools list to tear off a floating tool palette. Click the button at the top right (Windows) or top left (Mac OS) of the floating tool palette to close it.

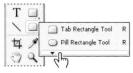

Clicking the triangle to "tear off" a floating tool palette

To cycle through hidden tools

You can select a preference that allows you to cycle through a set of hidden tools by holding down the Shift key. When this preference is not selected, you can cycle through a set of hidden tools by pressing the shortcut key (without holding down Shift).

1 Choose Edit > Preferences > General (Windows) or Photoshop > Preferences > General (Mac OS).

2 Select Use Shift Key For Tool Switch.

To display or hide tool tips

1 Do one of the following:

• (Windows) Choose Edit > Preferences > General.

• (Mac OS) Choose Photoshop > Preferences > General or choose ImageReady > Preferences > General.

2 Select or deselect Show Tool Tips.

Note: Tool tips may not be available in some dialog boxes.

About tool pointers

In most cases, the pointer for a tool is the same as the icon for that tool; you see that pointer when you select the tool. The default pointer for the marquee tools is the cross-hair pointer $+$; for the text tool, the default pointer is the I-beam $\mathbf{I}$; and for the painting tools the default pointer is the Brush Size icon.

Each default pointer has a different *hotspot*, where an effect or action in the image begins. With most tools, you can switch to precise cursors, which appear as cross hairs centered around the hotspot.

To change tool pointers

1 Do one of the following:

• (Photoshop) Choose Edit > Preferences > Display & Cursors (Windows) or choose Photoshop > Preferences > Display & Cursors (Mac OS).

• (ImageReady) Choose Edit > Preferences > Cursors (Windows) or choose ImageReady > Preferences > Cursors (Mac OS).

2 Choose a tool pointer setting under Painting Cursors and/or Other Cursors:

Standard Displays pointers as tool icons.

Precise Displays pointers as cross hairs.

Brush Size (painting cursors only) Displays the painting tool cursors as brush shapes representing the size of the current brush. Brush Size cursors may not appear for very large brushes.

3 (Photoshop) Select Brush Cursor options if you selected Brush Size as the tool pointer setting:

Normal The pointer outline corresponds to approximately 50% of the area that the tool will affect. This option shows the pixels that would be most visibly affected.

Full Size The pointer outline corresponds to nearly 100% of the area that the tool will affect, or nearly all the pixels that would be affected.

Always Show Crosshair Displays cross hairs in the center of the brush shape.

4 Click OK.

The Painting Cursors options control the pointers for the following tools:

- (Photoshop) Eraser, Pencil, Paintbrush, Healing Brush, Rubber Stamp, Pattern Stamp, Smudge, Blur, Sharpen, Dodge, Burn, and Sponge tools

- (ImageReady) Paintbrush, Pencil, and Eraser tools

The Other Cursors options control the pointers for the following tools:

- (Photoshop) Marquee, Lasso, Polygonal Lasso, Magic Wand, Crop, Slice, Patch, Eyedropper, Pen, Gradient, Line, Paint Bucket, Magnetic Lasso,

Magnetic Pen, Freeform Pen, Measure, and Color Sampler tools

- (ImageReady) Marquee, Lasso, Magic Wand, Eyedropper, Paint Bucket, and Slice tools

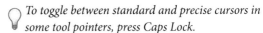 *To toggle between standard and precise cursors in some tool pointers, press Caps Lock.*

Using the options bar

The options bar appears below the menu bar at the top of the work area. The options bar is context sensitive—it changes as you select different tools. Some settings in the options bar (such as painting modes and opacity) are common to several tools, and some (such as the Auto Erase setting for the Pencil tool) are specific to one tool.

You can move the options bar in the work area by using the gripper bar, and you can dock it at the top or bottom of the screen. Tool tips appear when you position the pointer over a tool. To show or hide the options bar, choose Window > Options.

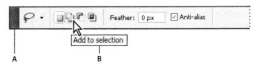

Lasso options bar
A. Gripper bar B. Tool tip

(Photoshop) To return tools to their default settings, right-click (Windows) or Control-click (Mac OS) the tool icon in the options bar, and then choose Reset Tool or Reset All Tools from the context menu.

(ImageReady) To return tools to their default settings, choose Edit > Preferences > General (Windows), or choose ImageReady > Preferences > General (Mac OS) and then click Reset All Tools.

For more information on setting options for a specific tool, search for the tool's name in Photoshop Help.

Using tool presets

Tool presets let you save and reuse tool settings. You can load, edit, and create libraries of tool presets using the Tool Preset picker in the options bar, the Tool Presets palette, and the Preset Manager.

To choose a tool preset, click the Tool Preset picker in the options bar, and select a preset from the pop-up palette. You can also choose Window > Tool Presets and select a preset in the Tools Presets palette.

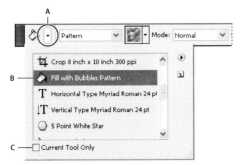

Viewing the Tool Preset picker
A. *Click the Tool Preset picker in the options bar to show the Tool Preset pop-up palette.* **B.** *Select a preset to change the tool's options to the preset, which applies each time you select the tool until you choose Reset Tool from the palette menu.* **C.** *Deselect to show all tool presets; select to show presets for only the tool selected in the toolbox.*

To create a tool preset

1 Choose a tool, and set the options you want to save as a tool preset in the options bar.

2 Do one of the following:

• Click the Tool Preset button next to the tool at the left of the options bar.

• Choose Window > Tool Presets to display the Tool Presets palette.

3 Do one of the following:

• Click the Create New Tool Preset button 🗐 .

• Choose New Tool Preset from the palette menu.

4 Enter a name for the tool preset, and click OK.

To change the list of tool presets

❖ Click the triangle to open the Tool Presets pop-up palette menu and choose one of the following:

Show All Tool Presets Shows all loaded presets.

Sort By Tool Sorts the presets by tool.

Show Current Tool Presets Shows only the loaded presets for the active tool. You can also select the Current Tool Only option in the Tool Presets pop-up palette.

Text Only, Small Text, or Large Text Determines how presets are displayed in the pop-up palette.

Note: To create, load, and manage libraries of tool presets, see 'About pop-up palettes' on page 20 and 'About the Preset Manager' on page 42.

Working with files

To close windows

❖ Do one of the following:

• Choose File > Close to close the active window.

• (Photoshop) Choose File > Close All to close all windows.

• (ImageReady and Windows) Choose Window > Arrange > Close All to close all windows.

To duplicate an image in Photoshop

You can duplicate an entire image (including all layers, layer masks, and channels) into available memory without saving to disk.

1 Open the image you want to duplicate.

2 Choose Image > Duplicate.

3 Enter a name for the duplicated image.

4 If you want to duplicate the image and merge the layers, select Duplicate Merged Layers Only. To preserve the layers, make sure this option is deselected.

5 Click OK.

💡 *To duplicate an image in Photoshop and automatically append the word "copy" to its file name, hold down Alt (Windows) or Option (Mac OS) when you choose Image > Duplicate.*

To duplicate an image in ImageReady

💡 *Using duplicates in ImageReady lets you experiment and then compare several versions of the optimized image to the original.*

1 Open the image you want to duplicate.

2 Do one of the following:

• Select the Original tab at the top of the image window.

• Select the Optimized tab at the top of the image window.

3 Do one of the following:

• Hold down Alt (Windows) or Option (Mac OS), and drag the Original or Optimized tab from the image window.

• Choose Image > Duplicate.

4 Name the duplicate, specify whether to flatten the layers, and click OK.

Note: When you duplicate an image in Optimized, 2-Up, or 4-Up view, the duplicate image appears in the Original view in the duplicate image window. If you want a duplicate optimized image to appear in the Optimized, 2-Up, or 4-Up view, duplicate the original image, and then select the Optimized, 2-Up, or 4-Up tab in the duplicate image window.

To close a file

1 Choose File > Close or File > Close All (Photoshop).

2 Choose whether or not to save the file:

• Click Yes (Windows) or Save (Mac OS) to save the file.

- Click No (Windows) or Don't Save (Mac OS) to close the file without saving it.

To quit Photoshop or ImageReady

1 Do one of the following:

- (Windows) Choose File > Exit.

- (Mac OS) Choose Photoshop > Quit or ImageReady > Quit.

2 Choose whether or not to save any open files:

- Click Yes (Windows) or Save (Mac OS) to save a file.

- Click No (Windows) or Don't Save (Mac OS) to close a file without saving it.

Viewing images

To change the screen mode

You can use the screen mode options to view your images on your entire screen. You can show or hide the menu bar, title bar, and scroll bars. You can choose from the following:

- The Standard screen mode is the default view, with menu bars, scroll bars, and other screen elements visible.

- Full Screen With Menu Bar view enlarges your view of an image but keeps the menu bar visible.

- (Photoshop) Full Screen mode lets you move the image around the screen to view different areas.

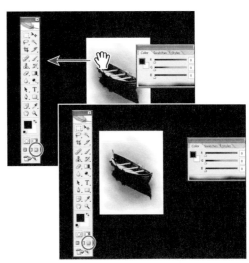

(Photoshop) Dragging an image in Full Screen mode

❖ Do one of the following:

- To display the default window, with the menu bar at the top and scroll bars on the side, choose View > Screen Mode > Standard, or click the Standard button 🔲 in the toolbox.

- To display a full-screen window with a menu bar and a 50% gray background, but no title bar or scroll bars, choose View > Screen Mode > Full Screen With Menu Bar, or click the Full Screen With Menu Bar button 🔲 in the toolbox.

- To display a full-screen window with only a black background (no title bar, menu bar, or scroll bars), choose View > Screen Mode > Full Screen, or click the Full Screen button 🔲 in the toolbox.

To view another area of an image

❖ Do one of the following:

• Use the window scroll bars.

• Select the Hand tool and drag to pan over the image.

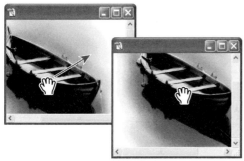

Dragging the Hand tool to view another area of an image

• Drag the colored box (proxy view area) in the Navigator palette.

💡 *To use the Hand tool while another tool is selected, hold down the spacebar as you drag in the image.*

To use the Navigator palette

You use the Navigator palette to quickly change the view of your artwork using a thumbnail display. The colored box in the Navigator (called the *proxy view area*) corresponds to the currently viewable area in the window.

❖ Do one or more of the following:

• To display the Navigator palette, select Window > Navigator.

• To change the magnification, type a value in the text box, click the Zoom Out or Zoom In button, or drag the zoom slider.

• To move the view of an image, drag the proxy view area in the image thumbnail. You can also click the image thumbnail to designate the viewable area.

• To change the color of the proxy view area, select Palette Options from the palette menu. Select a preset color from the Color pop-up menu, or double-click the color box to choose a custom color.

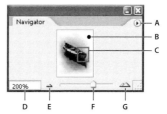

Navigator palette
A. Palette menu button B. Thumbnail display of artwork
C. Proxy preview area D. Zoom text box E. Zoom Out button
F. Zoom slider G. Zoom In button

To zoom in or out

❖ Do any of the following:

• (Photoshop) Select the Zoom tool 🔍 , and click either the Zoom In 🔍 or Zoom Out button 🔍 in the options bar. Click the area you want to magnify.

• Select the Zoom tool. The pointer becomes a magnifying glass with a plus sign in its center. Click the center of the area that you want to magnify, or hold down Alt (Windows) or Option (Mac OS) and click the center of the area that you want to reduce. Each click magnifies or reduces the view to the previous preset percentage.

Note: When you use the Zoom or Zoom Out tool, each click magnifies or reduces the image to the next preset percentage and centers the display around the point you click. When the image has reached its maximum magnification level of 1600% or minimum size of 1 pixel, the magnifying glass appears empty.

- Select the Zoom tool and drag a dotted rectangle, called a *marquee*, around the area you want to magnify. To move the marquee around the artwork, hold down the spacebar and continue dragging until the marquee is in the desired location.

- Choose View > Zoom In or View > Zoom Out. When the image reaches its maximum or minimum magnification, the command is dimmed.

- Set the zoom level at the lower left corner of the document window or in the Navigator palette (Photoshop).

- To display a file at 100%, choose View > Actual Pixels (Photoshop) or View > Actual Size (ImageReady).

- To change the view to fit the document window, choose View > Fit In Window.

(Photoshop) If your mouse has a scroll wheel, you can use it to zoom in or out after selecting the Zoom tool. Choose Edit > Preferences > General (Windows) or Photoshop > Preferences > General (Mac OS) and select the Zoom With Scroll Wheel option to enable this behavior.

To magnify by dragging

1 Select the Zoom tool.

2 Drag over the part of the image that you want to magnify.

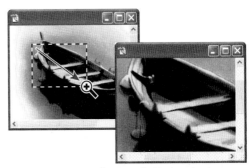

Dragging the Zoom tool to magnify the view of an image

The area inside the zoom marquee is displayed at the highest possible magnification. To move the marquee around the artwork in Photoshop, begin dragging a marquee and then hold down the spacebar while dragging.

To display an image at 100%

❖ Do one of the following:

- Double-click the Zoom tool in the toolbox.

- Choose View > Actual Pixels (Photoshop) or View > Actual Size (ImageReady).

- Enter 100% in the Status Bar and press Enter (Windows) or Return (Mac OS).

Note: The 100% view of an image displays an image as it will appear in a browser (based on the monitor resolution and the image resolution).

To fit an image to the screen

❖ Do one of the following:

- Double-click the Hand tool in the toolbox.

- Choose View > Fit On Screen.

- Select a zoom tool or the Hand tool, and click the Fit On Screen button in the options bar.

These options scale both the zoom level and the window size to fit the available screen space.

To automatically resize the window when zooming

❖ With the Zoom tool active, select Resize Windows To Fit in the options bar. The window is resized when you magnify or reduce the view of the image.

When Resize Windows To Fit is deselected (the default), the window maintains a constant size regardless of the image magnification. This can be helpful when using smaller monitors or working with tiled views.

Note: To automatically resize the window when using keyboard shortcuts to reduce or magnify an image view, choose Edit > Preferences > General (Windows) or Photoshop > Preferences > General (Mac OS), then select the Zoom Resizes Windows preference and click OK.

To view images in multiple windows

The document window is where your images appear. You can open multiple windows to display different images or different views of the same one. A list of open windows appears in the Window menu. To bring an open image to the front, choose the file name from the bottom of the Window menu. Available memory may limit the number of windows per image.

(ImageReady) The document window lets you switch easily between original and optimized views of an image using tabs, and to view the original image and multiple versions of an optimized image simultaneously.

1 Do one of the following:

- Choose Window > Arrange > New Window For *[Image File Name]*.

- (ImageReady) Drag any tab away from the document window.

2 If you want to arrange the windows, choose Window > Arrange and then choose one of the following:

Cascade Displays windows stacked and cascading from the upper left to the lower right of the screen.

Tile Horizontally or Tile Vertically Displays windows edge to edge. As you close images, the open windows are resized to fill the available space.

(Windows) Arrange Icons Aligns minimized image windows along the bottom of the screen.

💡 *(Photoshop) You can use the Hand tool's Scroll All Windows option to scroll through all open images. Select it in the options bar and drag in one image to scroll through all visible images.*

To zoom into or out of multiple images

1 Open one or more images, or copies of a single image.

2 Choose Window > Arrange > Tile Horizontally/Tile Vertically to display the images edge to edge.

3 Select the Zoom tool, and then do one of the following:

- Select Zoom All Windows in the options bar, and then click one of the images. The other images zoom in or out at the same time.

- Choose Window > Arrange > Match Zoom. Hold down the Shift key and click one of the images. The other images zoom in or out at the same magnification.

To match locations in images

1 Open one or more images, or multiple copies of a single image.

2 Choose either Window > Arrange > Tile Horizontally/Tile Vertically to display the images edge to edge.

3 Select the Hand tool, and then do one of the following:

- Select Scroll All Windows in the options bar, and then drag to view another area in one of the images.

- Choose Window > Arrange > Match Location, hold down the Shift key, and click or drag an area in one of the images. The other images snap to the corresponding area.

To match zoom and locations in images

1 Open one or more images, or multiple copies of a single image.

2 Choose Window > Arrange > Tile.

3 Choose Window > Arrange > Match Zoom And Location.

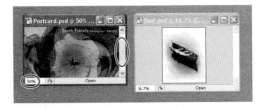
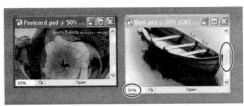

Without Match Zoom And Location (top), and with Match Zoom And Location (bottom) selected

4 Select the Zoom tool or the Hand tool.

5 Select one of the images, hold down the Shift key, and click in or drag an area of an image. The other images are magnified to the same percentage and snap to the area you clicked.

About the Info palette

The Info palette shows the color values beneath the pointer and, depending on the tool in use, gives other useful information. In Photoshop, the Info palette also displays a hint on using the selected tool, gives document status information, and can display 8-bit, 16-bit, or 32-bit values.

(Photoshop) The Info palette displays the following information:

- Depending on the option you specify, the Info palette displays 8-bit, 16-bit, or 32-bit values.

- When displaying CMYK values, the Info palette displays an exclamation point next to the CMYK values if the color beneath the pointer or color sampler is out of the printable CMYK color gamut.

- When a marquee tool is being used, the Info palette displays the *x* and *y* coordinates of the pointer position and the width (W) and height (H) of the marquee as you drag.

- When the Crop tool or Zoom tool is being used, the Info palette displays the width (W) and height (H) of the marquee as you drag. The palette also shows the angle of rotation of the crop marquee.

- When the Line tool, the Pen tool, or Gradient tool is being used, or when a selection is being moved, the Info palette displays the *x* and *y* coordinates of your starting position, the change in X (DX), the change in Y (DY), the angle (A), and the distance (D) as you drag.

- When a two-dimensional transformation command is being used, the Info palette displays the percentage change in width (W) and height (H), the angle of rotation (A), and the angle of horizontal skew (H) or vertical skew (V).

- When any color adjustment dialog box (for example, Curves) is being used, the Info palette displays before-and-after color values for the pixels beneath the pointer and beneath color samplers.

- If the Show Tool Hints option is enabled, you see hints for using the tool selected in the toolbox.

- Depending on the options selected, the Info palette displays status information, such as document size, document profile, document dimensions, scratch sizes, efficiency, timing, and current tool.

(ImageReady) The Info palette displays the following information:

- The RGB numeric values of the color beneath the pointer

- The Opacity value of the pixels beneath the pointer

- The hexadecimal value of the color beneath the pointer

- The position, in the indexed color table, of the color beneath the pointer

- The *x* and *y* coordinates of the pointer

- The *x* and *y* coordinates of your starting position (before you click the image) and your ending position (as you drag in the image) when you use the Marquee tool, the shape tools, the Crop tool, and the Slice tool

- The width (W) and height (H) of the selection as you drag when you use the Crop tool, the shape tools, the Slice tool, or the Zoom tool

- The percentage change in width (W) and height (H), the angle of rotation (A), and the angle of horizontal skew (H) or vertical skew (V) when you use a Transform or Free Transform command

To use the Info palette

The Info palette displays file information about an image and also provides feedback about the color values as you move a tool pointer over an image. Make sure the Info palette is visible in your work area if you want to view information while dragging in the image.

1 (Optional) Do one of the following if you need to display the Info palette:

- Click the Info palette tab if it's docked with other palettes.

- Choose Window > Info. File information about the image is displayed at the bottom of the Info palette. You can change the information displayed by clicking the triangle in the upper right corner of the palette and choosing Palette Options from the palette menu.

2 (Optional, Photoshop) Set the options for the information you want displayed in the Info Palette by doing any of the following:

- Choose Palette Options from the Info palette menu and specify options in the Info Palette Options dialog box.

- Click an eyedropper icon and choose display options from the pop-up menu. You can also use the pop-up menu to specify whether the Info palette displays 8-bit, 16-bit, or 32-bit values.

- Click the cursor coordinates icon ✛ and choose a unit of measurement.

3 Select a tool.

4 Move the pointer in the image, or drag in the image to use the tool. The following information may appear, depending on which tool you're using:

⚲ Displays the numeric values for the color beneath the pointer.

✛ Displays the *x* and *y* coordinates of the pointer.

⌗ Displays the width (W) and height (H) of a marquee or shape as you drag, or the width and height of an active selection.

To change the Info palette options

1 Click the triangle in the upper right corner to open the Info palette menu and choose Palette Options.

2 In the Info Palette Options dialog box, for First Color Readout, choose one of the following display options:

Actual Color Displays values in the current color mode of the image.

Proof Color Displays values for the output color space of the image.

A color mode Displays the color values in that color mode.

Total Ink Displays the total percentage of all CMYK ink at the pointer's current location, based on the values set in the CMYK Setup dialog box.

Opacity Displays the opacity of the current layer. This option does not apply to the background.

💡 *You can also set the readout options by clicking the eyedropper icon in the Info palette. In addition to the First Color Readout options, you can also display 8-bit, 16-bit, or 32-bit values.*

3 For Second Color Readout, choose a display option from the list in step 2. For the second readout, you can also click the eyedropper icon in the Info palette and choose readout options from the pop-up menu.

Clicking an eyedropper icon and choosing a readout mode from the pop-up menu

4 For Ruler Units, choose a unit of measurement.

5 Under Status information, select from the following to display file information in the Info palette:

Document Sizes Displays information on the amount of data in the image. The number on the left represents the printing size of the image—approximately the size of the saved, flattened file in Adobe Photoshop format. The number on the right indicates the file's approximate size including layers and channels.

Document Profile Displays the name of the color profile used by the image.

Document Dimensions Displays the dimensions of the image.

Scratch Sizes Displays information on the amount of RAM and the scratch disk used to process the image. The number on the left represents the amount of memory that is currently being used by the program to display all open images. The number on the right

represents the total amount of RAM available for processing images.

Efficiency Displays the percentage of time spent performing an operation instead of reading or writing to the scratch disk. If the value is below 100%, Photoshop is using the scratch disk and is therefore operating more slowly.

Timing Displays the amount of time it took to complete the last operation.

Current Tool Displays the name of the active tool.

6 (Optional) Select Show Tool Hints to display a hint for using a selected tool at the bottom of the Info palette.

7 Click OK.

To change measurement units, click the cross-hair icon in the Info palette and choose from the menu.

Rulers, the grid, and guides

About rulers

Rulers help you position images or elements precisely. When visible, rulers appear along the top and left side of the active window. Markers in the ruler display the pointer's position when you move it. Changing the ruler origin (the (0, 0) mark on the top and left rulers) lets you measure from a specific point on the image. The ruler origin also determines the grid's point of origin.

To show or hide rulers, choose View > Rulers.

To change a ruler's zero origin

1 (Optional) Choose View > Snap To, then choose any combination of options from the submenu. This snaps the ruler origin to guides, slices, or document bounds. In Photoshop, you can also snap to the grid.

2 Position the pointer over the intersection of the rulers in the upper left corner of the window, and drag diagonally down onto the image. A set of cross hairs appears, marking the new origin on the rulers.

💡 *In Photoshop, you can hold down Shift as you drag to make the ruler origin snap to the ruler ticks.*

To reset a ruler's origin to its default value, double-click the upper left corner of the ruler.

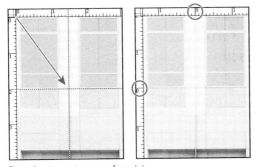

Dragging to create new ruler origin

For more information, see `To use snapping' on page 38.

To change the unit of measurement

1 Do one of the following:

- Double-click a ruler.

- (Windows) Choose Edit > Preferences > Units & Rulers, or right-click the ruler and then choose a new unit from the context menu.

- (Mac OS) Choose Photoshop > Preferences > Units & Rulers, or Control-click the ruler and then choose a new unit from the context menu.

2 For Rulers, choose a unit of measurement.

Note: Changing the units on the Info palette automatically changes the units on the rulers.

3 For Point/Pica Size, choose from the following options:

PostScript (72 points per inch) Sets a unit size compatible for printing to a PostScript device.

Traditional Uses 72.27 points per inch, as traditionally used in printing.

4 Click OK.

To specify columns for an image

Columns help you position images or elements precisely. The New, Image Size, and Canvas Size commands let you specify image width in terms of columns. Using columns is convenient when you plan to import an image into a page-layout program, such as Adobe InDesign®, and you want the image to fit exactly within a certain number of columns.

1 Choose Edit > Preferences > Units & Rulers (Windows) or Photoshop > Preferences > Units & Rulers (Mac OS).

2 Enter values for Width and Gutter.

About the Measure tool

The Measure tool 📏 helps you position images or elements precisely. The Measure tool calculates the distance between any two points in the work area.

When you measure from one point to another, a nonprinting line is drawn, and the options bar and Info palette show the following information:

- The starting location (X and Y)

- The horizontal (W) and vertical (H) distances traveled from the *x* and *y* axes

- The angle measured relative to the axis (A)

- The total distance traveled (D1)

- The two distances traveled (D1 and D2), when you use a protractor

All measurements except the angle are calculated in the unit of measure currently set in the Units & Rulers preference dialog box.

If your document has an existing measuring line, selecting the Measure tool causes it to be displayed.

To measure between two points

1 Select the Measure tool ✐ .

2 Drag from the starting point to the ending point. Hold down the Shift key to constrain the tool to 45˚ increments.

3 To create a protractor from an existing measuring line, Alt-drag (Windows) or Option-drag (Mac OS) at an angle from one end of the measuring line, or double-click the line and drag. Hold down the Shift key to constrain the tool to multiples of 45˚.

To edit a measuring line or protractor

1 Select the Measure tool ✐ .

2 Do one of the following:

- To resize the line, drag one end of an existing measuring line.

- To move the line, place the pointer on the line away from either endpoint, and drag the line.

- To remove the line, place the pointer on the line away from either endpoint, and drag the line out of the image.

Note: You can drag out a measure line on an image feature that should be horizontal or vertical, and then choose Image > Rotate Canvas > Arbitrary. The correct angle of rotation required to straighten the image is automatically entered into the Rotate Canvas dialog box.

About guides and the grid

Guides and the grid help you position images or elements precisely. Guides appear as nonprinting lines that float over the image. You can move and remove guides. You can also lock them so that you don't move them by accident.

The grid is useful for laying out elements symmetrically. The grid appears by default as nonprinting lines but can also be displayed as dots.

Guides and grids behave in similar ways:

- Selections, selection borders, and tools snap to a guide or the grid when dragged within 8 screen (not image) pixels. Guides also snap to the grid when moved. You can turn this feature on and off.

- Guide spacing, along with guide and grid visibility and snapping, is specific to an image.

- Grid spacing, along with guide and grid color and style, is the same for all images.

You can use Smart Guides to help align shapes, slices, and selections. They appear automatically when you draw a shape, or create a selection or slide. You can hide Smart Guides if you need to.

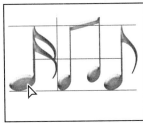

Smart guides appear automatically to help you align shapes, slices, and selections.

Note: *In ImageReady, you can create slices from guides.*

To show or hide a grid, guides, or smart guides

❖ Do one of the following:

- (Photoshop) Choose View > Show > Grid.

- Choose View > Show > Guides.

- View > Show > Smart Guides.

- Choose View > Extras. In Photoshop, this command also shows or hides layer edges, selection edges, target paths, slices, and annotations, and, in ImageReady, selection edges, slices, auto slices, image maps, text bounds, and text selections.

To place a guide

1 If the rulers are not visible, choose View > Rulers.

Note: *For the most accurate readings, view the image at 100% magnification or use the Info palette.*

2 Do one of the following to create a guide:

- (Photoshop) Choose View > New Guide. In the dialog box, select Horizontal or Vertical orientation, enter a position, and click OK.

- (ImageReady) Choose View > Create Guides. In the dialog box, specify guide options and click OK.

- Drag from the horizontal ruler to create a horizontal guide.

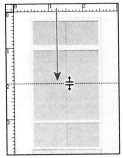

Dragging to create a horizontal guide

- Hold down Alt (Windows) or Option (Mac OS), and drag from the vertical ruler to create a horizontal guide.

- Drag from the vertical ruler to create a vertical guide.

- Hold down Alt (Windows) or Option (Mac OS), and drag from the horizontal ruler to create a vertical guide.

- (Photoshop) Hold down Shift and drag from the horizontal or vertical ruler to create a guide that snaps to the ruler ticks. The pointer changes to a double-headed arrow when you drag a guide.

3 (Optional) If you want to lock all guides, choose View > Lock Guides.

To move a guide

1 Select the Move tool ▸⊕ , or hold down Ctrl (Windows) or Command (Mac OS) to activate the Move tool. (This option does not work with the Hand tool or the Slice tool 🔪 .)

2 Position the pointer over the guide (the pointer turns into a double-headed arrow).

3 Move the guide in any of the following ways:

• Drag the guide to move it.

• Change the guide from horizontal to vertical, or vice versa, by holding down Alt (Windows) or Option (Mac OS) as you click or drag the guide.

• (Photoshop) Align the guide with the ruler ticks by holding down Shift as you drag the guide. The guide snaps to the grid if the grid is visible and View > Snap To > Grid is selected.

To remove guides from the image

❖ Do one of the following:

• To remove a single guide, drag the guide outside the image window.

• To remove all guides, choose View > Clear Guides.

To set guide and grid preferences

1 Do one of the following:

• (Windows) Choose Edit > Preferences > Guides, Grid, & Slices.

• (Mac OS) Choose Photoshop > Preferences > Guides, Grid, & Slices.

2 For Color, choose a color for the guides, the grid, or both. If you choose Custom, click the color box, choose a color, and click OK.

3 For Style, choose a display option for guides or the grid, or both.

4 For Gridline Every, enter a value for the grid spacing. For Subdivisions, enter a value by which to subdivide the grid.

If desired, change the units for this option. The Percent option creates a grid that divides the image into even sections. For example, choosing 25 for the Percent option creates an evenly divided 4-by-4 grid.

5 Click OK.

To use snapping

Snapping helps with precise placement of selection edges, cropping marquees, slices, shapes, and paths. However, sometimes snapping prevents you from correctly placing elements. You can enable or disable snapping using the Snap command. You can also specify different elements to which you want to snap when snapping is enabled.

❖ Choose View > Snap. A check mark indicates that snapping is enabled.

To specify what to snap to

❖ Choose View > Snap To, and choose one or more options from the submenu:

Guides Snaps to guides.

Grid Snaps to the grid. You cannot select this option when the grid is hidden.

Slices Snaps to slice boundaries. You cannot select this option when slices are hidden.

Document Bounds Snaps to the edges of the document.

All Selects all Snap To options.

None Deselects all Snap To options.

A check mark indicates that the option is selected and snapping is enabled.

If you want to enable snapping for only one option, make sure the Snap command is disabled, and then choose View > Snap To and choose an option. This automatically enables snapping for the selected option, and deselects all other Snap To options.

To show or hide Extras

Guides, grid, target paths, selection edges, slices, image maps, text bounds, text baselines, text selections, and annotations are nonprinting *Extras* that help you select, move, or edit images and objects. You can turn on or off an Extra or any combination of Extras without affecting the image. You can also show or hide Extras by choosing the Extras command in the View menu.

Hiding Extras only suppresses the display of Extras. It does not turn off these options.

❖ Do one of the following:

- To show or hide Extras, choose View > Extras. A check mark appears next to all shown Extras in the Show submenu.

- To turn on and show an Extra from a group of hidden Extras, choose View > Show and choose an Extra from the submenu.

- To turn on and show all available Extras, choose View > Show > All.

- To turn off and hide all Extras, choose View > Show > None.

Note: Showing Extras causes color samplers to be shown as well, even though color samplers are not an option in the Show submenu.

Customizing the work area

To manage workspaces

You can customize the palette locations in a workspace. You can save custom workspaces and switch between them. In Photoshop, you can also customize menu items and keyboard shortcuts. In ImageReady, preset workspaces are available for certain tasks.

❖ Choose Window > Workspace, and do one of the following:

- To switch to a workspace, choose a workspace from the submenu.

(Photoshop) Assign keyboard shortcuts to each workspace to navigate among them quickly.

- (ImageReady) To switch to a factory-preset workspace for authoring interactive images or optimizing images for the web, choose Interactivity Palette Locations or Optimization Palette Locations.

- To delete a custom workspace, choose Delete Workspace, select the workspace you want to delete, and click Delete.

- (Photoshop) To reset palettes, shortcuts, and menus to their default positions or states, choose Default Workspace.

- To reset palettes to their default positions, choose Reset Palette Locations (Photoshop) or Default Palette Locations (ImageReady).

- (Photoshop) To reset menus to Photoshop defaults, choose Reset Menus.

- (Photoshop) To reset keyboard shortcuts to Photoshop defaults, choose Reset Keyboard Shortcuts.

For more information, see ` To arrange palettes into a custom workspace' on page 40 and ` To define a set of menus' on page 40.

To change the font size in the work area

You can change the size of the small font text that appears in the options bar, palettes, and tool tips.

1 Choose Edit > Preferences > General (Windows) or Photoshop > Preferences > General (Mac OS).

2 Choose a size from the UI Font Size menu and click OK. The change takes effect the next time you start Photoshop.

To arrange palettes into a custom workspace

If you save the current palette locations, keyboard shortcut set, and menu set as a workspace, you can return to it even if you move or close a palette, or change to a different set of keyboard shortcuts or menus. In ImageReady, you can save the current palette locations.

1 With the workspace in the configuration you want to save, choose Window > Workspace > Save Workspace.

2 Enter a name for the workspace.

3 (Photoshop) Under Capture, select one or more options:

Palette Locations Saves the current palette locations.

Keyboard Shortcuts Saves the current set of keyboard shortcuts.

Menus Saves the current set of menus.

4 Click OK.

For more information, see ` To define a set of menus' on page 40.

To start with the last or default palette locations

Selecting the Save Palette Locations preference causes Photoshop or ImageReady to display palettes in their last locations upon startup. If you deselect this preference, Photoshop or ImageReady displays the palettes in their default locations upon startup.

❖ Do one of the following:

- (Windows) Choose Edit > Preferences > General, and then select/deselect Save Palette Locations.

- (Mac OS) Choose Photoshop > Preferences > General or choose ImageReady > Preferences > General, and then select/deselect Save Palette Locations.

The change takes effect the next time you start the application.

To define a set of menus

1 Do one of the following:

- Choose Edit > Menus.

• Choose Window > Workspace > Keyboard Shortcuts & Menus and click the Menus tab.

2 In the Keyboard Shortcuts and Menus dialog box, choose a set of menus from the Set menu (Photoshop Defaults is the only option until you create a new set). For information on customizing keyboard shortcuts, see Photoshop Help.

3 Choose a type from the Menu For menu:

Application Menus Lets you show, hide, or add color to items in the application menus.

Palette Menus Lets you show, hide, or add color to items in palette menus.

4 Click the triangle next to a menu or palette name.

5 Do one of the following:

• To hide a menu item, click the Visibility button 👁.

• To show a menu item, click the empty Visibility button.

• To add color to a menu item, click the color swatch and choose a color.

6 When you finish changing the menus, do one of the following:

• To save all changes to the current set of menus, click the Save Set button 💾 . Changes to a custom set are saved. If you're saving changes to the Photoshop Defaults set, the Save dialog box opens. Enter a name for the new set and click Save.

• To create a new set based on the current set of menus, click the Save Set As button 📄 .

Note: *If you haven't saved the current set of changes, you can click Cancel to discard all changes and close the dialog box.*

7 In the Save dialog box, enter a name for the set and click Save.

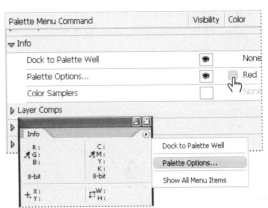

Choosing a color for a menu item using the Keyboard Shortcuts & Menus dialog box

To delete a set of menus

1 Do one of the following:

• Choose Edit > Menus.

• Choose Window > Workspace > Keyboard Shortcuts & Menus and click the Menu tab.

2 In the Keyboard Shortcuts & Menus dialog box, choose a set of menus from the Set menu.

3 Click the Delete Set icon 🗑 .

To temporarily show hidden menu items

It's possible to temporarily show items that you've hidden in a menu. After the menu closes, the items return to their hidden state.

❖ Do one of the following:

• From a menu with hidden items, choose Show All Menu Items.

• Shift-click a menu with hidden items.

To turn menu colors on or off

1 Choose Edit > Preferences > General (Windows) or Photoshop > Preferences > General (Mac OS).

2 Select or deselect Show Menu Colors.

About the Preset Manager

The Preset Manager lets you manage the libraries of preset brushes, swatches, gradients, styles, patterns, contours, custom shapes, and preset tools that come with Photoshop. For example, you can use the Preset Manager to change the current set of preset items or create new libraries. After you load a library in the Preset Manager, you can access the library's items in locations such as the options bar, palettes, dialog boxes, and so on.

In general, when you change a preset, Photoshop prompts you to save the changes as a new preset so that both the original and changed preset remain available.

Each type of library has its own file extension and default folder. Preset files are installed on your computer inside the Presets folder in the Adobe Photoshop CS2 application folder.

To open the Preset Manager, choose Edit > Preset Manager. Choose an option from the Preset Type menu to switch to a specific preset type.

You can adjust the configuration of presets by clicking the palette menu button and choosing a display mode from the top section of the menu:

Text Only Displays the name of each preset item.

Small Thumbnail or Large Thumbnail Displays a thumbnail of each preset item.

Small List or Large List Displays the name and thumbnail of each preset item.

Stroke Thumbnail Displays a sample brush stroke and brush thumbnail of each brush preset. (This option is available for brush presets only.)

To rearrange the list of items, drag an item up or down in the list.

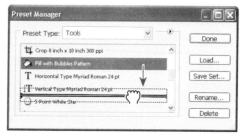

Rearranging tool presets in the Preset Manager

Note: *To delete a preset in the Preset Manager, select the preset and click Delete. You can always use the Reset command to restore the default items in a library.*

To load a library of preset items

❖ Do one of the following:

• Click the triangle to the right of the Preset Type pop-up menu and then choose a library file from the bottom of the palette menu. Click OK to replace the current list, or click Append to add the current list.

• To add a library to the current list, click Load, select the library file you want to add, and click Load.

- To replace the current list with a different library, choose Replace *[Preset Type]* from the palette menu. Select the library file you want to use, and click Load.

Note: Each type of library has its own file extension and default folder in the Presets folder in the Photoshop program folder.

To rename preset items

1 Select a preset item. Shift-click to select multiple items.

2 Do one of the following:

- Click Rename, and then enter a new name for the brush, swatch, and so on.

- If the Preset Manager currently displays presets as thumbnails, double-click a preset, enter a new name, and click OK.

- If the Preset Manager currently displays presets as a list or text only, double-click a preset, enter a new name inline, and press Enter (Windows) or Return (Mac OS).

To delete preset items

❖ Do one of the following:

- Select a preset item, and click Delete.

- Alt-click (Windows) or Options-click (Mac OS) the items you want to delete.

To create a new library of presets

1 Do one of the following:

- To save all the presets in the list as a library, make sure that no items are selected.

- To save a subset of the current list as a library, hold down Shift, and select the items you want to save.

2 Click Save Set, choose a location for the library, enter a file name, and click Save.

You can save the library anywhere. However, if you place the library file in the appropriate Presets folder inside the Photoshop program folder, the library name will appear at the bottom of the palette menu after you restart Photoshop.

To restore the default library of preset items

❖ Choose Reset from the palette menu. You can either replace the current list or append the default library to the current list.

Preferences

About preferences

Numerous program settings are stored in the Adobe Photoshop CS Prefs file, including general display options, file-saving options, cursor options, transparency options, and options for plug-ins and scratch disks. Most of these options are set in the Preferences dialog box. Preference settings are saved each time you quit the application.

Unexpected behavior may indicate damaged preferences. If you suspect damage to preferences, restore preferences to their default settings.

To open a preferences dialog box

1 Do one of the following:

- (Windows) Choose Edit > Preferences and choose the desired preference set from the submenu.

- (Mac OS) Choose Photoshop > Preferences or choose ImageReady > Preferences, and then choose the desired preference set from the submenu.

2 To switch to a different preference set, do one of the following:

- Choose the preference set from the menu at the top of the dialog box.

- Click Next to display the next preference set in the menu list; click Prev to display the previous preference set.

For information on a specific preference option, see the index.

To restore all preferences to default settings

❖ Do one of the following:

- Press and hold Alt+Control+Shift (Windows) or Option+Command+Shift (Mac OS) as you start Photoshop or ImageReady. You are prompted to delete the current settings.

- (Mac OS only) Open the Preferences folder in the Library folder, and drag the Adobe Photoshop CS Settings folder to the Trash.

New Preferences files are created the next time you start Photoshop or ImageReady.

To disable and enable warning messages

Sometimes you will see messages containing warnings or prompts. You can suppress the display of these messages by selecting the Don't Show Again option in the message. You can also globally redisplay all messages that have been suppressed.

1 Do one of the following:

- (Windows) Choose Edit > Preferences > General.

- (Mac OS) Choose Photoshop > Preferences > General or choose ImageReady > Preferences > General.

2 Click Reset All Warning Dialogs, and click OK.

About plug-in modules

Plug-in modules are software programs developed by Adobe Systems and by other software developers in conjunction with Adobe Systems to add features to Photoshop and ImageReady. A number of importing, exporting, and special-effects plug-ins come with your program. They are automatically installed in folders inside the Photoshop Plug-ins folder.

You can select an additional Plug-ins folder for compatible plug-ins stored with another application. You can also create a shortcut (Windows) or an alias (Mac OS) for a plug-in stored in another folder on your system. You can then add the shortcut or alias to the plug-ins folder and use that plug-in with Photoshop and ImageReady.

Once installed, plug-in modules appear as options in the Import or Export menu; as file formats in the Open, Save As, and Export Original (ImageReady) dialog boxes; or as filters in the Filter submenus.

Photoshop and ImageReady can accommodate a large number of plug-ins. However, if the list of installed plug-in modules becomes too long, Photoshop or ImageReady may not be able to display all the plug-ins in their appropriate menus. If so, newly installed plug-ins appear in the Filter > Other submenu.

To install a plug-in module

In Mac OS, you cannot run Photoshop in the Classic environment. Plug-ins originally intended to work on Mac OS 9 won't appear.

❖ Do one of the following:

• To install an Adobe Systems plug-in module, use the plug-in installer, if provided. You can also (Windows) install copy the module into the appropriate Plug-ins folder in the Photoshop program folder, or (Mac OS) drag a copy of the module to the appropriate Plug-ins folder in the Photoshop program folder. Make sure that the files are uncompressed.

• To install a third-party plug-in module, follow the installation instructions that came with the plug-in module. If you cannot run a third-party plug-in, it may require a legacy Photoshop serial number.

Note: If you want to use a plug-in only in Photoshop or only in ImageReady, or when a plug-in is compatible with only one of the applications, you can install the plug-in inside the Plug-ins folder in either the Adobe Photoshop Only folder or the Adobe ImageReady Only folder.

To specify a legacy serial number

1 Do one of the following:

• (Windows) Choose Edit > Preferences > Plug-ins & Scratch Disk.

• (Mac OS) Choose Photoshop > Preferences > Plug-ins & Scratch Disk.

2 Enter the serial number from Photoshop CS or earlier in the Legacy Photoshop Serial Number text box.

To select an additional plug-ins folder

1 Do one of the following:

• (Photoshop) Choose Edit > Preferences > Plug-ins & Scratch Disk (Windows) or choose Photoshop > Preferences > Plug-ins & Scratch Disk (Mac OS).

• (ImageReady) Choose Edit > Preferences > Plug-ins (Windows) or choose ImageReady > Preferences > Plug-ins (Mac OS).

2 Select Additional Plug-ins Folder.

3 Click Choose, and select a folder or directory from the list. Make sure that you do not select a location inside the Plug-ins folder. To display the contents of a folder, double-click the directory (Windows) or click Open (Mac OS).

4 When you have highlighted the additional plug-ins folder, click OK (Windows) or Choose (Mac OS).

5 Restart Photoshop or ImageReady for the plug-ins to take effect.

To suppress the loading of plug-ins

❖ Add a tilde ~ character at the beginning of the plug-in name, folder, or directory. That file (or all files in the folder) will be ignored by the application.

To view information about installed plug-ins

❖ Do one of the following:

- (Windows) Choose Help > About Plug-in and choose a plug-in from the submenu.

- (Mac OS) Choose Photoshop > About Plug-in or choose ImageReady > About Plug-in, and then choose a plug-in from the submenu.

Recovery and undo

To use the Undo or Redo commands

The Undo and Redo commands let you undo or redo operations. You can also use the History palette to undo or redo operations.

❖ Choose Edit > Undo or Edit > Redo.

If an operation can't be undone, the command is dimmed and changes to Can't Undo.

You can set the Redo keystroke preference to be the same for Photoshop and ImageReady. In the General area of the Preferences dialog box, select a preference for the Redo key. You can also set the key to toggle between Undo and Redo.

For more information, see`About the History palette' on page 47.

To revert to the last saved version

❖ Choose File > Revert.

Note: Revert is added as a history state in the History palette and can be undone.

To restore part of an image to its previously saved version

❖ Do one of the following:

- Use the History Brush tool to paint with the selected state or snapshot on the History palette.

- Use the Eraser tool with the Erase To History option selected.

- Select the area you want to restore, and choose Edit > Fill. For Use, choose History, and click OK.

Note: To restore the image with a snapshot of the initial state of the document, choose History Options from the Palette menu and make sure that the Automatically Create First Snapshot option is selected.

To cancel an operation

❖ Hold down Esc until the operation in progress has stopped. In Mac OS, you can also press Command+period.

To receive notification when an operation is completed

A progress bar indicates that an operation is being performed. You can interrupt the operation or have the program notify you when it has finished the operation.

1 Do one of the following:

- (Windows) choose Edit > Preferences > General.

- (Mac OS) choose Photoshop > Preferences > General or choose ImageReady > Preferences General.

2 Do one of the following:

- (Photoshop) Select Beep When Done.

- (ImageReady) Select Notify When Done. In Mac OS, you can then choose System Alert to be notified through your system alert or Text To Speech to receive a spoken notification.

3 Click OK.

About the History palette

You can use the History palette to jump to any recent state of the image created during the current working session. Each time you apply a change to an image, the new state of that image is added to the palette.

For example, if you select, paint, and rotate part of an image, each of those states is listed separately in the palette. When you select one of the states, the image reverts to how it looked when that change was first applied. You can then work from that state.

You can also use the History palette to delete image states and, in Photoshop, to create a document from a state or snapshot.

To display the History palette, choose Window > History, or click the History palette tab.

Photoshop History palette
A. *Sets the source for the history brush* **B.** *Thumbnail of a snapshot* **C.** *History state* **D.** *History state slider*

Keep the following in mind when using the History palette:

- Program-wide changes, such as changes to palettes, color settings, actions, and preferences, are not reflected in the History palette, because they are not changes to a particular image.

- By default, the History palette lists the previous 20 states (Photoshop), or 32 states (ImageReady). You can change the number of remembered states by setting a preference. Older states are automatically deleted to free more memory for Photoshop. To keep a particular state throughout your work session, make a snapshot of the state.

- Once you close and reopen the document, all states and snapshots from the last working session are cleared from the palette.

- By default, a snapshot of the initial state of the document is displayed at the top of the palette.

- States are added to the bottom of the list. That is, the oldest state is at the top of the list, the most recent one at the bottom.

- Each state is listed with the name of the tool or command used to change the image.

- By default, when you select a state, the states below it are dimmed. This way you can easily see which changes will be discarded if you continue working from the selected state.

- By default, selecting a state and then changing the image eliminates all states that come after it.

- If you select a state and then change the image, eliminating the states that came after, you can use the Undo command to undo the last change and restore the eliminated states.

- By default, deleting a state deletes that state and those that came after it. If you choose the Allow Non-Linear History option, deleting a state deletes only that state.

To revert to a previous image state

❖ Do any of the following:

- Click the name of the state.

- Drag the slider ▷ at the left of the state up or down to a different state.

- (Photoshop) Choose Step Forward or Step Backward from the History palette menu or the Edit menu to move to the next or previous state.

To delete one or more image states in Photoshop

❖ Do one of the following:

- Click the name of the state, and choose Delete from the History palette menu to delete that change and those that came after it.

- Drag the state to the Delete icon 🗑 to delete that change and those that came after it.

- Choose Clear History from the palette menu to delete the list of states from the History palette, without changing the image. This option doesn't reduce the amount of memory used by Photoshop.

- Hold down Alt (Windows) or Option (Mac OS), and choose Clear History from the palette menu to purge the list of states without changing the image. If you get a message that Photoshop is low on memory, purging states is useful, because the command deletes the states from the Undo buffer

and frees up memory. You can't undo the Clear History command.

- Choose Edit > Purge > Histories to purge the list of states for all open documents. You can't undo this action.

To delete all image states in ImageReady

❖ Choose Clear Undo/Redo History from the History palette menu.

Note: *This action cannot be undone.*

To create or replace a document with an image state

❖ Do one of the following:

- Drag a state or snapshot onto the New Document button 🖺 . The history list for the newly created document will be empty.

- Select a state or snapshot, and click the New Document button. The history list for the newly created document will be empty.

- Select a state or snapshot, and choose New Document from the History palette menu. The history list for the newly created document will be empty.

- Drag a state onto an existing document.

💡 *To save one or more snapshots or image states for use in a later editing session, create a new file for each state you save, and save each in a separate file. When you reopen your original file, plan to open the other saved files also. You can drag each file's initial snapshot to the original image to access the snapshots again from the original image's History palette.*

To set history options

You can specify the maximum number of items to include in the History palette and set other options to customize the palette.

1 Choose History Options from the History palette menu.

2 Select an option:

Automatically Create First Snapshot Automatically creates a snapshot of the initial state of the image when the document is opened.

Automatically Create New Snapshot When Saving Generates a snapshot every time you save.

Allow Non-Linear History Makes changes to a selected state without deleting the states that come after. Normally, when you select a state and change the image, all states that come after the selected one are deleted. In this way, the History palette can display a list of the editing steps in the order that they were made. By recording states in a nonlinear way, you can select a state, make a change to the image, and delete just that state. The change is appended at the end of the list.

Show New Snapshot Dialog By Default Forces Photoshop to prompt you for snapshot names even when you use the buttons on the palette.

Making a snapshot of an image

The Snapshot command lets you make a temporary copy (or *snapshot*) of any state of the image. The new snapshot is added to the list of snapshots at the top of the History palette. Selecting a snapshot lets you work from that version of the image.

Snapshots are similar to the states listed in the History palette, but they offer additional advantages:

- You can name a snapshot to make it easy to identify.

- Snapshots can be stored for an entire work session.

- You can compare effects easily. For example, you can take a snapshot before and after applying a filter. Then select the first snapshot, and try the same filter with different settings. Switch between the snapshots to find the settings you like best.

- With snapshots, you can recover your work easily. When you experiment with a complex technique or apply an action, take a snapshot first. If you're not satisfied with the results, you can select the snapshot to undo all the steps.

Note: Snapshots are not saved with the image—closing an image deletes its snapshots. Also, unless you select the Allow Non-Linear History option, selecting a snapshot and changing the image deletes all of the states currently listed in the History palette.

To create a snapshot

1 Select a state and do one of the following:

- To automatically create a snapshot, click the New Snapshot button on the History palette, or if Automatically Create New Snapshot When Saving is selected in the history options, choose New Snapshot from the History palette menu.

- To set options when creating a snapshot, choose New Snapshot from the History palette menu, or Alt-click (Windows) or Option-click (Mac OS) the New Snapshot button.

2 Enter the name of the Snapshot in the Name text box.

3 Choose the snapshot contents from the From menu:

Full Document Makes a snapshot of all layers in the image at that state

Merged Layers Makes a snapshot that merges all layers in the image at that state

Current Layer Makes a snapshot of only the currently selected layer at that state

To work with snapshots

❖ Do one of the following:

• To select a snapshot, click the name of the snapshot or drag the slider at the left of the snapshot up or down to a different snapshot.

• To rename a snapshot, double-click the snapshot and enter a name.

• To delete a snapshot, select the snapshot and either choose Delete from the palette menu, click the Delete icon 🗑 , or drag the snapshot to the Delete icon.

Painting with a state or snapshot of an image

The History Brush tool 🖌 lets you paint a copy of one image state or snapshot into the current image window. This tool makes a copy, or sample, of the image and then paints with it.

For example, you might make a snapshot of a change you made with a painting tool or filter (with the Full Document option selected when you create the snapshot). After undoing the change to the image, you could use the History Brush tool to apply the change selectively to areas of the image. Unless you select a merged snapshot, the History Brush tool paints from a layer in the selected state to the same layer in another state.

The History Brush tool copies from one state or snapshot to another, but only at the same location. In Photoshop, you can also paint with the Art History Brush tool to create special effects.

To paint with a state or snapshot of an image

1 Select the History Brush tool 🖌 .

2 Do one of the following in the options bar:

• Specify the opacity and blending mode.

• Choose a brush and set brush options.

3 In the History palette, click the left column of the state or snapshot to be used as the source for the History Brush tool.

4 Drag to paint with the History Brush tool.

About the Edit History Log

You may need to keep careful track of what's been done to a file in Photoshop, either for your own records, client records, or legal purposes. The Edit History Log helps you keep a textual history of changes made to an image. You can view the Edit History Log metadata using Adobe Bridge or the File Info dialog box.

You can choose to export the text to an external log file, or you can store the information in the metadata of edited files. Storing many editing operations as file metadata increases file size; such files may take longer than usual to open and save.

💡 *If you need to prove that the log file hasn't been tampered with, keep the edit log in the file's metadata, and then use Adobe Acrobat to digitally sign the log file.*

For more information, see`To add metadata using the File Info dialog box' on page 69.

To set Edit History Log options

1 Choose Edit > Preferences > General (Windows) or Photoshop > Preferences > General (Mac OS).

2 Click the History Log preference to toggle from on to off or vice versa.

3 In the History Log Options pane, choose one of the following options:

Metadata Stores metadata for each image.

Text File Exports the text to an external file. You are prompted to name the log file and choose a location in which to store it.

Both Stores metadata in the file and creates a text file.

Note: If you want to save the text file in a different location or save another text file, click the Choose button, specify where to save the text file, name the file if necessary, and click Save.

4 From the Edit Log Items menu, choose one of the following options:

Sessions Keeps a record of each time your start or quit Photoshop and each time you open and close files (each image's file name is included).

Concise Includes the text that appears in the history palette in addition to the Sessions information.

Detailed Includes the text that appears in the Actions palette in addition to the Concise information.

Choose Detailed if you need a complete history of all changes made to files.

Memory

Assigning scratch disks

When your system does not have enough RAM to perform an operation, Photoshop and ImageReady use a proprietary virtual memory technology, also called scratch disks. A *scratch disk* is any drive or drive partition with free memory. By default, Photoshop and ImageReady use the hard drive on which the operating system is installed as the primary scratch disk.

In the Plug-ins & Scratch Disks preferences in Photoshop, you can change the primary scratch disk and designate a second, third, or fourth scratch disk to be used when the primary disk is full. Your primary scratch disk should be your fastest hard disk; make sure it has plenty of defragmented space available.

The following guidelines can help you assign scratch disks:

- For best performance, scratch disks should be on a different drive than any large files you are editing.

- Scratch disks should be on a different drive than the one used for virtual memory.

- Scratch disks should be on a local drive. That is, they should not be accessed over a network.

- Scratch disks should be conventional (nonremovable) media.

- RAID disks/disk arrays are good choices for dedicated scratch disk volumes.

- Drives with scratch disks should be defragmented regularly.

To change the scratch disk assignment

1 Choose Edit > Preferences > Plug-ins & Scratch Disks (Windows) or Photoshop > Preferences > Plug-ins & Scratch Disks (Mac OS).

2 Choose the desired disks from the menus. You can assign up to four scratch disks of any size that your file system supports.

3 Click OK.

4 Restart Photoshop for the change to take effect.

To free memory

The Purge command lets you free memory used by the Undo command, the History palette, or the clipboard.

❖ Choose Edit > Purge, and choose the item type or buffer you want to clear. If it is already empty, the item type or buffer is dimmed.

Note: The Purge command permanently clears from memory the operation stored by the command or buffer; Purge cannot be undone. For example, choosing Edit > Purge > Histories deletes all history states from the History palette. Use the Purge command when the amount of information in memory is so large that Photoshop's performance is noticeably affected.

Chapter 3: Adobe Bridge

The basics of Bridge

About Adobe Bridge

Adobe Bridge is the control center for Adobe Creative Suite. You use it to organize, browse, and locate the assets you need to create content for print, the web, and mobile devices. Adobe Bridge keeps native PSD, AI, INDD, and Adobe PDF files as well as other Adobe and non-Adobe application files available for easy access. You can drag assets into your layouts as needed, preview them, and even add metadata to them. Bridge is available independently, as well as from within Adobe Photoshop, Adobe Illustrator, Adobe InDesign, and Adobe GoLive.

File browsing From Bridge you can view, search, sort, manage, and process image files. You can use Bridge to create new folders; rename, move, and delete files; edit metadata; rotate images; and run batch commands. You can also view information about files and data imported from your digital camera.

Version Cue If you have Adobe Creative Suite, you can use Bridge as a central location from which to use Adobe Version Cue. From Bridge, you can browse all the files in a project in one place without having to start the native application for each file, including non-Adobe application files. Also, you can create new Version Cue projects, delete projects, create versions, save alternates, and set access privileges in Bridge. See `Working with Version Cue in Bridge' on page 72.

Bridge Center If you have Adobe Creative Suite, Adobe Bridge includes Bridge Center, the "dashboard" of Adobe Creative Suite, where you can view news readers in your web browser, see your most recent activity, read about tips and tricks for using Adobe products, save groups of files, and more. Adobe Creative Suite users can also use Bridge to specify color management settings and access scripts that help automate your workflow. See `About Bridge Center' on page 64.

Camera Raw If you have Adobe Photoshop installed, you can open and edit camera raw files from Bridge and save them in a Photoshop-compatible format. You can edit the image settings directly in the Camera Raw dialog box without starting Photoshop. If you don't have Photoshop installed, you can still preview the camera raw files in Bridge. See `To open files in Bridge' on page 61.

Stock Photos Click Adobe Stock Photos from the Favorites pane in Bridge to search leading stock libraries for royalty-free images. You can download low-resolution, complementary versions of the images and try them out in your projects before purchasing them. See `About Adobe Stock Photos' on page 75.

Color management You can use Bridge to synchronize color settings across applications. This synchronization ensures that colors look the same no matter which Creative Suite application you view them in. See `To synchronize color settings across Adobe applications' on page 191.

The Bridge work area

These are the main components of the Adobe Bridge window:

The menu bar Contains commands specific to Bridge. In Windows®, the menu bar is at the top of the Bridge window. In Mac OS®, the menu bar is located at the top of the screen.

The Look In menu Lists the folder hierarchy, as well as favorite and recent folders. This menu gives you a quick way to find folders containing the items you want to display. The menu is at the top of the Bridge window.

The shortcut buttons Help you work efficiently with your files. They are located to the right of the Look In menu, at the top of the Bridge window.

The Favorites panel Gives you quick access to folders as well as to Version Cue, Adobe Stock Photos, collections, and Bridge Center (Adobe Creative Suite only). Like all panels, it's located on the left side of the Bridge window.

The Folders panel Shows the folder hierarchy. Use it to navigate to the correct folder.

The Preview panel Displays a preview of the selected file, separate from and typically larger than the thumbnail image displayed in the content area. You can reduce or enlarge the preview.

The Metadata panel Contains metadata information for the selected file. If multiple files are selected, shared data (such as keywords, date created, and exposure setting) is listed.

The Keywords panel Helps you organize your images by attaching keywords to them.

The content area Displays thumbnail previews of the items in the current folder, along with information about those items.

The bottom of the Bridge window displays status information and contains buttons for toggling the display of the panels, a slider for setting the size of thumbnails, and buttons for specifying the type of display in the content area.

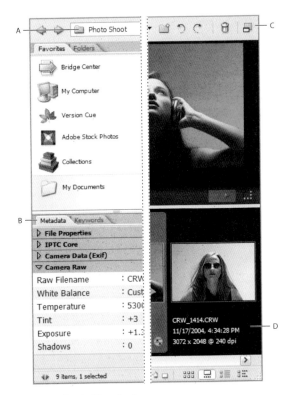

Bridge window in filmstrip view
A. *The Look In menu* **B.** *The Metadata panel* **C.** *The shortcuts buttons* **D.** *The content area*

To start and quit Bridge, and to return to an application

Do any of the following:

- To open Bridge from an application, choose File > Browse from your application.

- (Windows) To open Bridge directly, choose Adobe Bridge from the Start menu.

- (Mac OS) To open Bridge directly, double-click the Adobe Bridge icon 🔧 . By default, this is located in the Applications/Adobe Bridge folder.

- To quit Bridge, choose File > Exit (Windows) or Bridge > Quit Bridge (Mac OS).

- To return to the last open application that started Bridge, choose File > Return To *[Application]*.

To create and close Bridge windows

❖ Do one of the following:

- Choose File > New Window to create a full-size Bridge window.

- Choose File > Close Window. In Windows, this command quits Bridge as well.

To use Bridge in Compact mode

Switch to Compact mode when you want to shrink the Bridge window, hiding the panels and simplifying the content area. A subset of common Bridge commands remains available from the pop-up menu at the top right of the window.

By default, the Compact mode Bridge window floats on top of all windows. (In Full mode, the Bridge window can move behind application windows.) This floating window is useful because it is always visible

and usable as you work in different applications. For instance, you might use Compact mode after you select the files you plan to use, and then drag them into the application as you need them.

1 Click the Switch To Compact Mode button 🔲 .

2 Do any of the following:

- Choose commands from the menu at the top right of the Bridge window.

- Click the Switch To Ultra Compact Mode button 🔲 to hide the content area, further minimizing the Bridge window. You can click the button again to return to Compact mode.

- Click the Switch To Full Mode button 🔲 to return to Full mode, displaying the content area and the panels, and letting Bridge move behind the current application window.

To adjust the Bridge window

You can adjust the Bridge window by moving and resizing the panels. For example, you can enlarge the Preview panel to display bigger thumbnails. You can't, however, move panels outside the Bridge window.

❖ Do any of the following:

- Drag a panel by its tab up or down into another panel area.

- Drag the horizontal divider bar between panels to make them larger or smaller.

- Drag the vertical divider bar between the panels and the content area right or left to resize the panels or content area.

- Click the Show/Hide Panes button ◂▸ at the lower left of the Bridge window to display or hide the panels.

- Choose View, followed by the name of the panel you want to display or hide.

To select Bridge workspaces

A Bridge workspace is a certain configuration or layout of the work area. You can select either a premade one or a custom one that you have previously saved. You can use a preset configuration or switch between different configurations best suited for specific tasks, such as sorting photos.

Note: A Bridge workspace is different from a Version Cue Workspace. Your work in Bridge workspaces has no effect on the Version Cue Workspaces.

❖ Choose Window, followed by the name of the workspace you want, or choose Window > Workspace, followed by one of the following commands:

Lightbox Displays just the content area of Bridge, so that you can concentrate on viewing the files.

File Navigator Displays the content area in Thumbnails view, along with the Favorites panel and Folder panel.

Metadata Focus Displays the content area in Thumbnails view, along with the Metadata panel prominently shown.

Filmstrip Focus Displays just the content area, in Filmstrip view.

To save and delete Bridge workspaces

You can save the current Bridge layout (that is, the work area configuration) as a workspace and reuse it later. By saving Bridge in various configurations, you can work in (and quickly switch between) different layouts of the work area. For instance, you might use one workspace to sort new photos and another to work with Adobe InDesign files.

Note: A Bridge workspace is different from a Version Cue Workspace. Your work in Bridge workspaces has no effect on Version Cue Workspaces.

❖ Choose Window > Workspace, followed by one of these commands:

Save Workspace Saves the current Bridge layout as a workspace so that you can reuse it later, even if you move a panel or change the view in the content area. If you choose this command, enter a name for the workspace and click Save. You can also assign a keyboard shortcut to the workspace and specify whether to save the location of the Bridge window as part of the workspace.

Delete Workspace Deletes the saved workspace. If you choose this command, choose the workspace from the menu, and click Delete.

Reset To Default Workspace Restores the workspace to the default configuration.

To set Bridge preferences

1 Choose Edit > Preferences (Windows) or Bridge > Preferences (Mac OS).

2 Select any of the preferences categories on the left:

General Controls the general appearance settings. You can use this category to specify such preferences as how dark to make the content area for thumbnails, what information to show with thumbnails, and what to include in the Favorites panel. See `Bridge General preferences' on page 57.

Metadata Controls which sections and fields are displayed in the Metadata panel.

Labels Assigns names to each color label and specifies whether you need to press Control as part of the keyboard shortcut combination to apply labels and ratings to files.

File Type Associations Specifies which application to use from Bridge to open files of the named type. For any file type, you can click the name of the application (or None) and click Browse to locate an application to use. You can also reset the file type associations to their default settings as well as hide any file types that don't have an associated application. This affects only those files that you open with Bridge, and overrides the Explorer (Windows) and Finder (Mac OS) settings.

Adobe Stock Photos Specifies Adobe Stock Photos settings. See `To set Adobe Stock Photos preferences' on page 83.

Advanced Specifies advanced settings, including cache options and language options. See `Bridge Advanced preferences' on page 57.

3 Click OK.

Bridge General preferences

Set any of the following General preferences and click OK:

Background Specifies the darkness of the content area in which thumbnails are shown.

Show Tooltips Specifies whether to display Bridge help information when you position the pointer over an item. (This preference does not affect settings for Version Cue tool tips, which display metadata for items.)

Additional Lines Of Thumbnail Metadata Specifies whether to show additional metadata information with thumbnails in the content area. If you select this option, you can choose the type of metadata to show from the associated menu. You can display up to three extra lines of information.

Favorites Items Specifies what items to show in the Favorites panel. Certain options are dimmed if you do not have those items.

Reveal Scripts In Finder Opens the folder that contains scripts (the commands available in the Tools menu).

Reset All Warning Dialogs Resets warning notices in Bridge to their default settings.

Bridge Advanced preferences

Set any of the following Advanced preferences and click OK:

Do Not Process Files Larger Than Specifies the maximum file size of documents for which Bridge automatically creates thumbnails. Displaying large files can slow performance.

Number Of Recently Visited Folders To Display In The Look In Popup Sets the number of most recently viewed folders that appear in the Look In menu.

Language Sets the language used in the Bridge interface. Select Automatic to set the language to the one specified for Bridge by the program that installed it.

Show Camera Raw Interface On Open Opens camera raw files in the Adobe Camera Raw dialog box in Adobe Photoshop.

Use A Centralized Cache File Places the two cache files created for each folder you view in a centralized folder. A centralized cache is generally easier to use than a distributed cache. For instance, when the cache is centralized, you don't have to search in multiple, distributed locations if you want to remove the cache. To specify a new name or location for this centralized cache folder, click Choose.

Use Distributed Cache Files When Possible Places the two cache files created for each folder you view in the viewed folder, if possible. For instance, it's not possible to place the cache files in the viewed folder if that folder is on a burned CD. In that case, Bridge places the cache files in the centralized folder instead. However, if you are burning a CD, using a distributed cache means that you don't have to export the cache to the CD, because it is already in the folder you are burning to the CD. Also, using distributed cache files preserves the cache in a folder if you rename that folder. See `To work with the cache in Bridge' on page 58.

Note: Cache files are hidden files. To view them in Bridge, choose View > Show Hidden Files.

To work with the cache in Bridge

The cache stores thumbnail, metadata, and file information to shorten loading times when you return to a previously viewed folder. However, storing the cache takes up disk space.

Note: Purging the cache deletes the metadata cache and thumbnail cache. If the metadata can't be written to a file, label and rating information is lost as well.

❖ Choose any of the following commands from the Tools > Cache submenu:

Build Cache For Subfolders Builds, as a background process, a cache for the selected folder and all the folders within it (except aliases/shortcuts to other folders), shortening the time spent waiting for the cache to be displayed as you look in subfolders.

Purge Cache For This Folder Clears the cache for the selected folder. This command is useful if you suspect that the cache for a folder is old and needs to be regenerated.

Purge Central Cache Clears the entire centralized cache and any distributed cache in the currently viewed folder, freeing room on the hard drive. The command does not otherwise clear local caches.

Export Cache Exports the cache, allowing you to burn a CD with the cache already generated. Because the folder cache is written into the folder, the thumbnail cache and metadata cache are available after you burn the CD. This option is active only if you chose Use A Centralized Cache File in the Preferences dialog box.

Files and folders in Bridge

To view file and folder thumbnails in Bridge

The content area of Bridge displays thumbnails of the files and folders of the selected folder, along with information about them (depending on your view).

You can specify how you want files and folders are displayed in the content area; for instance, you can decide how big thumbnails should be, how they should appear, and whether file information should be displayed.

❖ Do any of the following:

- Drag the Thumbnail slider ⬠ at the bottom of the Bridge window to adjust the size of thumbnails. You can also click the buttons at either side of the Thumbnail slider to minimize or maximize the thumbnails.

- Click the Thumbnail View button ⬚⬚⬚ at the bottom of the Bridge window or choose View > As Thumbnails to display items in a grid.

- Click the Filmstrip View button ⬚ or choose View > As Filmstrip to display thumbnails in a scrolling list along with an extra-large thumbnail of the currently selected item. Click the Back button or Forward button directly below the extra-large thumbnail to go to the previous or next thumbnail. Click the Switch Filmstrip Orientation button ⟳ to change from a horizontal slide show to a vertical one. Note that you can page through a PDF preview in Filmstrip view.

- Click the Details View button ⬚☰ or choose View > As Details to display a scrollable list of thumbnails along with information about the selected file, such as its creation date, file type, pixel size, and file size. For Version Cue files, there is additional information about the number of versions or alternates as well as enhanced status information along with the current version comment.

- Click the Versions And Alternates View button ⬚⬚ or choose View > As Versions And Alternates to display a scrollable list of thumbnails along with thumbnails of any Version Cue alternates and versions for each item. (Only the current file appears unless you have created an alternates group containing the file or created previous versions of the file.) Click Alternates View or Versions View at the top right of the content area to display thumbnails of alternates or versions. In Alternates View, you can also create alternates groups containing files that are not in the current folder.

- Choose View > Show Thumbnail Only to view thumbnails without any text information listed. However, Version Cue tool tips still display Version Cue information when you position the pointer over the thumbnail.

- Choose View > Slideshow to view thumbnails as a slide show that takes over the entire screen. This is a quick and easy way to display and work with large versions of all the graphics files in a folder. Instructions on how to use the slide show are displayed on the screen when you choose this command.

💡 *Depending on the view you're in, you can display extra file information by positioning the pointer over a thumbnail in the content area. For files in Version Cue projects, you can also choose File > Versions or File Alternate. This command opens a dialog box that lets you work with the file's versions or alternates without having to select that view in the Bridge content area.*

To specify how files and folders are shown in Bridge

You can specify what type of files and folders you want to display as thumbnails in the content area, as well as the order in which to display them.

❖ Choose any of the following commands from the View menu:

- Sort, followed by the order in which you want to sort files. Choose Ascending to sort in ascending rather than descending order. Choose Manually to sort by the last order in which you dragged the files.

- Show Hidden Files to display hidden files, such as cache files and Version Cue files that have been provisionally removed (not permanently deleted) from Version Cue projects.

- Show Folders to display folders as well as individual files.

- Show All Files to display all files regardless of type, even non-Adobe files that Bridge doesn't normally display.

- Show Graphic Files Only to display only files in graphic file formats, such as EPS, JPEG, BMP, PS, TIFF, and GIF.

- Show Camera Raw Files Only to display only camera raw files.

- Show Vector Files Only to display only files created with drawing programs such as Adobe Illustrator, and EPS and PS files.

- Refresh (or choose Refresh from the Folders panel menu) to update the content area. This is useful, for instance, when you perform certain Version Cue actions that don't automatically refresh the view in the content area. Closing and reopening Bridge also refreshes the view.

You can also click Unfiltered at the top right of the Bridge window and choose the files you want to display based on their rating or label. The Unfiltered menu operates independently of the View > Sort commands.

To navigate folders and files with Bridge

❖ Do any of the following:

- Select the Folders panel and click to select the folder you want. Click the plus sign (Windows) or triangle (Mac OS) next to a folder or double-click the folder to open subfolders within it.

- Select the Favorites panel and click to select the folder you want.

- Choose a folder from the Look In menu. You can click the Go Back button, Go Forward button, or Go Up button next to the menu to navigate within the current folder listed in the menu.

To select files in Bridge

Before you can work with a file, you need to select it. You can select more than one file at a time.

❖ Do one of the following in the current folder:

- Click the thumbnail of a file.

- To select contiguous files, Shift-click them.

- To select noncontiguous files, Ctrl-click (Windows) or Command-click (Mac OS) them.

- To select all the files, choose Edit > Select All.

- To select all labeled files, choose Edit > Select Labeled.

- To select all unlabeled files, choose Edit > Select Unlabeled.

- To select the opposite of the current selection, choose Edit > Invert Selection.

- To deselect all selected files, choose Edit > Deselect All.

To open files in Bridge

You can open files in Bridge, even files that were not made with Adobe Creative Suite applications.

1 Select the file in the current folder.

2 Do one of the following:

- Choose File > Open.

- Press Enter (Windows) or Return (Mac OS).

- Double-click the file in the content area or Preview panel.

- Choose File > Open With, followed by the name of the application with which to open the file.

- Drag the file into the working area of an application, such as an open Illustrator document.

- Drag the file onto the application icon.

- Choose File > Open With Camera Raw to edit the Adobe camera raw settings for the file.

To manage files with Bridge

Adobe Bridge makes it easy to drag and drop files, move them between folders, copy and duplicate them, and otherwise manipulate them.

Note: From Bridge, you can also use Adobe Version Cue to manage files you author in Adobe Creative Suite applications. You can create and manage revisions to files kept in Version Cue projects. Version Cue is also a convenient environment for collaborative file management in workgroups. You can manage not only Adobe Creative Suite files but also non-Adobe files.

❖ Do any of the following:

To delete files Select the files and click the Delete button 🗑, click Delete on your keyboard, choose File > Send To Recycle Bin (Windows), choose File > Move To Trash (Mac OS), drag the file to the Recycle Bin or Trash, or choose Edit > Cut.

To copy files and folders Select the files or folders and choose Edit > Copy, or Ctrl-drag (Windows) or Option-drag (Mac OS) the file or folders to a different folder.

To duplicate files Select the files and choose Edit > Duplicate.

To paste files Choose Edit > Paste.

To move files to another folder Select the files and drag them to a different folder. (When you search for Adobe Stock Photos, you can't drag images to other areas, because some images may be comp thumbnails. To drag a comp image, first download it and then drag it from the downloaded comp's folder.)

💡 *To quickly attach an image to an e-mail message, drag the image from Bridge and drop it into the e-mail message.*

To rename files Click the file name, type a new name, and press Enter (Windows) or Return (Mac OS).

To manually reorder files in the content area Drag the file to a new location in the content area.

To display the location of a file in the operating system Select the file and choose File > Reveal In Explorer (Windows) or File > Reveal In Finder (Mac OS).

To find the location of a file in a collection Select a file and choose File > Reveal In Bridge. By default, if you select a file in a collection, it is listed as being located in the folder "File Results." Selecting Reveal In Bridge moves you to the folder in which the file is located.

To place files into an application Select the files and choose File > Place, followed by the name of the application. For instance, you can use this command to place a JPEG image into Illustrator. You can also drag files from Bridge into an application. Depending on the file, the document into which you want to place it may need to be open first.

To eject attached media such as CDs and DVDs Select the medium and choose File > Eject.

To drag files out of Bridge Select the files and drag them onto the desktop or into another folder. This action copies the file (Windows) or moves the file (Mac OS) onto the desktop or folder.

To drag files into Bridge Select one or more files on the desktop, in a folder, or in another application that supports drag and drop, and drag them into the content area in Bridge. The files are moved from their current folder into the one displayed in Bridge. (If the file you are dragging is in a different mounted volume than Bridge, the file is copied into Bridge.)

Drag a file or folder onto the Preview panel to display the contents of the folder in Bridge.

To manage folders with Bridge

❖ Do any of the following:

To create new folders Click the Create A New Folder button 🗀 or Choose File > New Folder. Then, enter a name when the folder appears in the content area.

To delete folders Select the folder and click the Delete button 🗑 , press Delete on your keyboard, or choose File > Move To Recycle Bin (Windows) or File > Move To Trash (Mac OS).

To add folders to Favorites Choose a folder from the Look In menu or Folders panel or select it in the content area. Then choose File > Add To Favorites. You can also drag the folder from the content area to the Favorites panel.

To remove folders from Favorites In the Favorites panel, select the folder you want to remove. Then choose File > Remove From Favorites.

To reorganize folders in the Favorites panel Drag the folder to the desired location in the panel.

To rename folders Click the folder name, type a new name, and press Enter (Windows) or Return (Mac OS).

To rotate images with Bridge

You can rotate the view of JPEG, PSD, TIFF, and camera raw file images in Bridge. Rotating an image in Bridge may rotate it in the application in which it was created as well. Rotating does not affect the data in the image file.

1 Select one or more images in the content area.

2 Do one of the following:

- To rotate the images 90˚ clockwise, click the Rotate 90˚ Clockwise button ⟳ or choose Edit > Rotate 90˚ Clockwise.

- To rotate the images 90˚ counterclockwise, click the Rotate 90˚ Counterclockwise button ⟲ or choose Edit > Rotate 90˚ Counterclockwise.

- To rotate the image 180˚, choose Edit > Rotate 180˚.

To label files with Bridge

Labeling files with a color is a flexible way to quickly mark a large number of files. Using the View > Sort menu or Unfilter button, you can choose to view files according to their label.

For example, suppose you've just imported a large number of images and are viewing them in Bridge. As you review each new image, you can label those you want to keep. After this initial pass, you can use the Unfilter button to display and work on files you've labeled with a particular color.

You can assign names to labels through the Preferences dialog box. The name is then added to the file's metadata when you apply the label.

Note: When you view folders, Bridge shows both labeled and unlabeled files until you choose another option. Also, purging the cache deletes labels from files that don't support XMP write (such as BMP, DCS, Pict, PS6 PDF, and PSB files), locked files, or read-only files (such as files on CDs).

1 Select one or more files.

2 Do one of the following:

- To label files, choose a color from the Label menu.

- To remove labels from files, choose Label > No Label.

To rate files with Bridge

You can assign ratings to files, awarding from zero to five stars. Using the View > Sort menu or Unfilter button, you can choose to view files according to their rating.

For example, suppose you've just imported a large number of images and are viewing them in Bridge. As you review each new image, you can rate them from best to worst. After this initial pass, you can view only files you've rated with four or five stars and work on those.

1 Select one or more files.

2 Do any of the following:

- In Thumbnail view, click the dot representing the number of stars you want to give the file. (Dots do not appear in very small thumbnail views. If necessary, rescale the thumbnail view until the dots appear.)

- Choose a rating from the Label menu.

- To add one star, choose Label > Increase Rating.

- To remove one star, choose Label > Decrease Rating.

- To remove all stars, choose Label > No Rating or click the No Rating icon ⊘ on the thumbnail of the file.

To search for files and folders with Bridge

You can perform searches with Bridge. You can narrow your search by adding multiple search criteria. You can even save your search criteria as a *collection*, so that you can perform the same search again later.

Note: For information on searching for Adobe Stock Photos with Bridge, see Help.

1 Choose Edit > Find.

2 In the Find dialog box, choose a source folder from the Look In menu. By default, the menu displays the currently active folder. Click the Browse button to navigate to another folder.

3 (Optional) Select Include All Subfolders to expand the search to any subfolders in the source folder.

4 (Optional) Select Search Past Versions Of Version Cue Files to include past versions of Adobe Version Cue files, as well as current ones, in the search.

5 (Optional) Select Show Find In A New Browser Window to display the search results in a new Bridge window. If left unselected, the search results appear in the content area of the current window.

6 Choose a criterion for your search by selecting an option from the leftmost Criteria menu.

7 Select a limiter from the center Criteria menu.

8 Enter the search text in the text box at the right, if needed. You can enter basic search terms such as AND, OR, and * (for wild cards).

9 To add search criteria, click the plus sign button. To remove search criteria, click the minus sign button.

10 Click Find. Bridge displays the files that match the search criteria, and you can navigate through the files.

11 (Optional) To save the search criteria to perform the same search again, click Save As Collection. Enter a name for the collection. Select Start Search From Current Folder to search from the same folder in the future. Then, click Save. The search criteria are saved in the Collections folder listed in the Favorites panel.

To search with criteria saved as collections

If you saved search criteria by using the Save As Collection option in the Find dialog box, you can run that search again by using that collection.

1 Select Collections in the Favorites panel or Look In menu.

2 Double-click the collection you want.

A new Bridge window appears containing the results of the search.

Bridge Center

About Bridge Center

If you are working with the Adobe Creative Suite, Bridge Center gives you quick access to your most recent files and folders, RSS newsreaders for the latest information, tips and tricks for using Adobe products, color management features, and Help documentation. It even lets you start new Version Cue projects.

To display Bridge Center, select it in the Favorites panel.

Note: If you don't see Bridge Center in the Favorites panel, make sure that Center is selected in the General preferences. See `To set Bridge preferences' on page 56.

Adobe Stock Photos Opens the Adobe Stock Photos home page in Bridge.

Saved File Groups Lists sets of files that you have saved as a group, even if they are being used in separate applications. When you create a saved file group, you assemble and name a set of files, which Bridge then closes. When you open a saved file group, Bridge reopens the current version of those files, launching the appropriate Adobe Creative Suite applications as needed. See `To work with saved file groups in Bridge Center' on page 65.

Note: Saved file groups do not preserve versions of files; groups always contain the most current version of the files. For instance, suppose you include the file logo.jpg in a saved file group. If you open the saved file group later, edit the logo.jpg file, and save it in another group, both saved file groups will contain the same logo.jpg file.

Recent Folders Lists your most recently visited folders. See `To use recent folders or files from Bridge Center' on page 66.

Recent Files Displays the most recently opened files.

RSS Reader RSS displays shared web content, such as headlines from different websites and the latest information on products from Adobe. RSS stands for *Really Simple Syndication* and is an XML format used to gather and distribute web content while reducing traffic to websites. See `To use RSS content in Bridge Center' on page 66.

Tips And Tricks Lists helpful tips and tricks for getting the most out of Adobe Creative Suite and other Adobe

applications. Click the Next button or Previous button to go to the next or previous tips and tricks topic.

Note: Click Close or Open located above the bottom tabs to hide or reveal the RSS Reader area and Tips And Tricks area.

New Version Cue Project Opens the New Version Cue project and displays a dialog box for creating a new project.

Color Management/Open Color Settings Opens the Color Settings dialog box so that you can manage color for Adobe Creative Suite applications. Also displays the Adobe Creative Suite Color Settings state (Synchronize or Unsynchronize).

Open Help Starts Adobe Help Center.

To work with saved file groups in Bridge Center

1 Click Bridge Center in the Favorites panel.

Note: Bridge Center is available with Adobe Creative Suite only.

2 In the Saved File groups, do any of the following:

- To save your currently open files as a group, click the text Save Open Files into a File Group.

- To open a saved file group, select the group and click the text Open this File Group.

- To display a group in the content area, click the name of that file group.

- To delete a saved file group, select the group and click Delete at the bottom.

To use recent folders or files from Bridge Center

1 Click Bridge Center in the Favorites panel.

Note: Bridge Center is available with Adobe Creative Suite only.

2 In the Recent Folders or Recent Files Group, do any of the following:

- To display a folder in the content area, click that folder.

- To sort the folders by name or date, click Name or Date.

- To open a file in the default application, click the file thumbnail or file name.

- To display the folder that contains a file, click the Shell icon 🗁 next to the file name. The folder is displayed in the content area.

- To sort the folders by name, date, or type, click Name, Date, or Type.

To use RSS content in Bridge Center

RSS (Really Simple Syndication) is an XML format for gathering and distributing web content. It displays web content, such as the latest information on Adobe products.

1 Click Bridge Center in the Favorites panel.

Note: Bridge Center is available with Adobe Creative Suite only.

2 In the RSS Reader section, do any of the following:

- To view content, click to select an RSS site from the list on the left, and then click to select a specific topic from the list on the right. If you want, click More to start your default web browser and display

further information on the topic from that RSS website.

- To add the URL of an RSS site, click the plus sign (+) at the top of the tab.

- To delete an RSS site from the list, select the site and click the minus sign (-).

- To specify how often to check RSS sites for updates, click Open Settings and enter a number specifying the interval, in hours.

- To check the RSS sites for updates manually, Click Update Now.

Running automated tasks with Bridge

To run automated tasks with Bridge

The Tools menu contains submenus for various commands available in the different Adobe Creative Suite applications. For instance, if you have Adobe Photoshop installed, you can use the commands under the Tools > Photoshop submenu to make picture packages and create Photomerge panoramas using photos you select in Bridge. Running these tasks from Bridge saves time because you don't have to open each file individually.

Note: Third parties can also create and add their own items to the Tools menu for added functionality in Bridge. For information about creating your own scripts, see Bridge JavaScript Scripting Reference.

1 Select the files or folders you want to use. If you select a folder, the command is applied where possible to all files in the folder.

2 Choose Tools > *[Application]*, followed by the command you want. (If your application doesn't have any automated tasks available, no application name appears in the menu.)

For information about a particular command, see the documentation for that application.

To batch-rename files with Bridge

You can rename files and folders in a group, or batch. When you batch-rename files, you can choose the same settings for all the selected files, saving time.

1 Do one of the following:

• Select the files that you want to rename.

• Select a folder in the Folders panel. The new setting will apply to all the files in the folder.

2 Choose Tools > Batch Rename.

3 Set the following options and click Rename:

• For Destination Folder, select whether you want to place the renamed files in the same folder or in a different folder, move them to another folder, or place a copy in another folder. If you select Move To Other Folder or Copy To Other Folder, click Browse to select the folder.

• For New Filenames, choose elements from the menus or enter text into the text boxes. The specified elements and text are combined to create the new file name. You can click the + button or - button to add or delete elements. A preview of the new file name appears at the bottom of the dialog box.

Note: If you choose Sequence Number, enter a number. The number is automatically incremented for each file named.

• Select Preserve Current File Name In XMP Metadata if you want to retain the original file name in the metadata.

• For Compatibility, select the operating systems with which you want renamed files to be compatible. The current operating system is selected by default, and you can't deselect it.

Metadata in Bridge

About metadata

Metadata is information about the file, such as its author, resolution, color space, copyright, and keywords applied to it. You can use metadata to streamline your workflow and organize your files. This information is stored in a standardized way using the Extensible Metadata Platform (XMP) standard on which Adobe Bridge and the Adobe Creative Suite applications are built. XMP is built on XML, and in most cases the information is stored in the file so that it isn't lost. If it is not possible to store the information in the file itself, XMP metadata is stored in a separate file called a *sidecar file.*

Many of the powerful Bridge features that allow you to organize, search, and keep track of your files and versions depend on XMP metadata in your files. Bridge provides two ways of working with metadata: through the Bridge Metadata panel and through the File Info dialog box. These methods provide different views into the XMP metadata stored in the file. In some cases, multiple views may exist for the same property; for example, a property may be labeled Author in one view and Creator in another, but both refer to the same underlying property. Even if you customize these views for specific workflows, they remain standardized through XMP. The Advanced view in the File Info dialog box displays the fundamental values being stored.

Metadata that is stored in other formats, such as EXIF, IPTC (IIM), GPS, and TIFF, is synchronized and described with XMP so that it can be more easily viewed and managed. Other applications and features (for example, Adobe Version Cue) also use XMP to communicate and store information such as version comments. For instance, when you save a file in Version Cue, you might add the comment that you rotated the file when you worked on it. Later on, you could use Bridge to navigate to that Version Cue project and search for the term "rotate" to locate that file.

In most cases the metadata remains with the file even when the file format changes, for example, from PSD to JPG. Metadata is also retained when those files are placed in an Adobe InDesign layout.

You can use the XMP Software Development Kit to customize the creation, processing, and interchange of metadata. For example, you can use the XMP SDK to add fields to the File Info dialog box. More information on XMP and the XMP SDK is available from the Adobe Solutions Network (www.adobe.com/xmp).

About the Metadata panel in Bridge

From the Metadata panel, you can view and edit the metadata for selected files, use metadata to search for files, and use templates to append and replace metadata. Metadata preserves information about the contents, copyright status, origin, and history of documents. Version Cue uses metadata to manage files.

You can specify the types of metadata displayed in the Metadata panel.

Note: *If you have applied metadata to an Adobe Acrobat® PDF file, some keywords may not appear; however, these keywords are still attached to the PDF file.*

Depending on the selected file, the following types of metadata appear in the Bridge Metadata panel:

File Properties Describes the characteristics of the file, including the size, creation date, and modification date.

IPTC Core Displays editable metadata. You can add captions to your files as well as copyright information. IPTC Core is a new specification that was approved by IPTC (International Press Telecommunications Council) in October 2004. It differs from the older IPTC (IIM, legacy) in that new properties have been added, some property names have changed, and some properties have been deleted. You can display the older IPTC (IIM, legacy) metadata by selecting it from the Metadata options in the Preferences dialog box.

IPTC (IIM, legacy) Displays editable metadata. As with IPTC Core, you can add captions to your files as well as copyright information. This set of metadata is hidden by default, because it has been superseded by IPTC Core. However, you can choose it by selecting it from the Metadata options in the Preferences dialog box.

Fonts Lists the fonts used in Adobe InDesign files.

Swatches List the swatches used in Adobe InDesign files.

Camera Data (Exif) Displays information assigned by digital cameras. EXIF information includes the camera settings used when the image was taken.

GPS Displays navigational information from a global positioning system (GPS) available in some digital cameras. Photos without GPS information don't have GPS metadata.

Camera Raw Displays settings applied by the Camera Raw plug-in.

Edit History Keeps a log of changes made to images with Photoshop.

Adobe Stock Photos Lists information about images obtained from Adobe Stock Photos.

Version Cue Lists any Version Cue version information about the file.

Note: Depending on the applications you are using, custom panels for various properties may appear here as well.

To view metadata with Bridge

❖ Do any of the following:

• Select one or more files and view the information in the Metadata panel. If you select multiple files, only metadata that is common to the files appears. Use the scroll bars to view hidden categories. Click the triangle to display everything within a category.

You can change the font size in the panel by choosing Increase Font Size or Decrease Font Size from the panel menu.

• Select one or more files and choose File > File Info. Then, select any of the categories listed on the left.

• Choose View > As Details or View > As Versions And Alternates to display the metadata next to the thumbnails in the content area. This is especially useful for viewing Version Cue files.

• Position the pointer over a thumbnail in the content area. (Metadata appears in a tool tip only if Show Tooltips is selected in General preferences.)

To edit metadata with Bridge

1 Click the pencil icon to the far right of the metadata field you want to edit.

2 Type in the text box to edit or add metadata.

3 Press Tab to move through metadata fields.

4 When you have finished editing the metadata, click the Apply button ✔ at the bottom of the Metadata panel. To cancel any changes you've made, click the Cancel button ⊘ at the bottom of the panel.

To specify the metadata displayed in the Metadata panel

1 Do one of the following:

• Choose Preferences from the Metadata panel menu.

• Choose Edit > Preferences (Windows) or Bridge > Preferences (Mac OS), and then click Metadata from the list on the left side of the dialog box.

2 Select the metadata fields that you want to display in the Metadata panel.

3 Select the Hide Empty Fields option if you don't want to view fields with no information in them.

4 Click OK.

To add metadata using the File Info dialog box

The File Info dialog box displays camera data, other file properties, an edit history, copyright and authorship information (if any), and custom metadata panels (if the application has installed them). You can add metadata directly from the File Info dialog box. If you select multiple files, the dialog box shows where different values exist for a text field. Any information you add to a field is applied to all selected files.

Note: You can also view metadata in the Metadata panel, in certain views in the content area, and by placing the pointer over the thumbnail in the content area.

1 Select one or more files.

2 Choose File > File Info.

3 Select any of the following from the list on the left side of the dialog box:

Description Lets you enter document information about the file, such as document title, author, description, and keywords that can be used to search for the document. You can also choose text from the menu to the right of the text fields. To specify copyright information, select Copyrighted from the Copyright Status pop-up menu. Then enter the copyright notice string and the URL of the person or company holding the copyright.

Categories Lets you enter information based on Associated Press categories. You can also choose text from the menu to the right of the text fields. The Categories option appears only if Adobe Photoshop is installed.

History Displays Adobe Photoshop history log information for images saved with Photoshop. The History option appears only if Adobe Photoshop is installed.

Camera Data 1 Displays read-only information about the camera and settings used to take the photo, such as make, model, shutter speed, and f-stop. The Camera Data 1 option appears only if Adobe Photoshop is installed.

Camera Data 2 Lists read-only file information about the photo, including pixel dimensions and resolution. The Camera Data 2 option appears only if Adobe Photoshop is installed.

Adobe Stock Photos Lists read-only information about images obtained from Adobe Stock Photos.

Origin Lets you enter file information that is useful for news outlets, including when and where the file was created, transmission information, special instructions for handling the file, and headline information. You can also choose text from the menu to the right of the text fields.

Advanced Displays fields and structures for storing metadata using namespaces and properties, such as file format and XMP, EXIF, and PDF properties. You can do any of the following with the information listed:

• Click Save to export the metadata to a text (.xmp) file.

• Click Replace to replace the metadata in the existing files with metadata saved in an .xmp file. Values in existing properties are replaced with the new values.

• Click Append to add the metadata in the existing files to metadata saved in an .xmp file. Values in existing properties are not replaced, and new values are appended or inserted where appropriate.

• Click Delete to remove the currently selected Advanced property. You can Shift-click to select multiple properties.

Note: Hold down the Option key to change these commands to Replace All, Append All, and Delete All. These commands then affect all information in the file; that is, EXIF information that is not modifiable by the user, such as the f-stop and the Photoshop file ID information, as well as user-modifiable information, such as document title and keywords. Holding down Option also displays the Reset button to restore the previous settings.

4 Click OK to apply the changes.

To work with metadata templates in Bridge

You can modify the metadata in the File Info dialog box and save it as a template for use with other files.

1 Create a new file using an Adobe Creative Suite application. This creates a file without metadata from any other source.

2 Select the file.

3 Choose File > Info.

4 Enter the desired information in the File Info dialog box.

5 Choose any of the following from the menu at the upper right of the File Info dialog box:

• To save the metadata in the File Info dialog box as a template for use with other files, choose Save Metadata Template. Enter a name for the template and click Save.

• To delete an existing metadata template, choose Delete Metadata Template. Choose the template you want to delete from the menu in the dialog box and click Delete.

• To open the folder containing metadata templates, choose Show Templates.

6 Click OK. You can now also apply metadata templates to files with the Append Metadata and Replace Metadata commands in the Tools menu and in the Metadata panel menu.

To apply metadata templates to files in Bridge

After you have saved metadata for one file, you can apply it to others.

1 Select one or more files.

2 Choose either of the following commands from the Metadata panel menu or the Tools menu:

• Append Metadata, followed by the name of the template. This command applies the template metadata only where no metadata value or property currently exists in the file.

• Replace Metadata, followed by the name of the template. This command completely replaces any existing metadata in the file with the metadata in the template.

To apply keywords to files with Bridge

The Keyword panel lets you create and apply Bridge keywords to files. Keywords can be organized into categories called *keyword sets*. Using keywords, you identify files based on their content. Later, you can view all files with shared keywords as a group.

Note: Bridge keywords are distinct from XMP keywords created with the File Info dialog box. The latter are displayed in Version Cue files in the "Other Metadata" section of the File Info dialog box.

❖ Do any of the following:

• To add a keyword to files, select one or more files. In the Keywords panel, click the box next to the name of the keyword you want to add. A check mark appears in the box next to the keyword when it's added to a file.

• To add a set of keywords to files, select one or more files. In the Keywords panel, click the box next to the name of the keyword set. A check mark appears in the box next to the keyword set when it's added to a file.

💡 *Create a group of frequently used keywords so that you can apply them as a group.*

• To remove keywords from a file, select the file, and then click the box next to the name of the keyword or keyword set that you want to remove.

• To create a new keyword, click the New Keyword button ⬛ at the bottom of the panel or choose New Keyword from the panel menu. A new default keyword name appears in the panel. To create the new keyword, type over the default name and press Return.

• To create a new keyword set, click the New Keyword Set button 📁 at the bottom of the panel or choose New Keyword Set from the panel menu. A new default keyword set name appears in the panel. To create the new keyword set, type over the default name and press Return.

• To rename a keyword or keyword set, select the keyword or keyword set and choose Rename from the panel menu. Then, type over the name in the panel and press Return.

Note: When you rename a keyword, the keyword's name isn't changed in files that currently contain it. The original name stays in the file.

• To move a keyword to a different keyword set, drag the keyword from one set to another.

• To delete a keyword, select the keyword by clicking its name, and then click the Delete Keyword button 🗑 at the bottom of the panel or choose Delete from the panel menu.

Note: Keywords that you get from other users appear in the Other Keywords category until you recategorize them. To make these keywords permanent in Bridge, select the keyword and then choose Persistent from the context menu.

• To find a file using the keyword, choose Find from the panel menu.

Note: You can't modify keywords in search results for Adobe Stock Photos.

Using Version Cue with Bridge

Working with Version Cue in Bridge

Adobe Bridge and Version Cue work together to give you an intuitive way to access and manage Version Cue files and projects.

Bridge provides comprehensive visualization of and centralized command over all aspects of Version Cue files and projects. You can use Bridge to access Version

Cue Workspaces, create a project in any of those workspaces, and create a project folder hierarchy. You can drag files into project folders and drag files from a project folder into non-project folders on your hard drive. You can also copy and move files within and between project folders.

The search capabilities of Bridge enable you to locate project files using file information such as version comments, or keywords or fonts contained in your files. You can view files that have been deleted (but not permanently deleted) in projects and you can restore deleted files using Bridge.

Working with versions in Bridge As you save versions of project files as they evolve, you can use the Versions View in Bridge to see all previous versions of the files, delete previous versions, and promote previous versions. You can get information not only about the current version of a file, but also about the version comment for each previous version without having to open the files in their native applications. However, if you need to view a previous version in more detail, you can use Bridge and Version Cue to open that version. You can view Version Cue file info (metadata) in the Details view, Versions And Alternates view, in tooltips, and in the Metadata panel. Bridge is instrumental in helping you create and track versions of non-Adobe file types that are in the projects in your Version Cue Workspace. When you use Bridge to open a file in a project, you can create a Version Cue version even if an application doesn't have a Save A Version command. You can manage and use those versions as you would if they were created from files made by Adobe Creative Suite components.

Working with alternates in Bridge Bridge also makes it easy to work with Version Cue alternates. You can use Bridge to designate files as alternates of each other,

or to generate alternates from previous versions of a file. In the Alternates view, you can see the complete group of alternates that have been designated for a project file as well as which of these alternates is the primary (preferred) member of the group. A file's inclusion in a group of alternates is indicated by an icon in all Bridge views as well as by text indications in the Details and Versions And Alternates views. Alternates don't have to be located within a single folder, and you can use Bridge to add files to an alternates group no matter where they are located in a project. In Alternates View, it's easy to navigate to the folders that contain alternates. You can remove files from a group of alternates as well as dissolve the group completely in Bridge.

Viewing Workspace, project, and file information
Because you may not always be connected to the network on which a particular Version Cue Workspace is located, Bridge indicates the availability of the workspaces and projects you've accessed by displaying different icons of workspaces and projects. When your Version Cue Workspace is online, you can view up-to-date status for all files you've created with Adobe Creative Suite components. This helps you understand whether a file is already in use, or whether another user has created a newer version. Normally, when you start editing a project file in a Version Cue Workspace, the file's status changes to In Use because you're making changes to the file. However, you can use Bridge to mark a file In Use without having to open the file. You can cancel the Mark In Use indication at any time. You can also use Mark In Use to prepare project files for offline editing when you know you'll be disconnected from a remote Version Cue Workspace. When you come back online, you can use Bridge to synchronize your files with your

workspace once the workspace is available again. For more information about working with Version Cue, see "Adobe Version Cue" in Help.

Version Cue Workspace and project icons in Bridge

Bridge displays status icons for Version Cue Workspaces and projects to let you know if they're available, shared, local, or remote.

- Available and Not Shared Indicates a project that's available and not shared with other users.

- Available and Shared Indicates a project that's available and shared with other users.

- Local Files Only Indicates a project that contains only local files.

- Workspace Not Available Indicates a workspace that's offline.

- Workspace On Own Hard Drive Indicates a workspace that's local to your computer.

- Remote Workspace Online Indicates a remote workspace that's available.

Chapter 4: Adobe Stock Photos

Adobe Stock Photos

About Adobe Stock Photos

Welcome to Adobe Stock Photos, the newest way to view, try, and buy royalty-free images from leading stock libraries. With Adobe Stock Photos, you won't have to interrupt your design process to find quality images. Instead, from inside your favorite applications, you can use the powerful search capabilities of Adobe Stock Photos to find and download images.

From Bridge, the Favorites pane gives you quick access to these stock images. With your computer connected to the Internet, simply click the Adobe Stock Photos icon to start browsing thousands of available images. Because of the tight integration between Stock Photos and Adobe Creative Suite components, you can download images from Adobe Stock Photos directly into your Illustrator, InDesign, and GoLive projects. From Photoshop, you can open any downloaded image.

In the design process, you need the flexibility to try different images before deciding which one you want. Adobe Stock Photos gives you the option to download low-resolution, complementary (comp) versions of images you're considering. You can work with the comps until you make your final decision, at which point you can purchase and download a high-resolution image.

For maximum convenience, you can open an account with Adobe. The benefit of opening an account is that you enter your personal information only once,

greatly simplifying the checkout process. You can also look back at previous purchases, and even download photos again after you purchase them.

Searching for images in Adobe Stock Photos

There are a few ways to search for images in Stock Photos. If you need help getting a project started, a broad search may yield a fund of possibilities and suggest areas to explore. If you have a clear idea of what you need, then you can use Advanced Search to narrow the field.

Related keywords also help you find photos. After you find photos, you can start a new search by selecting one or more related keywords. Each image is associated with keywords that help you find similar images. The more keywords you select, the narrower the search results.

Photos matching the search criteria appear as thumbnails in the main window. You can resize the thumbnail by dragging the Thumbnail slider at the bottom of the screen. When you click an image in search results, a comp image appears in the Preview pane (it may take several seconds for the image to appear in the pane). To enlarge the comp, simply resize the Preview pane. You can view metadata information about the image in the Metadata pane under Adobe Stock Photos Metadata.

Your previous searches are automatically saved in Stock Photos in the Favorites pane. Click Previous Searches to display the list. To see the search results, double-click a search. To delete a search, select it and press the Delete key (Windows), right-click the search and then choose Send To Recycle Bin (Windows), or Control-click the search and choose Move To Trash (Mac OS).

All thumbnails from recent searches are saved on your computer. Having the thumbnails available offline is helpful if you want to browse through the images when your computer isn't connected to the Internet. However, the thumbnails do take up some space on your hard drive. At some point, if you want to delete these thumbnails, delete the searches (as described above), or remove them manually from the default file location: My Documents/AdobeStock-Photos/Previous Searches (Windows), or Documents/AdobeStockPhotos/Previous Searches (Mac OS).

To search for stock photos

1 In Bridge, click Adobe Stock Photos in the Favorites pane.

2 In the text box at the top of the screen, type the word or phrase that describes the subject of the photos you want to search for.

3 Click the Search button 👓 or press Enter.

Images matching the search criteria are displayed in batches. (There is a preference for changing the number of images displayed in a batch.) To view more images, click More Results. Click a photo to view more information, such as its price and keywords associated with it.

To use Advanced Search

Advanced Search is a powerful tool that helps you find exactly the right photo. You can combine several search criteria to narrow your results.

1 In Bridge, click Adobe Stock Photos in the Favorites pane.

2 Click the Advanced Search button 👓⁺.

3 Search using any combination of the following options:

- Type a descriptive keyword or keywords in the text box to find related images. Alternatively, type an image ID, if you know the ID of the photo you want to use.

- To restrict searches to a specific media type, choose one or more options under Media Types.

- To search by the orientation of the photo, select the acceptable shapes under Orientation.

- Select the name of one or more providers to limit the search.

4 Click the Search button to display images matching the search criteria.

To search with related keywords

1 In Bridge, click Adobe Stock Photos from the Favorites pane.

2 In the text box at the top of the screen, type the word or phrase that describes the subject of the photos you want to search for.

3 In the search results, click a photo to select it.

4 Do one of the following:

- Click the Get Price & Keywords button.

- Right-click the image (Windows) and choose Get Price & Keywords from the menu.

5 When the Price & Keywords dialog box appears, select keywords under Keywords For This Image. The more keywords you select, the narrower the search.

6 When you finish selecting keywords, click the Search Again button to begin a new search using the keywords.

To view image price and keywords

You can view size and price information, as well as related keywords, in the Image Detail dialog box.

1 In the search results window, click an image to select it.

2 Do one of the following:

- Click the Get Price & Keywords button.

- Right-click the image (Windows) and choose Get Price & Keywords from the menu.

3 To close the dialog box, click the Close button.

Note: The currency displayed in the Price & Keywords dialog box may not be the native currency of your billing country; it is the supported currency for purchases made from your country. When you purchase photos from Adobe Stock Photos, your credit card will be billed in the supported currency.

Search tips

Here are some helpful pointers for refining your searches:

Misspelled words Double-check your search entries to make sure they're spelled correctly.

Trademarked names Brand names may not return full search results. Instead, search for the item by its general name.

Exact phrase searches To view images that exactly match a phrase, type the whole phrase in the Search text box. You can enter Boolean operators such AND, OR, or NOT to narrow your search.

Search by subject To search for a specific subject, use nouns that describe the main subject of a photo, such as "bicycle" or "house," as well as adjectives that modify the nouns, such as "vintage" or "red." To narrow the search further, use verbs that describe an action in the photo.

Search by concept Try searching with concepts, or perceptions, such as "romance," "vitality", "frustration," or "excitement," to find an inspiring image.

Search by style To find photos that reflect a specific photographic or artistic technique, try searching on terms such as "profile", "studio shot," or "clipping path."

Comp images

About comp images

Comp images are free, nonwatermarked, low-resolution versions of stock photos that you can download to use in mock-ups or other preliminary work. You can use comps to capture a feeling, idea, or concept before choosing the final image for a project. Comps are not licensed for production, but you can use them in mock-ups or other preliminary work. Because comps are low-resolution images, they're not suitable for printing or publishing. After an evaluation period, you can purchase a high-resolution version of the image to continue working with the photo.

Metadata is bundled with comp images. This metadata is read by Photoshop, InDesign, Illustrator, and GoLive, and is used in each application to recognize images as stock photos, even if you rename them. Metadata allows you to purchase high-resolution versions of images later, even after you move a comp to a project folder or create other versions of the image. If you are about to send the photo to be printed, InDesign and Illustrator display a warning that you are using a comp image.

You can view your downloaded comps by clicking Downloaded Comps in the Favorites pane, or you can navigate to the default folder where comps are saved: My Documents/AdobeStockPhotos (Windows) or Documents/AdobeStockPhotos (Mac OS). You can move downloaded comps to any folder you want. To delete a comp in the Stock Photos window, right-click it and then choose Send To Recycle Bin (Windows) or Control-click it and choose Move To Trash (Mac OS).

For more information on using comps, see the terms of service (TOS), which describe when and for how long you can use a comp. A Terms Of Service link is available on the main Adobe Stock Photos screen.

To download comps from Adobe Stock Photos

1 In the search results, click a photo to select it.

2 Do one of the following:

- Click the Download Comp button.
- Right-click the photo (Windows) and select Download Comp from the menu.

- Click Get Prices & Keywords and select Free Comp Image in the dialog box. Click the icon to download the comp.

To view comps in an Adobe Creative Suite application

From Adobe Stock Photos, you can open and edit a comp in Photoshop, Illustrator, InDesign, or GoLive. You can also drag a comp into an application.

1 In the search results window, right-click the image you want to open.

2 In the context menu, position the pointer over Open With, and then choose the name of the application in which you want to view a comp version of the image.

To view saved comps in Stock Photos

To help you keep track of downloaded comps, you can view them in Bridge. If you decide to purchase a comp, put the comp in your shopping cart.

1 In the Favorites pane, click Adobe Stock Photos.

2 Click Downloaded Comps to see the comps.

Buying stock photos

Buying stock photos

It's simple to buy images through Adobe Stock Photos. When you find the photos you want to buy, put them in your *shopping cart*. The photos remain in your cart until you're ready to complete your purchase. When you finish browsing, you can check out and have your images automatically downloaded to your computer.

Having an account with Adobe speeds the checkout process. Because your contact and billing information is saved, you can complete your purchase with just a few clicks.

Adobe Stock Photos maintains a secure site, and you can rest assured that your personal information is kept in strict confidence. Any information you enter is used only for Adobe Stock Photos purposes.

To view your photos, click Purchased Images in the Favorites pane, or navigate to the default Stock Photos folder: My Documents/AdobeStockPhotos (Windows) or Documents/AdobeStockPhotos (Mac OS).

To place photos in the shopping cart

As you find photos you want to purchase, add them to the shopping cart until you're ready to check out.

1 In the search results window, right-click a photo, and then choose Add To Cart from the context menu. You see a dialog box confirming that the photo is your shopping cart.

2 Click OK to continue, or click View Shopping Cart to see the contents of your cart.

If you want to disable this dialog box, select Don't Show Again.

To buy photos

1 To access your shopping cart, click the Shopping Cart icon.

2 Choose a resolution for the photos you want to buy. (You can remove an item from the shopping cart at any time by clicking the Delete icon 🗑 .)

3 Click Check Out.

4 Do one of the following:

- If you have an Adobe account, enter your ID and password.

- If you want to open an Adobe account, click Set Up An Account. You are prompted to enter your billing and account information.

- If you want to buy the images without an account, click Continue As Guest. You are prompted to enter your billing information. Click Continue.

5 Do one of the following:

- If you have an Adobe account, confirm your billing information and click Continue.

- If you don't have an Adobe account, enter your billing information and click Continue.

6 In the Order Summary page, confirm your choices. To delete a photo from the shopping cart, click the Delete icon.

7 If you have a promotion code, enter it in the Promotion Code text box and click Apply. You see any changes made to your order as a result of applying the promotion code.

8 Click the check box to accept the terms of the Adobe Stock Photos License Agreement (click the blue text to read the agreement).

9 Finally, click the Purchase Now button to complete the checkout process. Your purchase is processed, then you're prompted to download your photos.

10 Click Start Download. After the photos are saved, click View Purchased Images if you want to start working with them right away.

11 To view the receipt for your purchase, in the Thank You page click View Receipt. You can also monitor the progress of the download by clicking Open Download Status. When you finish, click Find More Images if you want to find new photos, or click Go To Your Account.

If you have been working with a comp version of the image you purchased, you need to replace the comp with the high-resolution image in your art.

Note: To delete the list of high-resolution images waiting for download from the Download Status screen, choose Edit > Preferences (Windows) or Bridge > Preferences (Mac OS). Select Adobe Stock Photos, and then click the Clear Now button.

To buy photos directly from InDesign or Illustrator

To seamlessly integrate Adobe Stock Photos into your design process, you can use the Place command to use downloaded comps in your work. When you're ready to purchase a photo, you can start the process from InDesign or Illustrator. Then, you can use the Links palette to replace the comp with the full image.

1 In Illustrator or InDesign, right-click a comp image and then choose Purchase This Image from the menu.

2 Adobe Stock Photos starts, and the photo is automatically placed in your shopping cart.

3 After purchasing the image, return to Illustrator or InDesign, and then click Re-link in the Links palette.

4 Navigate to the Purchased Images folder in the Adobe Stock Photos folder: My Documents/Adobe-StockPhotos (Windows), or Documents/AdobeStock-Photos (Mac OS).

5 Select the purchased image and then click OK. The comp is replaced with the full version of the photo.

To view order details

A benefit of having an Adobe account is that you can go back and view your previous orders.

1 In Adobe Stock Photos, click the Your Account button ♟ .

2 In the Your Account page, click View Order History.

3 The Your Order History page shows all of your previous orders. To view details about a particular order, click the order number (highlighted in blue).

4 In the Order Detail page, you can see the billing information, as well as a description of the photos you purchased. Click Return To Your Account if you're done, or click Return To Order History if you want to review other orders.

You can also redownload the photos you purchased.

Stock Photos accounts

Benefits of Stock Photos accounts

Creating an Adobe account makes purchasing photos quick and easy. When you log in with your e-mail address and password, you can work with your account in several ways:

Manage your profile After you complete the registration process, modify your account information anytime by clicking the Your Account link in the navigation bar.

See your order history Track orders made through Adobe Creative Suite Stock Photos to check the specific items ordered, the total cost of the purchase, or the order date.

Download previously purchased items again Access your order history and click Re-download to replace a lost or corrupted file for up to one year from the original purchase date.

Shop with ease Purchase photos without providing profile information. Adobe Stock Photos automatically enters your name and address when you make any purchases. All your personal information is securely stored.

To create a Stock Photos account

1 In Adobe Stock Photos, do one of the following:

- Click the Your Account button 🔒 , and then click the Continue button under Set Up An Account.

- If you have photos in the shopping cart, click the Shopping Cart icon, and then click Checkout. Click Set Up An Account.

2 If you haven't chosen your billing country, you see a dialog box with a list of countries. Choose the country of your billing address and click Continue.

3 In the text boxes, type your e-mail address and choose a password (at least six characters long and containing a mix of letters and numbers).

4 Enter your billing address, and then type your payment information. The billing address must exactly match the address where your credit card statements are mailed.

5 When you finish, click Continue.

After you create your account, Adobe Stock Photos sends a confirmation e-mail to the address you entered.

To log into your Stock Photos Account

1 In Adobe Stock Photos, click the Your Account button 🔒 .

2 When prompted, type your e-mail address and password, and then click Continue. If your login is successful, the Your Account page appears.

If you're having trouble logging into your account, make sure that you have spelled your e-mail address and password correctly. Also make sure that you haven't pressed the Caps Lock or Number Lock keys.

To edit your Stock Photos account profile

Your account profile includes your name and password settings.

1 Click the Your Account button 🔒 .

2 Log into your account.

3 In the Your Account page, click Edit Your Profile. Do any of the following:

- To change your password, type a new word in the Password text box. Passwords can contain only letters and numbers and must be at least six characters long.

- To sign up to get e-mail from Adobe Stock Photos about promotions or other special information, select the check box.

4 To confirm your changes, click Save. To go back to the main Your Account page without saving changes, click Return To Your Account.

To change Stock Photos account address information

You can change your default billing address or add other addresses. Make sure that any new addresses match the address on your credit card billing statements exactly to avoid any problems.

1 Click the Your Account button 👤 .

2 Log into your account.

3 In the Your Account page, click Edit Your Address.

4 Do any of the following:

- To change the nickname associated with the default address, type a new name in the Billing Address Nickname text box.

- Type any changes to the default address in the text boxes.

- To add a new address to your account, click Add New Address, and then enter the information in the text boxes.

- To edit a non-default address, click Edit under the address, and make any changes.

- To make an address the default, click Set Default under the address.

- To delete an address, click Delete under the address.

5 To confirm your changes, click Save. To go back to the main Your Account page without saving changes, click Return To Your Account.

To change Stock Photos account payment information

You can change your saved credit card information, or add additional credit cards. Enter your credit card number without spaces or dashes. You can give each credit card a nickname to keep track of which card you're using.

1 Click the Your Account button 👤 .

2 Log into your account.

3 In the Your Account page, click Edit Your Payment Information.

4 Do any of the following:

- To change the nickname of the default credit card, type a new name in the Payment Nickname text box.

- To change the default credit card number, type the new number in the Credit Card Number text box, and then choose the expiration date for the new card from the month and year menus.

- To add a new card to your account, click Add New Payment Method, and then type a nickname and the card number. Enter the expiration date.

- To delete a payment method, click Delete under the payment nickname.

5 To confirm your changes, click Save. To go back to the main Your Account page without saving changes, click Return To Your Account.

To download previously purchased images from Stock Photos

To download images, you need to have a Stock Photos Account. You can download images onto a different computer than the one you used to purchase the photos originally (see the license agreement for information about restrictions).

1 Click the Your Account button 🔒.

2 In the Your Account page, click View Order History.

3 In the Your Order History page, click the order number (highlighted in blue) of the photo you want to download again.

4 In the Order Detail page, click the arrow under Download. The photo is downloaded. By default, purchased images are located at My Documents/AdobeStockPhotos/PurchasedItems (Windows) or Documents/AdobeStock-Photos/PurchasedItems (Mac OS).

To set Adobe Stock Photos preferences

1 In Adobe Bridge, choose Edit > Preferences (Windows) or Bridge > Preferences (Mac OS).

2 Select Adobe Stock Photos from the list on the left.

3 Set any of the following preferences, and then click Save:

Thumbnails displayed per group To set how many thumbnail images are displayed in a search group, choose an option from the Thumbnails Per Search Group menu.

Search language To search using a different language, select the language from the Search Language menu. Note that you get the best results from most providers if you search in English. This setting doesn't affect the interface display language.

Destination folder for downloads To select a new default folder in which to store photos, downloaded comps, and purchased photos, click Change Location. Click Reset to restore the default location.

Billing Country To change your default billing country, choose the name of the country from the Billing Country menu. The currency displayed next to the Billing Country menu may not be the native currency of that country (not all currencies are supported). Instead, it's the currency Adobe allows for that country. Your credit card is billed in the supported currency.

Alert messages To enable or disable the messages that appear when you download a comp or add a photo to your shopping cart, select or deselect Display Message After Downloading Comp or Display Message After Adding Image To Shopping Cart.

Automatic downloading to default folder To save your photos automatically to your default folder, select Auto-Download Images After Purchasing Them. Deselect this option if you want to choose a location in which to save the photos (for example, in a Version Cue project or other project-specific folder on your computer).

Downloading after lost connection To resume downloading automatically after a connection is lost, select Resume Interrupted Downloads When Bridge Starts.

Chapter 5: Adobe Version Cue

Using Adobe Version Cue

Version Cue managed projects

Adobe Version Cue® is an innovative set of features designed to increase your productivity when you work alone or collaborate with others. Version Cue integrates design management into your existing workflows within and across Adobe Creative Suite components, including Adobe Photoshop CS2, Adobe InDesign CS2, Adobe Illustrator CS2, Adobe GoLive CS2, Adobe Acrobat 7, and Adobe Bridge. You can also work with Version Cue in Adobe InCopy CS2.

Version Cue streamlines the following tasks in Adobe Creative Suite:

- Creating historical versions and branched alternates of your files.

- Maintaining file security.

- Organizing files into private or shared projects.

- Browsing with file thumbnails, and searching file information and version comments.

- Reviewing file information, comments, and file status in private and shared projects while you browse.

In addition, you can use the Version Cue Workspace Administration for more advanced tasks:

- Initiating and managing online reviews of PDF documents.

- Duplicating, exporting, backing up, and restoring projects.

- Viewing information about projects in the Version Cue Workspace.

- Importing files to the Version Cue Workspace using FTP or WebDAV.

- Deleting file versions in batches and removing file locks.

- Creating a roster of project users and defining their project privileges.

- Restricting access to a specific project.

For more information on any of these Administration features, see "About the Version Cue Administration utility" in Help.

Availability of Version Cue features

Different Version Cue features are available in different environments:

- If you use Adobe Creative Suite, you have access to the full set of Version Cue features, including Version Cue Administration.

- If you use only one component of Adobe Creative Suite, or if you use InCopy and not Adobe Creative Suite, you have access to the features of the Adobe dialog box only. You can use Bridge, rather than the Adobe dialog box, for file browsing.

Note: Acrobat 7 and GoLive access Version Cue features differently than other Adobe Creative Suite components and don't use the Adobe dialog box.

- If you don't have Adobe Creative Suite, you can gain access to the full Version Cue feature set by participating in a shared project; that is, if another user on your network installs Adobe Creative Suite and gives you access to a Version Cue project in a Version Cue Workspace.

Getting the most out of Version Cue

In Version Cue, you create *projects* that you and other users access through Adobe Creative Suite components. Projects keep related files together in one place. Version Cue manages the files in these projects. Because Version Cue works in all Adobe Creative Suite components, your design process isn't interrupted when you work on individual files within a project.

You can use Version Cue in a single application, such as Photoshop CS2, to track changes to a file as you work on it. In addition, workgroups or an individual worker can use Version Cue across applications. Multiple users can manage projects that contain files from all Adobe Creative Suite components. Projects can include non-Adobe files, such as text documents, billing forms, or spreadsheets. When you keep all managed files related to a project in one place, you eliminate the task of tracking down important files.

Here's an example of how you might use Version Cue with Adobe Creative Suite: You start by creating a new project and adding a Photoshop file containing the main image for a printed piece. Then, you add art from Illustrator and text from InDesign. Next, you add GoLive web elements to leverage your printed content for use in a web page. As you and your team work on each piece of the project, Version Cue creates *versions* to keep track of changes. When it's time to present the project, you create a PDF of each project file and use the Version Cue Administration utility to set up an

online *PDF review*. Your customers, supervisors, or peer reviewers view and comment on the project using Acrobat.

Working with Version Cue in GoLive

Version Cue is tightly integrated with GoLive to manage the tasks specific to web page creation. Although you access Version Cue differently in GoLive than in Photoshop, Illustrator, InCopy, and InDesign, most of the same features are available. For more information, search for "opening Version Cue projects in GoLive" in Help.

Working with Version Cue in Acrobat

You access Version Cue from within Acrobat 7 much as you do in the other Adobe Creative Suite components; however, there are some differences. Most Version Cue features are available in Acrobat 7. For more information on using Version Cue in Acrobat 7, see Acrobat 7 Help.

About the Adobe dialog box

In Adobe Creative Suite 2.0 components (except for GoLive and Acrobat 7) and InCopy CS2, you can use the Adobe dialog box when you choose the Open, Import, Export, Place, Save, or Save As commands, even if you don't use Version Cue. The Adobe dialog box displays additional information, including thumbnails, which make it easy to identify files. You can use the Adobe dialog box when working with both Adobe and non-Adobe files.

Note: *In InDesign, if you deselect Always Save Preview Images With Documents in either the File Handling preferences or the Save As dialog box, you won't see thumbnails for InDesign files in the Adobe dialog box or in Bridge.*

By default, when you choose the Open, Import, Export, Place, Save, or Save As commands, the operating system (OS) dialog box appears. To use the Adobe dialog box instead and set it as the default, click Use Adobe Dialog. Use the View menu options to customize the display. You can change back to the OS dialog box at any time by clicking Use OS Dialog.

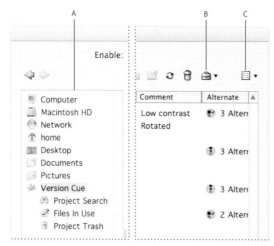

The Adobe Dialog Box
A. Favorites panel B. Project Tools menu C. View menu

You can use the Adobe dialog box to accomplish these tasks:

- Add frequently used files and folders to the Favorites panel for quick access.

- View thumbnail images of files.

- Determine whether a file is open in another Adobe Creative Suite application on your computer.

- Rename or delete files (Mac OS only).

- Connect to Bridge by using the Reveal In Bridge command.

- View metadata about files in the Properties panel. Metadata includes author, keyword, and copyright information.

- Access Version Cue projects and files as well as non-Version Cue files.

- View detailed information about Version Cue projects, such as the status of individual files.

- View and work with Version Cue versions and alternates.

- Search for files in a Version Cue project.

- Move Version Cue files to the Project Trash.

- Determine which Version Cue files are in use, and who is using them.

- Create a new Version Cue project, or connect to an existing Version Cue project.

What's new in Version Cue CS2

In addition to enhanced performance and reliability, here are some key new features in Version Cue CS2:

Integration with Adobe Bridge View Version Cue projects, work with versions, and make groups of alternates, all from one central place. From Bridge, you can search for and view all Version Cue files without opening individual Adobe Creative Suite components. You can manipulate files directly in Bridge to avoid delays as files open or as the components start up. For more information, search for "Using Version Cue in Bridge" in Help.

Alternates Alternates allow you to leverage an asset and take your designs in a different direction. For example, if you want to radically transform a photo that is currently used in a project, but you don't want to alter the original, you can create an alternate and work with it instead. Use alternates, in addition to versions, to manage your assets. See `About Version Cue alternates' on page 116. For more information, search for "Version Cue alternates" in Help.

Version Cue PDF Review Host online PDF reviews from your own computer or another Version Cue Workspace. You can include in the review any PDF file in the project, and use the Automatic e-mail generation to quickly invite users to the review. Review comments are collected in the Version Cue Workspace where all reviewers can see and reference them as the review progresses. For more information, search for "starting reviews" in Help.

Ability to manage non-Adobe files Store non-Adobe files, such as text documents, schedule spreadsheets, and billing forms, in a Version Cue project. You can also create versions of non-Adobe files. See `To save a version of a non-Adobe file' on page 112. For more information, search for "To save a version of a non-Adobe file" in Help.

To set Version Cue Workspace preferences

Note: You can perform this task only if you have access to the full Version Cue feature set, which is available in Adobe Creative Suite or in a shared workspace. See `Availability of Version Cue features' on page 85 for more information.

Use Version Cue preferences to turn Version Cue off (it is on by default), specify Version Cue Workspace settings, choose the locations of Version Cue folders that hold data and backup files, export projects in your workspace, and check for updates to Version Cue.

1 Do one of the following to access Version Cue CS2 preferences:

- In Windows, double-click the Version Cue icon ![icon] in the system tray at the bottom right of the screen.

- In Mac OS, click the Version Cue icon ![icon] in the menu bar at the top of the screen and choose Version Cue CS2 Preferences from the menu.

2 Choose an option from the Version Cue CS2 menu. Choose On to turn on the Version Cue Workspace, or Off to turn the workspace off.

3 To automatically turn on Version Cue when the computer starts (recommended), select Turn Version Cue CS2 On When The Computer Starts.

4 Choose one of the following from the Workspace Access menu:

This Workspace Is Visible To Others Gives others access to your shared Version Cue projects.

This Workspace Is Private Keeps your Version Cue Workspace hidden from other users.

Note: If Version Cue is installed on a computer that uses a firewall and you want to share the workspace with others, make sure that TCP ports 3703 and 427 are left open and deselect the Internet Connection Firewall option (Windows only). For information, see Windows Help.

5 In the Settings tab, do any of the following:

- From the Workgroup Size menu, choose the number of people who use the Version Cue

Workspace on a typical day. This setting controls how the workspace handles the potential load.

- From the Optimize For menu, choose the type of project you generally create. By default, this option is set to Mixed Media, to support workflows that involve both print media (such as InDesign files) and web content (created in GoLive). If you typically produce only print media, or if you create only web content, choose either Print Media or Web Media from the Optimize menu.

- In the Memory Usage text box, enter the amount of RAM that you want to make available to Version Cue. The default is 128 MB. This setting allocates RAM to optimize interoperability between Version Cue and Adobe Creative Suite components. For more robust requirements, such a larger workgroup or many assets, set the RAM to 256 MB or higher.

6 Select Show Version Cue CS2 Tray Icon (Windows) or Show Version Cue CS2 Status In Menu Bar (Mac OS) to keep the Version Cue menu icon visible, giving you quick access to Version Cue Administration and preferences.

7 Click the Locations tab and do one of the following:

- To move the Data folder, where projects, file versions, and user IDs are stored, click the Choose button next to the current folder location. Select a new location (not a network drive) for the folder. You must choose a location on the computer in which the Version Cue Workspace is installed. Click OK.

- To move the Backup folder, where project backups are stored, click the Choose button next to the current folder location. Select a new location for the folder. You must choose a location on the computer

in which the Version Cue Workspace is installed. Click OK.

Important: The workspace must be turned off before you change the folder locations. Do not attempt to move these folders manually or edit any of the files in the Version Cue Data folder. The Data folder contains files that maintain the integrity of the Version Cue file versions, metadata, and project information.

8 To export workspace data, click the Export tab, choose an export version and a location for the exported data, and then click Export.

9 Click the Updates tab, and then click Check For Updates to see whether any updates are available online. If so, you're prompted to install the updates.

10 Click OK (Windows) or Apply Now (Mac OS).

If prompted, click Yes (Windows) or Restart (Mac OS) to restart the Version Cue Workspace. (If Version Cue was running when you changed the settings, you are prompted to restart.)

To turn Version Cue on or off

By default, access to Version Cue is turned on in InCopy CS2 and in all Adobe Creative Suite components, except for Acrobat 7. If you disable Version Cue, you won't have access to any Version Cue Workspace, which could affect files in a project. If you disable or enable Version Cue in any Adobe Creative Suite component, that change affects all other Adobe Creative Suite components except Acrobat 7 (you must always enable or disable Version Cue manually in Acrobat 7), Bridge, and GoLive (Version Cue is always enabled in Bridge and GoLive), and the Version Cue Workspace (this is controlled through the Version Cue CS 2 preferences).

Photoshop CS2 Choose Edit > Preferences > File Handling (Windows) or Photoshop > Preferences > File Handling (Mac OS). Then select or deselect Enable Version Cue Workgroup File Management, and click OK.

Illustrator CS2 Choose Edit > Preferences > File Handling & Clipboard (Windows) or Illustrator > Preferences > File Handling & Clipboard (Mac OS). Then select or deselect Enable Version Cue, and click OK.

InDesign CS2 Choose Edit > Preferences > File Handling (Windows) or InDesign > Preferences > File Handling (Mac OS). Then select or deselect Enable Version Cue, and click OK.

InCopy CS2 Choose Edit > Preferences > File Handling (Windows) or InCopy > Preferences > File Handling (Mac OS). Then select or deselect Enable Version Cue, and click OK.

Acrobat 7 You must manually turn Version Cue on in Acrobat 7 to use it. Choose Edit > Preferences > General (Windows) or Acrobat > Preferences > General (Mac OS). Then select or deselect Enable Version Cue Workgroup File Management.

Bridge Version Cue is always turned on in Bridge.

GoLive Version Cue is always turned on in GoLive.

Working with Version Cue projects

About Version Cue projects

Version Cue uses *projects* to store related files and folders. If you work independently, you create a project to gather all the files you need, view the files in Bridge, and use Version Cue features such as versions and alternates. In a workgroup, depending on your workflow, you can create one Version Cue project for files that everyone in your workgroup collaborates on, a different project for files that don't require collaboration, and yet another project restricted to specific users.

When you first open a Version Cue project, Version Cue creates a folder named "Version Cue" in your My Documents (Windows) or Documents (Mac OS) folder, and adds a folder for the project to it. When you open a file from that project, Version Cue adds a *working copy* of the file to the project folder. As you edit and save intermediate changes to your file, you are actually editing in the working copy; the original file on the Version Cue Workspace is protected.

After you open a Version Cue project, a shortcut to that project appears in the list with other Version Cue Workspaces in Bridge, or in the Open, Place, or Save dialog boxes. Remote Version Cue Workspaces also appear in this list after you access them.

Version Cue uses a special folder for each project: the *documents* folder. This folder is where Version Cue stores non-GoLive files for each project. When you access the project from Bridge, InCopy, or any Adobe Creative Suite component except Acrobat 7, Version Cue automatically opens the documents folder and temporarily displays the project title as the folder name. (If you access the project using Acrobat 7, the folder is named "documents".) You'll also see the documents folder if you open the working copies folder.

If you create a new Version Cue project from GoLive, or if you add a new or existing website to a project, Version Cue creates three additional folders for that project:

Web-content folder Contains the home page (index.html) as well as any website content, including pages, images, styles, and scripts. You can create separate Pages, Images, and Styles subfolders if necessary. Any files or folders uploaded to a production server should be stored in the web-content folder. Because GoLive uses this folder to manage a site as it's created, be careful not to store other types of files in this folder. You can create any type and number of subfolders in the web-content folder.

Web-data folder Stores different types of reusable site objects, such as Smart Objects, components, and templates. This folder contains data used to create the final site. To avoid broken links, missing styles, and similar problems, never store final website content in the web-data folder.

Web-settings folder Stores only the saved settings in the GoLive Site Window and Site Settings dialog boxes.

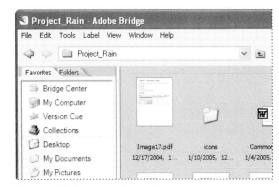

Viewing a Version Cue project in Bridge

To open a project

Note: You can perform this task only if you have access to the full Version Cue feature set, available in Adobe Creative Suite or in a shared workspace. See `Availability of Version Cue features' on page 85 for more information.

1 Do one of the following:

• In Illustrator, InCopy, InDesign, or Photoshop choose File > Open. If the button is visible, click Use Adobe Dialog (if you see the Use OS Dialog button, you are already using the Adobe dialog box). Click Version Cue in the Favorites panel.

• In Bridge, click Version Cue in the Favorites panel. Double-click Workspaces to view all available workspaces.

• In Acrobat 7, choose File > Open. Click Version Cue.

2 To open a Version Cue Workspace, double-click it.

Note: If you don't see a desired Version Cue Workspace, choose Refresh from the Tools menu.

3 To open a project, double-click it.

If the Use Adobe Dialog button doesn't appear in the Open, Save As, Save A Copy, or Place dialog boxes, make sure that you've turned on the Version Cue preference in InCopy or in the Adobe Creative Suite component you're using.

To connect to a remote project

Note: You can perform this task only if you have access to the full Version Cue feature set, available in Adobe Creative Suite or in a shared workspace. See `Availability of Version Cue features' on page 85 for more information.

When you need to work on Version Cue projects that are located remotely, on a different subnet, you can use the IP address of the computer to access that Version Cue Workspace. Workspaces on computers within your subnet should be visible automatically.

1 Do one of the following:

• In Illustrator, InCopy, InDesign, or Photoshop, choose File > Open. If you are using the OS Dialog box, click Use Adobe Dialog. Click Version Cue in the Favorites panel. Choose Connect To from the Project Tools menu ⬛ .

• In Bridge, choose Tools > Version Cue > Connect To.

• In Acrobat, choose File > Open. Click Version Cue. Choose Connect To from the Project Tools menu.

2 In the Connect To dialog box, enter the Version Cue Client URL (the Version Cue IP or DNS address), a colon, and the port number (3703), for example, http://153.32.235.230:3703. If you have connected to the workspace before, it's not necessary to enter the port number.

You can display the Version Cue Workspace Administration utility login page to identify the Version Cue Client URLs that remote users and WebDAV applications need to access the workspace.

3 Click OK. After you connect to a remote Version Cue Workspace, the dialog box displays all available Version Cue projects in that workspace.

A shortcut to the remote workspace is automatically included in your list of available Version Cue Workspaces.

To connect to a project using WebDAV

The Version Cue Workspace can communicate with applications that are WebDAV enabled. When Version Cue is running on a server, you can use it as a WebDAV server. However, Version Cue's native versioning features are more sophisticated than those available through WebDAV. WebDAV capabilities are provided for legacy workflows.

❖ Refer to your application's documentation for information on using its WebDAV features, and then use the Version Cue WebDAV Client URL, the port number (3703), "webdav", and the project name to identify the project you want to work with, for example, http://153.32.235.230:3703/webdav/*project_name*

To view Version Cue Workspace, project, and file information

Note: You can perform this task only if you have access to the full Version Cue feature set, available in Adobe Creative Suite or in a shared workspace. See `Availability of Version Cue features' on page 85 for more information.

For help on viewing information in Acrobat 7, see Acrobat Help.

1 In Illustrator, InCopy, InDesign, or Photoshop, choose File > Open.

2 If the button is available, click Use Adobe Dialog (if you see the Use OS Dialog button instead, you are already using the Adobe dialog box).

3 Click Version Cue in the Favorites panel.

You can resize the Favorites panel to display items with long names: place your cursor over the vertical line to the right of the Favorites panel and drag it to the right.

4 To change the display of Version Cue Workspaces, projects, or files in the dialog box, do any of the following:

• To view the properties of a file, click the toggle to display the Properties panel.

• To change the display of project, choose a display option from the View menu .

• To sort items in a column, while in detail view, click the column heading. Click the column heading again to reverse the order.

• To show or hide columns of information while in list view, right-click (Windows) or Control-click (Mac OS) the Name column heading, and choose Show All, Hide All, or a column name. (The Name column can't be hidden.) Visible columns have a check mark to the left of the column name.

• To change the location of a column, drag the column heading to the left or right of another column heading (Windows), or press Command+Option and drag the column heading

to the left or right of another column heading (Mac OS). The Name column can't be moved.

• To resize a column of information, drag the vertical dividing line between column headings or double-click the line to automatically resize the column to fit the widest item in it.

5 To display information about a file, project, or Version Cue Workspace, do one of the following:

• Place the pointer over the item. A summary of file information appears in a tool tip.

• Right-click (Windows) or Control-click (Mac OS) the file and choose Versions (to display information about a file's versions) or Alternates (to display information about a file's alternates).

Note: If you've already opened the file in an Adobe Creative Suite component, file status information appears at the bottom of the file's window.

To view Version Cue Workspace, project, and file information in Bridge

Note: You can perform this task only if you have access to the full Version Cue feature set, available in Adobe Creative Suite or in a shared workspace. See `Availability of Version Cue features' on page 85 for more information.

In Bridge, you can choose between two display views: Versions And Alternates View and Details View. Use the Versions And Alternates View to view thumbnails of files along with thumbnails of Version Cue alternates and versions. Use the Details View to view thumbnails as well as information about the number of versions or alternates, enhanced status information, and the current version comment.

1 Start Bridge, and then click Version Cue in the Favorites panel.

2 Click the Version Cue Workspace, project, or file to view its information, or place the pointer over the item to display a summary of information in a tool tip.

Creating and editing projects

To begin using Version Cue, you need to create a Version Cue project. When you work with Version Cue, you decide what a project entails. For example, you can create a project to organize files for an entire publishing effort, or you can create a project to manage files for specific aspects of an advertising campaign. You can use a project to organize assets related to a particular customer or use a project to separate private files from files that are worked on collaboratively. You can add files to projects at any time by using Bridge, InCopy, or any Adobe Creative Suite component.

When you create a Version Cue project, you specify a project name, the Version Cue Workspace that hosts the project, and a project description. You specify whether to share the project or keep it private. Shared projects are available to other users; however, you can password-protect shared projects to restrict access to specific users. You can create private projects on a workspace installed on your computer. If you create a project on a computer that is used as a server, it must be shared to be accessible.

You can create projects by using Bridge, InCopy, any Adobe Creative Suite component, or the Version Cue Administration utility. The Version Cue Administration utility provides options for specifying advanced project properties. You create new Version Cue projects with it by importing a folder of files. These files are used as the project starting point.

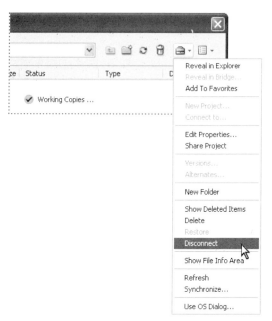

The Project Tools menu contains frequently used commands

To create a project

Note: You can perform this task only if you have access to the full Version Cue feature set, available in Adobe Creative Suite or in a shared workspace. See `Availability of Version Cue features' on page 85 for more information.

For information on creating a project in Acrobat 7, see Acrobat Help.

1 In Illustrator, InCopy, InDesign, or Photoshop, choose File > Open. Click Use Adobe Dialog if you're using the OS dialog box.

2 Click Version Cue in the Favorites panel.

3 Choose New Project from the Project Tools menu 🖺 .

4 Choose a location for the project from the Location menu.

5 Enter a name for the project in the Project Name box and a description in the Project Info box. (The description you enter appears as a tool tip when the pointer is over the project in the list of workspaces.)

6 To make this project and its files available to others, select Share This Project With Others. (If the Version Cue Workspace is on a computer other than your own, the Version Cue project is shared by default.)

7 Click OK.

To create a project in Bridge

Note: You can perform this task only if you have access to the full Version Cue feature set, available in Adobe Creative Suite or in a shared workspace. See `Availability of Version Cue features' on page 85 for more information.

1 Start Bridge, and then click Version Cue in the Favorites panel.

2 Choose Tools > Version Cue > New Project.

3 Choose a location for the project from the Location menu.

4 Enter a name for the project in the Project Name box and a description in the Project Info box. The description you enter appears as a tool tip when the pointer is over the project in the list of workspaces.

5 To make this project and its files available to others, select Share This Project With Others. (If the Version Cue Workspace is on a computer being used as a server, the Version Cue project is shared by default.)

6 Click OK. The project opens automatically. No Items To Display appears in the Content Area until you add files to the project.

To edit the properties of a project

Note: You can perform this task only if you have access to the full Version Cue feature set, available in Adobe Creative Suite or in a shared workspace. See `Availability of Version Cue features' on page 85 for more information.

1 Do one of the following:

• In Illustrator, InCopy, InDesign, or Photoshop, choose File > Open. Click Use Adobe Dialog if you're using the OS dialog box. Double-click the host Version Cue Workspace. Select the project, and then choose Edit Properties from the Project Tools menu.

• In Bridge, select the project and then choose Tools > Version Cue > Edit Properties.

• In Acrobat 7, choose File > Open. Click Version Cue. Select the project, and then choose Edit Properties from the Project Tools menu.

2 In the Edit Properties dialog box, do any of the following, and click Save:

• To change the project name, enter a name in the Project Name text box. The new name will not be reflected on your (or your workgroup's) working copies project folder until you disconnect from and reconnect to the project.

- To change the description of the project, enter text in the Project Info box.

- To make this project and its files available to other users, select Share This Project With Others. (If the Version Cue Workspace is on a computer being used as a server, the Version Cue project is shared by default.) To unshare a shared project, deselect Share This Project With Others. Note, however, that this action does not delete any working copies currently in project folders on the workgroup's computers.

- To view the location of working copies on your computer, expand Local Project Files. To open the folder, choose Show Files (Windows) or Show Files in Finder (Mac OS). To change the location of the files, click Change Location and choose the new location for working copies.

Note: Make sure that you use the Change Location feature to relocate working copies, rather than moving the project folder manually in the file system.

- Click Advanced Administration to enable lock protection, edit or assign users, or require users to log into the project. When prompted, log into Version Cue Administration. Depending on your privileges, this option may not be available.

3 Click Cancel to close the Open dialog box (Version Cue saves your settings even though you clicked Cancel).

See "To log into Version Cue Administration from a Creative Suite application" in Help for more information.

To share or unshare a project

Note: You can perform this task only if you have access to the full Version Cue feature set, available in Adobe Creative Suite or in a shared workspace. See 'Availability of Version Cue features' on page 85 for more information.

At any time, you can change a project's shared status. Projects on a Version Cue Workspace that other users can access are shared by default and can't be made private. Note that unsharing a project does not delete any working copies currently in the working copies project folders of your workgroup.

Note: If the Version Cue Workspace is installed on a computer that uses a firewall and you want to share the workspace with others, make sure that TCP ports 3703 and 427 are left open. If you're using a Windows machine, deselect the Internet Connection Firewall option. (For information on the Internet Connection Firewall option, see Windows Help.)

1 Do one of the following:

- In Illustrator, InCopy, InDesign, or Photoshop, choose File > Open. Click Use Adobe Dialog if you're using the OS Open dialog box.

- In Acrobat 7, choose File > Open.

2 Click Version Cue in the Favorites panel, and then double-click the host Version Cue Workspace.

3 Select the project, and then do one of the following:

- To share the project, choose Share Project from the Project Tools menu 🖾 .

- To unshare the project, choose Unshare Project from the Project Tools menu.

- Choose Edit Properties from the Project Tools menu. Select or deselect Share This Project With

Others, and click Save. After you edit the project properties, click Cancel to close the Open dialog box (your settings are saved even though you clicked Cancel).

To share or unshare a project from Bridge

Note: You can perform this task only if you have access to the full Version Cue feature set, available in Adobe Creative Suite or in a shared workspace. See 'Availability of Version Cue features' on page 85 for more information.

At any time, you can make a project shared or unshared. You can keep a Version Cue project unshared only if it is on your own computer. Projects that you create on a Version Cue Workspace that is not located on your own computer are shared by default and can't be made private. Note that unsharing a project does not delete any working copies that others may already have in the working copies project folder on their own computer.

1 Start Bridge, and then click Version Cue in the Favorites panel.

2 Double-click Workspaces.

3 Right-click (Windows) or Ctrl-click (Mac OS) the project and choose either Share Project or Unshare Project from the menu.

You can also choose Edit > Properties, and then select or deselect Share This Project With Others, and click Save.

Working with files in Version Cue

Using working copies

Version Cue projects and files reside in the Version Cue Workspace on the host computer. The master copies of files added to the project, including file versions and other file data, such as comments, version dates, and user IDs, are saved on this host computer. When you work in files from a Version Cue project, you're editing a *working* copy of the master file on your computer, not the master file on the Version Cue Workspace, which remains protected and untouched.

As you work, use the Save command to save changes periodically. This command does not create a new version of the master file but updates your working copy. A new version is created only when you choose the Save A Version command. This command first updates the working copy, and then adds a new version to the master file on the Version Cue Workspace. When the working copy of a file matches (is the same version as) the current version in the workspace, the file is *synchronized*.

Using working copies of master files, several people can work with the most recent version of a master file. For example, if two people need access to the same illustration during overlapping periods of time, Version Cue lets each person work with a working copy of the most recent file version. The second person to access the illustration is informed that the file is already in use. At that time, the second person can decide whether to continue working with the file.

Working copies give everyone flexible access to project files and allow work to proceed concurrently when necessary.

Note: Two users can't edit a file simultaneously in InCopy.

Working copies allow you to work on a file even when the host workspace is unavailable, or offline. Though some features, such as versions and alternates, can't be used when you're working offline, you can edit files and save your work. When the workspace is online again, you can save a version to update the master file.

There are times when you may wish to delete the working copies of your project files. For example, you may want to free up space on your hard drive, or are completely finished working on the project. Version Cue lets you delete your working copies of project files by disconnecting from the project. Disconnecting from a project deletes the working copies project folder on your hard drive. You can do this at any time if none of the working copies are In Use by you. If you accidentally disconnect from a project, new working copies are recreated the next time you access the project files. If a project is deleted from either the host workspace or your local computer, you can use working copies to recreate the project with the most current versions of the files.

To relocate working copies of a project, edit the project's properties and use the Change Location feature. For instructions, see `To edit the properties of a project' on page 95.

Note: Make sure that you use the Change Location feature to relocate working copies, rather than moving the project folder manually in the file system.

File protection in Version Cue

Version Cue automatically informs others that a file is being edited. Version Cue assigns In Use status to a file when you open and edit a file that isn't being edited by another user. When you save a version, Version Cue removes the file's In Use status.

Note: In InCopy, you must choose File > Checkin after saving a version to remove the file's In Use status.

At times two people may need to work with a file simultaneously. For example, User A may begin editing a file but be called away before saving a version. If User B works on the file while User A is away, Version Cue ensures that the two files don't overwrite each other in the project. User A's working copy won't reflect the changes made by User B, and vice versa. When finished with the file, both users can save a new version of the file to the Version Cue Workspace. Version Cue alerts all current users of the file about the presence of a new version in the Version Cue Workspace and gives them the option of downloading the latest version or continuing their current edits. Alternatively, users can save their edits as an alternate.(Version Cue alerts users who have the file open or who re-open a file that was previously closed while In Use.)

Note: Two users can't edit a file simultaneously in InCopy.

You can use the Version Cue Workspace Administration utility to assign lock protection to a Version Cue project. Only the first user to begin editing an available file in a lock-protected project can save the next version of that file to the Version Cue project. Other users who edit that file simultaneously can't save changes to a new version of that file, even after the first user saves a version. These other users must save the changes as completely new files with their own version thread; however, they can designate their file as an alternate of the original file.

The ability to access a file in a lock-protected project provides the flexibility to create proofs or experiment with the design, for example, and then close the file without saving changes.

Version Cue file statuses

Files that are managed by Version Cue are always marked with a status icon that describes the state of the file on the Version Cue Workspace. You can view a file's status while browsing the files in a Version Cue project, in Bridge, and also in the document window's Status area after opening a file from the Version Cue Workspace in an Adobe Creative Suite component. In Acrobat, the status is displayed in the title bar. A file can have more than one status at the same time (in some cases only one status is shown).

Each file status has a corresponding icon:

Open The file is open on your computer. This status lets you make informed decisions about whether it's appropriate, for example, to place a file into a layout while the file is still being edited. The Open status is indicated only for files on your computer.

In Use By Me You are editing the file. Version Cue assigns this status to a file when you make an edit to the file that changes its content. You can manually mark a file in use before you edit it to indicate to others that you intend to make changes to the content.

Synchronized The latest known version of the file is available for editing and you have a working copy of it on your computer. Version Cue assigns this status

when you save a version of the file you're editing, or when you manually synchronize a project.

No Working Copy No local copy of the file exists. This status indicates that it will take a few moments to create a working copy before you can edit the file.

In Use By <user name> Another user is editing the file and has not yet saved a new version.

Conflicted Copies There is a version conflict, or both you and another user are editing the file.

Only Copy The file in the working copies folder is the only copy known to Version Cue and has not been synchronized with the Version Cue Workspace. This scenario can occur when a file has been saved in an existing project for the first time while the workspace is offline. Because the workspace is offline, Version Cue displays the Offline Copy status until the workspace is back online, and then changes the status to Only Copy. Version Cue also displays this status if you drag a file from one folder into the working copies folder using the file system instead of Bridge (not recommended). You can edit the file, but it's important to synchronize (upload the file to the workspace) after you save your changes.

Offline Copy There is a local copy of the file in your working copies folder, but the Version Cue Workspace is offline. There is no way of checking whether the local copy is synchronized with the latest version on the workspace. You can edit an offline copy and save these changes; however, you must save a version or synchronize the file once the workspace comes back online.

Outdated Copy A local copy exists, but there is a newer version of the file in the workspace. This status indicates that it will take a few moments to create an up-to-date working copy before you can edit the file.

Unavailable ❓ The Version Cue Workspace is offline or you don't have access privileges. There is no way of checking the status of the local copy with the workspace. You can edit the local copy and save these changes; however, you must save a version or synchronize the file once the workspace comes back online.

Deleted 🗑 The file or folder has been deleted from the project, but not yet permanently erased. (You can restore a deleted file or folder).

To open a file from a project

Note: You can perform this task only if you have access to the full Version Cue feature set, available in Adobe Creative Suite or in a shared workspace. See `Availability of Version Cue features' on page 85 for more information.

After you add or save a file to a Version Cue project, the file is automatically managed by Version Cue. Managed files can't be overwritten. If you open a file that's in use by another user or that has been previously edited and saved as a new version, you are prompted to edit the most recent version.

1 Do one of the following:

- In Illustrator, InCopy, InDesign, or Photoshop, choose File > Open. Click Use Adobe Dialog if you're using the OS dialog box, and then click Version Cue in the Favorites panel.

- In Acrobat 7, choose File > Open, and then click Version Cue in the dialog box that appears.

- In Bridge, click Version Cue in the Favorites panel.

2 Double-click the host Version Cue Workspace.

3 Double-click the project that contains the file you want to open.

4 Select the file and click Open.

To reveal a file in Bridge

❖ Right-click (Windows) or Ctrl-click (Mac OS) the file in the Open dialog box in InCopy or an Adobe Creative Suite component, and choose Reveal In Bridge.

The file appears in the Bridge window.

To edit a file in use by another user

Note: You can perform this task only if you have access to the full Version Cue feature set, available in Adobe Creative Suite or in a shared workspace. See `Availability of Version Cue features' on page 85 for more information.

If you don't notice that a file's status is In Use when you open it, Version Cue displays an In Use By alert to remind you that someone else is already editing a working copy of the file.

Note: In InCopy, you can't edit a file that's in use by another user.

1 Open the file, and click one of the following options when the In Use By alert appears:

No, Close Document Closes the file without any alterations.

Yes, Keep Open Keeps the file open so you can work on the document.

2 If you continue working with the document and make a change to the content, Version Cue displays an alert to remind you that there is the possibility of creating conflicting copies. Click one of the following:

Discard Changes Displays the most recent version of the file from the Version Cue Workspace and discards your changes to the working copy.

Continue Editing Lets you edit the working copy without overwriting the changes made in another user's working copy of the same file (Version Cue will prompt each user to save a new version of the file).

3 If the project doesn't have lock protection applied to it, you can save a new version of your edits. Version Cue displays an alert warning you that conflicting edits will occur if you continue. Click one of the following:

Cancel Returns you to the open document without saving a version.

Save Version Anyway Updates the master file in the Version Cue Workspace with the new version. (Version Cue displays an alert to the other user to note that a newer version of the file has been created by you.)

At any point, you can close the document and discard any changes you've made.

To update a file with the most recent version

Note: You can perform this task only if you have access to the full Version Cue feature set, available in Adobe Creative Suite or in a shared workspace. See `Availability of Version Cue features' on page 85 for more information.

If another user creates a new version of a file that you have open or that is still marked In Use By Me, Version Cue prompts you to update your document with the latest version when you open it or attempt to make changes to it, or when you bring the document window frontmost in a group of documents.

❖ When the prompt appears, click one of the following:

Discard Changes Updates the document with the most recent version from the Version Cue project. You can continue editing the file after it is updated. You lose any changes you've made even if you have already saved those changes to the working copy with a Save command.

Continue Editing Leaves the document as is. You can continue editing the file without overwriting the changes in the more recent version. Instead, you're prompted to either save a new version of the file when you close it, or to discard your changes.

Adding files and folders to a project

To save versions of a file and take advantage of Version Cue file management, you must add or save the file to a Version Cue project. You can add assets such as swatch libraries to projects to share them with your workgroup. You can also add non-Adobe files to Version Cue projects You can add files using any of the following methods:

- Add files one at a time from within InCopy or in Adobe Creative Suite.

- Drag one or more files or folders to a Version Cue project using Bridge. Use this method to copy files from one Version Cue project to another.

- Drag files and folders from open windows on your computer's desktop to a Version Cue project displayed in a Bridge window.

- Place files directly in the project's working copies folder, and then synchronize the project to add the files. For more information, see 'About Version Cue projects' on page 90.

To add a file to a project

Note: *You can perform this task only if you have access to the full Version Cue feature set, available in Adobe Creative Suite or in a shared workspace. See 'Availability of Version Cue features' on page 85 for more information.*

For information on adding a file to a project in Acrobat 7, see Acrobat Help.

1 Open the file in Illustrator, InCopy, InDesign, or Photoshop.

2 Choose File > Save As. Click Use Adobe Dialog if you're using the OS dialog box.

3 Double-click the host Version Cue Workspace.

4 Double-click the project to open it.

5 Enter a comment for the first version in the Version Comments box, and click Save.

To add a file or folder to a project in Bridge

Note: *You can perform this task only if you have access to the full Version Cue feature set, available in Adobe Creative Suite or in a shared workspace. See 'Availability of Version Cue features' on page 85 for more information.*

1 Start Bridge. In Folders (in the Favorites panel), navigate to the folder in the Version Cue project to which you want to add files.

2 Navigate to the folder that contains the files or folders you want to add to the project.

3 Select one or more files or folders, and drag them to the Version Cue folder icon you navigated to in step 1.

Note: *To copy (not move) the files to a project, hold down Ctrl (Windows) or Option (Mac OS) as you drag the files to the project.*

To add a file or folder from a desktop folder to a project in Bridge

Note: *You can perform this task only if you have access to the full Version Cue feature set, available in Adobe Creative Suite or in a shared workspace. See 'Availability of Version Cue features' on page 85 for more information.*

1 Start Bridge, and click Version Cue in the Favorites panel.

2 Double-click Workspaces.

3 Double-click the Version Cue project and browse to the folder to which you want to add files.

4 Select files and folders in the open folder on your desktop.

5 Drag these items from the open folder to the Bridge content area displaying the Version Cue folder to which you want to add files.

Note: *To copy (not move) the files to a project, hold down Ctrl (Windows) or Option (Mac OS) as you drag the files to the project.*

To add files to a project folder without Bridge

Note: You can perform this task only if you have access to the full Version Cue feature set, available in Adobe Creative Suite or in a shared workspace. See `Availability of Version Cue features' on page 85 for more information.

It's best to add files using Bridge, but you can add files by dragging them into the documents folder of a Version Cue project.

1 Do one of the following:

• Locate the project folder inside the My Documents/Version Cue (Windows) or Documents/Version Cue (Mac OS) folder on your computer.

• If the project folder isn't already in the My Documents/Version Cue (Windows) or Documents/Version Cue (Mac OS) folder on your hard disk, create a new folder inside the Version Cue folder. Give the folder the same name as the existing Version Cue project on the Version Cue Workspace. Inside the new project folder, create a new folder and name it *documents*.

Note: These steps work only if the project already exists. You cannot create a new project using this method.

2 Move or copy the items you want to add to the documents folder.

3 In Illustrator, InCopy, InDesign, Photoshop, or Acrobat, choose File > Open. Click Use Adobe Dialog if you're using the OS dialog box.

4 Click Version Cue in the Favorites panel. Open the Version Cue Workspace, and select the project.

5 Choose Synchronize from the Project Tools menu . (Alternatively, you can select the project in Bridge and synchronize it.) Once the synchronization is complete, the files are added to the project.

To copy or move files between projects or from a project to a desktop folder

❖ Do one of the following:

• To copy a file between projects, start Bridge and navigate to the project folder that contains the file you want to copy. Choose File > New Window to open a new Bridge window, and navigate to the project folder to which you want to add the file. Drag the file from the first project folder to the destination project folder in the second Bridge window.

• To copy a file from a project to a desktop folder, drag it from the project folder in Bridge to the desktop folder.

Note: When you copy a file between projects or from a project to a desktop folder, Version Cue copies only the most current version.

• To move a file between projects, copy it from one project folder to another in Bridge, and then permanently delete the file from the first project folder. For instructions on permanently deleting files, see `To delete files or folders from a project' on page 109 and `To delete a file or folder permanently' on page 111.

• To move a file from a project to a desktop folder, drag it from the project folder in Bridge to the desktop folder, and then permanently delete the file from the first project folder. For instructions on permanently deleting files, see `To delete files or folders from a project' on page 109 and `To delete a file or folder permanently' on page 111.

To save changes to a file

Note: You can perform this task only if you have access to the full Version Cue feature set, available in Adobe Creative Suite or in a shared workspace. See `Availability of Version Cue features' on page 85 for more information.

If you want to save changes, but aren't ready to save a new version as you edit a file you have opened from a Version Cue project, you can use the File > Save command to save your changes to the working copy on your computer. Until you save a new version to the shared Version Cue Workspace, these changes won't be available to any other user. You can also close the file once you save changes to a file, and then reopen it and save a version later.

❖ To save changes to your working copy, choose File > Save.

To place a file from a project into a document

Note: You can perform this task only if you have access to the full Version Cue feature set, available in Adobe Creative Suite or in a shared workspace. See `Availability of Version Cue features' on page 85 for more information.

While you're working with a Version Cue project in Illustrator, InCopy, InDesign, or Photoshop, you can add a file to a document just as you normally would—by using the Place command. The Links palette (in Illustrator, InCopy, and InDesign) displays additional information about placed files from Version Cue

projects, identifying whether a linked file is being edited, which user is doing the editing, whether it is a member of a group of alternates, and if so, whether it is the primary (preferred) alternate. You can also use the Links palette to determine whether the linked file needs to be updated to a newer version from the Version Cue Workspace.

1 In Illustrator, InCopy, InDesign, or Photoshop, choose File > Place.

2 Click Version Cue in the Favorites panel.

3 Double-click the host Version Cue Workspace.

4 Double-click the project containing the file you want to place.

5 Select the file, and click Place.

For complete information on placing files into documents in Adobe Creative Suite, see the specific application's Help.

Note: When you place a file from a Version Cue project, a copy of that file is placed in your My Documents/Version Cue (Windows) or Documents/Version Cue (Mac OS) folder of working copies for that project. As a result, you can edit that file offline, while it's disconnected from the Version Cue Workspace.

To place a non-Version Cue file into a document

Note: You can perform this task only if you have access to the full Version Cue feature set, available in Adobe Creative Suite or in a shared workspace. See `Availability of Version Cue features' on page 85 for more information.

1 With the document open in Illustrator, InCopy, InDesign, or Photoshop, navigate to the file you want to place.

2 Select the file, and click Place (Illustrator) or Open.

For complete information on placing files into documents in Adobe Creative Suite, see the specific application's Help.

You should always add assets to a Version Cue project before placing them in a Version Cue-managed file. When you place a non-Version-Cue managed file into a managed file, you cannot keep track of the placed asset's versions, alternates, or status.

Using the Links palette with project files

When Version Cue is enabled in Illustrator, InCopy, or InDesign, the Links palette identifies who is editing a linked file from a Version Cue project. It also displays a linked file's versions and alternates so that you can promote and use previous versions, update the document with the linked file's alternates; you can even create versions of linked non-Adobe files.

The Links palette, including the File Status column, functions the same with Version Cue-managed files as it does with non-Version Cue-managed files. For example, if a newer version of a linked file is on the Version Cue Workspace, the Modified Artwork icon ⚠ appears; if a file is missing, the Missing Artwork icon ❓ appears. To update a linked file from a Version Cue project, you use the same procedures used for files that aren't managed by Version Cue.

The Version Cue Edit Status column in the Links palette displays nothing if the linked file is available, or it displays a status icon.

See Illustrator Help, InCopy Help, or InDesign Help for more information about working with the Links palette and placed files.

To view alternates and versions in the Links palette

Note: You can perform this task only if you have access to the full Version Cue feature set, available in Adobe Creative Suite or in a shared workspace. See `Availability of Version Cue features' on page 85 for more information.

When Version Cue is enabled in Illustrator, InCopy, or InDesign, you can view versions and alternates of a placed file from the Links palette.

❖ Do one of the following:

• To view versions of a placed file, choose Versions from the Links palette menu.

• To view alternates of a placed file, choose Alternates from the Links palette menu.

To replace a placed file with an alternate

1 In Illustrator, InCopy, or InDesign, select the file in the Links palette.

2 Choose Alternates from the Links palette menu.

3 Choose an alternate, and click Relink.

To replace a placed file with an alternate derived from a previous version

1 In Illustrator, InCopy, or InDesign, select the file in the Links palette.

2 Click Edit Original and edit the file in its native application.

3 Choose File > Save As, and select Save As Alternate (rename the file if you save it in the original folder).

4 Close the file.

5 In Illustrator, InCopy, or InDesign, select the placed file in the Links palette.

6 Choose Alternates from the Links palette menu.

7 Select the Alternate you created in step 3, and click Relink.

To replace a placed file with a previous version

1 In Illustrator, InCopy, or InDesign, select the file in the Links palette.

2 Choose Versions from the Links palette menu.

3 Select a version and click Promote To Current. Enter a version comment if desired, and click Save.

To search for files in a project

Note: *You can perform this task only if you have access to the full Version Cue feature set, available in Adobe Creative Suite or in a shared workspace. See 'Availability of Version Cue features' on page 85 for more information.*

Metadata is automatically added to Version Cue project files as you work with them. In addition, you can manually add other information to files in Adobe Creative Suite through the File Info dialog box. You can quickly locate files in a Version Cue project by searching for specific information such as titles, authors, copyright data, keywords, dates, and locations. The search feature searches through existing files, as well as files deleted from projects. For information on searching in Acrobat 7, see Acrobat Help. You can also search for Version Cue project files in Bridge, both by version comment and past versions.

1 In Illustrator, InCopy, InDesign, or Photoshop, choose File > Open.

2 If the button is visible, click Use Adobe Dialog (if you see the Use OS Dialog button instead, you are already using the Adobe dialog box).

3 Click Version Cue in the Favorites panel.

4 Double-click the host Version Cue Workspace.

5 Double-click the project you want to search.

6 Click Project Search .

7 Enter information in Project Search.

If you open an older version of a file found as the result of a search, the file name will be prefaced with Version <X> -.

Note: *It is best to treat older versions as view-only when opened as the result of a search. Although you can edit an older version in its native application, do so only if you intend for this version to become a separate asset or to be used as an alternate. To edit a previous version, first promote it to the new, current version, and then make changes.*

Disconnecting from projects

Disconnecting from projects

Disconnecting from a project erases the working copies of files on your computer while leaving the master copies on the Version Cue Workspace intact. Disconnecting also removes shortcuts to the project from Bridge and the Adobe dialog box. You may want to disconnect to free up more space on your hard drive. Or, you might disconnect from a project if someone else in your workgroup deletes a project from the Version Cue Workspace (your working copies are not touched by that deletion).

As long as you have saved a version of the working copies there is no harm in discarding them by disconnecting. When you access the project again, new working copies will be created for the current versions of the files you open. If you have working copies with the In Use By Me status, you will not be permitted to disconnect from a project until you have saved a version of those files.

When you disconnect from a project, only the working copies and shortcuts on your computer are erased. Leaving the project intact on the workspace allows others, as well as yourself, to access the master files. When you delete a project, all working copies and shortcuts on your own computer, along with the master copies of files and folders in the Version Cue Workspace, are erased. However, any working copies and shortcuts on other computers your co-workers or you previously used to access the project are not erased. To completely remove the project and erase

those working copies and shortcuts, you must select the shortcut or project folder and disconnect, even though the project has already been deleted.

You can disconnect from a Version Cue project by using Bridge, Photoshop CS2, Illustrator CS2, InCopy CS2, or InDesign CS2. GoLive CS2 uses a different method for deleting working copies of site files. Disconnect is not available in Acrobat 7.

To disconnect from a project

Note: You can perform this task only if you have access to the full Version Cue feature set, available in Adobe Creative Suite or in a shared workspace. See `Availability of Version Cue features' on page 85 for more information.

Disconnecting from a project removes the files from your computer but doesn't delete the project from the host Version Cue Workspace. Disconnect is not available in Acrobat 7.

1 In Illustrator, InCopy, InDesign, or Photoshop, choose File > Open. Click Use Adobe Dialog if you're using the OS dialog box.

2 Click Version Cue in the Favorites panel.

3 Open the Version Cue Workspace and select the project from which you want to disconnect.

4 Choose Disconnect from the Project tools menu.

Note: You can select any project icon or shortcut to the project when you want to disconnect.

To disconnect from a project in Bridge

Note: You can perform this task only if you have access to the full Version Cue feature set, available in Adobe Creative Suite or in a shared workspace. See `Availability of Version Cue features' on page 85 for more information.

Disconnecting from a project removes working copies of the project files from your computer but doesn't delete the project from the host Version Cue Workspace.

1 Start Bridge, and click Version Cue in the Favorites panel.

2 Double-click Workspaces, and navigate to the project from which you want to disconnect.

3 Right-click (Windows) or Ctrl-click (Mac OS) the project, and then choose Disconnect from the menu.

Note: You can select any project icon or shortcut to the project when you want to disconnect.

Deleting files, folders, and projects

Deleting files and folders

Deleting a file or folder from Version Cue is a two-step process that safeguards against accidental deletions. The first step is deleting the file or folder and giving it the Deleted status. Deleting hides the file or folder from normal view but does not erase it. The second step is permanently deleting and erasing the file or folder and its previous versions.

When you delete a folder, the folder and all folders and files nested inside it are hidden and given a Deleted status. When you permanently delete a folder, its entire contents are erased.

Any user with appropriate privileges can delete files and folders unless the files or folders are marked In Use. In a workgroup, if a user is editing a file that you need to delete, you can reset the file's lock by using the Version Cue Administration utility.

You can restore files or folders that have a Deleted status. Restoring reinstates Version Cue management. Restored files and folders appear in their previous location in the project folder hierarchy. (Deleted files and folders maintain their relationship within the project hierarchy until they are permanently deleted.)

In Bridge, InCopy, and in Adobe Creative Suite, you can show hidden and deleted files or folders, and view them in search results. Additionally, Version Cue has a Project Trash view from which you can view all deleted files in a project. Use Project Trash to view and handle all deleted files without navigating through the project folder hierarchy.

You can delete individual files or folders in Bridge, InCopy, or any Adobe Creative Suite component.

For more information, see "To delete a Version Cue project in the Version Cue Administration utility".

Deleting projects

Deleting a project from Version Cue permanently erases all of its master files (including versions and alternates) and folders from the Version Cue Workspace. This is a one-step process (with confirmation). Deleting a project automatically deletes the working copies of files on your computer as well as any shortcuts to that project. However, the working copies of files created on other users' computers are not deleted until they disconnect from the deleted project. You cannot restore deleted projects directly in Version Cue, nor can you delete a project if any user has files that are marked In Use. You can delete an entire Version Cue project in Bridge, InCopy, or any Adobe Creative Suite component. You can also delete projects by using the Version Cue Administration utility, if you have privileges to do so.

To delete a project

Note: You can perform this task only if you have access to the full Version Cue feature set, available in Adobe Creative Suite or in a shared workspace. See `Availability of Version Cue features' on page 85 for more information.

For information about deleting a project from Acrobat 7, see Acrobat Help.

1 In Illustrator, InCopy, InDesign, or Photoshop, choose File > Open. Click Use Adobe Dialog if you're using the OS dialog box.

2 Click Version Cue in the Favorites panel.

3 Do one of the following:

• Double-click the host Version Cue Workspace and select the project.

• Click the project shortcut.

4 Choose Delete from the Project Tools 🗄 menu.

5 Click OK in the confirmation dialog box.

You can also delete projects using the Version Cue Administration utility. See "To delete a Version Cue project in the Version Cue Administration utility" in Help.

To delete a project in Bridge

Note: You can perform this task only if you have access to the full Version Cue feature set, available in Adobe Creative Suite or in a shared workspace. See `Availability of Version Cue features' on page 85 for more information.

1 Start Bridge, and then click Version Cue in the Favorites panel.

2 Double-click Workspaces.

3 Right-click the project or the project shortcut, and then choose Delete Project from the menu.

4 Click OK to confirm the deletion.

To remove working copies of the files from the deleted project, you need to disconnect from the project.

To delete files or folders from a project

Note: You can perform this task only if you have access to the full Version Cue feature set, available in Adobe Creative Suite or in a shared workspace. See `Availability of Version Cue features' on page 85 for more information.

Once you delete a file or folder from a project, you can then choose to permanently delete it or restore it with its original data, including file versions and related information. For information about deleting files or folders from Acrobat 7, see Acrobat Help.

1 In Illustrator, InCopy, InDesign, or Photoshop, choose File > Open. Click Use Adobe Dialog if you're using the OS dialog box.

2 Click Version Cue in the Favorites panel.

3 Double-click the host Version Cue Workspace.

4 Double-click the project that contains the file or folder you want to delete.

5 Select the file or folder you want to delete.

6 Do one of the following:

- Choose Delete from the Project Tools menu 🖼

- Drag the file to the Project Trash 🗑.

Note: If Show Deleted files is not selected in the Project Tools menu, the file will become hidden and removed from view. If Show Deleted Files is selected, the file or folder will remain visible with the status Deleted.

To delete files from a project in Bridge

Note: You can perform this task only if you have access to the full Version Cue feature set, available in Adobe Creative Suite or in a shared workspace. See `Availability of Version Cue features' on page 85 for more information.

Once you delete a file from a project, you can then choose to permanently delete it or restore it with its original data, including file versions and related information.

1 In Bridge, click Version Cue in the Favorites panel, then double-click Workspaces.

2 Double-click the host Version Cue Workspace.

3 Double-click the project that contains the file you want to delete.

4 Select the file and click the Delete Item 🗑 icon in the toolbar.

Note: If Show Hidden and Deleted files is not selected in the View menu, the file will become hidden and removed from view. If Show Hidden and Deleted Files is selected, the file will remain visible with the status Deleted.

To restore a file or folder deleted from a project

Note: You can perform this task only if you have access to the full Version Cue feature set, available in Adobe Creative Suite or in a shared workspace. See `Availability of Version Cue features' on page 85 for more information.

For information on restoring files or folders in Acrobat 7, see Acrobat Help.

1 In Illustrator, InCopy, InDesign, or Photoshop, choose File > Open. Click Use Adobe Dialog if you're using the OS dialog box.

2 Click Version Cue in the Favorites panel.

3 Double-click the host Version Cue Workspace.

4 Double-click the project that contains the file or folder you want to restore and do one of the following:

- Click Project Trash in the Favorites panel, select the file you want to restore, and choose Restore from the Project Tools menu 🖼 .

- Choose Show Deleted Items from the Project Tools menu (deleted file and folder names appear in gray in the dialog box). Select the file or folder you want to restore, and choose Restore from the Project Tools menu.

5 Choose Refresh from the Project Tools menu to update the dialog box.

The file or folder is restored to its original location in the Version Cue project.

Note: To restore a file in a previously deleted folder, you must first restore the folder. Doing so restores the folder and all its contents.

To delete a file or folder permanently

Note: You can perform this task only if you have access to the full Version Cue feature set, available in Adobe Creative Suite or in a shared workspace. See `Availability of Version Cue features' on page 85 for more information.

You can permanently delete and erase files or folders that have a Deleted status. For information about deleting a file or folder permanently in Acrobat 7, see Acrobat Help.

1 In Illustrator, InCopy, InDesign, or Photoshop, choose File > Open. Click Use Adobe Dialog if you're using the OS dialog box.

2 Click Version Cue in the Favorites panel.

3 Open the Version Cue Workspace and project that contains the file or folder you want to delete permanently.

4 Choose Show Deleted Items from the Project tools menu.

5 Select the file or folder you want to permanently delete, and choose Delete Permanent from the Project Tools menu.

6 Click OK.

To delete a file permanently in Bridge

Note: You can perform this task only if you have access to the full Version Cue feature set, available in Adobe Creative Suite or in a shared workspace. See `Availability of Version Cue features' on page 85 for more information.

You can permanently delete and erase files that have a Deleted status.

1 Start Bridge. In the Favorites panel, click Version Cue.

2 Double-click Workspaces, then double-click the project that contains the file you want to delete permanently.

3 Right-click (Windows) or Control-click (Mac OS) the file, and choose Delete Permanent.

4 Click OK to confirm the deletion.

Version Cue versions

About Version Cue versions

Versions provide a convenient method of retaining work that was performed in different stages. At any point in your design process, you can save a version of the file, which Version Cue saves and tracks. Each version is a snapshot of the file. You can use versions to review ideas or changes with team members or a client before selecting a final version, or to recover from destructive changes.

Version Cue prevents users from overwriting each other's work. With this protection capability, multiple users can work on a file simultaneously. When more than one user is working on a file, Version cue alerts them all when one user saves a new version, allowing everyone to update the file and work in the latest version.

Note: Two users cannot edit a file simultaneously in InCopy.

You don't have to save a version every time you save your changes. Using the File > Save command works the same way in Version Cue-managed files as in non-Version Cue files. You need only save a version when you want to create a snapshot of the file. For example, if you change the background color or some text in the layout, and then save a version, you can go back to the previous version without damaging your file. Instead of choosing File > Save As and saving a new copy of a design, you save a version, which allows you to track changes as they occur.

If you want to continue your work using a previous version instead of the current version, promote the previous version to the next current version (do this instead of opening the previous version directly). This process keeps the previous version intact, should you decide to return to it again in the future. If you want a previous version, along with the current version, to be available for use in a project, you can save the previous version as a separate asset. When you do this, you can then make the previous version a member of a group of alternates, if desired.

You can view previous versions in their native applications. When you no longer need to keep previous versions of files, you can delete them individually or in batches.

To save a version

Note: You can perform this task only if you have access to the full Version Cue feature set, available in Adobe Creative Suite or in a shared workspace. See 'Availability of Version Cue features' on page 85 for more information.

To save a new version of a file, you use the Save A Version command, which saves your changes to the Version Cue Workspace. Versions of a file can be subsequently compared using thumbnails, and viewed, deleted, or promoted using the Versions command.

1 Do one of the following:

- In Photoshop, Illustrator, InCopy, InDesign, or Acrobat 7, choose File > Save A Version.

- In Bridge, choose Tools > Version Cue > Save A Version.

2 In the Save A Version dialog box, enter comments you want to associate with this version.

3 Click Save.

To save a version of a non-Adobe file

Note: You can perform this task only if you have access to the full Version Cue feature set, available in Adobe Creative Suite or in a shared workspace. See 'Availability of Version Cue features' on page 85 for more information.

Bridge opens files in their native applications so that you can make changes. You can save versions of non-Adobe files only if (1) the files are in a Version Cue project and (2) the files have been opened through Bridge. After you create versions with this procedure, you can access them from the Versions dialog box in Adobe Creative Suite components, from InCopy, and from the Versions View of Bridge.

1 Start Bridge.

2 In the Favorites panel, click Version Cue, and then navigate to the project containing the file you want to save as a version.

3 Double-click the file to open it.

4 When the file opens in its native application, make your changes, and save and close the file.

5 In Bridge, choose Tools > Version Cue > Save A Version.

6 In the Save A Version dialog box, enter comments you want to associate with the version, and then click Continue.

Note: You can save versions of nonembedded graphics, image, and text files in InCopy, InDesign, and Illustrator by using the Edit Original command in the Links palette. After editing the file, save it in its native application. Then, in the Links palette, select the file and use the Save Link Version command to save a version in the Version Cue project. For more information, see InCopy Help, InDesign Help, or Illustrator Help.

Viewing and comparing versions

Versions are always available for you to view and compare. Each version is treated as a separate file, which you can access through the Versions dialog box in all Adobe Creative Suite components and in InCopy. The Versions dialog box displays thumbnails of all file versions alongside comments, dates, and the login name of the user who created the version. Each version is numbered sequentially. You can view any version at any time. You can also *promote* a version,

that is, make a previous version the current one. You can also delete versions if they are irrelevant or if you need to save disk space. When you delete older versions, the version numbers of the remaining versions remain the same.

The Versions And Alternates view in Bridge displays versions of all the files in a project. This view is useful for comparing versions, because all the versions are available in one place for you to view or promote—you don't need to search your hard drive for saved files. When you want to compare details of versions, you can choose to view each version in its native application.

The commenting features of Version Cue maintain a descriptive history of files. Each time you save or promote a version, you can describe what changes you made. This history helps you track changes made at different stages. Also, your version comments are searchable; you can search for a particular word to find a version quickly.

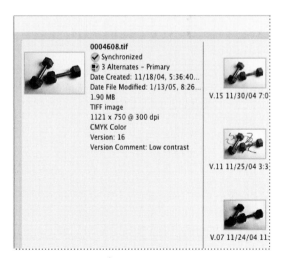

Viewing versions in Bridge

To view versions

Note: You can perform this task only if you have access to the full Version Cue feature set, available in Adobe Creative Suite or in a shared workspace. See `Availability of Version Cue features' on page 85 for more information.

After opening a file from a Version Cue Workspace, you can quickly access the previous version thumbnails, version comments, and version dates by using the Versions dialog box.

1 In Illustrator, InCopy, InDesign, or Photoshop, choose File > Open. Click Use Adobe Dialog if you're using the OS dialog box.

2 Click Version Cue in the Favorites panel.

3 Double-click the host Version Cue Workspace. Double-click the project to open it.

4 Click the name of the file whose versions you want to view.

5 Choose Versions from the Project Tools menu 🖨 .

6 In the Versions dialog box, do any of the following:

- To create a new file version from an older version, select the version and click Promote To Current Version.

- To open an earlier version in its own window and view details only or create a separate asset from the earlier version, click View Version. The version number appears in the file's title bar to remind you that you shouldn't edit it.

- To delete a version, select the version and click Delete.

In Acrobat 7, you can view the Versions dialog box by choosing File > Versions when a Version Cue-managed PDF file is open.

💡 *You can view versions of a file while it's open in an Adobe Creative Suite component: Choose Versions from the status menu at the bottom of the file window.*

To view versions in Bridge

Note: You can perform this task only if you have access to the full Version Cue feature set, available in Adobe Creative Suite or in a shared workspace. See `Availability of Version Cue features' on page 85 for more information.

In Bridge, you can use the Versions And Alternates view to see all versions of all files in a project.

1 Start Bridge, and then select Version Cue in the Favorites panel.

2 Choose View > As Versions And Alternates, or click the Versions And Alternates View icon (located at the lower right corner).

3 Click the Versions View button in the upper right corner of the window.

4 Double-click a project to view the files.

💡 *You can also see previous versions of a file while in other Bridge views. Right-click (Windows) or Ctrl-click (Mac OS) any file in a Version Cue project and choose Versions.*

To view a previous version in its native application

Note: You can perform this task only if you have access to the full Version Cue feature set, available in Adobe Creative Suite or in a shared workspace. See `Availability of Version Cue features' on page 85 for more information.

❖ Do one of the following:

• In the Versions dialog box, click the version you want to open and click View.

Note: The version number appears in the file's title bar to remind you that it is not the current version and you shouldn't edit the file.The file status is Never Saved, because the previous version is only a snapshot of a previous stage of a file.

• In Bridge, use the Versions And Alternates view, click the Versions View button in the upper-right corner of the window, right-click (Windows) or Control-click (Mac OS) a version, and choose View from the menu.

Version Cue opens the previous version in its own window. You can then edit the previous version and save it as a new asset or as an alternate. If you edit the previous version, your changes won't be reflected in the current version unless you promote the earlier version.

To promote a version

Note: You can perform this task only if you have access to the full Version Cue feature set, available in Adobe Creative Suite or in a shared workspace. See `Availability of Version Cue features' on page 85 for more information.

Promoting a previous version automatically saves a copy of that previous version as the current version. Any changes made between its creation and promotion don't appear in the new current version.

1 Do one of the following:

• In the Versions dialog box, select the version you want to promote, and click Promote To Current Version.

• In Bridge, using the Versions and Alternates view, click the Versions View button in the upper right corner of the window, right-click (Windows) or Control-click (Mac OS) a version, and then choose Promote To Current Version from the menu. If you have a working copy of the file, the status of the file changes to Outdated Copy until you open the file or synchronize.

2 Type a version comment in the Save A Version dialog box. Then click Continue to complete the promotion.

To revert to the last version in Bridge

Note: You can perform this task only if you have access to the full Version Cue feature set, available in Adobe Creative Suite or in a shared workspace. See `Availability of Version Cue features' on page 85 for more information.

❖ In Bridge, choose Tools > Version Cue > Revert To Last Version.

To delete a version

Note: You can perform this task only if you have access to the full Version Cue feature set, available in Adobe Creative Suite or in a shared workspace. See 'Availability of Version Cue features' on page 85 for more information.

❖ Do one of the following:

• In the Versions dialog box, click the version you want to delete and click Delete. To delete multiple versions, Shift-click (Windows) or Control-click (Mac OS) the versions and click Delete. When prompted, confirm the deletion.

• In Bridge, use the Versions And Alternates view, click the Versions View button in the upper right corner of the window, Right-click (Windows) or Control-click (Mac OS) the version, and then choose Delete from the menu.

Note that the remaining versions are not renumbered.

Using the Version Cue Administration utility, you can delete multiple previous versions of all files in a project simultaneously if you have access privileges. By using this method, you can retain past versions by date or by number of versions to keep. See "About the Version Cue Administration utility" in Help for more information.

Version Cue alternates

About Version Cue alternates

Version Cue makes it easy to manage variations of a design through the use of *alternates*. For example, you can create alternates for variations of a design based on different versions or completely different photos for different editions of a publication.

You can use alternates in several ways. For instance, if you make extensive changes to a file, it may make more sense to save it as an alternate than a version. When you use alternates, your original file remains untouched and you're free to continue your design work in a new direction. You can also create alternates for art you're planning to use in different media, for example, a high-resolution alternate for print and a lower-resolution alternate for web use. Or, you can make alternates from files with totally different content. For example, suppose you are creating an article about fruit production. You might use a photo of an orange for the California edition, a photo of a banana for the Florida edition, and a photo of an apple for the Washington edition. You can save each photo as an alternate.

You can access alternates from Bridge or directly from the Links palette in InCopy, InDesign, or Illustrator, making it easy to present a variety of design ideas to clients and creative directors. Version Cue protects alternates the same way as other assets. When you save an alternate, it appears as a separate file in its project, but Version Cue maintains a relationship between the original file and any alternates you create.

Version Cue maintains relationships between alternates by creating *alternates groups*, which you can view together in the Alternates dialog box. You can manually group files into an alternates group by using the Make Alternates command. You create alternates from files in different folders by dragging them between Bridge windows. Using this method you can add files from additional folders to the group as well. Thus, an alternates group can contain multiple files from multiple folders. You can make an alternate the primary, or preferred, alternate in a group. The primary alternate is designated by a special status icon, and its name is in bold in the Alternates View. In the Alternates dialog box that appears in Adobe Creative Suite components and in InCopy (in the Links palette or Open dialog box), the primary alternate appears at the top of the list in the Alternates dialog box.

You can change the primary alternate and remove alternates from the group by using Bridge or the Alternates dialog box in Adobe Creative Suite components or in InCopy.

Note: *Although you can create many alternates groups, a given file can be included in only one of these groups. Also, alternates must be located within a single project. Alternates are not available in Acrobat 7.*

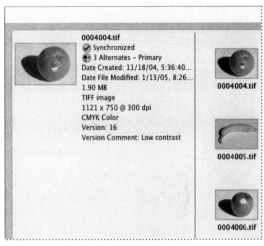

Viewing alternates in Bridge

To save an alternate

Note: *You can perform this task only if you have access to the full Version Cue feature set, available in Adobe Creative Suite or in a shared workspace. See `Availability of Version Cue features' on page 85 for more information.*

If you have a file open and want to create your current work as an alternate to the previous versions, you must use the Save As command.

1 Choose File > Save As.

2 In the Save As dialog box, select the Save As Alternate option at the bottom of the dialog box.

3 Click Save, and do one of the following:

• If you want to keep the same file name, save the alternates to a different folder.

• If you want to save the alternate in the same folder, change the file name.

The alternate is saved in the project file.

Note: If you don't change the folder or file name, Version Cue prompts you to create a new version of the file (not an alternate).

To view alternates from Bridge

Note: You can perform this task only if you have access to the full Version Cue feature set, available in Adobe Creative Suite or in a shared workspace. See 'Availability of Version Cue features' on page 85 for more information.

To quickly see which files have alternates, use the Versions And Alternates view in Bridge. This view includes thumbnails of each alternate, shows the number of alternates, and indicates which alternate is the primary alternate in the group. From this view, you can make changes to the alternates groups.

1 Start Bridge, and then select Version Cue in the Favorites panel.

2 Click the Versions And Alternates View icon. Then click Alternates View at the top of the screen.

3 Double-click a project to view alternates. To reveal an alternate's location, right-click (Windows) or Control-click (Mac OS) the alternate and choose Show File In Browser.

A file's inclusion in a group of alternates is indicated by the Alternates icon 🔘 and status information that displays how many alternates are associated with the file and whether the file is the primary alternate 🔘.

💡 *You can also see alternates of a file while in other Bridge views. Right-click (Windows) or Ctrl-click (Mac OS) any file in a Version Cue project Select and choose Alternates.*

To view alternates

Note: You can perform this task only if you have access to the full Version Cue feature set, available in Adobe Creative Suite or in a shared workspace. See 'Availability of Version Cue features' on page 85 for more information.

You can identify files with alternates in the Open, Place, Save, Import, and Export dialog boxes by looking in the Alternates column, where the number of alternates is displayed. Alternates aren't available in Acrobat 7.

1 In Illustrator, InCopy, InDesign, or Photoshop, choose File > Open. Click Use Adobe Dialog if you're using the OS dialog box.

2 Click Version Cue in the Favorites panel.

3 Double-click the host Version Cue Workspace and the project containing the alternates.

4 Click the file for the alternates you want to view.

5 Choose Alternates from the Project Tools menu 🗃 .

Note: You can also view alternates from the Links palette in Illustrator or InDesign, or from the status menu at the bottom of a file window while the file is open in an Adobe Creative Suite component. To view alternates from the Links palette, choose Alternates from the Links palette menu. To view alternates while a file is open in an Adobe Creative Suite component, choose Alternates from the menu at the bottom of the file's window.

To make an alternate the primary

Note: You can perform this task only if you have access to the full Version Cue feature set, available in Adobe Creative Suite or in a shared workspace. See `Availability of Version Cue features' on page 85 for more information.

❖ Do one of the following:

- In Bridge, click the Versions And Alternates View icon, and then click Alternates View at the top of the screen. Right-click (Windows) or Control-click (Mac OS) an alternate, and then choose Make Primary Alternate from the menu.

- In the Alternates dialog box, select the alternate and then click Make Primary Alternate. Click Done to close the dialog box. (To learn how to access the Alternates dialog box, see `To view alternates' on page 118.)

- In the Open, Save, Place, Import, and Export dialog boxes, right-click (Windows) or Ctrl-click (Mac OS) a file in a Version Cue project and choose Make Primary Alternate.

To remove an alternate

Note: You can perform this task only if you have access to the full Version Cue feature set, available in Adobe Creative Suite or in a shared workspace. See `Availability of Version Cue features' on page 85 for more information.

❖ Do one of the following:

- In Bridge, click the Versions And Alternates View icon, and then click Alternates View at the top of the screen. Right-click (Windows) or Control-click (Mac OS) an alternate from the group on the right

side of the window, and then choose Remove From Alternates Group.

- In the Alternates dialog box, select the alternate, and then click Remove. Click Done to close the dialog box. (To learn how to access the Alternates dialog box, see `To view alternates' on page 118.)

- In Open, Save, Place, Import and Export dialog boxes, right-click (Windows) or Ctrl-click (Mac OS) a file in a Version Cue project and choose Remove Alternate.

To use the Make Alternates command

Note: You can perform this task only if you have access to the full Version Cue feature set, available in Adobe Creative Suite or in a shared workspace. See `Availability of Version Cue features' on page 85 for more information.

When you use the Make Alternates command, you can make different files alternates of each other in an alternates group. You can select multiple files from more than one folder to make alternates.

1 In Illustrator, InCopy, InDesign, or Photoshop choose File > Open.

2 Navigate to the project containing the files you want to make alternates.

3 Shift-click or Control-click to select the files you want to make alternates. To view files in more than one folder, click the triangle to the left of the folder name.

4 Right-click (Windows) or Control-click (Mac OS) one of the selected files, and then choose Make Alternates from the menu.

Note: Although it is possible to reveal files in different projects by using the disclosure triangles, only files within a single project can be made alternates of each other.

To make alternates in Bridge

Note: You can perform this task only if you have access to the full Version Cue feature set, available in Adobe Creative Suite or in a shared workspace. See `Availability of Version Cue features' on page 85 for more information.

When you make alternates in Bridge, you can make different files alternates of each other in an alternates group. Alternates are not available in Acrobat 7.

❖ To make alternates in Bridge, do one of the following:

• To make alternates from files in one folder in Bridge, navigate to the project containing the files you want to make alternates. In the Bridge window, Shift-click or Control-click to select the files you want to make alternates and choose Tools > Version Cue > Make Alternates.

• To make alternates from files in multiple folders in Bridge, navigate to the project containing the files you want to make alternates, and click Alternates View in the upper right corner of the Bridge window. (If Alternates View doesn't appear, click Versions and Alternates View in the lower right corner of the window.) Choose File > New Window, and navigate to a different folder in the same Version Cue project. Shift-click or Control-click to select the files you want to make alternates, and drag them to the right of the larger thumbnail showing the file being viewed in the Alternates view of the first Bridge window.

• To make alternates from a past version of a file in Bridge, navigate to the project containing the file you want to make an alternate. Right-click the file and choose View. When the file opens in its native application, choose File > Save As, and either save the file in a different folder or change the file name. Select Alternates, and then click Save.

To move an alternate to another alternates group

Note: You can perform this task only if you have access to the full Version Cue feature set, available in Adobe Creative Suite or in a shared workspace. See `Availability of Version Cue features' on page 85 for more information.

A file cannot be a member of more than one alternates group. To move an alternate to another group, you must first remove it from it's original group and then add it to a new group.

1 Remove the alternate from its group. For instructions, see `To remove an alternate' on page 119.

2 Add the file to a new alternates group. For instructions, see `To save an alternate' on page 117 or `To make alternates in Bridge' on page 120.

Editing and synchronizing offline files

Editing and synchronizing offline files

When you need to work on files from a Version Cue project while the Version Cue Workspace is unavailable on the network, you can edit working copies on your computer. When the Version Cue Workspace is available again, you must *synchronize* your files with the workspace to save your latest version to the Version Cue Workspace. You can synchronize an entire project, just a folder in the project, or a selected file.

Working copies are normally copied on your computer when you open a project from an online workspace. However, if you haven't yet edited the file, you can prepare to work offline by synchronizing the entire Version Cue project, or just the files you need, while the workspace is still online to ensure that you have working copies.

When you are working offline, you can't create multiple versions because the Save A Version command is unavailable.

In Version Cue CS2, if you intend to work on a file offline, you can manually mark the file In Use before you take your work offline. When you mark a file In Use, Version Cue creates a working copy of the file for you. (You can mark a file In Use even if you don't intend to work offline.) Typically, when you're editing a file, In Use appears when other users access a file. When a file's status is In Use, Version Cue protects the

file. When you synchronize your file, the status of the file returns to Synchronized. Mark In Use is not available in Acrobat 7.

 If you have edited an offline file recently, you can open it from the File > Open Recent menu.

To manually mark a file as In Use

Note: You can perform this task only if you have access to the full Version Cue feature set, available in Adobe Creative Suite or in a shared workspace. See `Availability of Version Cue features' on page 85 for more information.

1 Do one of the following:

- In Bridge, click Version Cue in the Favorites panel. Navigate to the file. Select one or more files. Right-click (Windows) or Ctrl-click (Mac OS) a file, and then choose Mark In Use.

- In Illustrator, InCopy, InDesign, or Photoshop, choose File > Open. Click Version Cue in the Favorites panel, and then navigate to the file. Select one or more files. Right-click (Windows) or Control-click (Mac OS) a file, and then choose Mark In Use. (Mark In Use is not available in Acrobat 7.)

2 When you finish editing the file offline and the Version Cue workspace is again available, synchronize the file in Bridge or in any Adobe Creative Suite component. Version Cue automatically creates a new version of the file. If the workspace becomes available while you still have the file open, simply save a version.

If you haven't made any changes, you can manually cancel the In Use By Me status, by choosing Cancel Mark In Use from the context menu.

To edit working copies of files from an offline project

Note: You can perform this task only if you have access to the full Version Cue feature set, available in Adobe Creative Suite or in a shared workspace. See `Availability of Version Cue features' on page 85 for more information.

For information on editing offline files in Acrobat 7, see Acrobat Help.

1 In Illustrator, InCopy, InDesign, or Photoshop, choose File > Open. Click Use Adobe Dialog if you're using the OS dialog box.

2 Click Version Cue in the Favorites panel.

3 Double-click the host Version Cue Workspace.

4 Double-click the Version Cue project that contains the file. It may take Version Cue a few seconds to verify that a Version Cue Workspace or project is unavailable.

5 Double-click a file to open it (the Offline Copy status allows you to open the file).

6 When you finish editing the file, choose File > Save to save the changes to the working copy. When the Version Cue Workspace becomes available again, synchronize your files.

To synchronize files in Bridge

Note: You can perform this task only if you have access to the full Version Cue feature set, available in Adobe Creative Suite or in a shared workspace. See `Availability of Version Cue features' on page 85 for more information.

1 Start Bridge. In the Favorites panel, click Version Cue.

2 Double-click Workspaces.

3 Select the project that contains the master file, and do one of the following:

- To synchronize the entire project, right-click (Windows) or Control-click (Mac OS) the project, and then choose Synchronize.

- To synchronize a file in the project, open the project, right-click (Windows) or Control-click (Mac OS) the folder or file, and choose Synchronize from the Project Tools menu.

4 If the master file on the Version Cue Workspace is newer than your working copy and you've edited the working copy, a File Conflict dialog box appears. Specify one or more of the following:

Apply The Following Action To All Subsequent Conflicts Automatically applies the selected option every time there is a file conflict.

Save A Version Saves your working copy as a new file version to the Version Cue Workspace.

Skip This File Prevents the most recent version from the Version Cue Workspace from being downloaded. (This option also prevents a version of your working copy form being saved to the workspace.) Choose this option only if you want to keep your edits and disregard the other changes in the master file.

To synchronize files

Note: You can perform this task only if you have access to the full Version Cue feature set, available in Adobe Creative Suite or in a shared workspace. See `Availability of Version Cue features' on page 85 for more information.

For information on synchronizing files in Acrobat, see Acrobat Help.

1 In Illustrator, InCopy, InDesign, or Photoshop, choose File > Open. Click Use Adobe Dialog if you're using the OS dialog box.

2 Click Version Cue in the Favorites panel.

3 Select the project that contains the master file, and do one of the following:

- To synchronize the entire project, choose Synchronize from the Project Tools menu 📇 .

- To synchronize just a folder or one or more files, open the project, select the folder or files that you want to synchronize, and choose Synchronize from the Project Tools menu.

4 If the master file on the Version Cue Workspace is newer than your working copy and you've edited the working copy, a File Conflict dialog box appears. Specify one or more of the following:

Apply The Following Action To All Subsequent Conflicts Automatically applies the selected option every time there is a file conflict.

Save a Version Saves your working copy as a new file version to the Version Cue Workspace.

Skip This File Prevents the most recent version from the Version Cue Workspace from being downloaded. (This option also prevents a version of your working copy from being saved to the workspace.) Choose this option only if you want to keep your edits and disregard the other changes in the master file.

The Version Cue Administration utility

About the Version Cue Administration utility

Using the Version Cue Administration utility, you can do more advanced tasks that affect a specified project or an entire Version Cue Workspace. For instance, you can specify backup configurations, create projects from existing folders, delete batches of versions, host PDF reviews, and more.

Important: *For more information, see "About the Version Cue Administration utility" in Help.*

About Version Cue Administration integrity checks

Each time the Version Cue Workspace restarts, it performs an integrity check and performs repairs if necessary. To ensure best performance, restart the Version Cue Workspace periodically so it can perform the integrity check and self-repair.

Chapter 6: Getting images into Photoshop and ImageReady

Bitmap images and vector graphics

Bitmap images and vector graphics

Computer graphics fall into two main categories—
bitmap and *vector*. You can work with both types of
graphics in Photoshop and ImageReady; moreover, a
Photoshop file can contain both bitmap and vector
data. It's helpful to understand the difference between
the two categories as you create, edit, and import
artwork.

Bitmap images

Bitmap images—technically called *raster images*—are
made up of a grid of dots known as pixels. When
working with bitmap images, you edit pixels rather
than objects or shapes. Bitmap images are the most
common electronic medium for continuous-tone
images, such as photographs or digital paintings,
because they can represent subtle gradations of shades
and color.

Bitmap images can lose detail when scaled on-screen
because they are resolution-dependent, they contain a
fixed number of pixels, and each pixel is assigned a
specific location and color value. Bitmapped images
can look jagged if they're printed at too low a
resolution because the size of each pixel is increased.

Example of a bitmap image at different levels of magnification

> *For information about working with painting tools,
> see Photoshop Help.*

Vector graphics

Vector graphics are made up of mathematically
defined lines and curves called *vectors*. You can move,
resize, or change the color of a line without losing the
quality of the graphic.

Vector graphics are resolution-independent—that is,
they can be scaled to any size and printed at any
resolution without losing detail or clarity. As a result,
vector graphics are the best choice for representing
bold graphics that must retain crisp lines when scaled
to various sizes (logos, for example).

Example of a vector graphic at different levels of magnification

Note: *Because computer monitors can display images only on a grid, both vector graphics and bitmap images are displayed as pixels on-screen.*

For information about working with vector graphics and using the drawing and type tools, see Photoshop Help.

Image size and resolution

Pixel dimensions and image resolution

The number of pixels along the height and width of a bitmap image is called the *pixel dimensions* of an image. The number of pixels per inch (ppi) printed on a page determines the *image resolution*.

The amount of detail in an image depends on its pixel dimensions, whereas the image resolution controls how much space the pixels are printed over. For example, you can modify the resolution of an image without changing the actual pixel data in the image— all you change is the printed size of the image. However, if you want to maintain the same output dimensions, changing the resolution of the image requires a change in the total number of pixels.

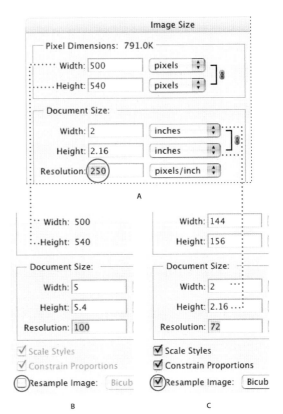

Pixel dimensions equal document (output) size times resolution.
A. Original dimensions and resolution B. Decreasing the resolution without changing pixel dimensions (no resampling)
C. Decreasing the resolution at same document size decreases pixel dimensions (resampling).

In Photoshop, you can change the resolution of an image. In ImageReady, the resolution of images is always 72 ppi, to optimize the images for online media.

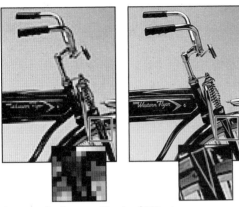

Example of an image at 72 ppi and 300 ppi

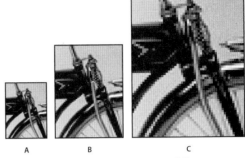

Printing the same low-resolution image at different sizes
A. Small print size **B.** Medium print size **C.** Large print size

When printed, an image with a high resolution contains more, and therefore smaller, pixels than an image with a low resolution. Higher-resolution images can reproduce greater detail and subtler color transitions than lower-resolution images because of the density of the pixels in the images. High-quality images often look good at any print size.

You can't improve a lower-quality image by printing it at a high resolution. Changing the print resolution of an image simply makes each pixel larger, which results in *pixelation*—output with large, coarse-looking pixels. Increasing the print resolution of an image doesn't add any pixel information to the image. You can make a low-resolution image look its best by picking a print size that makes the most of the pixels it has.

Important: *Video files are displayed only at 72 ppi. Even if an image has a higher resolution than 72 ppi, the quality may not be very good when it's displayed in a video-editing application.*

File size

The file size of an image is the digital size of the image file, measured in kilobytes (K), megabytes (MB), or gigabytes (GB). File size is proportional to the pixel dimensions of the image. Images with more pixels may produce more detail at a given printed size, but they require more disk space to store and may be slower to edit and print. Image resolution thus becomes a compromise between image quality (capturing all the data you need) and file size.

Another factor that affects file size is file format. Because of the varying compression methods used by GIF, JPEG, and PNG file formats, file sizes can vary considerably for the same pixel dimensions. Similarly, color bit-depth and the number of layers and channels in an image affect file size.

Photoshop supports a maximum pixel dimension of 300,000 by 300,000 pixels per image. This restriction places limits on the print size and resolution available to an image.

Monitor resolution

Image data is translated directly into monitor pixels. This means that when the image resolution is higher than the monitor resolution, the image appears larger on-screen than its specified print dimensions.

Monitor resolution depends on the size of the monitor plus its pixel setting. For example, a large image (800-by-600-pixel dimension) shown on a 15-inch monitor would almost fill the screen, but on a larger monitor, the same image would take up less room on the screen, and each pixel would appear larger.

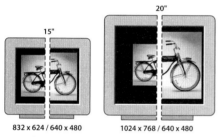

Example of an image displayed on monitors of various sizes and resolutions

Note: *When you are preparing an image for online display, pixel dimensions become especially important. Make sure that the size of an image allows room for the web browser window controls on smaller monitors.*

Printer resolution

Printer resolution is measured by the number of ink dots per inch (dpi) produced by all laser printers, including imagesetters.

Inkjet printers produce a microscopic spray of ink, not actual dots; however, most inkjet printers have an approximate resolution of 240 to 720 dpi. Many inkjet printer drivers offer simplified print settings for choosing higher quality printing. To determine your printer's optimal resolution, check your printer documentation.

For more information, see `About desktop printing' on page 381.

Screen frequency

Screen frequency is the number of printer dots or halftone cells per inch used to print grayscale images or color separations. Also known as *screen ruling* or *line screen*, screen frequency is measured in lines per inch (lpi)—or lines of cells per inch in a halftone screen. The higher the resolution of the output device, the finer (higher) a screen ruling you can use.

The relationship between image resolution and screen frequency determines the quality of detail in the printed image. To produce a halftone image of the highest quality, you generally use an image resolution that is from 1.5 to at most 2 times the screen frequency. But with some images and output devices, a lower resolution can produce good results. To determine your printer's screen frequency, check your printer documentation or consult your service provider.

Note: *Some imagesetters and 600-dpi laser printers use screening technologies other than halftoning. If you are printing an image on a nonhalftone printer, consult your service provider or your printer documentation for the recommended image resolutions.*

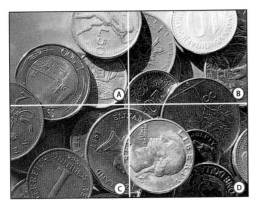

Screen frequency examples
A. *65 lpi: Coarse screen typically used to print newsletters and grocery coupons* **B.** *85 lpi: Average screen typically used to print newspapers* **C.** *133 lpi: High-quality screen typically used to print four-color magazines* **D.** *177 lpi: Very fine screen typically used for annual reports and images in art books*

Changing image size and resolution

Adjusting image size and resolution

After you have scanned or imported an image, you may want to adjust its size. In Photoshop, you use the Image Size dialog box to adjust the pixel dimensions, print dimensions, and resolution of an image; in ImageReady, you can adjust only the pixel dimensions of an image.

For assistance with resizing and resampling images in Photoshop, choose Help > Resize Image. This interactive wizard helps you scale your images for print or online media.

Remember, bitmap and vector data can produce different results when you resize an image. Bitmap data is resolution-dependent; therefore, changing the pixel dimensions of a bitmap image can degrade image quality and sharpness. In contrast, vector data is resolution-independent; you can resize it without losing its crisp edges.

To display the current image size

You can display information about the current image size using the information box at the bottom of the application window (Windows) or the document window (Mac OS).

❖ Do one of the following:

• (Photoshop) Press Alt (Windows) or Option (Mac OS), position the pointer over the file information box, and hold down the mouse button. The box displays the width and height of the image (both in pixels and in the unit of measurement currently selected for the rulers), the number of channels, and the image resolution.

• (ImageReady) Click an image information box, and select Image Dimensions from the pop-up menu. The box displays the width and height of the image, in pixels.

Resampling

Resampling refers to changing the pixel dimensions (and therefore display size) of an image. When you *downsample* (decrease the number of pixels), information is deleted from the image. When you *resample up* (increase the number of pixels, or *upsample*), new pixels are added. You specify an *interpolation* method to determine how pixels are added or deleted.

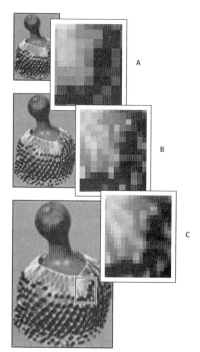

Resampling pixels
A. *Downsampled* **B.** *Original* **C.** *Resampled up (selected pixels displayed for each set of images)*

Keep in mind that resampling can result in poorer image quality. For example, when you resample an image to larger pixel dimensions, the image loses some detail and sharpness. Applying the Unsharp Mask filter to a resampled image can help refocus the image details.

You can avoid the need for resampling by scanning or creating the image at a sufficiently high resolution. If you want to preview the effects of changing pixel dimensions on-screen or to print proofs at different resolutions, resample a duplicate of your file.

For more information, see 'Sharpening images' on page 259.

Choosing an interpolation method

When an image is resampled, an *interpolation method* is used to assign color values to any new pixels that Photoshop creates, based on the color values of existing pixels in the image. Photoshop and ImageReady use sophisticated methods to preserve the quality and detail from the original image when you resample.

In the General Preferences dialog box, you can specify which default interpolation method to use whenever you resample images using the Image Size or transformation commands. The Image Size command also lets you specify an interpolation method other than the default.

To specify the default interpolation method

1 Do one of the following:

- In Windows, choose Edit > Preferences > General.

- (Photoshop) In Mac OS choose Photoshop > Preferences > General.

- (ImageReady) In Mac OS, choose ImageReady > Preferences > General.

2 For Interpolation, choose one of the following options:

Nearest Neighbor A fast but less precise method that replicates the pixels in an image. This method is for use with illustrations containing edges that are not anti-aliased, to preserve hard edges and produce a smaller file. However, this method can produce jagged effects, which become apparent when you distort or scale an image or perform multiple manipulations on a selection.

Bilinear A method that adds pixels by averaging the color values of surrounding pixels. It produces medium-quality results.

Bicubic A slower but more precise method based on an examination of the values of surrounding pixels. Using more complex calculations, Bicubic produces smoother tonal gradations than Nearest Neighbor or Bilinear.

Bicubic Smoother A good method for enlarging images based on Bicubic interpolation but designed to produce smoother results.

Bicubic Sharper A good method for reducing the size of an image based on Bicubic interpolation with enhanced sharpening. This method maintains the detail in a resampled image. If Bicubic Sharper oversharpens some areas of an image, try using Bicubic.

To change the pixel dimensions of an image in Photoshop

When preparing images for online distribution, it's useful to specify image size in terms of pixel dimensions. Changing pixel dimensions affects not only the size of an image on-screen but also its image quality and its printed characteristics—either its printed dimensions or its image resolution.

1 Choose Image > Image Size.

2 To maintain the current ratio of pixel width to pixel height, select Constrain Proportions. This option automatically updates the width as you change the height, and vice versa.

3 Under Pixel Dimensions, enter values for Width and Height. To enter values as percentages of the current dimensions, choose Percent as the unit of measurement. The new file size for the image appears at the top of the Image Size dialog box, with the old file size in parentheses.

4 Make sure that Resample Image is selected, and choose an interpolation method.

5 If your image has layers with styles applied to them, select Scale Styles to scale the effects in the resized image. This option is available only if you selected Constrain Proportions.

6 When you finish setting options, click OK.

For best results when you produce a smaller image, downsample and apply the Unsharp Mask filter. To produce a larger image, rescan the image at a higher resolution.

To change the pixel dimensions of an image in ImageReady

1 Choose Image > Image Size.

2 To maintain the current ratio of pixel width to pixel height, select Constrain Proportions.

3 Under New Size, enter values for Width, Height, or Percent. The New Size text field displays the new file size of the image.

4 (Optional) Select a interpolation method from the Quality pop-up menu.

Note: Action options are used to record an action with image size options in ImageReady.

Changing the print dimensions and resolution of an image

When creating an image for print media, it's useful to specify image size in terms of the printed dimensions and the image resolution. These two measurements, referred to as the *document size*, determine the total pixel count and therefore the file size of the image; document size also determines the base size at which an image is placed into another application. You can further manipulate the scale of the printed image using the Print With Preview command; however, changes you make using the Print With Preview command affect only the printed image, not the document size of the image file.

If you turn on resampling for the image, you can change print dimensions and resolution independently (and change the total number of pixels in the image). If you turn off resampling, you can change either the dimensions or the resolution—Photoshop adjusts the other value automatically to preserve the total pixel count. For the highest print quality, it's generally best to change the dimensions and resolution first, without resampling. Then resample only as necessary.

For more information, see`Positioning and scaling images' on page 384 and `To set Photoshop print options' on page 383.

To change the print dimensions and resolution of an image

1 Choose Image > Image Size.

2 Change the print dimensions, image resolution, or both:

- To change only the print dimensions or only the resolution and adjust the total number of pixels in the image proportionately, make sure that Resample Image is selected. Then choose an interpolation method.

- To change the print dimensions and resolution without changing the total number of pixels in the image, deselect Resample Image.

3 To maintain the current ratio of image width to image height, select Constrain Proportions. This option automatically changes the width as you change the height, and vice versa.

4 Under Document Size, enter new values for the height and width. If desired, choose a new unit of measurement. Note that for Width, the Columns option uses the width and gutter sizes specified in the Units & Rulers preferences.

5 For Resolution, enter a new value. If desired, choose a new unit of measurement.

To restore the initial values displayed in the Image Size dialog box, hold down Alt (Windows) or Option (Mac OS), and click Reset.

For information about using columns, see Photoshop Help

To view the print size on-screen

❖ Do one of the following:

- Choose View > Print Size.

- Select the Hand tool or Zoom tool, and click Print Size in the options bar.

The image is redisplayed in its approximate printed size, as specified in the Document Size area of the Image Size dialog box. The size and resolution of your monitor affect the on-screen print size.

To determine a suggested resolution for an image

If you plan to print your image using a halftone screen, the range of suitable image resolutions depends on the screen frequency of your output device. Photoshop can determine a recommended image resolution based on the screen frequency of your output device.

Note: If your image resolution is more than 2.5 times the screen ruling, an alert message appears when you try to print the image. This means that the image resolution is higher than necessary for the printer. Save a copy of the file, and then reduce the resolution.

1 Choose Image > Image Size.

2 Click Auto.

3 For Screen, enter the screen frequency for the output device. If necessary, choose a different unit of measurement. Note that the screen value is used only to calculate the image resolution, not to set the screen for printing.

Note: To specify the halftone screen ruling for printing, you must use the Halftone Screens dialog box, accessible through the Print With Preview command.

4 For Quality, select an option:

Draft Produces a resolution that is the same as the screen frequency (no lower than 72 pixels per inch).

Good Produces a resolution 1.5 times the screen frequency.

Best Produces a resolution 2 times the screen frequency.

Getting images from digital cameras

Acquiring digital images from cameras

You should copy images from a digital camera to your hard drive before editing them in Photoshop or ImageReady. If you use a media card reader, or if you connect to a camera that appears as a drive on your computer, you can use Adobe Bridge to move the files to your destination folder. You can also use the software that came with your camera, Windows Image Acquisition (WIA) or Image Capture (Mac OS). For more information on using Windows Image Acquisition or Image Capture, see your computer documentation.

To get images from a digital camera using Bridge

1 Connect your media card reader or camera to your computer. The media card reader or camera must appear as a drive (volume) on your computer for this procedure to work.

2 Open Bridge.

3 (Optional) If necessary, click the Folders tab, browse to the location where you want to store your images, and create a destination folder.

You can also click the Favorites tab and drag the destination folder into the Favorites palette. This makes it easier to access the folder in the future.

4 Click the Folders tab and browse to the drive with your images.

5 Select the images. Make sure that the destination folder is visible in either the Favorites palette or the Folders palettes.

6 Drag the images to the destination folder.

If your media card reader or camera appears as a volume on your desktop, you can also drag the image file from the volume into Bridge.

To import images from a digital camera using WIA

Certain digital cameras import images using Windows Image Acquisition (WIA) support. When you use WIA, Photoshop works with Windows and your digital camera or scanner software to import images directly into Photoshop.

Note: WIA is available only in Windows XP.

1 Choose File > Import > WIA Support.

2 Choose a destination in which to save your image files on your computer.

3 Make sure that Open Acquired Images in Photoshop is selected. If you are importing a large number of images, or if you want to edit the images later, deselect Open Acquired Images.

4 To save the imported images directly into a folder whose name is the current date, select Unique Subfolder.

5 Click Start.

6 Select the digital camera from which to import images.

Note: If the name of your camera does not appear in the submenu, verify that the software and drivers were properly installed and that the camera is connected.

7 Choose the image or images you want to import:

- Click the image from the list of thumbnails to import the image.

- Hold down Shift and click multiple images to import them at the same time.

- Click Select All to import all available images.

8 Click Get Picture to import the image.

Scanning images

About scanning

Before you scan an image, make sure to install the software necessary for your scanner. To ensure a high-quality scan, predetermine the optimum scanning resolution and dynamic range for your image. These preparatory steps can prevent unwanted color casts.

Scanner drivers are supported by the scanner manufacturer, not Adobe Systems Incorporated. If you have problems with scanning, make sure that you are using the latest version of the scanner driver.

When scanning images, try to scan similar images together. For example, it's better to scan dark images with other dark images. The scanned output will be better, and it will be easier to correct your images.

Importing scanned images

You can import scanned images directly from any scanner that has a Photoshop-compatible plug-in module or that supports the TWAIN interface. To import the scan using a plug-in module, choose the scanner name from the File > Import submenu. See your scanner documentation for instructions on installing the scanner plug-in.

If your scanner does not have Photoshop-compatible scanner driver, import the scan using the TWAIN interface.

If you can't import the scan using the TWAIN interface, use the scanner manufacturer's software to scan your images, and save the images as TIFF, PICT, or BMP files. Then open the files in Photoshop or ImageReady.

For more information, see 'About plug-in modules' on page 44.

Importing scanned images using the TWAIN interface

TWAIN is a cross-platform interface for acquiring images captured by certain scanners, digital cameras, and frame grabbers. The manufacturer of the TWAIN device must provide a Source Manager and TWAIN data source for your device to work with Photoshop and ImageReady.

You must install the TWAIN device and its software and restart your computer before you can use it to import images into Photoshop and ImageReady. See the documentation provided by your device manufacturer for installation information.

To import an image using the TWAIN interface in Photoshop

❖ Choose File > Import, and choose the device you want to use from the submenu.

To import an image using the TWAIN interface in ImageReady

1 If you're using the TWAIN device for the first time with ImageReady, choose File > Import > TWAIN Select. Then select the device you want to use. You do not need to repeat this step for subsequent uses of the TWAIN module.

If more than one TWAIN device is installed on your system and you want to switch devices, use the TWAIN Select command.

2 To import the image, choose File > Import > TWAIN Acquire.

To import images from a scanner using WIA Support

1 Choose File > Import > WIA Support.

2 Choose a destination on your computer for saving your image files.

3 Click Start.

4 Make sure that Open Acquired Images in Photoshop is selected. If you have a large number of images to import, or if you want to edit the images at a later time, deselect it.

5 Make sure that Unique Subfolder is selected if you want to save the imported images directly into a folder whose name is the current date.

6 Select the scanner that you want to use.

Note: If the name of your scanner does not appear in the submenu, verify that the software and drivers were properly installed and that the scanner is connected.

7 Choose the kind of image you want to scan:

Color Picture Uses the default settings for scanning color images.

Grayscale Picture Uses the default settings for scanning grayscale images.

Black And White Picture or Text Uses the default settings.

Adjust The Quality Of The Scanned Picture Uses custom settings.

8 Click preview to view the scan. If necessary, drag the handles of the bounding box to adjust the size of the crop.

9 Click Scan.

10 The scanned image is saved in BMP format.

Creating, opening, and importing images

To create a new image

Use the New command to create a new, blank image. If you've copied a selection to the clipboard, the image dimensions and resolution are automatically based on that image data.

1 Choose File > New.

2 If desired, type a name for the image, and set the width and height.

(Photoshop) To match the width and height of the new image to that of any open image, choose a file name from the bottom section of the Windows menu.

3 (Photoshop) Set the resolution and mode.

4 Select an option for the contents of the background layer (Photoshop) or first layer (ImageReady) of the image:

White Fills the background or first layer with white, the default background color.

Background Color Fills the background or first layer with the current background color.

Transparent Makes the first layer transparent, with no color values. The resulting document has a single, transparent layer as its contents.

5 Under Advanced, choose a color profile, or choose Don't Color Manage This Document. For Pixel Aspect Ratio, choose Square unless you're using the image for video. In that case, choose another option to use non-square pixels.

6 When you finish, you can save the settings as a preset by clicking Save Preset, or you can click OK to open the new file.

For more information, see `Color modes' on page 167 and `Saving images for use in video' on page 375.

Opening files

You can open files using the Open command and Open Recent command. In Photoshop, you can also open files using Adobe Bridge.

Sometimes Photoshop may not be able to determine the correct format for a file. This can happen, for example, because the file has been transferred between two operating systems. Sometimes a transfer between Mac OS and Windows can cause the file format to be mislabeled. In such cases, you must specify the correct format in which to open the file.

Note: Photoshop and ImageReady use plug-in modules to open and import many file formats. If a file format does not appear in the Open dialog box or in the File > Import submenu, you may need to install the format's plug-in module.

For information about using the Place command to import files, see Photoshop Help.

For more information, see 'About plug-in modules' on page 44.

To open a file using the Open command

1 Choose File > Open.

2 Select the name of the file you want to open. If the file does not appear, select the option for showing all files from the Files Of Type (Windows) or Show (Mac OS) pop-up menu.

3 (Mac OS) Click Show Preview to preview the selected file. This option requires the Apple QuickTime extension.

Note: Previews appear faster if they are saved with the file. In Photoshop, select Always Save For Image Previews in the File Handling preferences to always save a preview; select Ask When Saving to save previews on a file-by-file basis.

4 Click Open. In some cases, a dialog box appears, letting you set format-specific options.

Note: If a color profile warning message appears, specify whether to convert the pixels based on the file's color profile.

To open a recently used file

❖ Choose File > Open Recent, and select a file from the submenu.

To specify the number of files listed in the Open Recent submenu

1 Do one of the following:

- (Photoshop) Choose Edit > Preferences > File Handling (Windows), or choose Photoshop > Preferences > File Handling (Mac OS).

- (ImageReady) Choose Edit > Preferences > General (Windows), or choose ImageReady > Preferences > General (Mac OS).

2 Do one of the following:

- (Photoshop) Enter a number in the Recent File List Contains text box.

- (ImageReady) Enter a number in the Recent Files text box.

To specify the file format in which to open a file

❖ Do one of the following:

- (Windows) Choose File > Open As, and select the file you want to open. Then choose the desired format from the Open As pop-up menu, and click Open.

- (Mac OS) Choose File > Open, and choose All Documents from the Show pop-up menu. Then select the file you want to open, choose the desired file format from the Format pop-up menu, and click Open.

Note: If the file does not open, then the chosen format may not match the file's true format, or the file may be damaged.

Opening PDF files

Portable Document Format (PDF) is a versatile file format that can represent both vector and bitmap data. It has electronic document search and navigation features. PDF is the primary format for Adobe Illustrator and Adobe Acrobat.

Some PDF files contain a single image, and others contain multiple pages and images. When you open a PDF file in Photoshop, you can choose which pages or images to open and specify rasterization options. The pages or images are imported as Smart Objects in new documents.

In Photoshop, you can also import PDF data using the Place command, the Paste command, and the drag-and-drop feature. The page or image is placed on a separate layer as a Smart Object.

Note: You can't bring PDF data into ImageReady.

For more information, see `Smart Objects' on page 316.

To open a PDF file

After you open a PDF document, you can import pages or images from it into new documents in Photoshop. You can also import pages or images from a PDF document using the Place command.

For information about using the Place command, see Photoshop Help.

1 Do one of the following:

- (Photoshop) Choose File > Open.

- (Bridge) Select the PDF file and choose File > Open With > Adobe Photoshop CS2. Skip to step 3.

2 In the Open dialog box, select the name of the file, and click Open. You can change which types of files are listed by selecting an option from the Files Of Type (Windows) or Format (Mac OS) pop-up menu.

3 In the Import PDF dialog box, choose Page or Image from the Select menu, depending on what elements of the PDF document you want to import.

4 Select the pages or images you want to open by clicking the thumbnails. Shift-click to select more than one page or image. The number of selected items appears under the preview window.

Note: Use the Thumbnail Size menu to adjust the thumbnail view in the preview window. The Fit Page option fits one thumbnail in the preview window. A scroll bar appears if there are multiple items.

5 To give the new document a name, type it in the Name text box. If you're importing more than one page or image, multiple documents open with the base name followed by a number.

6 Under Page Options, choose from the Crop To menu to specify what part of the PDF document to include:

Bounding Box Crops to the smallest rectangular region that includes all the text and graphics of the page. This option eliminates extraneous white space.

Media Box Crops to the original size of the page.

Crop Box Crops to the clipping region (crop margins) of the PDF file.

Bleed Box Crops to the region specified in the PDF file for accommodating limitations inherent in production processes such as cutting, folding, and trimming.

Trim Box Crops to the region specified for the intended finished size of the page.

Art Box Crops to the region specified in the PDF file for placing the PDF data into another application.

7 Specify the following under Page Options:

Resolution Sets the resolution for the new document. See also `Pixel dimensions and image resolution' on page 126.

Mode Sets the color mode for the new document. See also `Color modes' on page 167.

Bit Depth Sets the bit depth for the new document. See also `About bit depth' on page 172.

Anti-aliased Minimizes jagged lines at the edges of an image. Deselect this option if you want a hard-edged transition between pixels.

Transparent Background Reveals text or graphics beneath the PDF page. Deselect this option to place the PDF page on a white background.

8 To suppress color profile warnings, select Suppress Warning.

9 Click OK.

Opening PostScript artwork

Encapsulated PostScript (EPS) can represent both vector and bitmap data and is supported by virtually all graphic, illustration, and page-layout programs.

Adobe applications that produce PostScript artwork include Adobe Illustrator, Adobe Dimensions, and Adobe Streamline. When you open an EPS file containing vector art, it is *rasterized*—the mathematically defined lines and curves of the vector artwork are converted into the pixels or bits of a bitmap image.

You can also bring PostScript artwork into Photoshop or ImageReady using the Place command, the Paste command, and the drag-and-drop feature.

High Dynamic Range images

About High Dynamic Range images

The dynamic range (ratio between dark and bright regions) in the visible world far exceeds the range of human vision and of images that are printed or displayed on a monitor. But whereas human eyes can adapt to very different brightness levels, most cameras and computer monitors can capture and reproduce only a fixed dynamic range. Photographers, motion picture artists, and others working with digital images must be selective about what's important in a scene because they are working with a limited dynamic range.

High Dynamic Range (HDR) images open up a world of possibilities because they can represent the entire dynamic range of the visible world. Because all the luminance values in a real-world scene are represented proportionately and stored in an HDR image, adjusting the exposure of an HDR image is like adjusting the exposure when photographing a scene in the real world. This capability lets you create blurs and other real-world lighting effects that look realistic. Currently, HDR images are used mostly in motion pictures, special effects, 3D work, and some high-end photography.

Merging images of different exposures to create an HDR image **A.** *Image with shadow detail but highlights clipped* **B.** *Image with highlight detail but shadows clipped* **C.** *HDR image containing the dynamic range of the scene*

In Photoshop, the luminance values of an HDR image are stored using a floating-point numeric representation that's 32 bits long (32-bits-per-channel). The luminance values in an HDR image are directly related to the amount of light in a scene. This is not so with (non-floating point) 16-bits-per-channel and 8-bits-per-channel image files, which can store luminance values only from black to paper white; this represents an extremely small segment of the dynamic range in the real world.

You can create an HDR image using multiple photographs, each captured at a different exposure. In Photoshop, the Merge To HDR command lets you create HDR images from multiple photographs. Because an HDR image contains brightness levels that far exceed the display capabilities of a standard 24-bit monitor or the range of tones in a printed image, Photoshop lets you adjust the preview of the HDR image so it can be viewed on a computer monitor. Some Photoshop tools, adjustments, and filters can be used with HDR images. If you need to print the image or use Photoshop tools and filters that don't work with HDR images, you can convert the HDR image to an 8- or 16-bits-per-channel image.

Working with HDR images

Photoshop lets you use the following tools, adjustments, and filters with 32-bits-per-channel HDR images:

Adjustments Channel Mixer, Photo Filter, and Exposure.

Note: Although the Exposure command can be used with 8- and 16-bits-per-channel images, it is designed for making exposure adjustments to 32-bits-per-channel HDR images.

Blend Modes Normal, Darken, Multiply, Lighten, Linear Dodge, and Difference.

Editing Commands Fill, Stroke, Free Transform, Transform, Image Size, Canvas Size, Rotate Canvas, Crop (with rotation and resize), and Trim.

File Formats Photoshop (PSD, PSB), Radiance (HDR), Portable Bit Map (PFM), OpenEXR, and TIFF.

Note: Although Photoshop cannot save an HDR image in the LogLuv TIFF file format, it can open and read a LogLuv TIFF file.

Filters Average, Box Blur, Gaussian Blur, Motion Blur, Radial Blur, Shape Blur, Surface Blur, Add Noise, Fibers, Lens Flare, Smart Sharpen, Unsharp Mask, De-Interlace, NTSC Colors, High Pass, and Offset.

Modes RGB Color, Grayscale, conversion to 8 Bits/Channel or 16 Bits/Channel.

Tools Marquee tools, Move tool, lasso tools, Crop tool, Slice tool, Clone Stamp tool, History Brush tool, Path Selection tool, Direct Selection tool, pen tools, annotation tools, Eyedropper tool, Color Sampler tool, Measure tool, Hand tool, and Zoom tool. Some tools work with supported blend modes only.

The Merge To HDR command

Use the Merge To HDR command to combine multiple images (with different exposures) of the same image or scene, capturing the dynamic range of a scene in a single HDR image. You can choose to save the merged image as a 32-bits-per-channel HDR image.

Note: It's also possible to use the Merge To HDR command to save the merged image as an 8- or 16-bits-per-channel image. However, only a 32-bits-per-channel image can store all the HDR image data; 8- and 16-bits-per-channel images will be clipped.

Keep the following tips in mind when you take photos to be combined with the Merge To HDR command:

- Secure the camera to a tripod.
- Take enough photos to cover the full dynamic range of the scene. You can try taking at least five to seven photos, but you might need to take more exposures depending on the dynamic range of the scene. The minimum number of photos should be three.

- Vary the shutter speed to create different exposures. Changing the aperture changes the depth of field in each exposure and can produce lower-quality results. Changing the ISO or aperture may also cause noise or vignetting in the image.

- In general, don't use your camera's auto-bracket feature, because the exposure changes are usually too small.

- The exposure differences between the photos should be one or two EV (exposure value) steps apart (equivalent to about one or two f-stops apart).

- Don't vary the lighting; for instance, don't use a flash in one exposure but not the next.

- Make sure that nothing is moving in the scene. Exposure Merge works only with differently exposed images of the identical scene.

To use the Merge To HDR command

1 Do one of the following:

- (Photoshop) Choose File > Automate > Merge To HDR.

- (Bridge) Select the images you want to use and choose Tools > Photoshop > Merge To HDR. Skip to step 3.

2 In the Merge To HDR dialog box, click Browse, browse to select the images, and click Open.

To remove an item, select it in the Merge To HDR dialog box and click Remove.

Note: *If you want to add a folder of images or images that are open in Photoshop, choose Folder or Open Files from the Use menu.*

3 (Optional) Select the Attempt To Automatically Align Source Images option if you held the camera in your hands when you photographed the multiple images.

4 Click OK.

A second Merge To HDR dialog box displays thumbnails of the images being used in the merged result, a preview of the merged result, a Bit Depth menu, and a slider for setting the white point preview.

5 If necessary, do one of the following to set the view options for the merged result preview:

- Click the Minus or Plus buttons below the preview image to zoom out or zoom in.

- Choose a view percentage or mode from the pop-up menu below the preview image.

6 (Optional) Deselect or select the thumbnails in the Sources filmstrip to specify which images to use in the merged image.

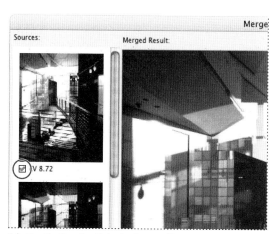

Selecting the thumbnails in the Sources filmstrip

7 Choose a bit depth for the merged image from the Bit Depth menu.

Note: *Be sure to choose 32 Bits/Channel if you want the merged image to store the entire dynamic range data of the HDR image.*

8 Move the slider below the histogram to set the white point for previewing the merged image.

Important: *If the merged image is being saved as a 32-bits-per-channel image, moving the slider adjusts the image preview only. All the HDR image data remains intact in the 32-bits-per-channel HDR image file. The preview adjustment is stored in the 32-bits-per-channel HDR image file and applied whenever the file is opened in Photoshop. If you choose to save the merged image as an 8- or 16-bits-per-channel image, moving the slider applies exposure edits to the image file. Any discarded image data will not be recoverable after the merged 8- or 16-bits-per-channel image is created.*

9 Click OK to create the merged image.

To adjust HDR image viewing

The dynamic range of HDR images exceeds the display capabilities of standard computer monitors. When you open an HDR image in Photoshop, it can look very dark or washed out. Photoshop lets you adjust the preview so that the monitor displays an HDR image whose highlights and shadows aren't washed out or too dark. The preview settings are stored in the HDR image file and are applied whenever the file is opened in Photoshop. Preview adjustments don't affect the HDR image file, all the HDR image information remains intact. Use the Exposure adjustment to make exposure edits to the 32-bits-per-channel HDR image.

To view 32-bit readouts in the Info palette, click the Eyedropper icon in the Info palette and choose 32-Bit from the pop-up menu.

1 Open a 32-bits-per-channel HDR image in Photoshop, and choose View > 32-Bit Preview Options.

2 In the 32-bit Preview Options dialog box, choose an option from the Method menu:

Exposure And Gamma Adjusts the brightness and contrast.

Highlight Compression Compresses the highlight values in the HDR image so they fall within the luminance values range of the 8- or 16-bits-per-channel image file.

3 If you chose Exposure And Gamma, move the Exposure and Gain sliders to adjust the brightness and contrast of the image preview.

4 Click OK.

You can also adjust the preview of an HDR image open in Photoshop by clicking the triangle in the status bar of the document window and choosing 32-Bit Exposure from the pop-up menu. Move the slider to set the white point for viewing the HDR image. Since the adjustment is made per view, you can have the same HDR image open in multiple windows, each with a different preview adjustment. Preview adjustments made with this method are not stored in the HDR image file.

To convert from 32 bits to 8 or 16 bits per channel

HDR images contain luminance levels that far exceed the luminance data that can be stored in 8- or 16-bits-per-channel image files. Photoshop lets you make exposure and contrast corrections so that converting a 32-bits-per-channel HDR image to 8 or 16 bits per channel results in an image with the dynamic range (tonal range) you want.

1 Open a 32-bits-per-channel image and choose Image > Mode > 16 Bits/Channel or 8 Bits/Channel.

2 In the HDR Conversion dialog box, choose a method for adjusting the brightness and contrast in the image:

Exposure And Gamma Lets you manually adjust the brightness and contrast of the HDR image.

Highlight Compression Compresses the highlight values in the HDR image so they fall within the luminance values range of the 8- or 16-bits-per-channel image file. No further adjustments are necessary; this method is automatic. Click OK to convert the 32-bits-per-channel image.

Equalize Histogram Compresses the dynamic range of the HDR image while trying to preserve some contrast. No further adjustments are necessary; this method is automatic. Click OK to convert the 32-bits-per-channel image.

Local Adaptation Adjusts the tonality in the HDR image by calculating the amount of correction necessary for local brightness regions throughout the image.

3 (Optional) Click the arrow to display the toning curve and histogram. The histogram shows the luminance values in the original HDR image. The red tick marks along the horizontal axis are in 1 EV (approximately 1 f-stop) increments. The toning curve is active only for the Local Adaptation method.

4 Do any of the following:

- If you chose Exposure And Gamma, move the Exposure slider to adjust the gain and move the Gamma slider to adjust the contrast.

- If you chose Local Adaptation, move the Radius slider to specify the size of the local brightness regions. Move the Threshold slider to specify how far apart two pixels' tonal values must be before they're no longer part of the same brightness region. You can also use the toning curve to make adjustments.

Note: The toning curve usually lets you make limited changes from point to point and attempts to equalize your changes across the points. If you select the Corner option after inserting a point on the curve, the limit is removed and no equalization is performed when you insert and move a second point. You'll notice that the curve becomes angular at a point with the Corner option applied.

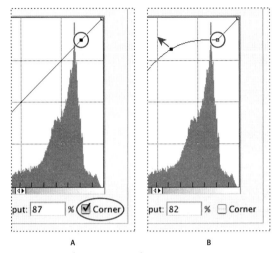

Toning curve adjustment using the Corner option
A. Inserting a point displays the Corner option. B. Adjusting new point makes the curve angular at the point where the Corner option is used.

5 (Optional) To save your 32-bit toning options as a file, click Save. Type a name for the file in the Save dialog box and click Save.

You can reuse the saved 32-bit toning option file. Click Load to convert another 32-bits-per-channel image to an 8- or 16-bits-per-channel image.

6 Click OK to convert the 32-bits-per-channel image.

Chapter 7: Camera raw files

Camera raw files in Photoshop and Bridge

Camera raw files

A *camera raw* file contains unprocessed picture data from a digital camera's image sensor. Many digital cameras can save images files in camera raw format. In this way, photographers can interpret the image data rather than having the camera make the adjustments and conversions automatically.

Camera raw image files contain the actual data captured by the sensor without any in-camera processing; these are the only files containing "pure" data. Working with camera raw files gives you maximum control; you can set the white balance, tonal range, contrast, color saturation, and sharpening. Think of camera raw files as your photo negative. You can reprocess the file at any time to achieve the results you want.

To create raw files, you need to set your camera to save files in its own raw file format. In Adobe Bridge or Photoshop, you can process only those camera raw files obtained from supported cameras. Visit the adobe.com website to view a list of supported cameras.

The Camera Raw plug-in

The Camera Raw plug-in processes camera raw files with default image setting files based on Camera Raw's built-in camera profiles for supported camera models and the EXIF data. Every camera model saves the camera raw image in a unique format, but Camera Raw can process many camera raw file formats. When you first view thumbnails and preview camera raw files in Bridge, you see the files with the default image settings applied. By default, Camera Raw also uses an Auto Adjustments option that applies image settings to a file by evaluating the image data in addition to using the Camera Raw default settings and the EXIF data. You can change the default settings, make advanced adjustments, and specify file saving options using the tools and controls in the Camera Raw dialog box. You can save settings for reuse or make them the default settings for a specific camera model.

Use the Camera Raw plug-in to perform the following tasks:

- Preview camera raw images in Bridge using the default image settings.

- Apply settings to camera raw files in Bridge without opening the Camera Raw dialog box.

- Copy and paste the settings from one camera raw image to another in Bridge.

- Use the default image settings and open camera raw image files directly in Photoshop without opening the Camera Raw dialog box.

- Process the files in the Camera Raw dialog box and open the images in Photoshop, where you can do further editing and save them in a supported file format.

- Process the files in the Camera Raw dialog box and either simply close the dialog box or save the camera raw images in a file format supported by Photoshop.

- Automate the processing of a batch of camera raw files and save them in a Photoshop-supported file format using the Image Processor, the Batch command, or a droplet.

- Mark camera raw files for deletion as you process a batch of images in the Camera Raw dialog box, and

send the rejected files to the Recycle Bin (Windows) or Trash (Mac OS) when you finish.

- Save adjusted settings as the default image settings for a specific camera. See `To adjust the rendering of non-neutral colors in Camera Raw' on page 159.

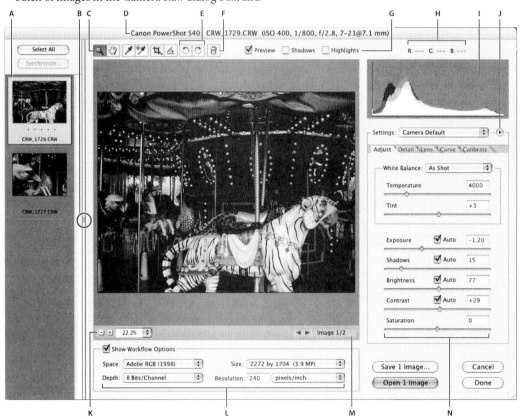

Camera Raw dialog box
A. Filmstrip B. Toggle Filmstrip C. Tools D. Camera, file name, and some EXIF information E. Rotate buttons
F. Mark for Delete button G. View options H. RGB values I. Histogram J. Camera Raw plug-in menu K. Zoom levels
L. Workflow options M. Navigation arrows N. Adjustment sliders

Note: You must have Photoshop installed to open camera raw files in Bridge. However, if Photoshop is not installed, you can still preview the camera raw files in the Preview tab and as thumbnails. If a third-party application is associated with the camera raw file type, it's possible to open the camera raw file in the third-party application from Bridge.

When you make adjustments (including straightening and cropping the image) from the Camera Raw dialog box, the original camera raw file data is preserved. The adjustment settings are stored on a per-image basis in either the Camera Raw database file or in *sidecar* XMP files (files that accompany the original camera raw image file in the same folder). Choose a preference to specify where the settings are stored. The XMP files are useful if you plan to move the image files to a storage medium or another computer and want to retain the camera raw settings. You can use the Export Settings command to copy the settings in the Camera Raw database to sidecar XMP files or embed the settings in Digital Negative (DNG) files.

From the Camera Raw dialog box, you can save the processed files in Digital Negative (DNG), JPEG, TIFF, or Photoshop (PSD) formats. If you open the file in Photoshop, you can save the camera raw image in Photoshop-compatible formats such as PSD, JPEG, Large Document Format (PSB), TIFF, Cineon, Photoshop Raw, PNG, or Portable Bit Map. For more information on the Digital Negative format, see Photoshop Help or visit the adobe.com website.

Note: The Camera Raw dialog box is automatically suppressed when you use a batch of camera raw files for a web photo gallery, picture package, or contact sheet, or when you use the Place command with camera raw files.

You can save the camera raw settings for a specific camera or a specific lighting condition and reuse them to process another camera raw image file or a batch of files.

For more information, see `Camera Raw settings' on page 161 and `To process camera raw files in Camera Raw' on page 148.

Camera raw and Photoshop Raw files

Although Photoshop can open and edit a camera raw image file, it cannot save an image in camera raw format. A Photoshop Raw format is available in Photoshop, but it's not the same format used in camera raw image files. A camera raw image file contains the unprocessed bits from the camera's CCD or CMOS. This data needs significant processing of the type performed by the Camera Raw plug-in. The Photoshop Raw format (.raw) is a flexible file format for transferring images between applications and computer platforms.

Caches for camera raw files in Bridge

When you view camera raw files in Adobe Bridge, the thumbnails and previews use either the camera raw default settings or your adjusted settings. The cache in Bridge and the Camera Raw cache store data for the file thumbnails, metadata, and file information. Caching this data shortens the loading time when you return to a previously viewed folder.

The Camera Raw cache speeds loading of the Camera Raw dialog box and the recalculation of previews in Bridge after changes are made to the Camera Raw settings. The Camera Raw cache holds preparsed raw image data for the most recently accessed camera raw files.

The cache in Bridge stores the calculated thumbnails, previews, and metadata for all kinds of images.

Because the caches can become very large, you may want to purge the cache or limit its size. You can also purge and regenerate the cache if you suspect that it is corrupted or old. Purging the cache deletes thumbnail information and metadata added since the camera raw file was opened in Bridge.

Note: The Camera Raw cache holds data for about 200 images for each gigabyte of disk storage allocated to it. By default, the Camera Raw cache is set to a maximum size of 1 GB. You can increase its limit in the Camera Raw Preferences.

To work with the camera raw cache in Bridge

1 In Bridge, do one of the following:

- In the Camera Raw dialog box, click the triangle next to the Settings menu and choose Preferences from the Camera Raw menu.

- (Windows) Choose Edit > Camera Raw Preferences.

- (Mac OS) Choose Bridge > Camera Raw Preferences, or, with the Camera Raw dialog box open, choose Photoshop > Camera Raw Preferences.

2 Do any of the following:

- To change the cache size, type a value in the Maximum Size text box.

- To purge the camera raw cache, click the Purge Cache button.

- To change the location of the camera raw cache, click Select Location, browse to the new location, and click Select.

3 Click OK.

For more information, see `To work with the cache in Bridge' on page 58.

Processing and opening camera raw files in Photoshop

To open camera raw images in Photoshop

You can open one or more camera raw image files directly in Photoshop without opening the Camera Raw dialog box. Photoshop apples either the default camera raw image settings or your adjusted settings.

❖ In Bridge, do one of the following:

- Select one or more camera raw image files, hold down the Shift key, and choose File > Open.

- Hold down the Shift key and double-click a camera raw image file.

To process camera raw files in Camera Raw

1 Do one of the following:

- (Bridge) Select one or more camera raw files, and choose File > Open With > Photoshop CS2. The Camera Raw dialog box appears, with Open as the default button for opening the images in Photoshop.

- (Bridge) Select one or more camera raw files and choose File > Open In Camera Raw. The Camera Raw dialog box appears, with Done as the default button for closing the dialog box after you adjust settings.

- (Photoshop) Choose File > Open, browse to select one or more camera raw files, and click Open. The Camera Raw dialog box appears, with Open as the default button for opening the images in Photoshop.

The Camera Raw dialog box opens with the camera raw image displayed in a preview window. The histogram shows the tonal range of the image with the current settings. As you make setting adjustments, the histogram automatically updates. If you selected more than one image, the Filmstrip appears on the left side of the Camera Raw dialog box. (You can show or hide the Filmstrip by clicking Toggle Filmstrip ▯.)

2 If you're processing several camera raw files, select them from the Filmstrip. Use the arrows in the lower right corner of the preview window to navigate to the image you want to adjust.

Note: A caution icon ⚠ *appears in the thumbnails and preview image while the preview is generated from the cache.*

3 (Optional) Adjust the image view using controls and options such as zoom, shadows, and highlights. See `Camera Raw view controls' on page 151.

Note: Selecting the Preview check box turns on a preview of any setting changes made to the current tab (Adjust, Detail, Lens, Curve, or Calibrate) combined with the settings in the hidden tabs. Deselecting the Preview check box displays the camera raw image with the original settings of the current tab combined with the settings in the hidden tabs.

4 (Optional) Click the Rotate Image buttons ↺ ↻ to rotate the image 90˚ counterclockwise or 90˚ clockwise.

5 (Optional) Select the Color Sampler tool ✒ to place up to four color samplers in the preview image. The RGB readouts for each sampler appear above the preview image. Click Clear Samplers to remove all the color samplers. See `Using the histogram and RGB levels in Camera Raw' on page 152 and `To view color values in an image' on page 220.

6 (Optional) Choose workflow options (target color space profile, bit depth, pixel dimension, and resolution). Select or deselect Show Workflow Options to show or hide the menus. See `Camera Raw Workflow settings' on page 152.

7 (Optional) To apply the settings used in the previous camera raw image or the default settings for your camera, choose an option from the Settings menu. In this way, you can quickly process images with similar lighting conditions. See `Camera Raw settings' on page 161 and `To apply saved Camera Raw settings' on page 162.

8 Set options to adjust the white balance. See `White balance controls for camera raw files' on page 153.

💡 *You can monitor the RGB values of pixels in your image as you adjust it in the Camera Raw dialog box. Position the Zoom tool, Hand tool, White Balance tool, Color Sampler tool, or Crop tool over the preview image to display the RGB values directly beneath the pointer. You can also place up to four color samplers in the preview image. The RGB values of each color sampler appear beneath the preview image.*

9 Make tonal adjustments using the Exposure, Shadow, Brightness, Contrast, and Saturation sliders, or select the Auto check boxes to make these adjustments automatically. There is no Auto check box for Saturation. See `Tonal adjustment controls for camera raw files' on page 154.

Click an Auto check box to undo your manual adjustments and make the adjustments automatically. To restore all options to their initial settings, press Alt (Windows) or Option (Mac OS) and click Reset.

Note: By default, the Auto check boxes are always selected in the Camera Raw dialog box. You change this default by choosing Use Auto Adjustments from the Camera Raw menu or changing the Camera Raw default so that all or some Auto check boxes are always unselected. See `To turn on or off the Auto adjustments in Camera Raw' on page 155.

10 (Optional) Click the following tabs to make further adjustments:

Detail Adjusts sharpening, or applies luminance smoothing or color noise reduction. See `To adjust sharpening in camera raw files' on page 156 and `Reducing noise in camera raw files' on page 157.

Lens Compensates for chromatic aberration and vignetting introduced by a digital camera. See `To compensate for chromatic aberration in Camera Raw' on page 158 and `To compensate for lens vignetting' on page 158.

Curve Adjusts tonality using a Curves adjustment. Use the Tone Curve menu to choose a preset adjustment.

Calibrate Lets you correct a color cast in the shadows and adjust non-neutral colors to compensate for the difference between the behavior of your camera and Camera Raw's built-in profile for your camera model. To save adjustments as the default settings for a specific camera, click the triangle next to the Settings menu. Then, from the Camera Raw dialog box menu, choose Save New Camera Raw Defaults. See `To remove a shadow color cast in camera raw files' on

page 159 and `To adjust the rendering of non-neutral colors in Camera Raw' on page 159.

You can save image settings or a subset of settings for reuse on other camera raw images. You can also save adjusted settings as the default for a specific camera. For example, if you find that the Linear setting in the Curve tab works best with the images from your camera, you can choose Linear from the Tone Curve menu and then choose Save New Camera Raw Defaults from the Adobe Camera Raw dialog box menu. In the future, a Linear tone curve will be applied to images from the same camera. See `To save or reset Camera Raw settings' on page 162

11 (Optional) If you are processing several images and want to delete one or more of them, select them in the Thumbnail pane and click Mark For Deletion 🗑 .

A red cross appears over a marked image in the Thumbnail pane. The file is sent to the Recycle Bin (Windows) or Trash (Mac OS) when you close the Camera Raw dialog box. (If you decide to keep an image that you marked for deletion, select it in the Thumbnail pane and click Mark For Deletion again.)

12 (Optional) To crop or straighten an image when the Camera Raw settings are applied, select the Crop tool 🔲 or Straighten tool 📐 and drag over the image. To cancel the operation, press Esc or click the Crop tool and choose Clear Crop from the context menu. See `To crop or straighten images in Camera Raw' on page 156.

If you selected more than one image in the Camera Raw dialog box, they are all cropped by the same amount and at the same place.

13 Click one of the following buttons:

Open Opens copies of the camera raw image files (with the Camera Raw settings applied) in Photoshop. You can edit the image further and save the images in a Photoshop-supported format. The original camera raw image file remains unaltered. The settings applied to the camera raw image are stored either in the camera raw database file or as a sidecar XMP file.

Done Closes the Camera Raw dialog box and stores file settings either in the camera raw database file or as a sidecar XMP file.

Save Applies the Camera Raw settings to the images and saves copies of them in a Photoshop-supported file format. In the Camera Raw Save Options dialog box, specify the destination for the saved files, a file-naming convention, and a file format: Digital Negative (DNG), JPEG, TIFF, or Photoshop. Press Alt (Windows) or Option (Mac OS) to suppress the Camera Raw Save Options dialog box and save the files using the last set of save options. See `To save camera raw images in Camera Raw' on page 160.

💡 *When using the Save command in the Camera Raw dialog box, files are placed in a queue to be processed and saved. This is useful if you are processing several files in the Camera Raw dialog box and saving them in the same format. Click Alt+Save (Windows) or Option+Save (Mac OS) to suppress the Camera Raw Save Options dialog box when saving a file. The file is placed into the queue and saved in the background while you work on another file. In this way, the Camera Raw dialog box lets you set up an efficient "assembly line" for processing and saving images.*

Cancel Cancels the adjustments specified in the Camera Raw dialog box.

After you process and edit a camera raw file using the Camera Raw plug-in, an icon 🖼 appears in the image thumbnail in Bridge.

Camera Raw view controls

Zoom tool 🔍 Sets the preview zoom to the next preset value when you click the preview image. Press Alt/Option and click to set the next lower zoom value. Drag the Zoom tool in the preview image to zoom in on a selected area. To return to 100%, double-click the Zoom tool.

Hand tool Moves the image in the preview window if the preview image is set at a zoom level higher than 100%. Hold down the spacebar to use the Hand tool while using another tool. Double-click the Hand tool to fit the preview image to the window.

Select Zoom Level Sets the magnification of the preview image. Choose a zoom setting from the menu or click the Select Zoom Level buttons.

Preview Turns on a preview reflecting the changes to the current settings tab (Adjust, Detail, Lens, Curve, or Calibrate) combined with the settings in the hidden tabs. Turn Preview off to view the camera raw image with the original settings for the current tab combined with the settings in the hidden tabs.

RGB Indicates the red, green, and blue values of the area of pixels directly below the pointer as you move it over the preview image. The values appear when you use the Zoom tool, Hand tool, White Balance tool, Color Sampler tool, Crop tool, or Straighten tool.

Shadows and Highlights Displays shadow and highlight clipping. Clipped shadows appear in blue, and clipped highlights appear in red. Highlight clipping is shown if any one of the three RGB channels is clipped (fully saturated with no detail). Shadow clipping is shown if all three RGB channels are clipped (black with no detail).

Using the histogram and RGB levels in Camera Raw

The Camera Raw histogram shows all three channels (red, green, and blue) of the image simultaneously. The histogram changes automatically as you adjust the settings in the Camera Raw dialog box.

As you move the Zoom tool, Hand tool, White Balance tool, Color Sampler tool, Crop tool, or Straighten tool over the preview image, you see, in the upper right corner of the dialog box, the RGB values of the area below the pointer.

You can also select the Color Sampler tool and place up to four color samplers in the preview image. The RGB values appear above the preview image. To clear the color samplers, click Clear Samplers.

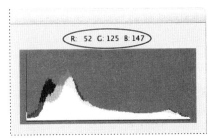

The Camera Raw dialog box displays the RGB values of the area of pixels below the pointer.

For more information, see 'About histograms' on page 215 and 'Viewing the color values of pixels' on page 219.

Camera Raw Workflow settings

Space Specifies the *target* color space profile. Generally, this should be set to the same value as your Photoshop RGB working space. Keep in mind that the *source* profile for camera raw image files is usually the camera-native color space. The profiles listed in the Space menu are built into the Camera Raw plug-in. If you want to use a color space that's not listed in the Space menu, choose ProPhoto RGB, and then convert to the working space of your choice when the file opens in Photoshop.

Depth Specifies whether the file opens as an 8- or 16-bits-per-channel image in Photoshop.

Size Specifies the pixel size at which to open the image. The default is the pixel size used to photograph the image. Use the Size menu if you want to resample the image.

For square-pixel cameras, the Size menu is mostly a convenience for the user. However, choosing a smaller-than-native size is useful to speed processing when you are planning a smaller final image anyway. Picking a larger size is similar to upsampling in Photoshop.

For non-square pixel cameras, the native size is the one that most closely preserves the total pixel count. Selecting a different size minimizes the resampling Camera Raw needs to perform, resulting in slightly higher image quality. The best quality size is marked with an asterisk (*) in the Size menu.

Note: *You can always change the pixel size of the image after it opens in Photoshop.*

Resolution Specifies the printing resolution at which the image will be printed or the amount of data in the image. This setting does not affect the actual pixels (pixel size of the image). For example, a 2048 x 1536 pixel image, when printed at 72 dpi, is approximately 28-1/2 x 21-1/4 inches. When printed at 300 dpi, the same image is approximately 6-3/4 x 5-1/8 inches. You can also use the Image Size command to adjust resolution in Photoshop.

Making tonal adjustments in Camera Raw

White balance and camera raw files

A digital camera records the white balance at the time of exposure as a metadata entry. The Camera Raw plug-in reads this value and makes it the initial setting when you open the file in the Camera Raw dialog box. This setting usually yields the correct color temperature, or nearly so. You can adjust it if the white balance is not quite right.

The Adjust tab in the Photoshop Camera Raw dialog box has three controls for correcting a color cast in your image. The Calibrate tab also has a control for correcting a shadow color cast (a color cast that remains in the shadows even after the white balance is adjusted).

White balance controls for camera raw files

White Balance Sets the color balance of the image to reflect the lighting conditions under which the photo was taken. In some cases, choosing a white balance from the White Balance menu provides satisfactory

results. In many cases, you may want to customize the white balance using the Temperature and Tint adjustments.

Note: The Camera Raw plug-in can read the white balance settings of some cameras. Leave White Balance set to As Shot to use the camera's white balance settings. For cameras whose white balance settings are not recognized by the Camera Raw plug-in, leaving White Balance set to As Shot is the same as choosing Auto: the Camera Raw plug-in reads the image data and automatically adjusts the white balance.

Temperature Fine-tunes the white balance to a custom color temperature. Set the color temperature using the Kelvin color temperature scale. Move the slider to the left to correct a photo taken with a lower color temperature of light; the plug-in makes the image colors bluer to compensate for the lower color temperature (yellowish) of the ambient light. Conversely, move the slider to the right to correct a photo taken with a higher color temperature of light; the plug-in makes the image colors warmer (yellowish) to compensate for the higher color temperature (bluish) of the ambient light.

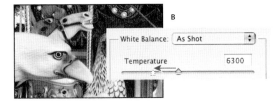

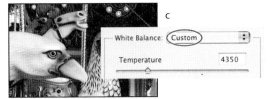

Using White Balance to click a neutral white area and resulting correction

Correcting the white balance
A. *Moving the Temperature slider to the right corrects a photo taken with a higher color temperature of light* **B.** *Moving the Temperature slider to the left corrects a photo taken with a lower color temperature of light* **C.** *Photo after color temperature adjustment*

Tint Fine-tunes the white balance to compensate for a green or magenta tint. Move the slider to the left (negative values) to add green to the photo; move it to the right (positive values) to add magenta.

💡 *To adjust the white balance quickly, select the White Balance tool, and then click an area in the preview image that should be a neutral gray or white. The Temperature and Tint sliders automatically adjust to make the selected color exactly neutral (if possible). If you're clicking whites, choose a highlight area that contains significant white detail rather than a specular highlight.*

Tonal adjustment controls for camera raw files

Exposure Adjusts the brightness or darkness of the image. Move the slider to the left to darken the image; move it to the right to brighten the image. The values are in increments equivalent to f-stops. An adjustment of +1.50 is similar to widening the aperture 1-1/2 stops. Similarly, an adjustment of –1.50 is similar to reducing the aperture 1-1/2 stops.

💡 *Hold down Alt (Windows) or Option (Mac OS) while moving the Exposure slider to preview where the highlights are clipped. (Clipping is the shifting of pixel values to either the highest highlight value or the lowest shadow value. Clipped areas are either completely white or completely black and have no image detail.) Move the slider until the highlights (not specular highlights) are completely clipped, and then reverse the adjustment slightly. Black indicates unclipped areas, and color indicates areas clipped in only one or two channels.*

Hold down Alt (Windows) or Option (Mac OS) while moving the Exposure slider to show clipped highlights.

Shadows Specifies which input levels are mapped to black in the final image. Moving the slider to the right increases the areas that are mapped to black. This sometimes creates the impression of increased contrast in the image. Using the Shadows slider is similar to using the black point slider for input levels in the Photoshop Levels command.

Hold down Alt (Windows) or Option (Mac OS) while moving the Shadow slider to preview where the shadows are clipped. Move the slider until the shadows begin to get clipped, and then reverse the adjustment slightly. Color indicates areas that are being clipped in one or two channels, and white indicates unclipped areas.

Brightness Adjusts the brightness or darkness of the image, much as the Exposure slider does. However, instead of clipping the image in the highlights (areas that are completely white, no detail) or shadows (areas that are completely black, no detail), Brightness compresses the highlights and expands the shadows when you move the slider to the right. In general, use the Brightness slider to adjust the overall brightness or

darkness after you set the white and black clipping points with the Exposure and Shadow sliders.

Contrast Adjusts the midtones in an image. Higher values increase the midtone contrast, and lower values produce an image with less contrast. Generally, you use the Contrast slider to adjust the contrast of the midtones after setting the Exposure, Shadow, and Brightness values.

Saturation Adjusts the color saturation of the image from –100 (pure monochrome) to +100 (double the saturation).

To turn on or off the Auto adjustments in Camera Raw

By default, the Auto check boxes are always selected in the Camera Raw dialog box. You change this default so that all or some Auto check boxes are always unselected.

❖ Do any of the following:

• In the Camera Raw dialog box, click the triangle next to the Settings menu and choose Use Auto Adjustments from the Camera Raw menu.

When Use Auto Adjustments is unchecked, all or some Auto check boxes are always unselected. When Use Auto Adjustments is checked, the Auto check boxes are always selected.

• Deselect the Auto check boxes, click the triangle next to the Settings menu, and choose Save New Camera Raw Defaults from the Camera Raw menu.

Transforming images in Camera Raw

To rotate images in Camera Raw

❖ Click a Rotate Image button ⟳ ⟲ to rotate the image 90˚ counterclockwise or 90˚ clockwise.

To crop or straighten images in Camera Raw

1 In the Camera Raw dialog box, select the Crop tool ⊐ or Straighten tool ⊿ .

2 (Optional) If you want the crop area constrained to specific proportions, click the Crop tool icon and choose a proportion from the pop-up menu. Choosing Custom opens the Custom Crop dialog box, where you can specify the proportions or the dimensions of the crop. Click OK.

3 Do one of the following:

- To crop the image, drag the Crop tool over the image.

- To straighten the image, drag the Straighten tool in the preview image to establish what's horizontal or vertical.

4 (Optional) To adjust the crop area, do one of the following:

- To scale or rotate the crop area, drag just outside the bounding box handles.

- To move the crop area, click in the bounding box and drag.

If you selected several images in the Camera Raw dialog box, they are all cropped to the same size, with the crop applied in the same position.

Note: To cancel the crop operation, press Esc with the Crop tool selected or click the Crop tool and choose Clear Crop from the pop-up menu. To cancel the crop and close the Camera Raw dialog box without processing the camera raw image file, click the Cancel button or deselect the Crop tool and press Esc.

5 Click Open, Done, or Save to apply the crop and process the camera raw image file.

For more information, see 'Cropping images' on page 253.

To adjust sharpening in camera raw files

The Sharpness slider adjusts the image sharpening to provide the edge definition you wish. The Sharpness adjustment is a variation of the Photoshop Unsharp Mask filter, which locates pixels that differ from surrounding pixels based on the threshold you specify and increases the pixels' contrast by the amount you specify. When opening a camera raw image file, the Camera Raw plug-in calculates the threshold to use based on camera model, ISO, and exposure compensation. You can choose whether sharpening is applied to all images or just to previews.

1 Zoom the preview image to at least 100%.

2 Move the slider to the right to increase sharpening and to the left to decrease it. A value of zero turns off sharpening. In general, set the Sharpness slider to a lower value for cleaner images.

💡 *If you don't plan to edit the image extensively in Photoshop, use the Camera Raw's Sharpness slider. If you do plan to edit the image extensively in Photoshop, turn off Camera Raw sharpening. Then use the sharpening filters in Photoshop as the last step after all other editing and resizing is complete.*

To specify whether the image or preview is sharpened

1 Do one of the following:

- In the Camera Raw dialog box, click the triangle next to the Settings menu and choose Preferences from the Camera Raw menu.

- (Windows) In Adobe Bridge, choose Edit > Camera Raw Preferences.

- (Mac OS) In Bridge, choose Bridge > Camera Raw Preferences, or with the Camera Raw dialog box opened in Photoshop, choose Photoshop > Camera Raw Preferences.

2 In the Camera Raw Preferences dialog box, choose one of the following:

All Images Applies sharpening to the camera raw image.

Preview Images Only Applies sharpening only to the preview image and not the actual camera raw image. This option is for users who do not want to apply sharpening with the Camera Raw plug-in.

Reducing noise in camera raw files

The Detail tab of the Camera Raw dialog box has controls for reducing image *noise*, the extraneous visible artifacts that degrade image quality. Image noise includes luminance (grayscale) noise, which makes an image look grainy, and chroma (color) noise, which is usually visible as colored artifacts in the image. Photos taken with high ISO speeds or less-sophisticated digital cameras can have noticeable noise.

The Luminance Smoothing slider reduces grayscale noise, and the Color Noise Reduction slider reduces chroma noise. Moving a slider to zero turns off its noise reduction.

When making Luminance Smoothing or Color Noise Reduction adjustments, first zoom in on the preview image for a better view.

Moving the Luminance Smoothing slider to the right reduces grayscale noise, and moving the Color Noise Reduction slider to the right reduces chroma noise.

Chromatic aberration

Chromatic aberration is a common defect caused by the failure of the lens to focus different frequencies (colors) to the same spot. In one type of chromatic aberration, the image from each color of light is in focus, but each image is a slightly different size. This type of aberration is seen as a complementary color fringing in areas away from the center of the image. For example, you may see a red fringe on the side of an object toward the center of the image, and cyan fringe on the side of the object away from the center of the image.

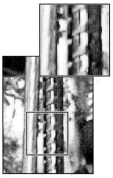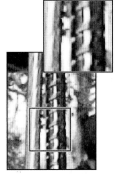

Original image (left), and after fixing chromatic aberration (right)

To compensate for chromatic aberration in Camera Raw

1 Zoom into an area near the corner of the preview image. For the best results, the area should contain very dark or black detail against a very light or white background. Look for the color fringing.

2 In the Lens tab, move one or more of the following sliders:

Fix Red/Cyan Fringe Adjusts the size of the red channel relative to the green channel. This compensates for red/cyan color fringing.

Fix Blue/Yellow Fringe Adjusts the size of the blue channel relative to the green channel. This compensates for blue/yellow color fringing.

Look at the preview image as you move the slider to the left or right. If you're adjusting red/cyan color fringing, you can hold down Alt (Windows) or Option (Mac OS) to hide the blue/yellow color fringing. Similarly, hold down Alt (Windows) or Option

(Mac OS) while adjusting the blue/yellow color fringing to hide the red/cyan color fringing. Your goal is to reduce the color fringing as much as possible.

To compensate for lens vignetting

Vignetting is a lens defect that causes the edges, especially the corners, of an image to be darker than the center.

1 In the Lens tab, move the Vignetting Amount slider to the right (positive values) to lighten the corners of the image or move the slider to the left (negative values) to darken the corners of the image. You can also enter values in the Vignetting Amount text box.

2 Move the Vignetting Midpoint slider to the left (lower value) to apply the Vignetting Amount adjustment to a larger area away from the corners, or move the slider to the right (higher value) to restrict the adjustment to an area closer to the corners. You can also enter a value in the Vignetting Midpoint text box.

Calibrating color in camera raw images

To remove a shadow color cast in camera raw files

Sometimes a color cast remains in the shadow areas after you adjust the highlight white balance using the Temperature and Tint sliders. The Calibrate tab has a Shadow Tint slider to correct this remaining shadow color cast.

❖ In the Calibrate tab, move the Shadow Tint slider to remove the color cast in the shadows. The camera's sensor and the white balance affect which colors are adjusted. Usually, moving the slider to the left (negative values) adds green to the shadow areas, and moving the slider to the right (positive values) adds magenta.

To adjust the rendering of non-neutral colors in Camera Raw

Sometimes colors rendered by the Camera Raw plug-in do not look as expected. The cause may be a difference between a camera's profile and Camera Raw's built-in profile for that camera model. Alternatively, the photo may have been taken under nonstandard lighting conditions beyond the compensating range of the Adobe Camera Raw plug-in. The Calibrate tab has Hue and Saturation sliders to adjust the settings for Camera Raw's built-in camera profile

to render non-neutral colors differently. You can also specify whether to use the profiles built into Camera Raw or a profile built into the file itself.

1 In the Calibrate tab, choose a profile from the Camera Profile menu:

ACR 3.0 Uses the built-in camera profile of Camera Raw 3.0 for Photoshop CS2 and Adobe Creative Suite.

Important: The options that appear in the Camera Profile menu depend on whether a camera raw file has a profile embedded or whether it has been processed with a previous version of Camera Raw. Often, the Camera Profile menu only contains the ACR 3.0 option.

Embedded Uses the profile embedded in the camera raw file.

ACR 2.4 Uses the built-in camera profile of Camera Raw 2.4 for Photoshop CS. The option is available for only certain cameras. Users who have fine-tuned their settings for the older Camera Raw built-in profile can select this option to use that profile instead.

2 Use the Hue and Saturation sliders to adjust the red, green, and blue in the image. Look at the preview image as you make adjustments until the image looks correct to you. In general, adjust the hue first and then adjust its saturation. Moving the Hue slider to the left (negative value) is like a counterclockwise move on the color wheel, and moving it to the right (positive value) is like a clockwise move. Moving the Saturation slider to the left (negative value) desaturates the color, and moving it to the right (positive value) increases saturation.

💡 *Adjustments made in the Calibrate tab affect the selected image in the Camera Raw dialog box. If you want to save the adjustments and make them the default image settings for the files from a specific camera, click the triangle next to the Settings menu and choose Save New Camera Raw Defaults from the Camera Raw menu.*

Saving camera raw images

To save camera raw images in Camera Raw

The Camera Raw dialog box lets you save camera raw files in Photoshop-supported file formats.

1 In the Camera Raw dialog box, apply adjustments to one or more camera raw images.

2 Click the Save button.

3 In the Camera Raw Save Options dialog box, specify the following options:

Destination Specifies where to save the file. If necessary, click the Select Folder button and navigate to the location.

File Naming Specifies the naming convention used if you're processing and saving more than one camera raw file.

4 Choose a file format from the Format menu:

Digital Negative Saves a copy of the camera raw file in the DNG file format. Specify save options by selecting any of the following: Compressed (Lossless), Uncompressed, Preserve Raw Image, or Convert To Linear

Image. You can also specify a JPEG preview for the DNG file.

JPEG Saves copies of the camera raw files in JPEG format. To specify the amount of compression, enter a value from 0 to 12 or choose from the pop-up menu. Entering a higher value or choosing High or Maximum applies less compression, increasing file size and image quality.

TIFF Saves copies of the camera raw files in TIFF format. Specify whether to apply no compression, or LZW or ZIP file compression.

Photoshop Saves copies of the camera raw files in the PSD file format. You can specify whether to preserve cropped pixel data in the PSD file.

5 Click Save.

Note: The Digital Negative (DNG) format is Adobe's proposed standard format for camera raw image files. DNG files are useful for archiving camera raw images because they contain the raw camera sensor data and data specifying how the image should look. Camera Raw image settings can be store in DNG files instead of in sidecar XMP files or the Camera Raw database.

Digital Negative saving options for Camera Raw

Compressed (lossless) Applies a lossless compression to the DNG file.

Convert To Linear Image Stores the image data in an interpolated ("demosaiced") format.

Embed Original Raw File Stores the entire original camera raw image data in the DNG file.

JPEG Preview Specifies whether to embed a JPEG preview in the DNG file. If you decide to embed a

JPEG preview, you can choose the preview size. If you embed JPEG previews, other applications can view the contents of the DNG file without parsing the camera raw data.

Camera Raw settings

Camera Raw settings

In the Camera Raw dialog box, you can change the default image settings and save the adjusted settings as the new camera default. You can always restore the original Camera Raw default settings for the specific camera (click the triangle to the right of the Settings pop-up menu and choose Reset Camera Raw Defaults from the Camera Raw menu). Because Camera Raw can identify which camera was used to take an image, you can save different default image settings for different cameras.

You can also save Camera Raw settings for a specific lighting condition and reapply them to images taken under similar conditions. Alternatively, you can save only a subset of the Camera Raw plug-in settings. In this way, you can create presets for custom white balances, specific lens settings, and so forth. In Adobe Bridge, you can also update all settings or a subset of the settings applied to camera raw images.

When a camera raw image file is processed with Camera Raw, the image settings are stored in one of two places: the Camera Raw database file or a sidecar XMP file. You can set a preference to determine where settings are stored. Photoshop and Bridge remember the settings for each camera raw image file. When you reopen a camera raw image, all the settings sliders

default to the values used when the file was last opened. Image attributes (target color space profile, bit depth, pixel size, and resolution) are not the stored with the settings.

For more information, see`To specify where Camera Raw settings are stored' on page 161 and `To save or reset Camera Raw settings' on page 162.

To specify where Camera Raw settings are stored

1 Do one of the following:

- In the Camera Raw dialog box, click the triangle next to the Settings menu to open the Camera Raw menu and choose Preferences.

- (Windows) In Adobe Bridge, choose Edit > Camera Raw Preferences.

- (Mac OS) Choose Bridge > Camera Raw Preferences, or with the Camera Raw dialog box opened in Photoshop, choose Photoshop > Camera Raw Preferences.

2 In the Camera Raw Preferences dialog box, choose one of the following from the Save Image Settings In menu:

Camera Raw Database Stores the settings in a Camera Raw database file, generally located in the user's Application Data folder as Document and Settings/*user name*/Application Data/Adobe/CameraRaw (Windows) or the user's Preferences folder as Users/*user name*/Library/Preferences (Mac OS). This database is indexed by file content, so settings remain with the image even if you move or rename the image file.

Sidecar ".xmp" Files Stores the settings in an XMP file in the same folder as the raw file with the same base name and an .xmp extension. This option is useful for long-term archiving of raw files with their associated settings, and for the exchange of raw files with associated settings in multiuser workflows. These same sidecar XMP files can store IPTC (International Press Telecommunications Council) data or other metadata associated with a camera raw image file. If you open files from a read-only volume such as a CD or DVD, be sure to copy the files to your hard drive before opening them. The Camera Raw plug-in cannot write an XMP file to a read-only volume and writes the settings to the Camera Raw database file instead. You can view XMP files in Bridge by choosing View > Show Hidden Files.

💡 *If you store the camera raw settings in the Camera Raw database and plan to move the files to a different location (CD, DVD, another computer, and so forth), you can use the Export Settings command in the Camera Raw dialog box to export the settings to sidecar XMP files or embed them in DNG files.*

To save or reset Camera Raw settings

1 In the Camera Raw dialog box, adjust the settings that you want to save.

2 Click the triangle next to the Settings menu and choose one of the following from the Camera Raw menu:

Save Settings Saves the current settings and adds them to the Settings menu. In the Save Raw Conversion Settings dialog box, name and save the settings. Save the setting to the Camera Raw settings folder so that it is visible in the Settings menu. Settings saved elsewhere disappear from the Settings menu as soon as you choose another setting. If this happens, use the Load Settings command in the Camera Raw menu and browse to find the setting.

Save New Camera Defaults Saves the current settings as the new default settings for other images taken with the same camera.

Reset Camera Raw Defaults Restores the original default settings for a specific camera.

To save a subset of settings

1 Click the triangle next to the Settings menu to display the Camera Raw menu, and choose Save Settings Subset.

2 Specify the settings to be saved by doing one of the following:

• Choose an option from the Subset menu.

• Select or deselect settings in the Settings list.

3 Click Save.

4 In the Save Raw Conversion Settings dialog box, name the subset and save it to the Camera Raw settings folder. This saved subset appears at the bottom of the Settings menu.

To apply saved Camera Raw settings

1 Do one of the following

• Open one or more camera raw images in the Camera Raw dialog box, and click the triangle next to the Settings text box to display the Settings menu.

• (Bridge) Select one or more camera raw images and choose Edit > Apply Camera Raw Settings.

2 From the Settings menu or the Apply Camera Raw Settings submenu, choose one of the following:

Image Settings Uses the settings from the selected camera raw image. This option is available only from the Settings menu in the Camera Raw dialog box.

Camera Raw Defaults Uses the saved default settings for a specific camera.

Previous Conversion Uses the settings from the previous image of the same camera.

A saved setting Uses a setting that you saved.

Note: You can also open the Camera Raw menu, choose Load Settings, and then browse to select a saved setting.

To load Camera Raw settings

Saved settings are not listed in the Settings menu (Camera Raw dialog box) or the Apply Camera Raw Settings submenu (Bridge or Photoshop) unless you save them to the Camera Raw settings folder. However, you can use the Load command to browse for and apply settings saved elsewhere.

1 In the Camera Raw dialog box, click the triangle next to the Settings menu and choose Load Settings from the Camera Raw menu.

2 In the Load Raw Conversion Settings dialog box, browse to the settings file, select it, and click Load.

To copy and paste Camera Raw settings

In Bridge, you can copy and paste the Camera Raw settings from one camera raw image file to another.

1 In Bridge, select a camera raw image and choose Edit > Apply Camera Raw Settings > Copy Camera Raw Settings.

2 Select one or more camera raw images and choose Edit > Apply Camera Raw Settings > Paste Camera Raw Settings.

You can also right-click (Windows) or Control-click (Mac OS) camera raw files to copy and paste using the context menu.

3 In the Paste Camera Raw Settings dialog box, do one of the following and then click OK:

- To apply all settings including any crops, choose Everything from the Subset menu.

- To apply all settings but not any crops, choose Settings from the Subset menu.

- To apply one or more settings subsets, choose a setting from the Subset menu or select only the settings you want to apply. If necessary, deselect that settings that you don't want applied.

To apply settings to multiple camera raw image files in Camera Raw

You can process multiple camera raw image files using the current settings or a subset of the current settings in the Camera Raw dialog box.

1 In the Camera Raw dialog box, select an image in the Filmstrip and adjust the image settings if necessary.

2 Select more than one image in the Filmstrip and click the Synchronize button.

3 In the Synchronize dialog box, do one of the following:

- Choose a setting from the Synchronize menu.

- Select the settings that you want to apply.

4 Click OK.

To clear settings applied to camera raw image files

You can clear image settings applied to camera raw files and restore the Camera Raw default image settings.

1 In Bridge, select one or more camera raw image files.

2 Choose Edit > Apply Camera Raw Settings > Clear Camera Raw Settings.

To delete Camera Raw settings

1 Choose a saved setting from the Settings menu.

2 Click the triangle next to the Settings menu to display the Camera Raw menu.

3 Choose Delete Current Settings from the menu. The setting is deleted from the Camera Raw settings folder.

To export Camera Raw settings

If you store file settings in the Camera Raw database, you can use the Export Settings command to copy the settings to sidecar XMP files or embed them in DNG files. This is useful for preserving the image settings with your camera raw files when you move them.

1 Open the Camera Raw dialog box with the camera raw files whose settings you want to export. Make sure to select the thumbnails in the Filmstrip.

2 Click the triangle next to the Settings menu and choose Export Settings from the Camera Raw menu.

The sidecar XMP files are created in the same folder as the camera raw image files. If you saved the camera raw image files in DNG format, the Camera Raw settings are embedded in the DNG files themselves.

Automating the Camera Raw workflow

Automating processing of camera raw images

You can create an action to automate the processing camera raw image files. You can automate the editing process, and the process of saving the files in formats such as PSD, DNG, JPEG, Large Document Format (PSB), TIFF, and PDF. In Photoshop, you can also use the Batch command, the Image Processor, or the Create Droplet command to process one or more camera raw image files. The Image Processor is especially useful for saving camera raw image files in different file formats during the same processing session.

Here are some tips for automating the processing of camera raw image files:

• When you record an action, do so with Image Settings chosen from the Settings menu of the Camera Raw dialog box. In this way, the settings particular to each image (from the Camera Raw database or sidecar XMP files) are used to play back the action.

• If you plan to use the action with the Batch command, you may want to use the Save As command and choose the file format when saving the camera raw image.

- When you use an action to open a camera raw file, the Camera Raw dialog box reflects the settings that were in effect when the action was recorded. You may want to create different actions for opening camera raw image files with different settings.

- When using the Batch command, select Override Action "Open" Commands so that Open commands in the action refer to the batched files rather than the files specified by name in the action. Deselect Override Action "Open" Commands only if the action is to operate on open files or if the action contains Open commands for specific files required by the action.

- When using the Batch command, select Suppress File Open Options Dialogs to prevent the Camera Raw dialog box from opening for each camera raw image being processed.

- Using the Batch command, select Override Action "Save As" Commands if you want to use the Save As instructions from the Batch command instead of the Save As instructions in the action. If you select this option, the action must contain a Save As command, because the Batch command does not automatically save the source files. Deselect Override Action "Save As" Commands to save the files processed by the Batch command in the location specified in the Batch dialog box.

- When creating a droplet, in the Play area of the Create Droplet dialog box, select Suppress File Open Options Dialogs. This prevents the Camera Raw dialog box from opening for each camera raw image being processed.

Chapter 8: Color

Color modes

Color modes

Photoshop lets you choose a *color mode* for each document. The color mode determines what color method is used to display and print the image you're working on. By selecting a particular color mode, you are choosing to work with particular *color model* (a numerical method for describing color). Photoshop bases its color modes on the color models that are useful for images used in publishing. You can choose from RGB (Red, Green, Blue), CMYK (Cyan, Magenta, Yellow, Black), Lab Color (based on CIE L* a* b*), and Grayscale. Photoshop also includes modes for specialized color output such as Indexed Color and Duotone. Color modes determine the number of colors, the number of channels, and the file size of an image. Choosing a color mode also determines which tools and file formats are available.

Note: ImageReady only uses the RGB mode to work with images, because its documents are primarily intended for web display.

RGB Color mode

Photoshop's RGB Color mode uses the RGB model, assigning an intensity value to each pixel. In 8-bits-per-channel images, the intensity values range from 0 (black) to 255 (white) for each of the RGB (red, green, blue) components in a color image. For example, a bright red color might have an R value of 246, a G value of 20, and a B value of 50. When the values of all three components are equal, the result is a shade of neutral gray. When the values of all components are 255, the result is pure white; when the values are 0, pure black.

RGB images use three colors, or *channels*, to reproduce colors on-screen. In 8-bits-per-channel images, the three channels translate to 24 (8 bits x 3 channels) bits of color information per pixel. With 24-bit images, up to 16.7 million colors can be reproduced. With 48-bit (16-bits-per-channel) and 96-bit (32-bits-per-channel) images, even more colors can be reproduced. In addition to being the default mode for new Photoshop images, the RGB model is used by computer monitors to display colors. This means that when working in color modes other than RGB, such as CMYK, Photoshop interpolates the CMYK image to RGB for display on-screen.

Although RGB is a standard color model, the exact range of colors represented can vary, depending on the application or display device. Photoshop's RGB Color mode varies according to the working space setting that you specify in the Color Settings dialog box.

Note: ImageReady uses only the RGB mode to work with images.

CMYK Color mode

In the CMYK mode, each pixel is assigned a percentage value for each of the process inks. The lightest (highlight) colors are assigned small percentages of process ink colors; the darker (shadow) colors higher percentages. For example, a bright red might contain 2% cyan, 93% magenta, 90% yellow, and 0% black. In CMYK images, pure white is generated when all four components have values of 0%.

Use the CMYK mode when preparing an image to be printed using process colors. Converting an RGB image into CMYK creates a *color separation*. If you start with an RGB image, it's best to edit first in RGB and then convert to CMYK at the end of your process. In RGB mode, you can use the Proof Setup commands to simulate the effects of a CMYK conversion without changing the actual image data. You can also use CMYK mode to work directly with CMYK images scanned or imported from high-end systems.

Although CMYK is a standard color model, the exact range of colors represented can vary, depending on the press and printing conditions. Photoshop's CMYK Color mode varies according to the working space setting that you specify in the Color Settings dialog box.

Lab Color mode

The Lab Color mode has a lightness component (L) that can range from 0 to 100. In the Adobe Color Picker, the *a* component (green-red axis) and the *b* component (blue-yellow axis) can range from +127 to –128. In the Color palette, the *a* component and the *b* component can range from +127 to –128.

You can use Lab mode to work with Photo CD images, edit the luminance and the color values in an image independently, move images between systems, and print to PostScript Level 2 and Level 3 printers. To print Lab images to other color PostScript devices, convert to CMYK first.

Lab images can be saved in Photoshop, Photoshop EPS, Large Document Format (PSB), Photoshop PDF, Photoshop Raw, TIFF, Photoshop DCS 1.0, or Photoshop DCS 2.0 formats. You can save 48-bit (16-bits-per-channel) Lab images in Photoshop, Large Document Format (PSB), Photoshop PDF, Photoshop Raw, or TIFF formats.

Note: The DCS 1.0 and DCS 2.0 formats convert the file to CMYK when opened.

Lab color is the intermediate color model Photoshop uses when converting from one color mode to another.

Bitmap mode

Bitmap mode uses one of two color values (black or white) to represent the pixels in an image. Images in Bitmap mode are called bitmapped 1-bit images because they have a bit depth of 1.

Grayscale mode

Grayscale mode uses different shades of gray in an image. In 8-bit images, there can be up to 256 shades of gray. Every pixel of a grayscale image has a brightness value ranging from 0 (black) to 255 (white). In 16 and 32-bit images, the number of shades in an image is much greater than in 8-bit images. Grayscale values can also be measured as percentages of black ink coverage (0% is equal to white, 100% to black). Images produced using black-and-white or grayscale scanners typically are displayed in Grayscale mode.

Although Grayscale is a standard color model, the exact range of grays represented can vary, depending on the printing conditions. In Photoshop, Grayscale mode uses the range defined by the working space setting that you specify in the Color Settings dialog box.

These guidelines apply to converting images to and from Grayscale mode:

- You can convert both Bitmap mode and color images to grayscale.

- To convert a color image to a high-quality grayscale image, Photoshop discards all color information in the original image. The gray levels (shades) of the converted pixels represent the luminosity of the original pixels.

You can mix information from the color channels to create a custom grayscale channel by using the Channel Mixer command.

- When converting from grayscale to RGB, the color values for a pixel are based on its previous gray value. A grayscale image can also be converted to a CMYK image (for creating process-color quadtones without converting to Duotone mode) or to a Lab color image.

Duotone mode

Duotone mode creates monotone, duotone (two-color), tritone (three-color), and quadtone (four-color) grayscale images using one to four custom inks.

Indexed Color mode

Indexed Color mode produces 8-bit image files with at most 256 colors. When converting to indexed color, Photoshop builds a *color lookup table (CLUT),* which stores and indexes the colors in the image. If a color in the original image does not appear in the table, the program chooses the closest one or uses *dithering* to simulate the color using available colors.

Because the palette of colors is limited, indexed color can reduce file size yet maintain the visual quality needed for multimedia presentations, web pages, and the like. Limited editing is available in this mode. For extensive editing, you should convert temporarily to RGB mode. Indexed color files can be saved in Photoshop, BMP, GIF, Photoshop EPS, Large Document Format (PSB), PCX, Photoshop PDF, Photoshop Raw, Photoshop 2.0, PICT, PNG, Targa, or TIFF formats.

For information on converting images to Indexed Color mode, see Photoshop Help.

Multichannel mode

Multichannel mode uses 256 levels of gray in each channel. Multichannel images are useful for specialized printing. Multichannel mode images can be saved in Photoshop, Photoshop 2.0, Photoshop Raw, or Photoshop DCS 2.0 format.

These guidelines apply to converting images to Multichannel mode:

- Color channels in the original image become spot color channels in the converted image.

- When you convert a color image to a multichannel image, the new grayscale information is based on the color values of the pixels in each channel.

- Converting a CMYK image to Multichannel mode creates cyan, magenta, yellow, and black spot channels.

- Converting an RGB image to Multichannel mode creates cyan, magenta, and yellow spot channels.

- Deleting a channel from an RGB, CMYK, or Lab image automatically converts the image to Multichannel mode.

- To export a multichannel image, save it in Photoshop DCS 2.0 format.

Adjusting the monitor display

About monitors and color work

Although the RGB color model used by computer monitors can display much of the visible spectrum, the video system sending data to a given monitor often limits how many colors can be displayed at once. By understanding how color data is measured in digital files and on-screen, you can better adjust color display settings to offset the limitations of your video system. For critical work, your monitor should be calibrated and characterized for use in a color management system. At the very least, your monitor should be calibrated to display colors as accurately as possible.

To speed up previews by adjusting the monitor display

The Use Pixel Doubling preference option speeds up the preview of a tool or command's effects by temporarily doubling the size of the pixels (halving the resolution) in the preview. This option has no effect on the pixels in the file; it simply provides faster previews with the tools and commands.

1 Do one of the following:

- In Windows, choose Edit > Preferences > Display & Cursors.

- In Mac OS, choose Photoshop > Preferences > Display & Cursors.

2 Select Use Pixel Doubling, and click OK.

Adjusting color display for cross-platform variations

RGB color display on a computer monitor varies with the operating system used by the computer. For example, an image appears darker on a Windows system than on a Mac OS computer (because the standard RGB color space is darker in Windows than in Mac OS). The Preview commands in ImageReady let you compensate for cross-platform differences in RGB color display during image preview. In Photoshop, you can simulate cross-platform differences by using the Macintosh RGB, Windows RGB, and Monitor RGB commands in the View > Proof Setup menu.

RGB color display can also vary between Photoshop and ImageReady. In Photoshop, you can select from several RGB color spaces when editing images. As a result, images created in Photoshop may use an RGB color space that differs from the monitor RGB color space used by ImageReady. You can adjust the RGB color display during image preview to compensate for differences between Photoshop and ImageReady.

To adjust RGB color display for cross-platform variations (ImageReady)

❖ Choose View > Preview and choose an option for adjusting the color display:

Uncompensated Color Displays the image with the monitor gamma uncorrected.

Standard Macintosh Color Displays the image with a gamma value of 1.8.

Standard Windows Color Displays the image with a gamma value of 2.2.

Use Embedded Color Profile Uses the embedded profile to display the image.

These options adjust color display only. No changes are made to pixels in the image.

You can edit your image in one window and view the same image with a different gamma value in a second window. Choose Window > Arrange > New Window For [File Name]. With the new window active, choose View > Preview and then choose a different gamma than the one used in the first window.

To adjust RGB color display to match Photoshop color display (ImageReady)

❖ Choose View > Preview > Use Embedded Color Profile.

Note: *To use the Use Embedded Color Profile command in ImageReady, you must first save the original image, with the color profile embedded, in Photoshop. Keep in mind that ImageReady does not use profiles in PNG or TIFF files.*

Channels and bit depth

About color channels

A working knowledge of color channels and bit depth is key to understanding how Photoshop stores and displays color information in images. Every Photoshop image has one or more *channels,* each storing information about color elements in the image. The number of default color channels in an image depends on its color mode. For example, a CMYK image has at least four channels, one each for cyan, magenta, yellow, and black information. Think of a channel as analogous to a plate in the printing process, with a separate plate applying each layer of color.

In addition to these default color channels, extra channels, called *alpha channels,* can be added to an image for storing and editing selections as masks, and spot color channels can be added to add spot color plates for printing.

An image can have up to 56 channels. By default, bitmap, grayscale, duotone, and indexed-color images have one channel; RGB and Lab images have three; and CMYK images have four. You can add channels to all image types except Bitmap mode images.

For more information about channels see Photoshop Help.

For more information, see `About masks and alpha channels' on page 243.

About bit depth

Bit depth—also called pixel depth or color depth—measures how much color information is available for displaying or printing each pixel in an image.

Greater bit depth (more bits of information per pixel) means more available colors and more accurate color representation in the digital image. For example, a pixel with a bit depth of 1 has two possible values: black and white. A pixel with a bit depth of 8 has 28, or 256, possible values. And a pixel with a bit depth of 24 has 224, or roughly 16 million, possible values. Common values for bit depth range from 1 to 64 bits per pixel.

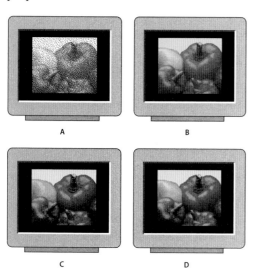

Pixel depth
A. *1-bit (Bitmap)* **B.** *8-bit (Grayscale)* **C.** *8-bit (Indexed Color)*
D. *24-bit (RGB)*

In most cases, Lab, RGB, grayscale, and CMYK images contain 8 bits of data per color channel. This translates to a 24-bit Lab bit depth (8 bits x 3 channels), a 24-bit RGB bit depth (8 bits x 3 channels), an 8-bit grayscale bit depth (8 bits x 1 channel), and a 32-bit CMYK bit depth (8 bits x 4 channels). Photoshop can also work with Lab, RGB, CMYK, multichannel, and grayscale images that contain 16 bits of data per color channel. Additionally, Photoshop can work with RGB and grayscale images that contain 32 bits of data per color channel.

For more information, see`About High Dynamic Range images' on page 139.

Converting between bit depths

A 16- or 32-bits-per-channel image provides finer distinctions in color (but larger file size) than an 8-bits-per-channel version of the same image.

Photoshop provides the following support for working with 16-bits-per-channel images:

- All tools in the toolbox, except the Art History Brush tool, can be used with 16-bits-per-channel images.

- All color and tonal adjustment commands, except Variations, are available.

- You can work with layers, including adjustment layers, in 16-bits-per-channel images.

- Some filters, including Liquify, can be used with 16-bits-per-channel images.

To take advantage of certain Photoshop features, such as Extract, Pattern Maker, and some filters, you can convert a 16-bits-per-channel image to an 8-bits-per-channel image. It's best if you do a Save As and convert a copy of the image file so the original file retains the full 16-bits-per-channel image data.

Photoshop provides the following support for working with 32-bits-per-channel images:

- Crop with rotation and resize

- Fill and stroke (no pattern fill, supported blend modes only)

- Image Size and Canvas Size commands

- Trim command

- Arbitrary rotation and 90˚ rotation and flips

- Blend modes: Normal, Multiply, Difference, Lighten, Darken, Linear Dodge

- Free Transform command

- The following tools in the toolbox: Clone Stamp tool (supported blend modes only), and History Brush (supported blend modes only)

- Display of floating-point values in the Info palette

- Conversion to 8- or 16-bits-per-channel documents, and conversion from 16-bits-per-channel to 32-bits-per-channel

- Conversion between RGB and Grayscale modes

- Support of the following file formats: PSD/PSB, TIFF, LogLUV TIFF (read-only), Radiance HDR, PFM, OpenEXR

- Support for the following image adjustment commands: Channel Mixer, Photo Filter, and Exposure.

- Support for the following plug-in filters: Average, Radial Blur, Fibers, Lens Flare, DeInterlace, and NTSC Colors

- Support for the following built-in filters: Surface Blur, Box Blur, Gaussian Blur, Motion Blur, Sampled/Shape Blur, Add Noise, Unsharp Mask, High Pass, Offset

- Save Selection and Load Selection commands

To work with certain Photoshop features, such as layers, filters, and adjustments, you can convert a 32-bits-per-channel image to a 16-bits-per-channel image. Do a Save As and convert a copy of the image file so that the original file retains the full 32-bits-per-channel image data.

Note: *It's also possible to convert a 32-bits-per-channel image to 8 bits per channel. See `To convert from 32 bits to 8 or 16 bits per channel' on page 143.*

For more information, see `About High Dynamic Range images' on page 139.

To convert between 8 bits and 16 bits per channel

❖ Choose Image > Mode > 16 Bits/Channel or 8 Bits/Channel.

To convert from 16 bits to 32 bits per channel

1 Open a 16-bit image. If necessary, flatten the image. Only flat images can be converted to 32-bits-per-channel mode.

2 Choose Image > Mode > 32 Bits/Channel.

Note: *It's also possible to convert a 32-bits-per-channel image to 8-bits-per-channel. See `To convert from 32 bits to 8 or 16 bits per channel' on page 143.*

For more information, see `About High Dynamic Range images' on page 139.

Converting between color modes

Converting an image to another mode

You can change an image from its original mode (source mode) to a different mode (target mode). When you choose a different color mode for an image, you permanently change the color values in the image. For example, when you convert an RGB image to CMYK mode, RGB color values outside the CMYK gamut (defined by the CMYK working space setting in the Color Settings dialog box) are adjusted to fall within gamut. As a result, some image data may be lost and can't be recovered if you convert the image from CMYK back to RGB.

Before converting images, it's best to do the following:

- Do as much editing as possible in the original image mode (usually RGB for images from most scanners or digital cameras, or CMYK for images from traditional drum scanners or imported from a Scitex system).

- Save a backup copy before converting. Be sure to save a copy of your image that includes all layers so that you can edit the original version of the image after the conversion.

- Flatten the file before converting it. The interaction of colors between layer blending modes changes when the mode changes.

To convert an image to another mode

❖ Choose Image > Mode and the mode you want from the submenu. Modes not available for the active image appear dimmed in the menu.

Images are flattened when converted to Multichannel, Bitmap, or Indexed Color mode, because these modes do not support layers.

Making a conditional mode change

You can specify conditions for a mode change so that the conversion can occur during an *action*, which is a series of commands applied sequentially to a single file or a batch of files. When a mode change is part of an action, an error can occur if the file being opened is not in the source mode specified in the action. For example, suppose one step in an action is to convert an image with a source mode of RGB to a target mode of CMYK. Applying this action to an image in Grayscale mode, or any other source mode besides RGB, results in an error.

When you record an action, you can use the Conditional Mode Change command to specify one or more modes for the source mode and a mode for the target mode.

To add a conditional mode change to an action

1 Start recording an action.

2 Choose File > Automate > Conditional Mode Change.

3 In the Conditional Mode Change dialog box, select one or more modes for the source mode. You can also use the All or None buttons to select all possible modes or no mode.

4 Choose a target mode from the Mode pop-up menu.

5 Click OK. The conditional mode change appears as a new step in the Actions palette.

To convert a color photo to black-and-white

1 Open the photo you want to convert to black-and-white.

2 Choose Image > Mode > Grayscale.

3 If asked to discard color info, click OK. Photoshop converts the colors in the image to black, white, and shades of gray.

Converting images to Bitmap mode

Converting an image to Bitmap mode reduces the image to two colors, greatly simplifying the color information in the image and reducing its file size.

When converting a color image to Bitmap mode, first convert it to Grayscale mode. This removes the hue and saturation information from the pixels and leaves just the brightness values. However, because only a few editing options are available for Bitmap mode images, it's usually best to edit the image in Grayscale mode and then convert it to Bitmap mode.

Note: Images in Bitmap mode are 1 bit per channel. You must convert a 16- or 32-bits-per-channel image to 8-bit Grayscale mode before converting it to Bitmap mode.

To convert an image to Bitmap mode

1 Do one of the following:

- If the image is in color, choose Image > Mode > Grayscale. Then choose Image > Mode > Bitmap.

- If the image is grayscale, choose Image > Mode > Bitmap.

2 For Output, enter a value for the output resolution of the Bitmap mode image, and choose a unit of

measurement. By default, the current image resolution appears as both the input and the output resolutions.

3 Choose one of the following bitmap conversion methods from the Use pop-up menu:

50% Threshold Converts pixels with gray values above the middle gray level (128) to white and pixels with gray values below that level to black. The result is a very high-contrast, black-and-white representation of the image.

Pattern Dither Converts an image by organizing the gray levels into geometric configurations of black and white dots.

Diffusion Dither Converts an image by using an error-diffusion process, starting at the pixel in the upper left corner of the image. If the pixel's value is above middle gray (128), the pixel is changed to white—if below it, to black. Because the original pixel is rarely pure white or pure black, error is inevitably introduced. This error is transferred to surrounding pixels and diffused throughout the image, resulting in a grainy, filmlike texture. This option is useful for viewing images on a black-and-white screen.

Halftone Screen Simulates the appearance of halftone dots in the converted image.

Custom Pattern Simulates the appearance of a custom halftone screen in the converted image.

Original grayscale image, and 50% Threshold conversion method

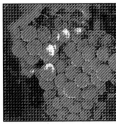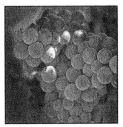

Pattern Dither conversion method, and Diffusion Dither conversion method

To convert a Bitmap mode image to Grayscale mode

You can convert a Bitmap mode image to Grayscale mode in order to edit it. Keep in mind that a Bitmap mode image edited in Grayscale mode may not look the same when you convert it back to Bitmap mode. For example, suppose a pixel that is black in Bitmap mode is edited to a shade of gray in Grayscale mode. When the image is converted back to Bitmap mode, that pixel is rendered as white if its gray value is above the middle gray value of 128.

1 Choose Image > Mode > Grayscale.

2 Enter a value between 1 and 16 for the size ratio.

The size ratio is the factor for scaling down the image. For example, to reduce a grayscale image by 50%, enter 2 for the size ratio. If you enter a number greater than 1, the program averages multiple pixels in the Bitmap mode image to produce a single pixel in the grayscale image. This process lets you generate multiple shades of gray from an image scanned on a 1-bit scanner.

Specifying the halftone screen for Bitmap mode images

The Halftone Screen option in the Bitmap dialog box lets you convert a grayscale image to simulated halftone dots.

Important: *The halftone screen becomes part of the image. If you print the image on a halftone printer, the printer will use its own halftone screen as well as the halftone screen that is part of the image. On some printers, the result is a moiré pattern.*

To specify the halftone screen for Bitmap mode images

1 Choose Image > Mode > Bitmap.

2 Choose Halftone Screen from the Use menu; then click OK. The Halftone Screen dialog box opens.

3 For Frequency, enter a value for the screen frequency, and choose a unit of measurement. Values can range from 1 to 999 for lines per inch and from 0.400 to 400 for lines per centimeter. You can enter decimal values.

The screen frequency specifies the ruling of the halftone screen in lines per inch (lpi). The frequency depends on the paper stock and type of press used for printing. Newspapers commonly use an 85-line screen. Magazines use higher resolution screens, such as 133-lpi and 150-lpi. Check with your print shop for correct screen frequencies.

4 Enter a value for the screen angle in degrees from -180 to +180.

The screen angle refers to the orientation of the screen. Continuous-tone and black-and-white halftone screens commonly use a 45˚ angle.

5 For Shape, choose the dot shape you want.

 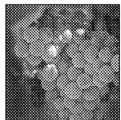

Original grayscale image, and Halftone Screen conversion: 53 lpi, 45˚ angle, round dot

You can save and reuse halftone screen settings by using the Save and Load buttons in the Halftone Screen dialog box.

Specifying custom halftone screens for Bitmap mode images

The Custom Pattern option in the Bitmap dialog box simulates the effect of printing a grayscale image through a custom halftone screen. This method lets you apply a screen texture, such as a wood grain, to an image. To use this option, you must first define a pattern.

You can create a pattern representing the texture you want and then screen the grayscale image to apply the texture. To cover the entire image, the pattern must be as large as the image. Otherwise, the pattern is tiled. For example, if you apply a 1-inch-by-1-inch pattern to a 4-inch-by-4-inch image, the pattern appears as 16 squares. Photoshop comes with several self-tiling patterns that can be used as halftone screen patterns.

Because the Custom Pattern option simulates dark and light colors by making the halftone pattern thicker and thinner, it makes sense to choose a pattern that lends itself to thickness variations, typically one with a variety of gray shades.

To prepare a black-and-white pattern for conversion, you can first convert the image to grayscale and then apply the Blur More filter several times. This blurring technique creates thick lines tapering from dark gray to white.

Choosing colors

About the Adobe Color Picker

You select a color in the Adobe Color Picker either by choosing from a color spectrum or by defining the color numerically. Through the Adobe Color Picker, you can set the foreground color, background color, and text color. In Photoshop, you can also use the Color Picker to set target colors in some color and tonal adjustment commands, the stop colors in the Gradient Editor, the filter color in the Photo Filter command, and the color in a fill layer, certain layer styles, and shape layers.

When you select a color in the Adobe Color Picker, it simultaneously displays the numeric values for HSB, RGB, Lab, CMYK, and hexadecimal numbers. This is useful for viewing how the different color modes describe a color.

In the Adobe Color Picker, you can select colors based on the HSB (hue, saturation, brightness) or RGB (red, green, blue) color models, or specify a color based on its hexadecimal values. In Photoshop, you can also select colors based on the Lab color model, and on the CMYK (cyan, magenta, yellow, black) color model. You can configure the Adobe Color Picker so that you can choose only from web-safe colors or choose from several custom color systems. The color field in the Adobe Color Picker can display color components in HSB color mode, RGB color mode, and (Photoshop) Lab color mode.

Note: *Although Photoshop and ImageReady use the Adobe Color Picker by default, you can set a preference to have Photoshop and ImageReady use a different color picker. For instance, you can use the built-in color pickers on your system or a plug-in color picker. Any plug-in color pickers you install appear under Color Picker in the General section of the Preferences dialog box.*

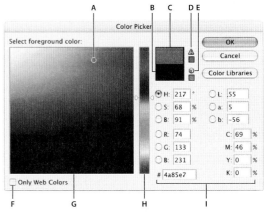

Adobe Color Picker
A. Picked color B. Original color C. Adjusted color D. Out-of-gamut alert icon E. Not web-safe alert icon F. Web Colors option G. Color field H. Color slider I. Color values

To display the Adobe Color Picker

Do one of the following:

- In the toolbox, click the foreground or background color selection box.

- In the Color palette, click the Set Foreground Color or Set Background Color selection box.

- In the text tool options bar, click the color swatch.

- (Photoshop) In the Layers palette, click the color swatch in a fill or shape layer.

- (Photoshop) In the Gradient Editor, double-click a color stop.

- (Photoshop) In the options bar of a shape or pen tool, click the color swatch.

- (Photoshop) In the Layer Style dialog box for certain layer styles (such as Outer Glow and Inner Glow), click the Set Color box.

- (Photoshop) In the dialog box of certain color and tonal adjustment commands, double-click an eyedropper or click a color swatch. Not every eyedropper lets you set a target color. For instance, double-clicking the eyedroppers in the Replace Color command does not open the Adobe Color Picker.

Specifying a color using the color field and color slider

With the HSB, RGB, and Lab color modes, you can use the color field and the color slider in the Color Picker dialog box to select a color.

Note: *The Lab color mode is available only in Photoshop.*

1 Click a component next to the HSB, RGB, or Lab values.

2 Select a color by doing one of the following:

- Drag the white triangles along the slider.

- Click in the color slider.

- Click in the color field.

When you select a color, a circular marker indicates the color's position in the color field.

As you adjust the color using the color field and color slider, the numerical values are adjusted accordingly. The color rectangle to the right of the color slider displays the new color in the top section of the rectangle. The original color appears at the bottom of the rectangle. Alerts appear if the color is not web-safe 🔲 or is (Photoshop) *out of gamut* ⚠ .

You can select a color outside the Adobe Color Picker. Moving the pointer over the document window changes it to the Eyedropper tool. You can then select a color by clicking in the image. The selected color is displayed in the Adobe Color Picker. You can move the Eyedropper tool anywhere on your desktop by clicking in the image and then holding down the mouse button. You can select a color by releasing the mouse button.

To specify a color using numeric values

In the Adobe Color Picker, you can select a color in any of the four color models by specifying numeric values for each color component.

Do one of the following:

- (Photoshop) In CMYK color mode (the mode PostScript printers use), specify each component value as a percentage of cyan, magenta, yellow, and black.

- In RGB color mode (the mode your monitor uses), specify component values from 0 to 255 (0 is black, and 255 is the pure color).

- In HSB color mode, specify saturation and brightness as percentages; specify hue as an angle from 0° to 360° that corresponds to a location on the color wheel.

- Enter a hexadecimal value in the # text box. For example, 000000 is black, ffffff is white, and ff0000 is red.

- (Photoshop) In Lab mode, enter a lightness value (L) from 0 to 100, and an A value (green to magenta) and a B value(blue to yellow) from -128 to +127.

To use the Adobe Color Picker in HSB mode

The Adobe Color Picker lets you select a color based on the HSB (hue, saturation, brightness) color model. When you select a color in HSB mode, the Adobe Color Picker updates the RGB, Lab, CMYK, and hexadecimal values accordingly. HSB mode is the default mode for the Adobe Color Picker.

1 Open the Adobe Color Picker.

2 In the HSB section of the dialog box, do one of the following:

• Click the H option to display all hues in the color slider. When you select a hue in the slider, the color field displays the saturation and brightness range of that hue, with the saturation increasing from left to right and the brightness increasing from bottom to top.

• Click the S option to display all hues in the color field, with their maximum brightness at the top of the color field and their minimum at the bottom. The color slider displays the color that's selected in the color field, with its maximum saturation at the top of the slider and its minimum saturation at the bottom.

• Click the B option to display all hues in the color field, with their maximum saturation at the top of the color field and their minimum saturation at the bottom. The color slider displays the color that's selected in the color field, with its maximum brightness at the top of the slider and its minimum brightness at the bottom.

3 Select a color with a specific hue, saturation, and brightness by using a combination of the color slider and the color field or entering a numeric values in the H, S, and B text boxes.

To work with the Adobe Color Picker in RGB mode

In RGB (red, green, blue) mode, the color slider displays the range of color levels available for the selected color component (R, G, or B). The color field displays the range for the remaining two components—one on the horizontal axis, one on the vertical. For example, if you click the red component (R), the color slider displays the range of color for red (0 is at the bottom of the slider, and 255 is at the top). The color field displays the values for blue on its horizontal axis and for green on its vertical axis.

1 Open the Adobe Color Picker.

2 In the RGB section of the dialog box, do one of the following:

• Click the R option to display the red color component in the color slider, with its maximum brightness (255) at the top of the slider and its minimum brightness (0) at the bottom. When you set the color slider to minimum brightness, the color field displays colors created by the green and blue color components. Using the color slider to increase the red brightness mixes more red into the colors displayed in the color field.

• Click the G option to display the green color component in the color slider, with its maximum brightness (255) at the top of the slider and its minimum brightness (0) at the bottom. When you set the color slider to minimum brightness, the color field displays colors created by the red and blue color components. Using the color slider to increase the green brightness mixes more green into the colors displayed in the color field.

• Click the B option to display the blue color component in the color slider, with its maximum brightness (255) at the top of the slider and its minimum brightness (0) at the bottom. When you set the color slider to minimum brightness, the color field displays colors created by the green and red color components. Using the color slider to increase the blue brightness mixes more blue into the colors displayed in the color field.

3 Select an RGB color using a combination of the color slider and the color field or entering numeric values in the R, G, and B text boxes.

To work with the Adobe Color Picker in Lab mode

The Adobe Color Picker lets you select a color based on the Lab color model. The L value specifies the luminance of a color. The A value specifies how red or green a color is. The B value specifies how blue or yellow a color is.

1 Open the Adobe Color Picker.

2 In the Lab section of the dialog box, do one of the following:

• Click the L option to display all hues in the color field. You select a hue by either clicking in the color field or entering values in the A and B text boxes. The color slider displays the selected hue, with its maximum luminance at the top and its minimum luminance at the bottom.

• Click the A option. Move the color slider to adjust the amount of red or green. Moving the slider or clicking in the color slider changes the range of

colors displayed in the color field. The color field also displays the luminance, with maximum luminance at the top and minimum luminance at the bottom. The B (blue or yellow) color component is represented in the color field with blue on the left and yellow on the right.

• Click the B option. Move the color slider to adjust the amount of yellow or blue. Moving the slider or clicking in the color slider changes the range of colors displayed in the color field. The color field also displays the luminance on the vertical axis, with maximum luminance at the top and minimum luminance at the bottom. The A (green or red) color component is represented in the color field with green on the left and red on the right.

3 Select a color using a combination of the color slider and the color field or entering numeric values in the L, A, and B text boxes.

Web-safe colors

The *web-safe colors* are the 216 colors used by browsers regardless of the platform. The browser changes all colors in the image to these colors when displaying the image on an 8-bit screen. The 216 colors are a subset of the Mac OS 8-bit color palettes. By working only with these colors, you can be sure that art you prepare for the web will not dither on a system set to display 256 colors.

To select web-safe colors in the Adobe Color Picker

❖ Select the Only Web Colors option in the lower left corner of the Color Picker. Any color you pick with this option selected is web-safe.

To change a nonweb color to a web-safe color

If you select a nonweb color, an alert cube 🔲 appears next to the color rectangle in the Adobe Color Picker.

❖ Click the alert cube to select the closest web color. (If no alert cube appears, the color you chose is web-safe.)

To select a web-safe color using the Color palette

1 Click the Color palette tab, or choose Window > Color to view the Color palette.

2 Choose an option for selecting a web-safe color:

• Choose Make Ramp Web Safe from the Color palette menu. Any color you pick with this option selected is web-safe.

• Choose Web Color Sliders from the Color palette menu (Photoshop), or choose any Slider option from the Color palette menu (ImageReady). By default, web color sliders snap to web-safe colors (indicated by tick marks) when you drag them. To override web-safe color selection, Alt-drag (Windows) or Option-drag (Mac OS) the sliders.

If you choose a nonweb color, an alert cube 🔲 appears above the color ramp on the left side of the Color palette. Click the alert cube to select the closest web color.

In ImageReady, drag around the alert icon to select other close web colors. (If no alert cube appears, the color you chose is web-safe.)

Note: In Photoshop, you must choose Web Color Sliders from the Color palette menu to view the web-safe alert cube. In ImageReady, you can view the alert cube with any color slider option.

To select the closest CMYK equivalent for a nonprintable color

Some colors in the RGB, HSB, and Lab color models, such as neon colors, cannot be printed because they have no equivalents in the CMYK model. When you select a nonprintable color, an alert triangle appears in the Color Picker dialog box and in the Color palette. The closest CMYK equivalent is displayed below the triangle.

Note: The alert triangle is not available if you are using web-safe sliders.

Click the alert triangle ⚠ that appears in the Color Picker dialog box or the Color palette.

Printable colors are determined by your current CMYK working space as defined in the Color Settings dialog box.

Choosing custom colors

The Adobe Color Picker lets you choose custom colors from the PANTONE MATCHING SYSTEM®, the Trumatch® Swatching System™, the Focoltone® Colour System, the Toyo Color Finder™ 1050 system, the ANPA-Color™ system, the HKS® color system, and the DIC Color Guide.

To ensure that the final printed output is the color you want, consult your printer or service bureau and choose your custom color based on a printed color swatch. Manufacturers recommend that you get a new swatch book each year to compensate for fading inks and other damage.

Important: Photoshop prints custom colors to CMYK (process color) plates in every image mode except Duotone. To print true spot color plates, create spot color channels.

To choose a custom color

1 Open the Adobe Color Picker, and click Color Libraries.

The Custom Colors dialog box displays the color closest to the color currently selected in the Adobe Color Picker.

2 For Book, choose a color system.

3 Locate the color you want by entering the ink number or by dragging the triangles along the scroll bar.

4 Click the desired color patch in the list.

Custom color systems

The Adobe Color Picker supports various color systems:

ANPA-COLOR Commonly used for newspaper applications. The *ANPA-COLOR ROP Newspaper Color Ink Book* contains samples of the ANPA colors.

DIC Color Guide Commonly used for printing projects in Japan. For more information, contact Dainippon Ink & Chemicals, Inc., in Tokyo, Japan.

FOCOLTONE Consists of 763 CMYK colors. Focoltone colors help avoid prepress trapping and registration problems by showing the overprints that make up the colors. A swatch book with specifications for process

and spot colors, overprint charts, and a chip book for marking up layouts are available from Focoltone. For more information, contact Focoltone International, Ltd., in Stafford, United Kingdom.

HKS swatches Used for printing projects in Europe. Each color has a specified CMYK equivalent. You can select from HKS E (for continuous stationery), HKS K (for gloss art paper), HKS N (for natural paper), and HKS Z (for newsprint). Color samplers for each scale are available. HKS Process books and swatches have been added to the color system menu.

PANTONE® Colors used for spot-color reproduction. The PANTONE MATCHING SYSTEM can render 1,114 colors. PANTONE color guides and chip books are printed on coated, uncoated, and matte paper stocks to ensure accurate visualization of the printed result and better on-press control. You can print a solid PANTONE color in CMYK. To compare a solid PANTONE color to its closest process color match, use the *PANTONE solid to process* guide. The CMYK screen tint percentages are printed under each color. For more information, contact Pantone, Inc., Carlstadt, NJ (www.pantone.com).

TOYO Color Finder 1050 Consists of more than 1000 colors based on the most common printing inks used in Japan. The *TOYO Process Color Finder* book and swatches have been added to the color system menu. The *TOYO Color Finder 1050 Book* contains printed samples of Toyo colors and is available from printers and graphic arts supply stores. For more information, contact Toyo Ink Manufacturing Co., Ltd., in Tokyo, Japan.

TRUMATCH Provides predictable CMYK color matching with more than 2000 achievable, computer-generated colors. Trumatch colors cover the visible spectrum of the CMYK gamut in even steps. The Trumatch Color displays up to 40 tints and shades of each hue, each originally created in four-color process and each reproducible in four colors on electronic imagesetters. In addition, four-color grays using different hues are included. For more information, contact Trumatch Inc., in New York City, New York.

To use the Windows Color Picker

(Windows only)

1 Choose Edit > Preferences > General.

2 Choose Windows from the Color Picker menu, and click OK.

For more information, see your Windows documentation.

To use the Apple Color Picker

(Mac OS only)

1 Do one of the following:

- (Photoshop) Choose Photoshop > Preferences > General.
- (ImageReady) Choose ImageReady > Preferences > General.

2 For Color Picker, do one of the following:

- (Photoshop) Choose Apple and click OK.
- (ImageReady) Choose System, and click OK.

For more information, see your Mac OS documentation.

To return to the Adobe Color Picker after using another color picker

1 Do one of the following:

- In Windows, choose Edit > Preferences > General.
- (Photoshop) In Mac OS, choose Photoshop > Preferences > General.
- (ImageReady) In Mac OS, choose ImageReady > Preferences > General.

2 Choose Adobe from the Color Picker menu, and click OK.

Using the color wheel

If you're new to adjusting color components, it helps to keep a diagram of the standard color wheel on hand when you work on color balance. You can use the color wheel to predict how a change in one color component affects other colors and also how changes translate between RGB and CMYK color models.

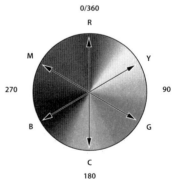

Color wheel
R. *Red* **Y.** *Yellow* **G.** *Green* **C.** *Cyan* **B.** *Blue* **M.** *Magenta*

For example, you can decrease the amount of any color in an image by increasing the amount of its opposite on the color wheel—and vice versa. Colors that lie opposite each other on the standard color wheel are known as *complementary* colors. Similarly, you can increase and decrease a color by adjusting the two adjacent colors on the wheel, or even by adjusting the two colors adjacent to its opposite.

In a CMYK image, you can decrease magenta either by decreasing the amount of magenta or by increasing its complement (by adding cyan and yellow). You can even combine these two corrections, minimizing their effect on overall lightness. In an RGB image, you can decrease magenta by removing red and blue or by adding green. All of these adjustments result in an overall color balance containing less magenta.

Chapter 9: Color management

Understanding color management

Why colors sometimes don't match

No device in a publishing system is capable of reproducing the full range of colors viewable to the human eye. Each device operates within a specific color space which can produce a certain range, or *gamut*, of colors.

A color model determines the relationship between values, and the color space defines the absolute meaning of those values as colors. Some color models have a fixed color space (such as Lab) because they relate directly to the way humans perceive color. These models are described as being *device-independent*. Other color models (RGB, HSL, HSB, CMYK, and so forth) can have many different color spaces. Because these models vary with each associated color space or device, they are described as being *device-dependent*.

Because of these varying color spaces, colors can shift in appearance as you transfer documents between different devices. Color variations can result from differences in image sources (scanners and software produce art using different color spaces); brands of computer monitors; the way software applications define color; print media (newsprint paper reproduces a smaller gamut than magazine-quality paper); and other natural variations, such as manufacturing differences in monitors or monitor age.

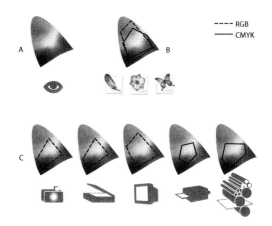

Color gamuts of various devices and documents
A. *Lab color space* **B.** *Documents (working space)* **C.** *Devices*

What is a color management system?

Color-matching problems result from various devices and software using different color spaces. One solution is to have a system that interprets and translates color accurately between devices. A color management system (CMS) compares the color space in which a color was created to the color space in which the same color will be output, and makes the necessary adjustments to represent the color as consistently as possible among different devices.

A color management system translates colors with the help of *color profiles*. A profile is a mathematical description of a device's color space. For example, a scanner profile tells a color management system how your scanner "sees" colors. Adobe applications use

ICC profiles, a format defined by the International Color Consortium (ICC) as a cross-platform standard. (See `About color profiles' on page 201.)

Because no single color-translation method is ideal for all types of graphics, a color management system provide a choice of *rendering intents,* or translation methods, so that you can apply a method appropriate to a particular graphical element. For example, a color translation method that preserves correct relationships among colors in a wildlife photograph may alter the colors in a logo containing flat tints of color. (See `About rendering intents' on page 210.)

Note: *Don't confuse color management with color correction. A color management system won't correct an image that was saved with tonal or color balance problems. It provides an environment where you can evaluate images reliably in the context of your final output.*

Do you need color management?

Without a color management system, your color specifications are device-dependent. You might not need color management if your production process is tightly controlled for one medium only. For example, you or your prepress service provider can tailor CMYK images and specify color values for a known, specific set of printing conditions.

The value of color management increases when you have more variables in your production process. Color management is recommended if you anticipate reusing color graphics for print and online media, using various kinds of devices within a single medium (such as different printing presses), or if you manage multiple workstations.

You will benefit from a color management system if you need to accomplish any of the following:

• Get predictable and consistent color output on multiple output devices including color separations, your desktop printer, and your monitor. Color management is especially useful for adjusting color for devices with a relatively limited gamut, such as a four-color process printing press.

• Accurately soft-proof (preview) a color document on your monitor by making it simulate a specific output device. (Soft-proofing is subject to the limitations of monitor display, such as room lighting conditions.)

• Accurately evaluate and consistently incorporate color graphics from many different sources if they also use color management, and even in some cases if they don't.

• Send color documents to different output devices and media without having to manually adjust colors in documents or original graphics. This is valuable when creating images that will eventually be used both in print and online.

• Print color correctly to an unknown color output device; for example, you could store a document online for consistently reproducible on-demand color printing anywhere in the world.

Creating a viewing environment for color management

Your work environment influences how you see color on your monitor and on printed output. For best results, control the colors and light in your work environment by doing the following:

* View your documents in an environment that provides a consistent light level and color temperature. For example, the color characteristics of sunlight change throughout the day and alter the way colors appear on your screen, so keep shades closed or work in a windowless room. To eliminate the blue-green cast from fluorescent lighting, you can install D50 (5000° Kelvin) lighting. You can also view printed documents using a D50 lightbox.

* View your document in a room with neutral-colored walls and ceiling. A room's color can affect the perception of both monitor color and printed color. The best color for a viewing room is polychromatic gray. Also, the color of your clothing reflecting off the glass of your monitor may affect the appearance of colors on-screen.

* Remove colorful background patterns on your monitor desktop. Busy or bright patterns surrounding a document interfere with accurate color perception. Set your desktop to display neutral grays only.

* View document proofs in the real-world conditions under which your audience will see the final piece. For example, you might want to see how a housewares catalog looks under the incandescent light bulbs used in homes, or view an office furniture catalog under the fluorescent lighting used in offices. However, always make final color judgements under the lighting conditions specified by the legal requirements for contract proofs in your country.

Keeping colors consistent

About color management in Adobe applications

Adobe's color management system helps you maintain the appearance of colors as you bring images in from external sources, edit documents and transfer them between Adobe applications, and output your finished compositions. This system is based on conventions developed by the International Color Consortium (ICC), a group responsible for standardizing profile formats and procedures so that consistent and accurate color can be achieved throughout a workflow.

By default, color management is turned on in Adobe applications. If you purchased the Adobe Creative Suite, color settings are synchronized across applications to provide consistent display for RGB and CMYK colors. This means that colors look the same no matter which application you view them in.

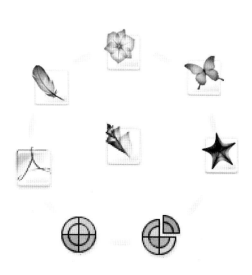

Color settings for each Creative Suite application are synchronized in a central location through Adobe Bridge.

If you decide to change the default settings, easy-to-use presets let you configure Adobe's color management system to match common output conditions. You can also customize color settings to meet the demands of your particular color workflow.

Keep in mind that the kinds of images you work with and your output requirements influence how you use color management. For example, there are different color-consistency issues for an RGB photo printing workflow, a CMYK commercial printing workflow, a mixed RGB/CMYK digital printing workflow, and an internet publishing workflow.

Basic steps for producing consistent color

1. Consult with your production partners (if you have any) to ensure that all aspects of your color management workflow integrate seamlessly with theirs.

Discuss how the color workflow will be integrated with your workgroups and service providers, how will software and hardware be configured for integration into the color management system, and at what level will color management be implemented. (See `Do you need color management?' on page 188.)

For more information on common color management workflows, see the Color Workflow Guide on your application CD.

2. Calibrate and profile your monitor.

A monitor profile is the first profile you should create. Seeing accurate color is essential if you are making creative decisions involving the color you specify in your document. (See `To calibrate and profile your monitor' on page 203.)

3. Add color profiles to your system for any input and output devices you plan to use, such as scanners and printers.

The color management system uses profiles to know how a device produces color and what the actual colors in a document are. Device profiles are often installed when a device is added to your system. You can also use third-party software and hardware to create more accurate profiles for specific devices and conditions. If your document will be commercially printed, contact your service provider to determine the profile for the printing device or press condition. (See `About color profiles' on page 201 and `To install a color profile' on page 204.)

4. Set up color management in Adobe applications.

The default color settings are sufficient for most users. However, you can change the color settings by doing one of the following:

- If you use multiple Adobe applications, use Bridge to choose a standard color management configuration and synchronize color settings across applications before working with documents. (See `To synchronize color settings across Adobe applications' on page 191.)

- If you use only one Adobe application, or if you want to customize advanced color management options, you can change color settings for a specific application. (See `To set up color management for Illustrator, InDesign, and Photoshop' on page 192 or `To set up color management for GoLive' on page 192.)

5. (Optional) Preview colors using a soft proof.

After you create a document, you can use a soft proof to preview how colors will look when printed or viewed on a specific device. (See `Soft-proofing colors' on page 197.)

Note: A soft proof alone doesn't let you preview how overprinting will look when printed on an offset press. If you work with Illustrator or InDesign documents that contain overprinting, turn on Overprint Preview to accurately preview overprints in a soft proof.

6. Use color management when printing and saving files.

Keeping the appearance of colors consistent across all of the devices in your workflow is the goal of color management. Leave color management options enabled when printing documents, saving files, and preparing files for online viewing. (See `Printing with color management' on page 199 and `Color-managing documents for online viewing' on page 196.)

To synchronize color settings across Adobe applications

When you set up color management using Adobe Bridge, color settings are automatically synchronized across applications. This synchronization ensures that colors look the same in all Adobe Creative Suite applications.

If color settings are not synchronized, a warning message appears at the top of the Color Settings dialog box in every Creative Suite application. Adobe recommends that you synchronize color settings before you work with new or existing documents.

1 Open Bridge.

To open Bridge from another Creative Suite application, choose File > Browse from the application. To open Bridge directly, either choose Adobe Bridge from the Start menu (Windows) or double-click the Adobe Bridge icon (Mac OS).

2 Choose Edit > Creative Suite Color Settings.

3 Select a color setting from the list, and click Apply.

If none of the default settings meet your requirements, select Show Expanded List Of Color Setting Files to view additional settings. To install a custom settings file, such as a file you received from a print service provider, click Show Saved Color Settings Files.

To set up color management for Illustrator, InDesign, and Photoshop

1 Choose Edit > Color Settings.

2 Select a color setting from the Settings menu, and click OK.

The setting you select determines the color working spaces used by the application, what happens when you open and import files with embedded profiles, and how the color management system converts colors. To view a description of a setting, select the setting and then position the pointer over the setting name. The description appears at the bottom of the dialog box.

In certain situations, such as if your service provider supplies you with a custom output profile, you may need to customize specific options in the Color Settings dialog box. However, customizing is recommended for advanced users only.

Note: If you work with more than one Adobe application, it is highly recommended that you synchronize your color settings across applications. (See `To synchronize color settings across Adobe applications' on page 191.)

To set up color management for GoLive

By default, GoLive's color management system uses a standard web workflow in which you author web pages and import images in the sRGB color space.

sRGB reflects the characteristic of the average PC monitor and is therefore applicable to the majority of web users. If you have a highly controlled distribution for your website (for example, you know that the majority of users will view the site using Apple Macintosh computers), you can override the standard web workflow.

1 Choose Edit > Color Settings.

2 If you want to author web pages in a color space other than sRGB, or you want to preserve embedded profiles in RGB images, deselect Use Standard Web Workflow.

Adobe recommends that you leave the Use Standard Web Workflow option selected.

3 Select a color setting from the Settings menu, and click OK.

The setting you select determines the color working space of the application, what happens when you open and import files with embedded profiles, and how the color management system converts colors. You can view the options for a color setting directly in the Color Settings dialog box.

In most cases, it is best to use a standard color setting and not change specific options in the Color Settings dialog box. Customizing the working spaces, color management policies, and color conversion options is recommended for advanced users only.

Note: If you work with more than one Adobe application, it is recommended that you synchronize your color settings across applications. (See `To synchronize color settings across Adobe applications' on page 191.)

To change the appearance of CMYK black

In Illustrator and InDesign, pure CMYK black (K=100) appears jet black (or rich black) when viewed on-screen, printed to a non-Postscript desktop printer, or exported to an RGB file format. If you prefer to see the difference between pure black and rich black as it will appear when printed on a commercial press, you can change the Appearance Of Black preferences. These preferences do not change the color values in a document.

1 Choose Edit > Preferences > Appearance Of Black (Windows) or *Application name* > Preferences > Appearance Of Black (Mac OS).

2 Choose an option for On Screen:

Display All Blacks Accurately Displays pure CMYK black as dark gray. This setting allows you to see the difference between pure black and rich black.

Display All Blacks As Rich Black Displays pure CMYK black as jet black (RGB=000). This setting makes pure black and rich black appear the same on-screen.

3 Choose an option for Printing/Exporting:

Output All Blacks Accurately When printing to a non-Postscript desktop printer or exporting to an RGB file format, outputs pure CMYK black as using the color numbers in the document. This setting allows you to see the difference between pure black and rich black.

Output All Blacks As Rich Black When printing to a non-Postscript desktop printer or exporting to an RGB file format, outputs pure CMYK black as jet black (RGB=000). This setting makes pure black and rich black appear the same.

Managing process and spot colors

When color management is on, any color you apply or create within an Adobe application automatically uses a color profile that corresponds to the document. If you switch color modes, the color management system uses the appropriate profiles to translate the color to the new color model you choose.

Keep in mind the following guidelines for working with process and spot colors:

• Choose a CMYK working space that matches your CMYK output conditions to ensure that you can accurately define and view process colors.

• Select colors from a color library. Adobe applications come with several standard color libraries, which you can load using the Swatches palette menu.

• (Illustrator and InDesign) Turn on Overprint Preview to get an accurate and consistent preview of spot colors.

• (Illustrator and InDesign) Use Lab values (the default) to display predefined spot colors (such as colors from the TOYO, PANTONE, DIC, and HKS libraries) and convert these colors to process colors. Using Lab values provides the greatest accuracy and guarantees the consistent display of colors across Creative Suite applications. If you want the display and output of these colors to match earlier versions of Illustrator or InDesign, use CMYK equivalent values instead. For instructions on switching between Lab values and CMYK values for spot colors, search Illustrator or InDesign Help

Note: Color-managing spot colors provides a close approximation of a spot color on your proofing device and monitor. However, it is difficult to exactly reproduce a spot color on a monitor or proofing device because many spot color inks exist outside the gamuts of many of those devices.

To share swatches between applications

You can share the solid swatches you create in one Adobe CS2 application with any other Adobe CS2 application by saving a swatch library for exchange. The colors appear exactly the same across applications as long as your color settings are synchronized.

1 In the Swatches palette, create the process and spot-color swatches you want to share, and remove any swatches you don't want to share.

Note: You cannot share the following types of swatches between applications: patterns, gradients, and the Registration swatch from Illustrator or InDesign; and book color references, HSB, XYZ, duotone, monitorRGB, opacity, total ink, and webRGB swatches from Photoshop. These types of swatches are automatically excluded when you save swatches for exchange.

2 Select Save Swatches For Exchange from the Swatches palette menu, and save the swatch libraries in an easily accessible location.

3 Load the swatch library into the Swatches palette for any other Adobe CS2 application. See that application's Help for additional instructions.

Color-managing imported images

Color-managing imported images

How imported images are integrated into a document's color space depends on whether or not the image has an embedded profile:

- When you import an image that contains no profile, the Adobe application uses the current document profile to define the colors in the image.

- When you import an image that contains an embedded profile, color policies in the Color Settings dialog box determine how the Adobe application handles the profile. (See `Color Management Policy options' on page 208.)

Using a safe CMYK workflow

In Illustrator and InDesign, a safe CMYK workflow ensures that CMYK color numbers are preserved all the way to the final output device, as opposed to being converted by your color management system. This workflow is beneficial if you want to incrementally adopt color management practices. For example, you can use CMYK profiles to soft-proof and hard-proof documents without the possibility of unintended color conversions occurring during final output.

Illustrator and InDesign support a safe CMYK workflow by default. As a result, when you open or import a CMYK image with an embedded profile, the application ignores the profile and preserves the raw color numbers. If you want your application to adjust color numbers based on an embedded profile, change the CMYK color policy to Preserve Embedded

Profiles in the Color Settings dialog box. You can easily restore the safe CMYK workflow by changing the CMYK color policy back to Preserve Numbers (Ignore Linked Profiles).

You can override safe CMYK settings when you print a document or save it to PDF. However, doing so may cause colors to be reseparated. For example, pure CMYK black objects may be reseparated as rich black. For more information on color management options for printing and saving PDF files, search in Help.

Preparing imported graphics for color management

Use the following general guidelines to prepare graphics for being color-managed in Adobe applications:

- Embed an ICC-compliant profile when you save the file. The file formats that support embedded profiles are JPEG, PDF, PSD (Photoshop), AI (Illustrator), INDD (InDesign), and TIFF. (See `To embed a color profile in a document' on page 204.)

- If you plan to reuse a color graphic for multiple final output devices or media, such as for print, video, and the web, prepare the graphic using RGB or Lab colors whenever possible. If you must save in a color model other than RGB or Lab, keep a copy of the original graphic. RGB and Lab color models represent larger color gamuts than most output devices can reproduce, retaining as much color information as possible before being translated to a smaller output color gamut.

To view or change profiles for imported bitmap images

InDesign allows you to view, override, or disable profiles for imported bitmap images. This may be necessary when you are importing an image containing no profile or an incorrectly embedded profile. For example, if the scanner manufacturer's default profile was embedded but you have since generated a custom profile, you can assign the newer profile.

1 Do one of the following:

- If the graphic is already in layout, select it and choose Object > Image Color Settings.

- If you're about to import the graphic, choose File > Place, select Show Import Options, locate and select the file, and click Place. Then choose Color Settings from the menu at the top of the Image Import Options dialog box that appears.

2 For Profile, choose the source profile to apply to the graphic in your document. If a profile is currently embedded, the profile name appears at the top of the Profile menu.

3 (Optional) For Rendering Intent, choose a rendering intent. In most cases, it's best to use the default rendering intent.

4 Click OK.

Color-managing documents for online viewing

Color-managing documents for online viewing

Color management for online viewing is very different from color management for printed media. With printed media, you have far more control over the appearance of the final document. With online media, your document will appear on a wide range of possibly uncalibrated monitors and video display systems, significantly limiting your control over color consistency.

When you color-manage documents that will be viewed exclusively on the web, Adobe recommends that you use the sRGB color space. sRGB is the default working space for most Adobe color settings, but you can verify that sRGB is selected in the Color Settings dialog box of any Creative Suite application. With the working space set to sRGB, any RGB graphics you create will use sRGB as the color space.

When working with images that have an embedded color profile other than sRGB, you should convert the image's colors to sRGB before you save the image for use on the web. If you want the application to automatically convert the colors to sRGB when you open the image, select Convert To Working Space as the RGB color management policy. In Photoshop and InDesign, you can also manually convert the colors to sRGB using the Edit > Convert To Profile command.

Color-managing PDF documents for online viewing

When you export Portable Document Format (PDF) files, you can choose to embed profiles. PDF files with embedded profiles reproduce color consistently in Acrobat 4.x or later running under a properly configured color management system. For information about color management in Acrobat software, see Acrobat online Help.

Keep in mind that embedding color profiles increases the size of PDF files. RGB profiles are usually small (around 3K); however, CMYK profiles can range from .5 to 2 MB.

Color-managing HTML documents for online viewing

Many web browsers do not support color management. Of the browsers that do support color management, not all instances can be considered color-managed because they may be running on systems where the monitors are not calibrated. In addition, few web pages contain images with embedded profiles. If you manage a highly controlled environment, such as the intranet of a design studio, you may be able to achieve some degree of HTML color management for images by equipping everyone with a browser that supports color management and calibrating all monitors.

You can approximate how colors will look on non-calibrated monitors by using the sRGB color space. In Adobe GoLive, you can also preview how colors will look in different browsers using options in the View palette. (See `To preview how colors will appear in a web browser' on page 199.) However, because color reproduction varies among uncalibrated monitors, you still won't be able to anticipate the true range of potential display variations.

Proofing colors

Soft-proofing colors

In a traditional publishing workflow, you print a hard proof of your document to preview how its colors will look when reproduced on a specific output device. In a color-managed workflow, you can use the precision of color profiles to soft-proof your document directly on the monitor. You can display an on-screen preview of how your document's colors will look when reproduced on a particular output device. If you are authoring a website in GoLive, you can also soft-proof how colors will look when viewed in different browsers and with different color profiles.

Keep in mind that the reliability of the soft proof depends upon the quality of your monitor, the profiles of your monitor and output devices, and the ambient lighting conditions of your work environment.

Note: A soft proof alone doesn't let you preview how overprinting will look when printed on an offset press. If you work with Illustrator or InDesign documents that contain overprinting, turn on Overprint Preview to accurately preview overprints in a soft proof.

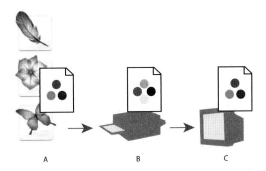

Using a soft proof to preview the final output of a document on your monitor
A. Document in the working space **B.** *Document's color values are translated to color space of chosen proof profile (usually the output device's profile).* **C.** *Monitor displays proof profile's interpretation of document's color values.*

To soft-proof colors

1 In Illustrator, InDesign, or Photoshop, choose View > Proof Setup, and do one of the following:

• Choose a preset that corresponds to the output condition you want to simulate. (See `Soft proof presets' on page 198.)

• Choose Custom (Photoshop and InDesign) or Customize (Illustrator) to create a custom proof setup for a specific output condition. This option is recommended for the most accurate preview of your final printed piece. (See `Custom soft proof options' on page 198.)

2 Choose View > Proof Colors to toggle the soft-proof display on and off. When soft proofing is on, a check mark appears next to the Proof Colors command, and the name of the proof preset or profile appears at the top of the document window.

💡 *To compare the colors in the original image and the colors in the soft proof, open the document in a new window before you set up the soft proof.*

Soft proof presets

Working CMYK Creates a soft proof of colors using the current CMYK working space as defined in the Color Settings dialog box.

Document CMYK (InDesign) Creates a soft proof of colors using the document's CMYK profile.

Working Cyan Plate, Working Magenta Plate, Working Yellow Plate, Working Black Plate, or Working CMY Plates (Photoshop) Creates a soft proof of specific CMYK ink colors using the current CMYK working space.

Macintosh RGB or Windows RGB (Photoshop and Illustrator) Creates a soft proof of colors in an image using either a standard Mac OS or Windows monitor as the proof profile space to simulate. Both options assume that the simulated device will display your document without using color management. Neither option is available for Lab or CMYK documents.

Monitor RGB (Photoshop and Illustrator) Creates a soft proof of colors in an RGB document using your current monitor color space as the proof profile space. This option assumes that the simulated device will display your document without using color management. This option is unavailable for Lab and CMYK documents.

Custom soft proof options

Device To Simulate Specifies the color profile of the device for which you want to create the proof. The usefulness of the chosen profile depends on how accurately it describes the device's behavior. Often, custom profiles for specific paper and printer combinations create the most accurate soft proof.

Preserve CMYK Numbers or Preserve RGB Numbers Simulates how the colors will appear without being converted to the color space of the output device. This option is most useful when you are following a safe CMYK workflow. (See `Using a safe CMYK workflow' on page 194.)

Rendering Intent (Photoshop and Illustrator) When the Preserve Numbers option is deselected, specifies a rendering intent for converting colors to the device you are trying to simulate. (See `About rendering intents' on page 210.)

Use Black Point Compensation (Photoshop) Ensures that the shadow detail in the image is preserved by simulating the full dynamic range of the output device. Select this option if you plan to use black point compensation when printing (which is recommended in most situations).

Simulate Paper Color Simulates the dingy white of real paper, according to the proof profile. Not all profiles support this option.

Simulate Black Ink Simulates the dark gray you really get instead of a solid black on many printers, according to the proof profile. Not all profiles support this option.

💡 *In Photoshop, if you want the custom proof setup to be the default proof setup for documents, close all document windows before choosing the View > Proof Setup > Custom command.*

To save or load a custom proof setup in Photoshop

1 Choose View > Proof Setup > Custom.

2 Do either of the following:

• To save a custom proof setup, click Save. To ensure that the new preset appears in the View > Proof Setup menu, save the preset in the default location.

• To load a custom proof setup, click Load.

To preview how colors will appear in a web browser

Different web browsers use different color spaces. For example, most Windows browsers display colors using the sRGB color space, while most Mac OS browsers display colors using the Apple RGB color space. You can preview how colors will look when viewed in different browsers using options in GoLive's View palette.

1 In GoLive, select the Layout Editor in the document window.

2 Click the Options tab in the View palette.

3 For Basic Profile, select the browser you want to emulate.

4 (Optional) For User Profiles, select an option from the Color submenu.

For example, if you want to preview how colors look when displayed using embedded profiles, select Use Embedded Profiles. Or, if you want to preview how colors look when displayed in grayscale, select Mac Grayscale (Gray Gamma 1.8) or Windows Grayscale (Gray Gamma 2.2).

Note: The Safari browser (listed under the Basic Profile > Other menu) is currently the only browser that supports embedded color profiles. Therefore, selecting User Profiles > Color > Use Embedded Profiles does not provide an accurate preview for any browser other than Safari.

Each User Profiles > Color option you select overrides existing Basic Profile and User Profiles options. For example, if you select Explorer 6 Win for Basic Profile and then select Mac Colors (Apple RGB) for User Profiles > Color, GoLive displays colors using the Apple RGB color space.

Color-managing documents when printing

Printing with color management

Color management options for printing let you specify how you want Adobe applications to handle the outgoing image data so the printer will print colors consistent with what you see on your monitor. Your options for printing color-managed documents depend on the Adobe application you use, as well as the output device you select. In general, you have the following choices for handling colors during printing:

• Let the printer determine colors. (See `Letting the printer determine colors when printing' on page 200.)

• Let the application determine colors. (See `Letting the application determine colors when printing' on page 200.)

- (Photoshop and InDesign) Do not use color management. In this workflow, no color conversion occurs. You may also need to turn off color management in your printer driver. This method is useful primarily for printing test targets or generating custom profiles.

Letting the printer determine colors when printing

In this workflow, the application does no color conversion, but sends all necessary conversion information to the output device. This method is especially convenient when printing to inkjet photo printers, because each combination of paper type, printing resolution, and additional printing parameters (such as high speed printing) requires a different profile. Most new inkjet photo printers come with fairly accurate profiles built into the driver, so letting the printer select the right profile saves time and alleviates mistakes. This method is also recommended if you are not familiar with color management.

If you choose this option, it is very important that you set up printing options and turn on color management in your printer driver. Search Help for additional instructions.

If you select a PostScript printer, you can take advantage of *PostScript color management*. PostScript color management makes it possible to perform color composite output or color separations at the raster image processor (RIP)—a process called *in-RIP separations*—so that a program need only specify parameters for separation and let the device calculate the final color values. PostScript color-managed output workflows require an output device that supports PostScript color management using PostScript level 2, version 2017 or higher; or PostScript 3.

Letting the application determine colors when printing

In this workflow, the application does all the color conversion, generating color data specific to one output device. The application uses the assigned color profiles to convert colors to the output device's gamut, and sends the resulting values to the output device. The accuracy of this method depends on the accuracy of the printer profile you select. Use this workflow when you have custom ICC profiles for each specific printer, ink, and paper combination.

If you choose this option, it is very important that you disable color management in your printer driver. Letting the application and the printer driver simultaneously manage colors during printing results in unpredictable color. Search Help for additional instructions.

Obtaining custom profiles for desktop printers

If the output profiles that come with your printer don't produce satisfactory results, you obtain custom profiles in the following ways:

- Purchase a profile for your type of printer and paper. This is usually the easiest and least expensive method.

- Purchase a profile for your specific printer and paper. This method involves printing a profiling target on your printer and paper, and providing that target to a company that will create a specific profile. This is more expensive than purchasing a standard profile, but can provide better results because it compensates for any manufacturing variations in printers.

- Create your own profile using a scanner-based system. This method involves using profile-creation software and your own flatbed scanner to scan the profiling target. It can provide excellent results for matte surface papers, but not glossy papers. (Glossy papers tend to have fluorescent brighteners in them that look different to a scanner than they do in room light.)

- Create your own profile using a hardware profile-creation tool. This method is expensive but can provide the best results. A good hardware tool can create an accurate profile even with glossy papers.

- Tweak a profile created using one of the previous methods with profile-editing software. This software can be complex to use, but lets you correct problems with a profile or simply adjust a profile to produce results more to your taste.

Color-managing PDF files for printing

When you create Adobe PDF files for commercial printing, you can specify how color information is represented. The easiest way to do this is using a PDF/X standard; however, you can also specify color-handling options manually in the Output section of the PDF dialog box. For more information about PDF/X and how to create PDF files, search Help.

In general, you have the following choices for handling colors when creating PDF files:

- (PDF/X-3) Do not convert colors. Use this method when creating a document that will be printed or

displayed on various or unknown devices. When you select a PDF/X-3 standard, color profiles are automatically embedded in the PDF file.

- (PDF/X-1a) Convert all colors to the destination CMYK color space. Use this method if you want to create a press-ready file that does not require any further color conversions. When you select a PDF/X-1a standard, no profiles are embedded in the PDF file.

- (Illustrator and InDesign) Convert colors that have embedded profiles to the destination color space, but preserve the numbers for those colors without embedded profiles. You can manually select this option in the Output section of the PDF dialog box. Use this method if the document contains CMYK images that aren't color-managed and you want to make sure that the color numbers are preserved. (See `Using a safe CMYK workflow' on page 194.)

Note: *All spot-color information is preserved during color conversion; only the process color equivalents convert to the designated color space.*

Working with color profiles

About color profiles

Precise, consistent color management requires accurate ICC-compliant profiles of all of your color devices. For example, without an accurate scanner profile, a perfectly scanned image may appear incorrect in another program, simply due to any difference between the scanner and the program displaying the image. This misleading representation may cause you to make unnecessary, time-wasting, and potentially damaging "corrections" to an already satisfactory image. With an accurate profile, a program importing the image can correct for any device differences and display a scan's actual colors.

A color management system uses the following kinds of profiles:

Monitor profiles Describe how the monitor is currently reproducing color. This is the first profile you should create because it is absolutely essential for managing color. If what you see on your monitor is not representative of the actual colors in your document, you will not be able to maintain color consistency. (See `To calibrate and profile your monitor' on page 203.)

Input device profiles Describe what colors an input device is capable of capturing or scanning. If your digital camera offers a choice of profiles, Adobe recommends that you select Adobe RGB. Otherwise, use sRGB (which is the default for most cameras). Advanced users may also consider using different profiles for different light sources. For scanner profiles, some photographers create separate profiles for each type or brand of film scanned on a scanner.

Output device profiles Describe the color space of output devices like desktop printers and a printing press. The color management system uses output device profiles to properly map the colors in an document to the colors within the gamut of an output device's color space. The output profile should also take into consideration specific printing conditions, such as the type of paper and ink. For example, glossy paper is capable of displaying a different range of colors than a matte paper.

Most printer drivers come with built-in color profiles. It's a good idea to try these profiles before you invest in custom profiles. For information on how to print using the built-in profiles, see `Letting the printer determine colors when printing' on page 200. For information on how to obtain custom profiles, see `Obtaining custom profiles for desktop printers' on page 200.

Document profiles Define the specific RGB or CMYK color space of a document. By assigning, or *tagging,* a document with a profile, the application provides a definition of actual color appearances in the document. For example, R=127, G=12, B=107 is just a set of numbers that different devices will display differently. But when tagged with the AdobeRGB color space, these numbers specify an actual color or wavelength of light; in this case, a specific color of purple.

When color management is on, Adobe applications automatically assign new documents a profile based on Working Space options in the Color Settings dialog box. Documents without associated profiles are known as *untagged* and contain only raw color numbers. When working with untagged documents, Adobe applications use the current working space profile to display and edit colors. (See `About color working spaces' on page 207.)

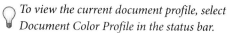 *To view the current document profile, select Document Color Profile in the status bar.*

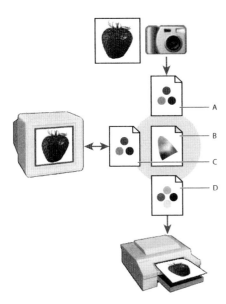

Managing color with profiles
A. Profiles describe the color spaces of the input device and the document. B. Using the profiles' descriptions, the color management system identifies the document's actual colors. C. The monitor's profile tells the color management system how to translate the numeric values to the monitor's color space. D. Using the output device's profile, the color management system translates the document's numeric values to the color values of the output device so the actual colors are printed.

About monitor calibration and characterization

Profiling software such as Adobe Gamma can both calibrate and characterize your monitor. *Calibrating* your monitor brings it into compliance with a predefined standard; for example, adjusting your monitor so that it displays color using the graphics arts standard white point color temperature of 5000 degrees Kelvin. *Characterizing* your monitor simply creates a profile that describes how the monitor is currently reproducing color.

Monitor calibration involves adjusting the following video settings, which may be unfamiliar to you.

Brightness and contrast The overall level and range, respectively, of display intensity. These parameters work just as they do on a television. Adobe Gamma helps you set an optimum brightness and contrast range for calibration.

Gamma The brightness of the midtone values. The values produced by a monitor from black to white are nonlinear—if you graph the values, they form a curve, not a straight line. Gamma defines the value of that curve halfway between black and white.

Phosphors The substances that CRT monitors use to emit light. Different phosphors have different color characteristics.

White point The color and intensity of the brightest white the monitor can reproduce.

To calibrate and profile your monitor

When you calibrate your monitor, you are adjusting it so it conforms to a known specification. Once your monitor is calibrated, the profiling utility lets you save a color profile. The profile describes the color behavior of the monitor—what colors can or cannot be displayed on the monitor and how the numeric color values in an image must be converted so that colors are displayed accurately.

1 Make sure your monitor has been turned on for at least a half hour. This gives it sufficient time to warm up and produce more consistent output.

2 Make sure your monitor is displaying thousands of colors or more. Ideally, make sure it is displaying millions of colors or 24-bit or higher.

3 Remove colorful background patterns on your monitor desktop and set your desktop to display neutral grays. Busy patterns or bright colors surrounding a document interfere with accurate color perception.

4 Do one of the following to calibrate and profile your monitor:

- In Windows, use the Adobe Gamma utility, located in the Control Panel.

- In Mac OS, use the Calibrate utility, located in the System Preferences/Displays/Color tab.

- For the best results, use third-party software and measuring devices. In general, using a measuring device such as a colorimeter along with software can create more accurate profiles because an instrument can measure the colors displayed on a monitor far more accurately than the human eye.

Note: Monitor performance changes and declines over time; recalibrate and profile your monitor every month or so. If you find it difficult or impossible to calibrate your monitor to a standard, it may be too old and faded.

Most profiling software automatically assigns the new profile as the default monitor profile. For instructions on how to manually assign the monitor profile, refer to the Help system for your operating system.

To install a color profile

Color profiles are often installed when a device is added to your system. The accuracy of these profiles (often called *generic profiles* or *canned profiles*) varies from manufacturer to manufacturer. You can also obtain device profiles from your service provider, download profiles from the web, or create *custom profiles* using professional profiling equipment.

- In Windows, right-click a profile and select Install Profile. Alternatively, copy the profiles into the WINDOWS\system32\spool\drivers\color folder (Windows XP) or the WINNT\system32\spool\drivers\color folder (Windows 2000).

- In Mac OS, copy profiles into the /Library/Application Support/Adobe/Color/Profiles/Recommended folder. You can also copy profiles into the /Users/*username*/Library/ColorSync/Profiles folder.

After installing color profiles, be sure to restart Adobe applications.

To embed a color profile in a document

In order to embed a color profile in a document you created in Photoshop, Illustrator, or InDesign, you must save or export the document in a format that supports ICC profiles.

1 Save or export the document in one of the following file formats: Adobe PDF, PSD (Photoshop), AI (Illustrator), INDD (InDesign), JPEG, or TIFF.

2 Select the option for embedding ICC profiles. The exact name and location of this option varies between applications. Search Help in the relevant CS2 application for additional instructions.

Changing the color profile for a document

There are very few situations that require you to change the color profile for a document. This is because your application automatically assigns the color profile based on the settings you select in the Color Settings dialog box. The only times you should manually change a color profile are when preparing a document for a different output destination or correcting a policy behavior that you no longer want implemented in the document. Changing the profile is recommended for advanced users only.

You can change the color profile for a document in the following ways:

- Assign a new profile. The color numbers in the document remain the same, but the new profile may dramatically change the appearance of the colors as displayed on your monitor.

- Remove the profile so that the document in no longer color-managed.

- (Photoshop and InDesign) Convert the colors in the document to the color space of a different profile. The color numbers are shifted in an effort to preserve the original color appearances.

To assign or remove a color profile from a document in Photoshop or Illustrator

1 Choose Edit > Assign Profile.

2 Select an option, and click OK:

Don't Color Manage This Document Removes the existing profile from the document. Select this option only if you are sure that you do not want to color-manage the document. After you remove the profile

from a document, the appearance of colors is defined by the application's working space profiles, and you can no longer embed a profile in the document.

Working [color model: working space] Assigns the working space profile to the document.

Profile Lets you select a different profile. The application assigns the new profile to the document without converting colors to the profile space. This may dramatically change the appearance of the colors as displayed on your monitor.

To assign or remove a color profile from a document in InDesign

1 Choose Edit > Assign Profiles.

2 For RGB Profile and CMYK Profile, select one of the following:

Discard (Use Current Working Space) Removes the existing profile from the document. Select this option only if you are sure that you do not want to color-manage the document. After you remove the profile from a document, the appearance of colors is defined by the application's working space profiles, and you can no longer embed a profile in the document.

Assign Current Working Space <working space> Assigns the working space profile to the document.

Assign Profile Lets you select a different profile. The application assigns the new profile to the document without converting colors to the profile space. This may dramatically change the appearance of the colors as displayed on your monitor.

3 Choose a rendering intent for each type of graphic in your document. For each graphic type, you can choose one of the four standard intents, or the Use

Color Settings Intent, which uses the rendering intent currently specified in the Color Settings dialog box. For more information on rendering intents, search in Help.

The graphic types include the following:

Solid Color Intent Sets the rendering intent for all vector art (solid areas of color) in InDesign native objects.

Default Image Intent Sets the default rendering intent for bitmap images placed in InDesign. You can still override this setting on an image-by-image basis. (See `To view or change profiles for imported bitmap images' on page 195.)

After-Blending Intent Sets the rendering intent to the proofing or final color space for colors that result from transparency interactions on the page. Use this option when your document includes transparent objects.

4 To preview the effects of the new profile assignment in the document, select Preview, and then click OK.

To convert colors in a document to another profile

1 In Photoshop or InDesign, choose Edit > Convert To Profile.

2 Under Destination Space, choose the color profile to which you want to convert the document's colors. The document will be converted to and tagged with this new profile.

3 Under Conversion Options, specify a color management engine, a rendering intent, and black point and dither options. (See `Color Conversion options' on page 209.)

4 To flatten all layers of the document onto a single layer upon conversion, select Flatten Image.

5 To preview the effects of the conversion in the document, select Preview. This preview becomes more accurate if you select Flatten Image.

Color settings

To customize color settings

For most color-managed workflows, it is best to use a preset color setting which has been tested by Adobe Systems. Changing specific options is recommended only if you are knowledgeable about color management and very confident about the changes you make.

After you customize options, you can save them as a preset. Saving color settings ensures that you can reuse them and share them with other users or applications.

- To save color settings as a preset, click Save in the Color Settings dialog box. To ensure that the application displays the setting name in the Color Settings dialog box, save the file in the default location. If you save the file to a different location, you must load the file before you can select the setting.

- To load a color settings preset that's not saved in the standard location, click Load in the Color Settings dialog box, select the file you want to load, and click Open.

About color working spaces

A *working space* is an intermediate color space used to define and edit color in Adobe applications. Each color model has a working space profile associated with it. You can choose working space profiles in the Color Settings dialog box.

A working space profile acts as the source profile for newly created documents that use the associated color model. For example, if Adobe RGB (1998) is the current RGB working space profile, each new RGB document that you create will use colors within the Adobe RGB (1998) gamut. Working spaces also determine the appearance of colors in untagged documents.

If you open a document embedded with a color profile that doesn't match the working space profile, the application uses a *color management policy* to determine how to handle the color data. In most cases, the default policy is to preserve the embedded profile. For more information on setting up color management policies, see `About missing and mismatched color profiles' on page 208 and `Color Management Policy options' on page 208.

Working Space options

To display working space options, choose Edit > Color Settings.

To view a description of any profile, select the profile and then position the pointer over the profile name. The description appears at the bottom of the dialog box.

RGB Determines the RGB color space of the application. In general, it's best to choose Adobe RGB or sRGB, rather than the profile for a specific device (such as a monitor profile).

sRGB is recommended when preparing images for the web, because it defines the color space of the standard monitor used to view images on the web. sRGB is also a good choice when working with images from consumer-level digital cameras, because most of these camera use sRGB as their default color space.

Adobe RGB is recommended when preparing documents for print, because Adobe RGB's gamut includes some printable colors (cyans and blues in particular) that can't be displayed using sRGB. Adobe RGB is also a good choice when working with images from professional-level digital cameras, because most of these camera use Adobe RGB as their default color space.

CMYK Determines the CMYK color space of the application. All CMYK working spaces are device-dependent, meaning that they are based on actual ink and paper combinations. The CMYK working spaces Adobe supplies are based on standard commercial print conditions.

Gray (Photoshop) Determines Grayscale color space of the application.

Spot (Photoshop) Specifies the dot gain to use when displaying spot color channels and duotones.

Adobe applications ship with a standard set of working space profiles that have been recommended and tested by Adobe Systems for most color management workflows. By default, only these profiles appear in the working space menus. To display additional color profiles that you have installed on your system, select Advanced Mode (Illustrator and InDesign) or More Options (Photoshop). A color profile must be bi-directional, that is, contain specifications for translating both into and out of color spaces in order to appear the working space menus.

Note: In Photoshop, you can create custom working space profiles. However, Adobe recommends that you use a standard working space profile rather than creating a custom working space profile. For more information, see the Photoshop support knowledgebase at http://www.adobe.com/support/products/photoshop.html.

About missing and mismatched color profiles

For a newly created document, the color workflow usually operates seamlessly: unless specified otherwise, the document uses the working space profile associated with its color mode for creating and editing colors.

However, some existing documents may not use the working space profile that you have specified, and some existing documents may not be color-managed. It is common to encounter the following exceptions to your color-managed workflow:

- You might open a document or import color data (for example, by copying and pasting or dragging and dropping) from a document that is not tagged with a profile. This is often the case when you open a document created in an application that either does not support color management or has color management turned off.

- You might open a document or import color data from a document that is tagged with a profile different from the current working space. This may be the case when you open a document that has been created using different color management settings, or a document that has been scanned and tagged with a scanner profile.

In either case, the application uses a *color management policy* to decide how to handle the color data in the document. (See 'Color Management Policy options' on page 208.)

If the profile is missing or does not match the working space, the application may display a warning message, depending on options you set in the Color Settings dialog box. Profile warnings are turned off by default, but you can turn them on to ensure the appropriate color management of documents on a case-by-case basis. The warning messages vary between applications, but in general you have the following options:

- (Recommended) Leave the document or imported color data as it is. For example, you can choose to use the embedded profile (if one exists), leave the document without a color profile (if one doesn't exist), or preserve the numbers in pasted color data.

- Adjust the document or imported color data. For example, when opening a document with a missing color profile, you can choose to assign the current working space profile or a different profile. When opening a document with a mismatched color profile, you can choose to discard the profile or convert the colors to the current working space. When importing color data, you can choose to convert the colors to the current working space in order to preserve their appearance.

Color Management Policy options

A color management policy determines how the application handles color data when you open a document or import an image. You can choose different policies for RGB and CMYK images, and you can specify when you want warning messages to appear. To display color management policy options, choose Edit > Color Settings.

To view a description of a policy, select the policy and then position the pointer over the policy name. The description appears at the bottom of the dialog box.

RGB, CMYK, and Gray Specifies a policy to follow when bringing colors into the current working space (either by opening files or importing images into the current document). (The Grayscale option is available for Photoshop and GoLive only.) Choose from the following options:

• **Preserve Embedded Profiles** Always preserves embedded color profiles when opening files. This is the recommended option for most workflows because it provides consistent color management. One exception is if you're concerned about preserving CMYK numbers, in which case you should select Preserve Numbers (Ignore Linked Profiles) instead.

• **Convert to Working Space** Converts colors to the current working space profile when opening files and importing images. Select this option if you want to force all colors to use a single profile (the current working space profile).

• **Preserve Numbers (Ignore Linked Profiles)** This option is available in InDesign and Illustrator for CMYK. Preserves color numbers when opening files and importing images, but still allows you to use color management to view colors accurately in Adobe applications. Select this option if you want to use a safe CMYK workflow. (See `Using a safe CMYK workflow' on page 194.) In InDesign, you can override this policy on a per-object basis by choosing Object > Image Color Settings.

• **Off** Ignores embedded color profiles when opening files and importing images, and does not assign the working space profile to new documents. Select this option if you want to discard any color metadata provided by the original document creator.

Profile Mismatches: Ask When Opening Displays a message whenever you open a document tagged with a profile other than the current working space. You will be given the option to override the policy's default behavior. Select this option if you want to ensure the appropriate color management of documents on a case-by-case basis.

Profile Mismatches: Ask When Pasting Displays a message whenever color profile mismatches occur as colors are imported into a document via pasting or dragging-and-dropping. You will be given the option to override the policy's default behavior. Select this option if you want to ensure the appropriate color management of pasted colors on a case-by-case basis.

Missing Profiles: Ask When Opening Displays a message whenever you open an untagged document. You will be given the option to override the policy's default behavior. Select this option if you want to ensure the appropriate color management of documents on a case-by-case basis.

Color Conversion options

Color conversion options let you control how the application handles the colors in a document as it moves from one color space to another. Changing these options is recommended only if you are knowledgeable about color management and very confident about the changes you make. To display conversion options, choose Edit > Color Settings, and select Advanced Mode (Illustrator and InDesign) or More Options (Photoshop).

Engine Specifies the Color Management Module (CMM) used to map the gamut of one color space to the gamut of another. For most users, the default Adobe (ACE) engine fulfills all conversion needs.

💡 *To view a description of an engine or intent option, select the option and then position the pointer over the option name. The description appears at the bottom of the dialog box.*

Intent Specifies the rendering intent used to translate one color space to another. Differences between rendering intents are apparent only when you print a document or convert it to a different working space.

Use Black Point Compensation Ensures that the shadow detail in the image is preserved by simulating the full dynamic range of the output device. Select this option if you plan to use black point compensation when printing (which is recommended in most situations).

Use Dither (Photoshop) Controls whether to dither colors when converting 8-bit-per-channel images between color spaces. When the Use Dither option is selected, Photoshop mixes colors in the destination color space to simulate a missing color that existed in the source space. Although dithering helps to reduce the blocky or banded appearance of an image, it may also result in larger file sizes when images are compressed for web use.

About rendering intents

A rendering intent determines how a color management system handles color conversion from one color space to another. Different rendering intents use different rules to determine how the source colors are adjusted; for example, colors that fall inside the destination gamut may remain unchanged, or they may be adjusted to preserve the original range of visual relationships when translated to a smaller destination gamut. The result of choosing a rendering intent depends on the graphical content of documents and on the profiles used to specify color spaces. Some profiles produce identical results for different rendering intents.

💡 *In general, it is best to use the default rendering intent for the selected color setting, which has been tested by Adobe Systems to meet industry standards. For example, if you choose a color setting for North America or Europe, the default rendering intent is Relative Colorimetric. If you choose a color setting for Japan, the default rendering intent is Perceptual.*

You can select a rendering intent when you set color conversion options for the color management system, soft-proof colors, and print artwork:

Perceptual Aims to preserve the visual relationship between colors so it's perceived as natural to the human eye, even though the color values themselves may change. This intent is suitable for photographic images with lots of out-of-gamut colors. This is the standard rendering intent for the Japanese printing industry.

Saturation Tries to produce vivid colors in an image at the expense of color accuracy. This rendering intent is suitable for business graphics like graphs or charts, where bright saturated colors are more important than the exact relationship between colors.

Relative Colorimetric Compares the extreme highlight of the source color space to that of the destination color space and shifts all colors accordingly. Out-of-gamut colors are shifted to the closest reproducible color in the destination color space. Relative colorimetric preserves more of the original colors in an image than Perceptual. This is the standard rendering intent for printing in North America and Europe

Absolute Colorimetric Leaves colors that fall inside the destination gamut unchanged. Out of gamut colors are clipped. No scaling of colors to destination white point is performed. This intent aims to maintain color accuracy at the expense of preserving relationships between colors and is suitable for proofing to simulate the output of a particular device. This intent is particularly useful for previewing how paper color affects printed colors.

Advanced controls

In Photoshop you display advanced controls for managing color by choosing Edit > Color Settings and selecting More Options.

Desaturate Monitor Colors By Determines whether to desaturate colors by the specified amount when displayed on the monitor. When selected, this option can aid in visualizing the full range of color spaces with gamuts larger than that of the monitor. However, this causes a mismatch between the monitor display and the output. When the option is deselected, distinct colors in the image may display as a single color.

Blend RGB Colors Using Gamma Controls how RGB colors blend together to produce composite data (for example, when you blend or paint layers using Normal mode). When the option is selected, RGB colors are blended in the color space corresponding to the specified gamma. A gamma of 1.00 is considered "colorimetrically correct" and should result in the fewest edge artifacts. When the option is deselected, RGB colors are blended directly in the document's color space.

Note: When you select Blend RGB Colors Using Gamma, layered documents will look different when displayed in other applications than they do in Photoshop.

Chapter 10: Making color and tonal adjustments

Color and tonal corrections

Before making color and tonal adjustments

The powerful tools in Photoshop and ImageReady can enhance, repair, and correct the color and tonality (lightness, darkness, and contrast) in an image. Here are some items to consider before making color and tonal adjustments.

- Work with a monitor that's calibrated and profiled. For critical image editing, this is absolutely essential. Otherwise, the image you see on your monitor will look different when printed.

- Whenever you make a color or tonal adjustment to an image, some image information is discarded. It's best to be judicious regarding the amount of correction you apply to an image.

- (Photoshop) For critical work and maximum preservation of image data, it's best if the image you work with is 16 bits per channel (16-bit image) rather than 8 bits per channel (8-bit image). Data is discarded when you make tonal and color adjustments. The loss of image information is more critical in an 8-bit image than a 16-bit image. Generally, 16-bit images have a larger file size than 8-bit images.

Note: If you jump back and forth between Photoshop and ImageReady, be aware that ImageReady converts 16-bit images to 8-bit for editing. After the images are saved in ImageReady, they are permanently converted to 8-bit images, and the discarded data is unrecoverable. However, if you are editing a 16-bit image in ImageReady and haven't saved it yet, you can return to Photoshop. Photoshop opens it as a 16-bit image without data loss.

- Duplicate or make a copy of the image file. Working on a copy of your image preserves the original in the event you need to use the image in its original state.

- Remove any flaws such as dust spots, blemishes, and scratches from the image before making color and tonal adjustments.

- (Photoshop) Plan to use adjustment layers to adjust the tonal range and color balance of your image rather than applying an adjustment directly to the image layer itself. Adjustment layers let you go back and make successive tonal adjustments without discarding data from the image layer. Keep in mind that using adjustment layers adds to the file size of the image and demands more RAM from your computer.

- (Photoshop) Open the Info or Histogram palette in Expanded view. As you evaluate and correct the image, both palettes display invaluable feedback on your adjustments.

- You can make a selection or use a mask to confine your color and tonal adjustments to part of an image. Another way to apply color and tonal adjustments selectively is to set up your document with image components on different layers. Color and tonal adjustments are applied to only one layer at a time and affect only the image components on the targeted layer.

Correcting images in Photoshop

Here is the general workflow you follow when you correct the tonality and color of an image:

1 Use the histogram to check the quality and tonal range of the image.

2 Adjust the color balance to remove unwanted color casts or to correct oversaturated or undersaturated colors. See `Color adjustment commands' on page 214.

3 Adjust the tonal range.

Begin tonal corrections by adjusting the values of the extreme highlight and shadow pixels in the image, setting an overall tonal range for the image. This process is known as *setting the highlights and shadows* or *setting the white and black points*.

Setting the highlights and shadows typically redistributes the midtone pixels appropriately. However, you may need to adjust your midtones manually. See `Tonal adjustment methods' on page 215.

4 (Optional) Make other color adjustments.

After you correct the overall color balance of your image, you can make optional adjustments to enhance colors or produce special effects.

5 Sharpen the edges of the image.

As one of the final steps, use the Unsharp Mask filter to sharpen the clarity of edges in the image. The amount of sharpening required for an image varies according to the image quality produced by the digital camera or scanner you use. See `Sharpening images' on page 259.

6 (Optional) Target the image for press characteristics.

Use the Output sliders in the Levels dialog box or the Curves dialog box to bring important details in the highlights and shadows into the gamut of an output device, like a desktop printer. Do this if your image is being sent out to a printing press and you know the characteristics of the press.

Because sharpening increases the contrast of neighboring pixels, it's possible that some pixels in critical areas might become unprintable on the press that you're using. For this reason, it's best to fine-tune the output settings after sharpening.

For more information on adjusting output settings, see "Setting highlight and shadow target values" in Photoshop Help.

Color adjustment commands

You can choose from the following color adjustment commands:

Auto Color command Quickly corrects the color balance in an image. Although its name implies an automatic adjustment, you can fine-tune how the Auto Color command behaves.

Levels command Adjusts color balance by setting the pixel distribution for individual color channels.

Curves command Provides up to 14 controls points for highlight, midtone, and shadow adjustments for individual channels.

Photo Filter command Makes color adjustments by simulating the effects of photographing with a Kodak Wratten or Fuji filter in front of a camera lens.

Color Balance command Changes the overall mixture of colors in an image.

Hue/Saturation command Adjusts the hue, saturation, and lightness values of the entire image or of individual color components.

Match Color command Matches the color from one photo to another photo, from one layer to another layer, and from a selection in an image to another selection in the same image or a different image. This command also adjusts the luminance and color range and neutralizes color casts in an image.

Replace Color command Replaces specified colors in an image with new color values.

Selective Color command Adjusts the amount of process colors in individual color components.

Channel Mixer command Modifies a color channel and makes color adjustments not easily done with other color adjustment tools.

For complete information about tonal and color adjustment commands, see Photoshop Help.

Tonal adjustment methods

There are several different ways to set an image's tonal range:

- Drag sliders along the histogram in the Levels dialog box.

- Adjust the shape of the graph in the Curves dialog box. This method lets you adjust any point along a 0–255 tonal scale and provides the greatest control over an image's tonal quality.

- Assign target values to the highlight and shadow pixels using either the Levels or Curves dialog box. This can help preserve important highlight and shadow details in images being sent to a printing press or laser printer. You might also need to fine-tune the target values after sharpening.

- Adjust the tonality in the shadow and highlight areas using the Shadow/Highlight command. This adjustment is especially useful for correcting photos in which strong backlighting silhouettes the subject or proximity to the camera flash overlightens the subject slightly.

Viewing histograms and pixel values

About histograms

A *histogram* illustrates how pixels in an image are distributed by graphing the number of pixels at each color intensity level. The histogram shows whether the image contains enough detail in the shadows (shown in the left part of the histogram), midtones (shown in the middle), and highlights (shown in the right part) to make a good correction.

The histogram also gives a quick picture of the tonal range of the image, or the image *key type*. A low-key image has detail concentrated in the shadows; a high-key image has detail concentrated in the highlights; and an average-key image has detail concentrated in the midtones. An image with full tonal range has a number of pixels in all areas. Identifying the tonal range helps determine appropriate tonal corrections.

How to read a histogram
A. *Overexposed photo* **B.** *Properly exposed photo with full tonality*
C. *Underexposed photo*

The Histogram palette offers many options for viewing tonal and color information about an image. By default, the histogram displays the tonal range of the entire image. To display histogram data for a portion of the image, first select that portion.

To open the Histogram palette

❖ Choose Window > Histogram or click the Histogram tab to open the Histogram palette. By default, the Histogram palette opens in Compact View with no controls or statistics, but you can adjust the view.

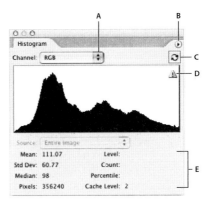

Histogram palette
A. *Channel menu* **B.** *Palette menu* **C.** *Uncached Refresh button*
D. *Cached Data Warning icon* **E.** *Statistics*

To adjust the view of the Histogram palette

❖ Choose a view from the Histogram palette menu ⊙.

Expanded View Displays the histogram with statistics and with controls for choosing the channel represented by the histogram, viewing options in the Histogram palette, refreshing the histogram to display uncached data, and choosing a specific layer in a multilayered document.

Compact View Displays a histogram with no controls or statistics. The histogram represents the entire image.

All Channels View Displays individual histograms of the channels in addition to all the options of the Expanded View. The individual histograms do not include alpha channels, spot channels, or masks.

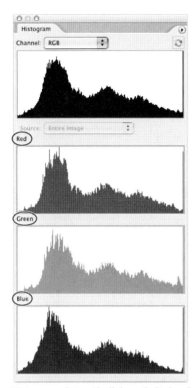

Histogram palette with all channels displayed and statistics hidden

To view a specific channel in the histogram

If you chose the Expanded View or All Channels View of the Histogram palette, you can choose a setting from the Channel menu. Photoshop remembers the channel setting if you switch from either Expanded View or All Channels View back to Compact View.

• Choose an individual channel to display a histogram of the document's individual channels, including color channels, alpha channels, and spot channels.

• Depending on the image's color mode, choose RGB, CMYK, or Composite to view a composite histogram of all the channels. This is the default view when you first choose Expanded View or All Channels View.

• If the image is RGB or CMYK, choose Luminosity to display a histogram representing the luminance or intensity values of the composite channel.

• If the image is RGB or CMYK, choose Colors to display a composite histogram of the individual color channels in color.

In the All Channels View, choosing from the Channels menu affects only the topmost histogram in the palette.

To view channel histograms in color

❖ From the Histogram palette, do one of the following:

• In the All Channels View, choose Show Channels In Color from the palette menu.

• In Expanded View or All Channels View, choose an individual channel from the Channel menu and choose Show Channels In Color from the palette menu. If you switch to Compact View, the channel continues to be shown in color.

• In Expanded View or All Channels View, choose Colors from the Channel menu to show a composite histogram of the channels in color. If you switch to Compact View the composite histogram continues to be shown in color.

To view histogram statistics

By default, the Histogram palette displays statistics in the Expanded View and All Channels View.

1 Choose Show Statistics in the Histogram palette menu.

2 Do one of the following:

- To view information about a specific pixel value, place the pointer in the histogram.

- To view information about a range of values, drag in the histogram to highlight the range.

The palette displays the following statistical information below the histogram:

Mean Represents the average intensity value.

Standard deviation (Std Dev) Represents how widely intensity values vary.

Median Shows the middle value in the range of intensity values.

Pixels Represents the total number of pixels used to calculate the histogram.

Level Displays the intensity level of the area underneath the pointer.

Count Shows the total number of pixels corresponding to the intensity level underneath the pointer.

Percentile Displays the cumulative number of pixels at or below the level underneath the pointer. This value is expressed as a percentage of all the pixels in the image, from 0% at the far left to 100% at the far right.

Cache Level Shows the current image cache used to create the histogram. When the cache level is higher than 1, the histogram is displayed faster because it is derived from a representative sampling of pixels in the image (based on the magnification). The original image is cache level 1. At each level above level 1, four adjacent pixels are averaged to arrive at a single pixel value. So, each level is half the dimensions (has 1/4 the number of pixels) of the one below. When Photoshop needs to do a quick approximation, it can use one of the upper levels. Click the Uncached Refresh button to redraw the histogram using the actual image pixels.

To view the histogram for a multilayered document

1 Choose Expanded View from the Histogram palette menu.

2 Choose a setting from the Source menu. (The Source menu is not available for single-layered documents.)

Entire Image Displays a histogram of the entire image, including all layers.

Selected Layer Displays a histogram of the layer that's selected in the Layers palette.

Adjustment Composite Displays a histogram of an adjustment layer selected in the Layers palette, including all the layers below the adjustment layer.

To preview histogram adjustments

You can preview the effect to the histogram of any color and tonal adjustments.

❖ Select the Preview option in the dialog boxes of any color or tonal adjustment command.

The Histogram palette displays a preview of how the adjustment affects the histogram.

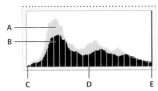

Preview of histogram adjustment in the Histogram palette
A. *Original histogram* **B.** *Adjusted histogram* **C.** *Shadows*
D. *Midtones* **E.** *Highlights*

To refresh the histogram display

When a histogram is read from a cache instead of the document's current state, the Cached Data Warning icon ⚠ appears in the Histogram palette. Histograms based on the image cache are displayed faster and are based on a representative sampling of pixels in the image. You can set the *cache level* (from 2 to 8) in the Memory And Image Cache preference.

❖ To refresh the histogram so that it displays all of the pixels of the original image in its current state, do one of the following:

- Double-click anywhere in the histogram.

- Click the Cached Data Warning icon ⚠.

- Click the Uncached Refresh button ⟳.

- Choose Uncached Refresh from the Histogram palette menu.

For information about cache level, see `To view histogram statistics' on page 218.

Viewing the color values of pixels

You can use the Info palette and the Color palette to see the color value of pixels as you make color corrections. This feedback is useful while you make color

adjustments. For instance, referring to the color values can help when neutralizing a color cast or can alert you that a color is saturated.

When you work with a color adjustment dialog box, the Info palette displays two sets of color values for the pixels under the pointer. The value in the left column is the original color value. The value in the right column is the color value after the adjustment is made.

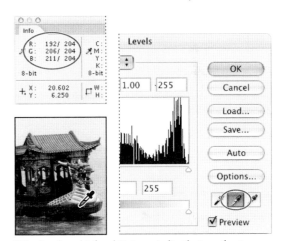

Using Levels and Info palette to neutralize the tone of an image

You can view the color of a single location using the Eyedropper tool 🖋, or you can use up to four Color Samplers ✛ to display color information for one or more locations in the image. These samplers are saved in the image, so you can refer to them repeatedly as you work, even if you close and reopen the image.

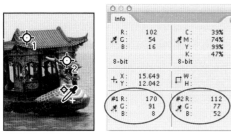

Color samplers and Info palette

To view color values in an image

1 Choose Window > Info to open the Info palette.

2 Select the Eyedropper tool ![eyedropper] or Color Sampler tool ![color sampler], and if necessary, choose a sample size in the options bar:

Point Sample Reads the value of a single pixel.

3 By 3 Average Reads the average value of a 3-by-3 pixel area.

5 By 5 Average Reads the average value of a 5-by-5 pixel area.

3 If you selected the Color Sampler tool ![color sampler], place up to four color samplers on the image. Click where you want to place a sampler.

4 Open an adjustment dialog box (under Image > Adjustments).

5 Make your adjustments in the dialog box and, before applying them, view the before and after color values in the Info palette:

- To view color values using the Eyedropper tool ![eyedropper], move the pointer over the area of the image you want to examine. Opening an adjustment dialog box activates the Eyedropper tool outside the dialog box. You still have access to the scroll controls and

to the Hand and Zoom ![zoom] tools using keyboard shortcuts.

- To view the color values under the color samplers, look at the lower half of the Info palette. To place additional color samplers in the image while the adjustment dialog box is open, Shift-click in the image.

💡 *The Color palette also shows the color value of pixels under the eyedropper.*

To move or delete a color sampler

1 Select the Color Sampler tool ![color sampler] .

2 Do one of the following:

- To move a color sampler, drag the sampler to the new location.

- To delete a color sampler, drag the sampler out of the document window. Alternatively, hold down Alt (Windows) or Option (Mac OS) until the pointer becomes a scissors and click the sampler.

- To delete all color samplers, click Clear in the options bar.

- To delete a color sampler while an adjustment dialog box is open, hold down Alt+Shift (Windows) or Option+Shift (Mac OS), and click the sampler.

To hide or show color samplers in an image

❖ Choose View > Extras. A check mark indicates that color samplers are visible.

To change the display of color sampler information in the Info palette

- To display or hide color sampler information in the Info palette, choose Color Samplers from the palette menu. A check mark indicates that the color sampler information is visible.

- To change the color space in which a color sampler displays values, move the pointer onto the color sampler icon ✖ in the Info palette, hold down the mouse button, and choose another color space from the menu.

Chapter 11: Selecting

Making selections

Selecting

Making a *selection* is isolating one or more parts of your image. By selecting specific areas, you can edit and apply effects and filters to portions of your image while leaving the unselected areas untouched.

There are separate sets of tools to make selections of bitmap and vector data. For example, to select bitmap pixels, you can use the marquee tools or the lasso tools. You can use commands in the Select menu to select all pixels, to deselect, or to reselect.

To select vector data, you can use the pen or shape tools, which produce precise outlines called *paths*. For 32-bits-per-channel images, only the pen tools are available to select vector data. You can convert paths to selections or convert selections to paths.

Selections can be copied, moved, and pasted, or saved and stored in an *alpha channel*. Alpha channels store selections as grayscale images. You can add alpha channels to create and store *masks*. A mask is a selection that protects portions of an image from any editing or manipulations you apply.

Note: To select a specified color or color subset within an existing selection or an entire image, you can use the Color Range command.

To select all pixels on a layer within the canvas boundaries

1 Select the layer in the Layers palette.

2 Choose Select > All.

To deselect selections

❖ Do one of the following:

• Choose Select > Deselect.

• If you are using the Rectangle Marquee tool, the Rounded Rectangle Marquee tool (ImageReady), the Elliptical Marquee tool, or the Lasso tool, click anywhere in the image outside the selected area.

To reselect the most recent selection

❖ Choose Select > Reselect.

To use the marquee tools

The marquee tools let you select rectangles, ellipses, rounded rectangles (ImageReady), and 1-pixel rows and columns. By default, a selection border is dragged from its corner.

1 Select a marquee tool:

Rectangular Marquee ⬚ Makes a rectangular selection.

Rounded Rectangle Marquee (ImageReady) ⬚ Selects a rounded rectangle, such as a web page button.

Elliptical Marquee ◯ Makes an elliptical selection.

Single Row ⋯ **or Single Column** ⦙ **Marquee** Defines the border as a 1-pixel-wide row or column.

2 Specify one of the selection options in the options bar.

Selection options
A. New B. Add To C. Subtract From D. Intersect With

3 Specify a feathering setting in the options bar. Turn anti-aliasing on or off for the Rounded Rectangle Marquee tool or the Elliptical Marquee tool.

4 For the Rectangle Marquee tool, the Rounded Rectangle Marquee tool, or the Elliptical Marquee tool, choose a style in the options bar:

Normal Determines marquee proportions by dragging.

Fixed Aspect Ratio Sets a height-to-width ratio. Enter values (decimal values are valid in Photoshop) for the aspect ratio. For example, to draw a marquee twice as wide as it is high, enter 2 for the width and 1 for the height.

Fixed Size Specifies set values for the marquee's height and width. Enter pixel values in whole numbers. Keep in mind that the number of pixels needed to create a 1-inch selection depends on the resolution of the image.

5 For aligning your selection to guides, a grid, slices, or document bounds, do one of the following to snap your selection:

• (Photoshop) Choose View > Snap, or choose View > Snap To and choose a command from the submenu. The marquee selection can snap to a document boundary and more than one Photoshop Extra. This is controlled in the Snap To submenu.

• (ImageReady) Choose View > Snap To > Guides.

6 Do one of the following to make a selection:

• With the Rectangle Marquee tool, the Rounded Rectangle Marquee tool, or the Elliptical Marquee tool, drag over the area you want to select. Hold down Shift as you drag to constrain the marquee to a square or circle (release the mouse button before Shift to keep the shape constrained). To drag a marquee from its center, hold down Alt (Windows) or Option (Mac OS) after you begin dragging.

Dragging a marquee from the corner of an image (left), and from the center of an image (right)

• With the Single Row or Single Column Marquee tool, click near the area you want to select, and then drag the marquee to the exact location. If no marquee is visible, increase the magnification of your image view.

 To reposition a rectangle, rounded rectangle, or elliptical marquee, first drag to create the border, keeping the mouse button depressed. Then hold down the spacebar and continue to drag. Release the spacebar, but keep the mouse button depressed, if you need to continue adjusting the selection border.

To use the Lasso tool

The Lasso tool is useful for drawing freeform segments of a selection border.

1 Select the Lasso tool ⌇ , and select options. See `To set options for the Lasso, Polygonal Lasso, and Magnetic Lasso tools' on page 226.

2 Drag to draw a freehand selection border.

3 To draw a straight-edged selection border, hold down Alt (Windows) or Option (Mac OS), and click where segments should begin and end. You can switch between drawing freehand and straight-edged segments.

4 To erase recently drawn segments, hold down the Delete key until you've erased the fastening points for the desired segment.

5 To close the selection border, release the mouse without holding down Alt (Windows) or Option (Mac OS).

To use the Polygonal Lasso tool

The Polygonal Lasso tool is useful for drawing straight-edged segments of a selection border.

1 Select the Polygonal Lasso tool ⋈ , and select options. See `To set options for the Lasso, Polygonal Lasso, and Magnetic Lasso tools' on page 226.

2 Click in the image to set the starting point.

3 Do one or more of the following:

• To draw a straight segment, position the pointer where you want the first straight segment to end, and click. Continue clicking to set endpoints for subsequent segments.

• To draw straight lines in 45˚ segments, hold down Shift as you move to click the next segment.

• To draw a freehand segment, hold down Alt (Windows) or Option (Mac OS), and drag. When you finish, release Alt or Option and the mouse button.

• To erase recently drawn straight segments, press the Delete key.

4 Close the selection border:

• Position the Polygonal Lasso tool pointer over the starting point (a closed circle appears next to the pointer), and click.

• If the pointer is not over the starting point, double-click the Polygonal Lasso tool pointer, or Ctrl-click (Windows) or Command-click (Mac OS).

To use the Magnetic Lasso tool

When you use the Magnetic Lasso tool ⧈ , the border snaps to the edges of defined areas in the image. The Magnetic Lasso tool is not available for 32-bits-per-channel images.

The Magnetic Lasso tool is especially useful for quickly selecting objects with complex edges set against high-contrast backgrounds.

1 Select the Magnetic Lasso tool and, if necessary, set options in the options bar.

2 Click in the image to set the first fastening point. Fastening points anchor the selection border in place.

3 To draw a freehand segment, either release or keep the mouse button depressed, and then move the pointer along the edge you want to trace.

The most recent segment of the selection border remains active. As you move the pointer, the active segment snaps to the strongest edge in the image, based on the detection width set in the options bar. Periodically, the Magnetic Lasso tool adds fastening points to the selection border to anchor previous segments.

4 If the border doesn't snap to the desired edge, click once to add a fastening point manually. Continue to trace the edge, and add fastening points as needed.

Fastening points anchor selection border to edges

5 To switch temporarily to the other lasso tools, do one of the following:

• To activate the Lasso tool, hold down Alt (Windows) or Option (Mac OS), and drag with the mouse button depressed.

• To activate the Polygonal Lasso tool, hold down Alt (Windows) or Option (Mac OS), and click.

6 To erase recently drawn segments and fastening points, press the Delete key until you've erased the fastening points for the desired segment.

7 Close the selection border:

• To close the border with a freehand Magnetic segment, double-click, or press Enter or Return.

• To close the border with a straight segment, hold down Alt (Windows) or Option (Mac OS), and double-click.

• To close the border, drag back over the starting point and click.

To set options for the Lasso, Polygonal Lasso, and Magnetic Lasso tools

The Lasso tool options let you customize how the different lasso tools detect and select edges.

1 If needed, select the tool.

2 Specify one of the selection options in the options bar.

A B C D

Selection options
A. New B. Add To C. Subtract From D. Intersect With

3 Specify feather and anti-aliasing options.

4 (Photoshop) For the Magnetic Lasso tool, set any of these options:

Width To specify a detection width, enter a pixel value for Width. The Magnetic Lasso tool detects edges only within the specified distance from the pointer.

To change the lasso pointer so that it indicates the lasso width, press the Caps Lock key. Change the pointer while the tool is selected but not in use.

Edge Contrast To specify the lasso's sensitivity to edges in the image, enter a value between 1% and

100% for Edge Contrast. A higher value detects only edges that contrast sharply with their surroundings; a lower value detects lower-contrast edges.

Frequency To specify the rate at which the lasso sets fastening points, enter a value between 0 and 100 for Frequency. A higher value anchors the selection border in place more quickly.

On an image with well-defined edges, try a higher width and higher edge contrast, and trace the border roughly. On an image with softer edges, try a lower width and lower edge contrast, and trace the border more precisely.

Stylus Pressure If you are working with a stylus tablet, select or deselect the Stylus Pressure option. When the option is selected, an increase in stylus pressure decreases the edge width.

While creating a selection, press the right bracket (]) to increase the Magnetic Lasso edge width by 1 pixel; press the left bracket ([) to decrease the width by 1 pixel.

To use the Magic Wand tool

The Magic Wand tool lets you select a consistently colored area (for example, a red flower) without having to trace its outline. You specify the color range, or *tolerance*, for the Magic Wand tool's selection.

You cannot use the Magic Wand tool on an image in Bitmap mode or on 32-bits-per-channel images.

1 Select the Magic Wand tool ✹ .

2 Specify one of the selection options in the options bar. The Magic Wand tool's pointer changes depending on which option is selected.

Selection options
A. New B. Add To C. Subtract From D. Intersect With

3 In the options bar, specify any of the following:

Tolerance Determines the similarity or difference of the pixels selected. Enter a value in pixels, ranging from 0 to 255. A low value selects the few colors very similar to the pixel you click. A higher value selects a broader range of colors.

Anti-aliased Defines a smooth edge.

Contiguous Selects only adjacent areas using the same colors. Otherwise, all pixels in the entire image using the same colors are selected.

Sample All Layers Selects colors using data from all the visible layers. Otherwise, the Magic Wand tool selects colors from the active layer only.

4 In the image, click the color you want to select. If Contiguous is selected, all adjacent pixels within the tolerance range are selected. Otherwise, all pixels in the tolerance range are selected.

Selecting a specific color or color subset

The Color Range command selects a specified color or color subset within an existing selection or an entire image. If you want to replace a selection, be sure to deselect everything before applying this command. The Color Range command is not available for 32-bits-per-channel images.

To refine an existing selection, use the Color Range command repeatedly to select a subset of colors. For example, to select the green areas in a cyan selection, select Cyans in the Color Range dialog box, and click OK. Then reopen the Color Range dialog box, and select Greens. (The results are subtle because the technique selects parts of colors within a color mix.)

To select a color range using sampled colors

1 Choose Select > Color Range.

2 For Select, choose the Sampled Colors tool 🖊 .

3 Select one of the display options:

Selection Previews only the selection as you build it.

Image Previews the entire image. For example, you might want to sample from a part of the image that isn't on-screen.

💡 *To toggle between the Image and Selection previews in the Color Range dialog box, press Ctrl (Windows) or Command (Mac OS).*

4 Position the pointer over the image or preview area, and click to sample the colors you want included.

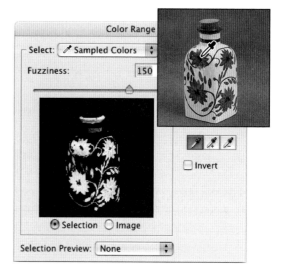

Sampling color

5 Adjust the range of colors using the Fuzziness slider or by entering a value. To decrease the range of colors selected, decrease the value. The Fuzziness option partially selects pixels by controlling the degree to which related colors are included in the selection (whereas the Tolerance option for the Magic Wand tool and the paint bucket increases the range of colors that are fully selected).

Increasing fuzziness expands selection

6 Adjust the selection:

- To add colors, select the plus eyedropper, and click in the preview area or image.

- To remove colors, select the minus eyedropper, and click in the preview area or image.

To activate the plus eyedropper temporarily, hold down Shift. Hold down Alt (Windows) or Option (Mac OS) to activate the minus eyedropper.

7 To preview the selection in the image window, choose an option for Selection Preview:

None Displays no preview in the image window.

Grayscale Displays the selection as it would appear in a grayscale channel.

Black Matte Displays the selection in color against a black background.

White Matte Displays the selection in color against a white background.

Quick Mask Displays the selection using the current quick mask settings.

8 To revert to the original selection, hold down Alt (Windows) or Option (Mac OS), and click Reset.

To select a color range using preset colors

1 Choose Select > Color Range.

2 For Select, choose a color or tonal range. The Out-Of-Gamut option works only on RGB and Lab images. (An out-of-gamut color is an RGB or Lab color that cannot be printed using process color printing.)

3 Click Selection to display the selected areas in the preview area.

4 To preview the selection in the image window, choose an option for Selection Preview:

None Displays no preview in the image window.

Grayscale Displays the selection as it would appear in a grayscale channel.

Black Matte Displays the selection in color against a black background.

White Matte Displays the selection in color against a white background.

Quick Mask Displays the selection using the current quick mask settings.

5 To revert to the original selection, hold down Alt (Windows) or Option (Mac OS), and click Reset.

Note: If you see the message "No pixels are more than 50% selected," the selection border will not be visible. You may have selected a color, such as red, when the image didn't contain the fully saturated color.

To save and load color range settings

❖ Use the Save and Load buttons in the Color Range dialog box to save and reuse the current settings.

Creating selections from slices (ImageReady)

If you create a slice in ImageReady, you can convert it to a selection.

1 Select a slice.

2 Choose Select > Create Selection From Slice.

Adjusting pixel selections

To move, hide, or invert a selection

You can move a selection border around an image, hide a selection border, and invert a selection so that the previously unselected part of the image is selected.

1 Using any selection tool, select New Selection ▣ from the options bar, and position the pointer inside the selection border. The pointer changes ▶⠿ to indicate that you can move the selection.

2 Drag the border to enclose a different area of the image. You can drag a selection border partly beyond the canvas boundaries. When you drag it back, the original border reappears intact. You can also drag the selection border to another image window.

Original selection border (left), and selection border moved (right)

💡 *You can apply geometric transformations to change the shape of a selection border.*

For more information, see 'Applying transformations' on page 265.

To control the movement of a selection

- To constrain the direction to multiples of 45°, begin dragging, and then hold down Shift as you continue to drag.

- To move the selection in 1-pixel increments, use an arrow key.

- To move the selection in 10-pixel increments, hold down Shift, and use an arrow key.

To hide or show selection edges

Do one of the following:

- Choose View > Extras. In Photoshop, this command shows or hides selection edges, grids, guides, target paths, slices, and annotations. In ImageReady, this command shows or hides selection edges, layer edges, grids, guides, smart guides, slices, auto slices, image maps, and text selections.

- Choose View > Show > Selection Edges. This toggles the view of the selection edges and affects the current selection only. The selection edges reappear when you make a different selection.

For more information, see 'To show or hide Extras' on page 39.

To select the unselected parts of an image

❖ Choose Select > Inverse.

💡 *You can use this option to select an object placed against a solid-colored background. Select the background using the Magic Wand tool and then inverse the selection.*

Adjusting selections manually

You can use the selection tools to add to or subtract from existing pixel selections.

Before manually adding to or subtracting from a selection, set the feather and anti-aliasing values in the options bar to the same settings used in the original selection.

To add to a selection or select an additional area

1 Make a selection.

2 Using any selection tool, do one of the following:

• Select the Add To Selection option 🖫 in the options bar, and drag.

• Hold down Shift, and drag to add another selection.

A plus sign appears next to the pointer when you're adding to a selection.

To subtract from a selection

1 Make a selection.

2 Using any selection tool, do one of the following:

• Select the Subtract From Selection option 🖫 in the options bar, and drag to intersect with other selections.

• Hold down Alt (Windows) or Option (Mac OS), and drag to subtract another selection.

A minus sign appears next to the pointer when you're subtracting from a selection.

To select only an area intersected by other selections

1 Make a selection.

2 Using any selection tool, do one of the following:

• Select the Intersect With Selection option 🖫 in the options bar, and drag.

• Hold down Alt+Shift (Windows) or Option+Shift (Mac OS) and drag over the portion of the original selection that you want to select.

An "x" appears next to the pointer when you're selecting an intersected area.

Intersected selections

Softening and refining the edges of selections

Methods for softening the edges of a selection

You can smooth the hard edges of a selection by anti-aliasing and by feathering.

Anti-aliasing Smooths the jagged edges of a selection by softening the color transition between edge pixels and background pixels. Because only the edge pixels change, no detail is lost. Anti-aliasing is useful when cutting, copying, and pasting selections to create composite images.

Anti-aliasing is available for the Lasso tool, the Polygonal Lasso tool, the Magnetic Lasso tool, the Rounded Rectangle Marquee tool (ImageReady), the Elliptical Marquee tool, and the Magic Wand tool. (Select a tool to display its options bar.) You must specify this option before using these tools. After a selection is made, you cannot add anti-aliasing.

Feathering Blurs edges by building a transition boundary between the selection and its surrounding pixels. This blurring can cause some loss of detail at the edge of the selection.

You can define feathering for the Marquee tool, the Lasso tool, the Polygonal Lasso tool, or the Magnetic Lasso tool as you use the tool, or you can add feathering to an existing selection. Feathering effects become apparent when you move, cut, copy, or fill the selection.

To use anti-aliasing

1 Select the Lasso tool, the Polygonal Lasso tool, the Magnetic Lasso tool, the Rounded Rectangle Marquee tool (ImageReady), the Elliptical Marquee tool, or the Magic Wand tool.

2 Select Anti-aliased in the options bar.

To define a feathered edge for a selection tool

1 Select any of the lasso or marquee tools.

2 Enter a Feather value in the options bar. This value defines the width of the feathered edge and can range from 0 to 250 pixels.

To define a feathered edge for an existing selection

1 Choose Select > Feather.

2 Enter a value for the Feather Radius, and click OK.

Note: A small selection made with a large feather radius may be so faint that its edges are invisible and thus not selectable. If you see the message "No pixels are more than 50% selected," either decrease the feather radius or increase the size of the selection. Or click OK to accept the mask at its current setting and create a selection in which you cannot see the edges.

A

B

Selection without feathering and with feathering.
A. *Selection with no feather, same selection filled with pattern*
B. *Selection with feather, same selection filled with pattern*

Removing fringe pixels from a selection

When you move or paste an anti-aliased selection, some of the pixels surrounding the selection border are included with the selection. This can result in a fringe or halo around the edges of the pasted selection. These Matting commands let you edit unwanted edge pixels:

- Defringe replaces the color of any fringe pixels with the colors of nearby pixels containing pure colors (those without background color). For example, if you select a yellow object on a blue background and then move the selection, some of the blue background is selected and moved with the object. Defringe replaces the blue pixels with yellow ones.

- Remove Black Matte and Remove White Matte are useful when a selection is anti-aliased against a white or black background and you want to paste it onto a different background. For example, anti-aliased black text on a white background has gray pixels at the edges, which are visible against a colored background.

You can also remove fringe areas by using the Advanced Blending sliders in the Layer Styles dialog box to remove, or make transparent, areas from the layer. In this case, you would make the black or white areas transparent. Alt-click (Windows) or Option-click (Mac OS) the sliders to separate them; separating the sliders allows you to remove fringe pixels and retain a smooth edge.

To decrease fringe on a selection

1 Choose Layer > Matting > Defringe.

2 Enter a value in the Width text box to specify the area in which to search for replacement pixels. In most cases, a distance of 1 or 2 pixels is enough.

3 Click OK.

To remove a matte from a selection

❖ Choose Layer > Matting > Remove Black Matte or Layer > Matting > Remove White Matte.

Moving, copying, and pasting selections and layers

Moving selections and layers within an image

The Move tool lets you drag a selection or layer to a new location in the image. With the Info palette open, you can track the exact distance of the move. You can also use the Move tool to align selections and layers and distribute layers within an image.

For more information, see`Selecting layers' on page 290.

To specify Move tool options

1 Select the Move tool ▸⊕ .

2 Select any of the following in the options bar:

Auto Select Layer Selects the topmost layer that has pixels under the Move tool, rather than the selected layer.

Auto Select Groups Selects the layer group that the selected layer is in.

Show Transform Controls Displays handles on the bounding box around the selected item.

To move a selection or layer

1 Select the Move tool ⊕.

To activate the Move tool when another tool is selected, hold down Ctrl (Windows) or Command (Mac OS). (This technique does not work with the Pen tool, the Freeform Pen tool, the Path Selection tool, the Direct Selection tool, the Hand tool, the Slice Select tool, or the anchor point tools.)

2 Do one of the following:

• Move the pointer inside the selection border, and drag the selection to a new position. If you have selected multiple areas, all move as you drag.

Original selection (left), and after the selection is moved with the Move tool (right)

• Select the layer you want to move. Then drag the layer to a new position.

To align selections and layers within an image

1 Do one of the following:

• To align the content of a layer to a selection, make a selection in the image. Then select a layer in the Layers palette.

• To align the contents of multiple layers to a selection border, make a selection in the image. In the Layers palette, select the layers you want to align. Shift-click to select contiguous layers, Ctrl-click (Windows) or Command-click to select noncontiguous layers.

• To align the contents of layers with the content of the active layer, select the layers you want to align to the active layer. Shift-click to select contiguous layers, Ctrl-click (Windows) or Command-click to select non-contiguous layers.

2 Select the Move tool ⊕.

3 Select one or more alignment options in the options bar.

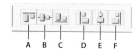

Alignment options
A. Top *B. Vertical Centers* *C. Bottom* *D. Left* *E. Horizontal Centers* *F. Right*

For more information, see 'To link and unlink layers' on page 292.

To distribute layers in an image

1 In the Layers palette, select three or more layers. Shift-click to select contiguous layers, Ctrl-click

(Windows) or Command-click to select noncontiguous layers.

2 Select the Move tool ▸⊕ .

3 Select one or more distribute options in the options bar.

Distribute options
A. Top **B.** *Vertical Centers* **C.** *Bottom* **D.** *Left* **E.** *Horizontal Centers* **F.** *Right*

For more information, see `To link and unlink layers' on page 292.

Copying selections or layers

You can use the Move tool to copy selections as you drag them within or between images, or you can copy and move selections using the Copy, Copy Merged, Cut, and Paste commands. Dragging with the Move tool saves memory because the clipboard is not used as it is with the Copy, Copy Merged, Cut, and Paste commands.

Copy Copies the selected area on the active layer.

Copy Merged Makes a merged copy of all the visible layers in the selected area.

Paste Pastes a cut or copied selection into another part of the image or into another image as a new layer. If you have a selection, the Paste command places the copied selection over the current selection. Without an active selection, Paste places the copied selection in the middle of the view area.

Paste Into (Photoshop) Pastes a cut or copied selection inside another selection in the same image or a different image. The source selection is pasted onto a new layer, and the destination selection border is converted into a layer mask.

Keep in mind that when a selection or layer is pasted between images with different resolutions, the pasted data retains its pixel dimensions. This can make the pasted portion appear out of proportion to the new image. Use the Image Size command to make the source and destination images the same resolution before copying and pasting, and then set the zoom of both images to the same magnification.

Depending on your color management settings and the color profile associated with the file (or imported data), you may be prompted to specify how to handle color information in the file (or imported data).

For more information, see `To determine a suggested resolution for an image' on page 133 and ` Masking layers' on page 321.

To copy a selection

1 Select the area you want to copy.

2 Choose Edit > Copy or Edit > Copy Merged.

To copy a selection while dragging

1 Select the Move tool ▸⊕ , or hold down Ctrl (Windows) or Command (Mac OS) to activate the Move tool.

2 Hold down Alt (Windows) or Option (Mac OS), and drag the selection you want to copy and move.

When copying between images, drag the selection from the active image window into the destination image window. If nothing is selected, the entire active layer is copied. As you drag the selection over another image window, a border highlights the window if you can drop the selection into it.

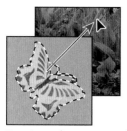

Dragging a selection into another image

To create multiple copies of a selection within an image

1 Select the Move tool ▸⊕ , or hold down Ctrl (Windows) or Command (Mac OS) to activate the Move tool.

2 Copy the selection:

• Hold down Alt (Windows) or Option (Mac OS), and drag the selection.

• To copy the selection and offset the duplicate by 1 pixel, hold down Alt or Option, and press an arrow key.

• To copy the selection and offset the duplicate by 10 pixels, press Alt+Shift (Windows) or Option+Shift (Mac OS), and press an arrow key.

As long as you hold down Alt or Option, each press of an arrow key creates a copy of the selection and offsets it by the specified distance from the last duplicate. In this case, the copy isn't made on a new layer.

To paste one selection into another

1 Cut or copy the part of the image you want to paste.

2 Select the part of the image into which you want to paste the selection. The source selection and the destination selection can be in the same image or in two different Photoshop images.

3 Choose Edit > Paste Into. The contents of the source selection appear masked by the destination selection.

In the Layers palette, the layer thumbnail for the source selection appears next to the layer mask thumbnail for the destination selection. The layer and layer mask are unlinked—that is, you can move each one independently.

Using the Paste Into command
A. *Window panes selected* **B.** *Copied image* **C.** *Paste Into command* **D.** *Layer thumbnails and layer mask in Layers palette* **E.** *Pasted image repositioned*

4 Select the Move tool ▶⊕ , or hold down the Ctrl (Windows) or Command (Mac OS) key to activate the Move tool. Then drag the source contents until the part you want appears through the mask.

5 To specify how much of the underlying image shows through, click the layer mask thumbnail in the Layers palette, select a painting tool, and edit the mask:

- To hide more of the image underlying the layer, paint the mask with black.

- To reveal more of the image underlying the layer, paint the mask with white.

- To partially reveal the image underlying the layer, paint the mask with gray.

6 If you are satisfied with your results, you can choose Layer > Merge Down to merge the new layer and layer mask with the underlying layer and make the changes permanent.

For more information, see`Masking layers' on page 321.

Using drag-and-drop to copy between applications

The drag-and-drop feature lets you copy and move images between Photoshop or ImageReady and other applications.

In Windows, the application must be OLE-compliant. To duplicate an entire image by dragging and dropping, use the Move tool to drag the image. To copy an OLE object that contains PSD data, use the OLE clipboard. (See your Windows documentation.)

Dragging vector artwork from Adobe Illustrator or from other applications that use the Illustrator clipboard rasterizes the artwork—the mathematically defined lines and curves of the vector art are converted into the pixels or bits of a bitmap image. To copy the vector artwork as a path in Photoshop, hold down Ctrl (Windows) or Command (Mac OS) as you drag from Adobe Illustrator. To copy type, you must first convert it to outlines.

Using the clipboard to copy between applications

You can often use the Cut or Copy command to copy selections between Photoshop or ImageReady and other applications. The cut or copied selection remains on the clipboard until you cut or copy another selection.

In some cases, the contents of the clipboard are converted to a raster image. Photoshop prompts you when vector artwork will be rasterized.

Note: The image is rasterized at the resolution of the file into which you paste it.

To save clipboard contents when you quit Photoshop

1 Do one of the following:

- (Windows) Choose Edit > Preferences > General.

- (Mac OS) Choose Photoshop > Preferences > General.

2 Select Export Clipboard to save any Photoshop contents on the clipboard when you quit Photoshop. If you leave this deselected, the contents are deleted when you quit the program.

To paste PostScript artwork from another application

1 In the supporting application, select your artwork, and choose Edit > Copy.

2 (Photoshop or ImageReady) Select the image into which you'll paste the selection.

3 Choose Edit > Paste.

4 (Photoshop) In the Paste dialog box, select from the following Paste As options:

Smart Object Places the artwork in a new layer as a smart object.

Pixels Rasterizes the artwork as it is pasted. Rasterizing converts mathematically defined vector artwork to pixels.

Paths Pastes the copy as a path in the Paths palette. When copying type from Illustrator, you must first convert it to outlines.

Shape Layer Creates a new shape layer that uses the path as a vector mask.

Note: When copying artwork from Adobe Illustrator, Illustrator's default clipboard preferences may prevent the Paste dialog box from appearing in Photoshop. Select AICB in the File Handling and Clipboard area of Illustrator's Preferences dialog box if you want the Paste options to appear when you paste the artwork in Photoshop.

5 If you chose Paste As Pixels in the previous step, you can choose Anti-aliased in the options bar to make a smooth transition between the edges of the selection and the surrounding pixels.

Note: You can use the Matting commands if you have already merged data and are trying to reextract the rasterized data.

For more information, see 'Smart Objects' on page 316 and 'Removing fringe pixels from a selection' on page 233.

Saving, loading, and deleting selections

To save a selection

1 Make a selection using any of the selection tools.

2 Choose Select > Save Selection.

3 Specify the following Destination options in the Save Selection dialog box:

Document Chooses the active file as the source.

Channel Chooses a new channel or the channel containing the selection you want to load.

Name Lets you enter a name for the selection.

4 Select an Operation option to specify how to combine the selections if the destination image already has a selection:

New Channel Saves the current selection in a new channel.

Add To Channel Adds the current selection to existing selections in the destination channel.

Subtract From Channel Subtracts the current selection from existing selections in the destination channel.

Intersect With Channel Saves a selection from an area intersected by the current selection and existing selections in the destination channel.

To remove (cut) an object from a photo

1 In the Layers palette, select the layer containing the object you want to remove.

2 Using a selection tool, select the object that you want to remove.

3 If you need to refine the selection, click the Quick Mask Mode button ▢ in the toolbox. Photoshop masks or covers the nonselected areas of the image in a translucent color. Select a brush and appropriate brush size in the options bar. Paint with black to add to the mask; paint with white to reveal more of the image.

4 To remove the selected object, choose Edit > Cut.

To delete a selection

❖ Choose Edit > Clear, or press Backspace (Windows) or Delete (Mac OS). To cut a selection to the clipboard, choose Edit > Cut.

Deleting a selection on a background or on a layer with the Lock Transparency option selected in the Layers palette replaces the original location with the background color. Deleting a selection on a layer without Lock Transparency selected replaces the original area with the layer transparency.

To load a saved selection into an image

1 Choose Select > Load Selection.

2 Specify the Source options in the Load Selection dialog box:

Document Chooses the active file as the source.

Channel Chooses the channel containing the selection you want to load.

Invert Makes the nonselected areas selected.

3 Select an Operation option to specify how to combine the selections if the image already has a selection:

New Selection Adds the loaded selection.

Add To Selection Adds the loaded selection to any existing selections in the image.

Subtract From Selection Subtracts the loaded selection from existing selections in the image.

Intersect With Selection Saves a selection from an area intersected by the loaded selection and existing selections in the image.

For more information, see 'To save a mask selection' on page 247.

To load a saved selection in ImageReady

❖ Choose Select > Load Selection, and then choose an option from the submenu.

For more information, see 'To save a mask selection' on page 247.

To load a selection from another image

1 Open the two images you want to use.

2 Make the destination image active, and choose Select > Load Selection.

3 Specify the following options in the Load Selection dialog box:

Document Chooses the source image.

Channel Chooses the channel containing the selection you want to load as a mask.

Invert Makes the nonselected areas selected.

Operation Specifies how to combine the selections if the destination image already has a selection.

💡 *You can drag a selection from one open Photoshop image into another.*

Extracting selections

The Extract filter

The Extract filter dialog box provides a sophisticated way to isolate a foreground object and erase its background on a layer. Even objects with wispy, intricate, or undefinable edges may be clipped from their backgrounds with a minimum of manual work. You use tools in the Extract dialog box to specify which part of the image to extract. You can resize the dialog box by dragging its lower right corner.

💡 *For simpler cases, try using the Background Eraser tool.*

When you extract the object, Photoshop erases its background to transparency. Pixels on the edge of the object lose their color components derived from the background, so they can blend with a new background without producing a color halo.

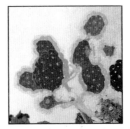

Selected area highlighted and filled, and extracted object

You can add back opacity to the background and create other effects by using the Edit > Fade command after an extraction.

For information about using the Background Eraser tool, see Photoshop Help.

For more information, see `To blend effects' on page 330.

To extract an object from its background

1 In the Layers palette, select the layer containing the object you want to extract. If you select a background layer, it becomes a normal layer after the extraction. If the layer contains a selection, the extraction erases the background only in the selected area.

To avoid losing the original image information, duplicate the layer or make a snapshot of the original image state.

2 Choose Filter > Extract, and then specify tool options:

Brush Size Enter a value, or drag the slider to specify the width of the Edge Highlighter tool ✎ . You also use the Brush Size option to specify the width of the Eraser, Cleanup, and Edge Touchup tools.

Highlight Choose a preset color option for the highlight that appears around objects when you use the Edge Highlighter tool, or choose Other to pick a custom color for the highlight.

Fill Choose a preset color option, or choose Other to pick a custom color for the area covered by the Fill tool.

Smart Highlighting Select this option if you are highlighting a well-defined edge. The option helps you keep the highlight on the edge, and applies a highlight

that is just wide enough to cover the edge, regardless of the current brush size.

Note: *If you use Smart Highlighting to mark an object edge that's near another edge, decrease the brush size if conflicting edges pull the highlight off the object edge. If the object edge has a uniform color on one side and high-contrast edges on the other side, keep the object edge within the brush area but center the brush on the uniform color.*

Specify Extraction options:

Textured Image Select this option if the foreground or background of your image contains a lot of texture.

Smooth Enter a value or drag the slider to increase or decrease the smoothness of the outline. It's usually best to begin with zero or a small value to avoid unwanted blurring of details. If there are sharp artifacts in the extraction result, you can increase the Smooth value to help remove them in the next extraction.

Channel Choose the alpha channel from the Channel menu to base the highlight on a selection saved in an alpha channel. The alpha channel should be based on a selection of the edge boundary. If you modify a highlight based on a channel, the channel name in the menu changes to Custom. Your image must have an alpha channel for the Channel option to be available.

Force Foreground Select this option if the object is especially intricate or lacks a clear interior.

3 Select the Edge Highlighter tool ✎ , and draw to define the edge of the object you want to extract. Drag so that the highlight slightly overlaps both the foreground object and its background. Use a large brush to cover wispy, intricate edges where the foreground blends into the background, as with hair or trees.

Use either the Zoom tool or the Hand tool to adjust the view as needed.

If you need to erase the highlight, select the Eraser tool ✐ , and drag over the highlight. To erase the entire highlight, press Alt+Backspace (Windows) or Option+Delete (Mac OS).

If the object has a well-defined interior, make sure that the highlight forms a complete enclosure. You do not need to highlight areas where the object touches the image boundaries. If the object lacks a clear interior, highlight the entire object.

Note: *You can't highlight the entire object if you've selected Textured Image or Force Foreground.*

4 Define the foreground area by doing one of the following:

- If the object has a well-defined interior, select the Fill tool ⬧ . Click inside the object to fill its interior. Clicking a filled area again with the Fill tool removes the fill.

- If you've selected Force Foreground, select the Eyedropper tool ⚲ , and click inside the object to sample the foreground color, or click in the Color text box and use a color picker to select the foreground color. This technique works best with objects that contain tones of a single color.

5 (Optional) Click Preview to preview the extracted object. Zoom in as needed, and set any of the following preview options:

Show Choose a menu option to switch between views of the original and the extracted image.

Display Choose a menu option to preview the extracted object against a colored matte background or a grayscale background. To display a transparent background, choose None.

Show Highlight Shows the object's highlight in the preview.

Show Fill Shows the object's fill in the preview.

6 (Optional) Improve the extraction by doing one of the following:

- Choose new Highlight and Fill options and draw again with the Edge Highlighter tool. Define the foreground area once more, and then preview the extracted object.

- Specify new Extraction settings (Smooth, Force Foreground, or Color) and then preview the extracted object.

When you are satisfied with the extraction, you can do the final touchups.

7 Touch up the extraction results by doing one of the following:

- To erase background traces in the extracted area, use the Cleanup tool ✐ . The tool subtracts opacity and has a cumulative effect. You can also use the Cleanup tool to fill gaps in the extracted object. Hold down Alt (Windows) or Option (Mac OS) while dragging to add back opacity.

- To edit the edge of the extracted object, use the Edge Touchup tool ✐ . The tool sharpens edges and has a cumulative effect. If there is no clear edge, the Edge Touchup tool adds opacity to the object or subtracts opacity from the background.

You can also clean up the image after an extraction by using the Background Eraser and History Brush tools in the toolbox.

8 Click OK to apply the final extraction. On the layer, all pixels outside the extracted object are erased to transparency.

Using masks

About masks and alpha channels

When you select part of an image, the area that is not selected is "masked" or protected from editing. So, when you create a mask, you isolate and protect areas of an image as you apply color changes, filters, or other effects to the rest of the image. You can also use masks for complex image editing such as gradually applying color or filter effects to an image.

Examples of masks
A. Opaque mask used to protect the background and edit the butterfly B. Opaque mask used to protect the butterfly and color the background C. Semitransparent mask used to color the background and part of the butterfly

In Photoshop, masks are stored in alpha channels. Masks and channels are grayscale images, so you can edit them like any other image. With masks and channels, areas painted black are protected, and areas painted white are editable.

Photoshop lets you create masks in the following ways:

Quick Mask mode Lets you edit any selection as a mask. The advantage of editing your selection as a mask is that you can use almost any Photoshop tool or filter to modify the mask. For example, if you create a rectangular selection with the Marquee tool, you can enter Quick Mask mode and use the Paintbrush tool to expand or decrease the selection, or you can use a filter to distort the edges of the selection. You can also use selection tools, because the quick mask is not a selection. You can also save and load selections you make using Quick Mask mode in alpha channels.

Alpha channels Let you save and load selections. You can edit alpha channels using any of the editing tools. When a channel is selected in the Channels palette, foreground and background colors appear as grayscale values. Storing selections as alpha channels creates more permanent masks than the temporary masks of Quick Mask mode. You can reuse stored selections or even load them into another image.

Selection saved as an alpha channel in Channels palette

Note: *In Photoshop and ImageReady, it's possible to create layer masks to isolate and protect areas of an image. Layer masks, and also vector masks in Photoshop, let you produce a mix of soft and hard masking edges on the same layer. By making changes to the layer mask or the vector masks, you can apply a variety of special effects. Because ImageReady doesn't let you work with channels, its layer masks aren't stored as alpha channels.*

For more information, see 'Masking layers' on page 321.

To create a temporary mask for use as a selection

To use Quick Mask mode, start with a selection and then add to or subtract from it to make the mask. You can also create the mask entirely in Quick Mask mode. Color differentiates the protected and unprotected areas. When you leave Quick Mask mode, the unprotected areas become a selection.

Note: *A temporary Quick Mask channel appears in the Channels palette while you work in Quick Mask mode. However, you do all mask editing in the image window.*

1 Using any selection tool, select the part of the image you want to change.

2 Click the Quick Mask mode button ◐ in the toolbox.

A color overlay (similar to a rubylith) covers and protects the area outside the selection. Selected areas are left unprotected by this mask. By default, Quick Mask mode colors the protected area using a red, 50% opaque overlay.

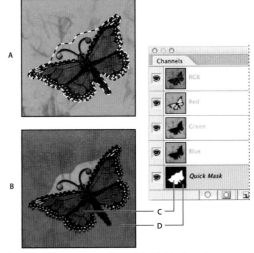

Selecting in Standard mode and Quick Mask mode
A. *Standard mode* **B.** *Quick Mask mode* **C.** *Selected pixels appear as white in channel thumbnail* **D.** *Rubylith overlay protects area outside selection, and unselected pixels appear as black in channel thumbnail*

3 To edit the mask, select a painting tool from the toolbox. The swatches in the toolbox automatically become black and white.

4 Paint with white to select more of an image (the color overlay is removed from areas painted with white). To deselect areas, paint over them with black (the color overlay covers areas painted with black). Painting with gray or another color creates a semitransparent area, useful for feathering or anti-aliased effects. (Semitransparent areas may not appear to be selected when you exit Quick Mask Mode, but they are.)

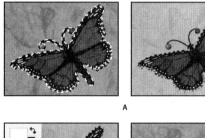

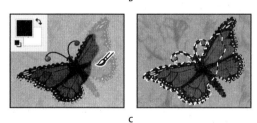

Painting in Quick Mask mode
*A. Original selection and Quick Mask mode with green chosen as mask color **B.** Painting with white in Quick Mask mode adds to the selection **C.** Painting with black in Quick Mask mode subtracts from the selection*

5 Click the Standard Mode button ▣ in the toolbox to turn off the quick mask and return to your original image. A selection border now surrounds the unprotected area of the quick mask.

If a feathered mask is converted to a selection, the boundary line runs halfway between the black pixels and the white pixels of the mask gradient. The selection boundary indicates the transition between pixels that are less than 50% selected and those that are more than 50% selected.

6 Apply the desired changes to the image. Changes affect only the selected area.

7 Choose Select > Deselect to deselect the selection, or save the selection by choosing Select > Save Selection.

You can convert this temporary mask to a permanent alpha channel by switching to standard mode and choosing Select > Save Selection

To change the Quick Mask options

1 Double-click the Quick Mask Mode button ▣ in the toolbox.

2 Choose from the following display options:

Masked Areas Sets masked areas to black (opaque) and selected areas to white (transparent). Painting with black increases the masked area; painting with white increases the selected area. When this option is selected, the Quick Mask button in the toolbox becomes a white circle on a gray background ▣ .

Selected Areas Sets masked areas to white (transparent) and selected areas to black (opaque). Painting with white increases the masked area; painting with black increases the selected area. When this option is selected, the Quick Mask button in the toolbox becomes a gray circle on a white background ⬤ .

💡 *To toggle between the Masked Areas and Selected Areas options for quick masks, Alt-click (Windows) or Option-click (Mac OS) the Quick Mask Mode button.*

3 To choose a new mask color, click the color box, and choose a new color.

4 To change the opacity, enter a value between 0% and 100%.

Both the color and opacity settings affect only the appearance of the mask and have no effect on how underlying areas are protected. Changing these settings may make the mask more easily visible against the colors in the image.

To create an alpha channel and add a mask

You can create a new alpha channel and then use painting tools, editing tools, and filters to create a mask from the alpha channel. You can also save an existing selection in a Photoshop or ImageReady image as an alpha channel that appears in the Channels palette in Photoshop.

1 Do one of the following:

- To create a new alpha channel using the current option settings, click the New Channel button 🔳 at the bottom of the Channels palette. Skip to the note in step 6.

- To create an alpha channel and specify option settings, either Alt-click (Windows) or Option-click (Mac OS) the New Channel button at the bottom of the Channels palette, or choose New Channel from the Channels palette menu.

2 If you are specifying option settings, begin by typing a name for the alpha channel in the Name text box of the New Channel dialog box.

3 To set a display option for the mask, select one of the following in the New Channel dialog box:

Masked Areas Sets masked areas to black (opaque) and selected areas to white (transparent). Painting with black increases the masked area; painting with white increases the selected area. When this option is selected, the Quick Mask button in the toolbox becomes a white circle on a gray background ⬤ .

Selected Areas Sets masked areas to white (transparent) and selected areas to black (opaque). Painting with white increases the masked area; painting with black increases the selected area. When this option is selected, the Quick Mask button in the toolbox becomes a gray circle on a white background ⬤ .

4 To specify the appearance of the mask, any of the following in the New Channel dialog box:

- To choose a new mask color, click the color box and then use the Adobe Color Picker to select a new color. Click OK to close the Adobe Color Picker after selecting a color.

- To change the opacity, enter a value between 0% and 100%.

Both the color and opacity settings affect only the appearance of the mask and have no effect on how underlying areas are protected. Changing these settings may make the mask more easily visible against the colors in the image.

5 Click OK to close the New Channel dialog box.

6 (Optional) Click the eye icon 👁 next to a color channel or the composite color channel, such as RGB, to display the image with a color overlay showing the mask.

Note: When the new channel appears at the bottom of the Channels palette, it is the only channel visible in the image window unless you click a color channel or the composite color channel.

7 Select a painting or editing tool and do one of the following to add or subtract from the mask created from the alpha channel:

- To remove areas in the new channel, paint with white.

- To add areas in the new channel, paint with black.

- Add or remove areas using opacities less than 100%, set the opacity in the options bar of the painting or editing tool and then paint with white or black. You can also paint with a color to achieve lower opacities.

🔍 *For information about using the painting or editing tools, or setting painting options such as opacity, see Photoshop Help.*

For more information, see 'About masks and alpha channels' on page 243.

Properties of alpha channels

An alpha channel has these properties:

- Each image can contain up to 56 channels, including all color and alpha channels.

- You can specify a name, color, mask option, and opacity for each channel. (The opacity affects the preview of the channel, not the image.)

- All new channels have the same dimensions and number of pixels as the original image.

- You can edit the mask in an alpha channel using painting tools, editing tools, and filters.

Original mask (left), and after a filter was applied (right)

- You can convert alpha channels to spot color channels.

To save a mask selection

You can save any selection as a mask in a new or existing alpha channel.

1 Select the area or areas of the image that you want to isolate.

2 Click the Save Selection button 🔲 at the bottom of the Channels palette. A new channel appears, named according to the sequence in which it was created.

To save a selection to a new or existing channel

1 In Photoshop or ImageReady, use a selection tool to select the area or areas of the image that you want to isolate.

2 Choose Select > Save Selection.

3 Specify the following in the Save Selection dialog box, and click OK:

Document Chooses a destination image for the selection. By default, the selection is placed in a channel in your active image. You can choose to save the selection to a channel in another open image with the same pixel dimensions or to a new image.

Channel Chooses a destination channel for the selection. By default, the selection is saved in a new channel. You can choose to save the selection to any existing channel in the selected image or to a layer mask if the image contains layers.

4 If you're saving the selection as a new channel, type a name for the channel in the Name text box. In ImageReady, you can change the default channel name if you want to.

5 If you're saving the selection to an existing channel, select how to combine the selections:

Replace Channel Replaces the current selection in the channel.

Add to Channel Adds the selection to the current channel contents.

Subtract From Channel Deletes the selection from the channel contents.

Intersect With Channel Keeps the areas of the new selection that intersect with the channel contents.

In Photoshop, you can select the channel in the Channels palette to see the saved selection displayed in grayscale. A selection saved in ImageReady will appear in a new or existing channel in the Photoshop Channels palette.

To change an alpha channel's options

1 In the Channel palette, do one of the following:

- Select the channel, click the triangle in the upper right corner of the Channels palette, and choose Channel Options from the palette menu.

- Double-click the channel thumbnail in the Channels palette.

2 If you want to rename the channel, type the new name in the Name text box of the Channel Options dialog box.

3 To set a display option for the mask, select one of the following in the Channel Options dialog box:

Masked Areas Sets masked areas to black (opaque) and selected areas to white (transparent). Painting with black increases the masked area; painting with white increases the selected area. When this option is selected, the Quick Mask button in the toolbox becomes a white circle on a gray background .

Selected Areas Sets masked areas to white (transparent) and selected areas to black (opaque). Painting with white increases the masked area; painting with black increases the selected area. When this option is selected, the Quick Mask button in the toolbox becomes a gray circle on a white background .

Spot Color Converts an alpha channel to a spot color channel.

4 To specify the appearance of the mask, do the following in the Channel Options dialog box:

- To choose a new mask color, click the color box, and choose a new color.

- To change the opacity, enter a value between 0% and 100%.

Both the color and opacity settings affect only the appearance of the mask and have no effect on how underlying areas are protected. Changing these settings may make the mask more easily visible against the colors in the image.

For information about channels and spot colors, see Photoshop Help.

To load a saved selection from an alpha channel

You can reuse a previously saved selection by loading it into an image. You can also load the selection into an image after you finish modifying an alpha channel.

❖ Do one of the following in the Channels palette:

• Select the alpha channel, click the Load Selection button ⬡ at the bottom of the palette, and then click the composite color channel near the top of the palette.

• Drag the channel containing the selection you want to load onto the Load Selection button.

• Ctrl-click (Windows) or Command-click (Mac OS) the channel containing the selection you want to load.

• To add the mask to an existing selection, press Ctrl+Shift (Windows) or Command+Shift (Mac OS), and click the channel.

• To subtract the mask from an existing selection, press Ctrl+Alt (Windows) or Command+Option (Mac OS), and click the channel.

• To load the intersection of the saved selection and an existing selection, press Ctrl+Alt+Shift (Windows) or Command+Option+Shift (Mac OS), and select the channel.

You can drag a selection from one open Photoshop image into another.

Chapter 12: Transforming and retouching

Changing the size of the work canvas

Changing the canvas size

The Canvas Size command lets you add or remove work space around an existing image. You can also use the command to crop an image by decreasing the canvas area. In ImageReady, added canvas appears in the same color or transparency as the background. In Photoshop, there are several options for the background of the added canvas. If your image has a transparent background, the added canvas is transparent.

To change the size of the canvas

1 Choose Image > Canvas Size.

2 Do one of the following:

- Enter the dimensions for the canvas in the Width and Height boxes. (Photoshop) Choose the units of measurement you want from the drop-down menus next to the Width and Height boxes.

- Select Relative, and enter the amount by which you want to increase or decrease the size of the canvas. (Enter a negative number to decrease the size of the canvas.)

3 For Anchor, click a square to indicate where to position the existing image on the new canvas.

4 (Photoshop) Choose an option from the Canvas Extension Color menu:

- Foreground to fill the new canvas with the current foreground color

- Background to fill the new canvas with the current background color

- White, Black, or Gray to fill the new canvas with that color

- Other to select a new canvas color using the Color Picker

Note: *The Canvas Extension Color menu isn't available if an image doesn't contain a background layer.*

5 Click OK.

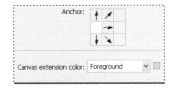

Original canvas, and canvas added to right side of image using the foreground color

To make a photo frame

You can make a photo frame by increasing the canvas size and filling it with a color.

You can also use one of the prerecorded actions to make a styled photo frame. It's best to do this on a copy of your photo.

1 Open the Actions palette. Choose Window > Actions.

2 Choose Photo Frames from the Actions palette menu.

3 Choose one of the photo frame actions from the list.

4 Click the Play Action button.

The action plays, creating the frame around your photo.

Rotating and flipping entire images

Rotating and flipping entire images

The Rotate Canvas commands let you rotate or flip an entire image. The commands do not work on individual layers or parts of layers, paths, or selection borders.

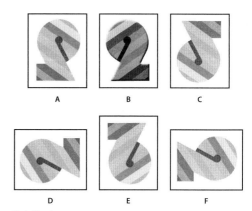

Rotating images
A. Flip Horizontal B. Original image C. Flip Vertical D. Rotate 90˚ CCW E. Rotate 180˚ F. Rotate 90˚ CW

To rotate or flip an entire image

❖ Choose Image > Rotate Canvas, and choose one of the following commands from the submenu:

180˚ Rotates the image by a half-turn.

90˚ CW Rotates the image clockwise by a quarter-turn.

90˚ CCW Rotates the image counterclockwise by a quarter-turn.

Arbitrary Rotates the image by the angle you specify. If you choose this option, enter an angle between -359.99 and 359.99 in the angle text box.
(In Photoshop, you can select CW or CCW to rotate clockwise or counterclockwise.) Then click OK.

Flip Canvas Horizontal (Photoshop) or Flip Horizontal (ImageReady) Flips the image horizontally, along the vertical axis.

Flip Canvas Vertical (Photoshop) or Flip Vertical (ImageReady) Flips the image vertically, along the horizontal axis.

Cropping images

Cropping images

Cropping is the process of removing portions of an image to create focus or strengthen the composition. You can crop an image using the Crop tool 🔲 and the Crop command. You can also trim pixels using the Crop And Straighten and the Trim commands.

Using the Crop tool

To crop an image using the Crop tool

1 Select the Crop tool 🔲 .

2 If necessary, use the options bar to set any Crop tool options.

3 Drag over the part of the image you want to keep to create a marquee. The marquee doesn't have to be precise—you can adjust it later.

4 If necessary, adjust the cropping marquee:

- To move the marquee to another position, place the pointer inside the bounding box and drag.

- To scale the marquee, drag a handle. To constrain the proportions, hold down Shift as you drag a corner handle.

- To rotate the marquee, position the pointer outside the bounding box (the pointer turns into a curved arrow), and drag. To move the center point around which the marquee rotates, drag the circle at the center of the bounding box.

Note: *In Photoshop, you can't rotate the marquee for an image in Bitmap mode.*

5 Do one of the following:

- To complete the crop, press Enter (Windows) or Return (Mac OS), click the Commit button ✔ in the options bar, or double-click inside the cropping marquee.

- To cancel the cropping operation, press Esc or click the Cancel button ⃠ in the options bar.

To set Crop tool options

❖ Choose from the following in the options bar to set the mode of the Crop tool:

- (Photoshop) To crop the image without resampling (default), make sure that the Resolution text box in the options bar is empty. You can click the Clear button to quickly clear all text boxes.

- (Photoshop) To resample the image during cropping, enter values for the height, width, and resolution in the options bar. The Crop tool won't resample the image unless the width and/or height, and resolution are provided. If you've entered height and width dimensions and want the values quickly exchanged, click the Swaps Height And Width icon ⇄ .

Note: *(Photoshop) You can click the triangle next to the Crop tool icon in the options bar to open the Tool Preset Picker and select a resampling preset. As with all Photoshop tools, you can create your own Crop tool preset. See also 'To create a tool preset' on page 25.*

- (ImageReady) To crop the image without resampling, make sure that Fixed Size is deselected in the options bar.

- (ImageReady) To resample the image during cropping, select Fixed Size, and enter a height and width in the options bar.

- To resample an image based on the dimensions and resolution of another image, open the other image, select the Crop tool, and click Front Image in the options bar. (In ImageReady, you must select the Fixed Size option to access the Front Image button.) Then make the image you want to crop active.

Resampling during cropping combines the function of the Image > Image Size command with that of the Crop tool.

- Specify whether you want to hide or delete the cropped area. Select Hide to preserve the cropped area in the image file. You can make the hidden area visible by moving the image with the Move tool. Select Delete to discard the cropped area.

Note: *In Photoshop, the Hide option is not available for images that contain only a background layer. If you want to crop a background by hiding, convert the background to a regular layer first. In ImageReady, cropping a background by hiding automatically converts the background to a regular layer.*

- Specify whether you want to use a cropping shield to shade the area of the image that will be deleted or hidden. When Shield is selected, you can specify a color and opacity for the cropping shield. When Shield is deselected, the area outside the cropping marquee is revealed.

For more information, see `Resampling' on page 129 and `About the background layer' on page 288.

To crop an image using the Crop command

In addition to the Crop tool, you can use the crop and trim commands to crop an image.

1 Use a selection tool to select the part of the image you want to keep.

2 Choose Image > Crop.

To crop an image using the Trim command

1 Choose Image > Trim.

2 In the Trim dialog box, select an option:

- Transparent Pixels to trim away transparency at the edges of the image, leaving the smallest image containing nontransparent pixels.

- Top Left Pixel Color to remove an area the color of the upper left pixel from the image.

- Bottom Right Pixel Color to remove an area the color of the lower right pixel from the image.

3 Select one or more areas of the image to trim away: Top, Bottom, Left, or Right.

Transforming perspective while cropping

The Crop tool in Photoshop has an additional option that allows you to transform the perspective in an image. This is very useful when working with images that contain *keystone distortion*. Keystone distortion occurs when an object is photographed from an angle rather than from a straight-on view. For example, if you take a picture of a tall building from ground level, the edges of the building appear closer to each other at the top than they do at the bottom.

Steps to transform perspective
A. *Draw initial cropping marquee* **B.** *Adjust cropping marquee to match the object's edges* **C.** *Extend the cropping bounds* **D.** *Final image*

To transform the perspective in an image

1 Select the Crop tool ⌗ and set the crop mode.

2 Drag the cropping marquee around an object that was rectangular in the original scene (although it doesn't appear rectangular in the image). You'll use the edges of this object to define the perspective in the

image. The marquee doesn't have to be precise—you'll adjust it later.

Important: *You must select an object that was rectangular in the original scene or Photoshop will not be able to transform the perspective in the image.*

3 Select Perspective in the options bar, and set the other options as desired.

4 Move the corner handles of the cropping marquee to match the object's edges. This defines the perspective in the image, so it is important to precisely match the object's edges.

5 Drag the side handles to extend the cropping bounds while preserving the perspective.

Note: *Do not move the center point of the cropping marquee. The center point needs to be in its original position in order to perform perspective correction.*

6 Do one of the following:

• Press Enter (Windows) or Return (Mac OS), click the Commit button ✔ in the options bar, or double-click inside the cropping marquee.

• To cancel the cropping operation, press Esc or click the Cancel button ⊘ in the options bar.

💡 *If Photoshop displays an error, it is probably due to improper placement of the corner handles or center point. Click Cancel to go back and adjust the cropping marquee; click Don't Crop to cancel the cropping operation. An error may also occur if you're working with a previously cropped image.*

To use the Crop And Straighten Photos command

The Crop and Straighten Photos command helps you make separate image files from multiple images in a single scan. For best results, you should keep 1/8 inch between the images in your scan, and the background (typically the scanner bed) should be a uniform color with little noise. The Crop and Straighten Photos command works best on images with clearly delineated outlines.

💡 *If the Crop And Straighten Photos command cannot process a complex image file, use the Crop tool.*

1 Open the scanned file that contains the images you want to separate.

2 Select the layer that contains the images. Alternatively, draw a selection border around one or more images to generate just those images into separate files.

3 Choose File > Automate > Crop And Straighten Photos. The scanned images are processed, and then each image opens in its own window.

💡 *If the Crop And Straighten Photos command incorrectly splits one of your images, make a selection border around the image and some background, and then hold down Alt (Windows) or Option (Mac OS) when you choose the command. The modifier key indicates only one image should be separated from the background.*

Correcting image distortion

The Lens Correction filter

The Lens Correction filter fixes common lens flaws such as barrel and pincushion distortion, vignetting, and chromatic aberration.

Barrel distortion is a lens defect that causes straight lines to bow out toward the edges of the image. *Pincushion distortion* is the opposite effect, where straight lines bend inward.

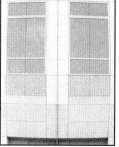

Examples of barrel distortion (left) and pincushion distortion (right)

Vignetting is a defect where the edges, especially the corners, of an image are darker than the center. *Chromatic aberration* appears as a color fringe along the edges of objects caused by the lens focusing on different colors of light in different planes.

Some lenses exhibit these defects depending on the focal length or the f-stop used. You can set the Lens Correction filter to use settings based on the camera, lens, and focal length used to make the image.

You can also use the filter to rotate an image or fix image perspective caused by vertical or horizontal camera tilt. The filter's image grid makes these adjustments easier and more accurate than using the Transform command.

To correct image perspective and lens flaws

1 Choose Filter > Distort > Lens Correction.

2 Set the grid and image zoom. As you work you may want to adjust the grid lines to help you judge the amount of correction to make. See `To adjust the Lens Correction preview and grid' on page 258.

3 (Optional) Choose a preset list of settings from the Settings menu. Lens Default uses settings that you previously saved for the camera, lens, focal length, and f-stop combination used to make the image. Previous Conversion uses the settings used in your last lens correction. Any group of custom settings you saved are listed at the bottom of the menu. See `Setting camera and lens defaults' on page 258.

4 Set any of the following options to correct your image.

Remove Distortion Corrects lens barrel or pincushion distortion. Move the slider to straighten horizontal and vertical lines that bend either away from or toward the center of the image. You can also use the Remove Distortion tool 🖳 to make this correction. Drag toward the center of the image to correct for barrel distortion and toward the edge of the image to correct for pincushion distortion. Adjust the Edge option to specify how you want to handle any resulting blank image edges.

Vignette Corrects images that have darkened edges caused by lens faults or improper lens shading.

Amount Sets the amount of lightening or darkening along the edges of an image.

Midpoint Specifies the width of area affected by the Amount slider. Specify a lower number to affect more of the image. Specify a higher number to restrict the effect to the edges of the image.

Chromatic Aberration Corrects color fringing. Zoom in on the image preview to get a closer view of the fringing as you make the correction. For more information see `Chromatic aberration' on page 157.

Fix Red/Cyan Fringe Compensates for red/cyan color fringing by adjusting the size of the red channel relative to the green channel.

Fix Blue/Yellow Fringe Compensates for blue/yellow color fringing by adjusting the size of the blue channel relative to the green channel.

Vertical Perspective Corrects image perspective caused by tilting the camera up or down. Makes vertical lines in an image parallel.

Horizontal Perspective Corrects image perspective, making horizontal lines parallel.

Angle Rotates the image to correct for camera tilt or to make adjustments after correcting perspective. You can also use the Rotate Straighten tool 🔺 to make this correction. Drag along a line in the image that you want to make vertical or horizontal.

Edge Specifies how to handle the blank areas that result from pincushion, rotation, or perspective corrections. You can fill blank areas with transparency or a color, or you can extend the edge pixels of the image.

Scale Adjusts the image scale up or down. The image pixel dimensions aren't changed. The main use is to remove blank areas of the image caused by pincushion, rotation, or perspective corrections. Scaling up effectively results in cropping the image and interpolating up to the original pixel dimensions.

To adjust the Lens Correction preview and grid

- To change the image preview magnification, use the Zoom tool or the zoom controls in the lower left side of the preview image.

- To move the image in the preview window, select the hand tool and drag in the image preview.

- To use the grid, select Show Grid at the bottom of the dialog box. Use the Size control to adjust the grid spacing and the Color control to change the color of the grid. You can move the grid to line it up with your image using the Move Grid tool .

Setting camera and lens defaults

You can save the settings in the Lens Correction dialog box to reuse with other images made with the same camera, lens, and focal length. Photoshop saves settings for distortion, vignetting, and chromatic aberration. Perspective correction settings are not saved. You can save and reuse settings in two ways:

- Manually save and load settings. Set options in the dialog box, and then choose Save Settings from the Settings menu . To use the saved settings, choose them from the Settings menu. You can also load saved settings that don't appear in the menu using the Load Settings command in the Settings menu.

- Set a lens default. If your image has EXIF metadata for the camera, lens, focal length, and f-stop, you can save the current settings as a lens default. To save the settings, click the Set Lens Default button. When you correct an image that matches the camera, lens, focal length, and f-stop, the Lens Default option becomes available in the Settings menu.

Reducing image noise

Reducing image noise

Image noise appears as random extraneous pixels that aren't part of the image detail. Noise can be caused by photographing with a high ISO setting on a digital camera, underexposure, or shooting in a dark area with a long shutter speed. Low-end consumer cameras usually exhibit more image noise than high-end cameras. Scanned images may have image noise caused by the scanning sensor. Often, the film's grain pattern appears in the scanned image.

Image noise can appear in two forms: luminance (grayscale) noise, which makes an image look grainy or patchy, and color noise, which is usually visible as colored artifacts in the image.

Luminance noise may be more pronounced in one channel of the image, usually the blue channel. You can adjust the noise for each channel separately in Advanced mode. Before opening the filter, examine each channel in your image separately to see if noise is prevalent in one channel. You preserve more image detail by correcting one channel rather than making an overall correction to all channels.

To reduce image noise and JPEG artifacts

1 Choose Filter > Noise > Reduce Noise.

2 Zoom in on the preview image to get a better view of image noise.

3 Set options:

Strength Controls the amount of luminance noise reduction applied to all image channels.

Preserve Details Preserves edges and image details such as hair or texture objects. A value of 100 preserves the most image detail, but reduces luminance noise the least. Balance the Strength and Preserve Details controls to fine-tune noise reduction.

Reduce Color Noise Removes random color pixels. A higher value reduces more color noise.

Sharpen Details Sharpens the image. Removing noise reduces image sharpness. Use the sharpening control in the dialog box or use one of the other Photoshop sharpening filters later to restore sharpness.

Remove JPEG Artifacts Removes blocky image artifacts and halos caused by saving a image using a low JPEG quality setting.

4 If luminance noise is more prevalent in one or two color channels, click the Advanced button and then choose the color channel from the Channel menu. Use the Strength and Preserve Details controls to reduce noise in that channel.

Sharpening images

Sharpening images

Sharpening enhances the definition of edges in an image. Whether your images come from a digital camera or a scanner, most images can benefit from sharpening. The degree of sharpening needed varies depending on the quality of the digital camera or scanner. Keep in mind that sharpening cannot correct a severely blurred image.

Notes and tips about sharpening:

- Sharpen your image on a separate layer so that you can resharpen it later if you need to output it to a different medium.

- If you sharpen your image on a separate layer, set the layer's blending mode to Luminance to avoid color shifts along edges.

- Sharpening increases image contrast. If you find that highlights or shadows are clipped after you sharpen, use the layer blending controls (if you sharpen a separate layer) to prevent sharpening in highlights and shadows. See `To specify a tonal range for blending layers' on page 304.

- If you need to reduce image noise, do so before sharpening so that you don't intensify the noise.

- Sharpen your image multiple times in small amounts. Sharpen the first time to correct blur caused by capturing your image (scanning it or taking it with your digital camera). After you've color corrected and sized your image, sharpen it again (or a copy of it) to add the appropriate amount of sharpening for your output medium.

- If possible, judge your sharpening by outputting it to the final medium. The amount of sharpening needed varies among output media.

For greatest control use the Unsharp Mask (USM) filter or the Smart Sharpen filter to sharpen your images. Although Photoshop also has the Sharpen, Sharpen Edges, and Sharpen More filter options, these filters are automatic and do not provide controls and options.

You can sharpen your entire image or just a portion defined by a selection or mask. Because the Unsharp Mask and Smart Sharpen filters can be applied to only one layer at a time, you might need to merge layers or flatten your file to sharpen all image layers in a multi-layered file.

Note: Don't be misled by the name Unsharp Mask, which comes from a darkroom technique used in traditional film-based photography. The filter sharpens images rather than the opposite.

To use the Smart Sharpen filter

The Smart Sharpen filter has sharpening controls not available with the Unsharp Mask filter. You can set the sharpening algorithm or control the amount of sharpening that occurs in shadow and highlight areas.

1 Zoom the document window to 100% to get an accurate view of the sharpening.

2 Choose Filter > Sharpen > Smart Sharpen.

3 Set the controls in the Sharpen tabs:

Amount Sets the amount of sharpening. A higher value increases the contrast between edge pixels, giving the appearance of greater sharpness.

Radius Determines the number of pixels surrounding the edge pixels affected by the sharpening. The greater the radius value, the wider the edge effects and the more obvious the sharpening.

Remove Sets the sharpening algorithm used to sharpen the image. Gaussian Blur is the method used by the Unsharp Mask filter. Lens Blur detects the edges and detail in an image, and provides finer sharpening of detail and reduced sharpening halos. Motion Blur attempts to reduce the effects of blur due to camera or subject movement. Set the Angle control if you choose Motion Blur.

Angle Sets the direction of motion for the Motion Blur option of the Remove control.

More Accurate Processes the file longer for a more accurate removal of blurring.

4 Adjust sharpening of dark and light areas using in the Shadow and Highlight tabs. (Click the Advanced button to display the tabs). If the dark or light sharpening halos appear too strong you can reduce them with these controls:

Fade Amount Adjusts the amount of sharpening in the highlights or shadows.

Tonal Width Controls the range of tones in the shadows or highlights that are modified. Move the slider to the left or right to decrease or increase the Tonal Width value. Smaller values restrict the adjustments to only the darker regions for shadow correction and only the lighter regions for highlight correction.

Radius Controls the size of the area around each pixel that is used to determine whether a pixel is in the shadows or highlights. Moving the slider to the left specifies a smaller area, and moving it to the right specifies a larger area.

5 Click OK.

The Unsharp Mask filter

The Unsharp Mask sharpens an image by increasing contrast along the edges in an image. The Unsharp Mask does not detect edges in an image. Instead, it locates pixels that differ in value from surrounding pixels by the threshold you specify. It then increases the contrast of neighboring pixels by the amount you specify. So, for neighboring pixels the lighter pixels get lighter and the darker pixels get darker.

In addition, you specify the radius of the region to which each pixel is compared. The greater the radius, the larger the edge effects.

Original image, and Unsharp Mask applied

The degree of sharpening applied to an image is often a matter of personal choice. However, oversharpening an image produces a halo effect around the edges.

Oversharpening an image produces a halo effect around the edges.

The effects of the Unsharp Mask filter are more pronounced on-screen than in high-resolution output. If your final destination is print, experiment to determine what settings work best for your image.

To sharpen a photo using Unsharp Mask

1 (Optional) If your image is multilayered, select the layer containing the image you want to sharpen. You can apply Unsharp Mask to only one layer at a time, even if layers are linked or grouped. You can merge the layers before applying the Unsharp Mask filter.

2 Choose Filter > Sharpen > Unsharp Mask. Make sure the Preview option is selected.

💡 *Click the image in the preview window and hold down the mouse to see how the image looks without the sharpening. Drag in the preview window to see different parts of the image, and click + or – to zoom in or out.*

Although there is a preview window in the Unsharp Mask dialog box, it's best to move the dialog box so you can preview the effects of the filter in the document window.

3 Drag the Radius slider or enter a value to determine the number of pixels surrounding the edge pixels that affect the sharpening. The greater the radius value, the wider the edge effects. And the wider the edge effects, the more obvious the sharpening.

The Radius value varies according to the subject matter, the size of the final reproduction, and the output method. For high-resolution images, a Radius value between 1 and 2 is usually recommended. A lower value sharpens only the edge pixels, whereas a higher value sharpens a wider band of pixels. This effect is much less noticeable in print than on-screen, because a 2-pixel radius represents a smaller area in a high-resolution printed image.

4 Drag the Amount slider or enter a value to determine how much to increase the contrast of pixels. For high-resolution printed images, an amount between 150% and 200% is usually recommended.

5 Drag the Threshold slider or enter a value to determine how different the sharpened pixels must be from the surrounding area before they are considered edge pixels and sharpened by the filter. For instance, a threshold of 4 affects all pixels that have tonal values that differ by a value or 4 or more, on a scale of 0 to 255. So, if adjacent pixels have tonal values of 128 and 129, they are not affected. To avoid introducing noise or posterization (in images with flesh tones, for example), use an edge mask or try experimenting with Threshold values between 2 and 20. The default Threshold value (0) sharpens all pixels in the image

If applying Unsharp Mask makes already bright colors appear overly saturated, choose Edit > Fade Unsharp Mask and choose Luminosity from the Mode menu.

Selective sharpening

You can sharpen parts of your image by using a mask or a selection. This is useful when you want to prevent sharpening in certain parts of your image. For example,

you can use an edge mask with the Unsharp Mask filter on a portrait to sharpen the eyes, mouth, nose, and outline of the head, but not the texture of the skin.

Using an edge mask to apply the Unsharp Mask only to specific features in an image

To sharpen a selection

1 With the image layer selected in the Layers palette, draw a selection.

2 Choose Filter > Sharpen > Unsharp Mask. Adjust the options and click OK.

Only the selection is sharpened, leaving the rest of the image untouched.

To sharpen an image using an edge mask

1 Create a mask to apply sharpening selectively. There are many ways to create an edge mask. Use your favorite method, or try this one:

- Open the Channels palette and select the channel that displays the grayscale image with the greatest contrast in the document window. Often, this is the green or the red channel.

Selecting a channel with the greatest contrast

- Duplicate the selected channel.

- With the duplicate channel selected, choose Filter > Stylize > Find Edges.

- Choose Image > Adjustments > Invert to invert the image.

Find Edges filter applied and image inverted

- With the inverted image still selected, choose Filter > Other > Maximum. Set the radius to a low number and click OK to thicken the edges and randomize the pixels.

- Choose Filter > Noise > Median. Set the radius to a low number and click OK. This averages the neighboring pixels.

- Choose Image > Adjustment > Levels and set the black point high to get rid of random pixels. If

necessary, you can also paint with black to retouch the final edge mask.

Setting the black point high in Levels to eliminate random pixels in the edge mask

- Choose Filter > Blur > Gaussian Blur to feather the edges.

Important: The Maximum, the Median, and the Gaussian Blur filters soften the edge mask so that the sharpening effects blend better in the final image. Although all three filters are used in this procedure, you can experiment using only one or two.

2 In the Channels palette, Ctrl-click (Windows) or Command-click (Mac OS) the duplicate channel to make the edge mask a selection.

3 In the Layers palette, select the image layer. Make sure the selection is still visible on the image.

4 Choose Select > Inverse.

5 With the selection active on the image layer, choose Filter > Sharpen > Unsharp Mask. Set the desired options and click OK.

To view your results, select the RGB channel in the Channels palette and deselect the selection in the image.

You can create an action to conveniently apply all the steps in the procedure.

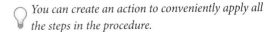

For more information, see 'About masks and alpha channels' on page 243.

Transforming objects

Specifying an item to transform

You can apply transformations to a selection, an entire layer, multiple layers, or a layer mask. In Photoshop, you can also apply transformations to a path, a vector shape, a vector mask, a selection border, or an alpha channel.

Important: *In Photoshop, you can apply transformations to 8-bit and 16-bit images. However, you must convert images to 8-bit RGB Color mode before you can edit them in ImageReady.*

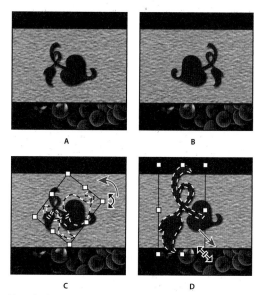

A

B

C

D

Transforming an image
*A. Original image **B.** Layer flipped **C.** Selection border rotated*
D. Part of object scaled

To calculate the color values of pixels that are added or deleted during transformations, Photoshop and ImageReady use the interpolation method selected in the General area of the Preferences dialog box. This setting directly affects the speed and quality of the transformation. Bicubic interpolation, the default, is slowest but yields the best results.

For more information, see 'Choosing an interpolation method' on page 130.

To select an item to transform

❖ Do one of the following:

• To transform an entire layer, make the layer active, and make sure nothing is selected.

Important: You cannot transform the background layer. To transform it, first convert it to a regular layer.

- To transform part of a layer, select the layer in the Layers palette, and then select part of the image on that layer.

- To transform multiple layers, link the layers together in the Layers palette.

- To transform a layer mask or a vector mask, unlink the mask and select the mask thumbnail in the Layers palette.

- (Photoshop) To transform a path or vector shape, use the Path Selection tool ▶ to select the entire path or the Direct Selection tool ▶ to select part of the path. If you select one or more points on a path, only those path segments connected to the points are transformed.

- (Photoshop) To transform a selection border, make or load a selection. Then choose Select > Transform Selection.

- (Photoshop) To transform an alpha channel, select the channel in the Channels palette.

For more information, see`To link and unlink layers' on page 292.

Applying transformations

The commands under the Transform submenu let you apply the following transformations to an item:

- Scaling enlarges or reduces an item relative to its *reference point*, the fixed point around which transformations are performed. You can scale horizontally, vertically, or both horizontally and vertically.

- Rotating turns an item around a reference point. By default, this point is at the center of the object; however, you can move it to another location.

- Skewing lets you slant an item vertically and horizontally.

- Distorting lets you stretch an item in all directions.

- Applying perspective lets you apply one-point perspective to an item.

- (Photoshop) Warping lets you manipulate the shape of an item.

In Photoshop, you can perform several commands in succession before applying the cumulative transformation. For example, you can choose Scale and drag a handle to scale, and then choose Distort and drag a handle to distort. Then press Enter or Return to apply both transformations. In ImageReady, you can perform multiple types of transformations at the same time using the Transform > Numeric command.

To set or move the reference point for a transformation

All transformations are performed around a fixed point called the *reference point*. By default, this point is at the center of the item you are transforming. However, you can change the reference point or move the center point to a different location using the reference point locator in the options bar.

1 Choose a transformation command. A bounding box appears in the image.

2 Do one of the following:

- In the options bar, click a square on the reference point locator ▦ . Each square represents a point on the bounding box. For example, to move the reference point to the upper left corner of the bounding box, click the top left square on the reference point locator.

- In the transform bounding box that appears in the image, drag the reference point ⊹. The reference point can be outside the item you want to transform.

To scale, rotate, skew, distort, apply perspective, or warp

1 Select what you want to transform.

2 Choose Edit > Transform > Scale, Rotate, Skew, Distort, Perspective, or Warp.

Note: (Photoshop) If you are transforming a shape or entire path, the Transform menu becomes the Transform Path menu. If you are transforming multiple path segments (but not the entire path), the Transform menu becomes the Transform Points menu.

3 (Optional) In the options bar, click a square on the reference point locator ▦ .

4 Do one or more of the following:

- If you chose Scale, drag a handle on the bounding box. Press Shift as you drag a corner handle to scale proportionately. When positioned over a handle, the pointer becomes a double arrow.

- If you chose Rotate, move the pointer outside the bounding border (it becomes a curved, two-sided arrow), and then drag. Press Shift to constrain the rotation to 15° increments.

- If you chose Skew, drag a side handle to slant the bounding box.

- If you chose Distort, drag a corner handle to stretch the bounding box.

- If you chose Perspective, drag a corner handle to apply perspective to the bounding box.

- (Photoshop) If you chose Warp, choose a warp from the Warp Style pop-up menu in the options bar, or to perform a custom warp, drag the control points, a line, or an area within the mesh to change the shape of the bounding box and mesh.

- For all types of transformations, enter a value in the options bar. For example, to rotate an item, specify degrees in the rotation ⊿ text box.

5 (Optional) If desired, switch to a different type of transformation by selecting a command from the Edit > Transform submenu.

Important: When you transform a bitmap image (versus a shape or path), the image becomes slightly less sharp each time you commit a transformation; therefore, performing multiple commands before applying the cumulative transformation is preferable to applying each transformation separately.

6 (Optional) If you want to warp the image, click the Switch Between Free Transform And Warp Mode button ⚓ in the options bar.

7 When you finish, do one of the following:

- Press Enter (Windows) or Return (Mac OS), click the Commit button ✔ in the options bar, or double-click inside the transformation marquee.

- To cancel the transformation, press Esc or click the Cancel button ⊘ in the options bar.

For more information, see 'To warp an item' on page 269.

To flip or rotate precisely

1 Select what you want to transform.

2 Choose Edit > Transform and choose one of the following commands from the submenu:

- Rotate 180˚ to rotate by a half-turn

- Rotate 90˚ CW to rotate clockwise by a quarter-turn

- Rotate 90˚ CCW to rotate counterclockwise by a quarter-turn

- Flip Horizontal to flip horizontally, along the vertical axis

- Flip Vertical to flip vertically, along the horizontal axis

Note: (Photoshop) If you are transforming a shape or entire path, the Transform command becomes the Transform Path command. If you are transforming multiple path segments (but not the entire path), the Transform command becomes the Transform Points command.

To repeat a transformation

❖ Choose Edit > Transform > Again, Edit > Transform Path > Again, or Edit > Transform Points > Again.

To duplicate an item when transforming it

❖ Hold down Alt (Windows) or Option (Mac OS) when selecting the Transform command.

To apply multiple transformations at the same time (ImageReady)

1 Select what you want to transform.

2 Choose Edit > Transform > Numeric.

3 Do one or more of the following, and click OK:

- Select Position and enter values for the new location in the X (horizontal position) and Y (vertical position) text boxes. Select Relative to specify the new position in relation to the current position.

- Select Scale. Enter the dimensions in the Width and Height text boxes, or enter a scaling percentage in the Scale text box. Select Constrain Proportions to maintain the aspect ratio.

- Select Skew and enter degrees in the Horizontal skew and Vertical skew text boxes.

- Select Rotate. Enter degrees of rotation in the Angle text box, or drag in the circle to the right of the text box.

The Free Transform command

The Free Transform command lets you apply transformations (rotate, scale, skew, distort, and perspective) in one continuous operation. In Photoshop, you can also apply a warp transformation. Instead of choosing different commands, you simply hold down a key on your keyboard to switch between transformation types.

Note: (Photoshop) If you are transforming a shape or entire path, the Transform command becomes the Transform Path command. If you are transforming multiple path segments (but not the entire path), the Transform command becomes the Transform Points command.

To transform freely

1 Select what you want to transform.

2 Do one of the following:

- Choose Edit > Free Transform.

- If you are transforming a selection, pixel-based layer, or selection border, choose the Move tool . Then select Show Transform Controls (Photoshop) or Show Transform Box (ImageReady) in the options bar.

- (Photoshop) If you are transforming a vector shape or path, select the Path Selection tool ▶ . Then select Show Transform Controls in the options bar.

3 Do one or more of the following:

- To scale by dragging, drag a handle. Press Shift as you drag a corner handle to scale proportionately.

- To scale numerically, enter percentages in the Width and Height text boxes in the options bar. Click the Link icon 🔗 to maintain the aspect ratio.

- To rotate by dragging, move the pointer outside the bounding border (it becomes a curved, two-sided arrow), and then drag. Press Shift to constrain the rotation to 15˚ increments.

- To rotate numerically, enter degrees in the rotation text box ◿ in the options bar.

- To distort relative to the center point of the bounding border, press Alt (Windows) or Option (Mac OS), and drag a handle.

- To distort freely, press Ctrl (Windows) or Command (Mac OS), and drag a handle.

- To skew, press Ctrl+Shift (Windows) or Command+Shift (Mac OS), and drag a side handle. When positioned over a side handle, the pointer becomes a white arrowhead with a small double arrow.

- To skew numerically, enter degrees in the H (horizontal skew) and V (vertical skew) text boxes in the options bar.

- To apply perspective, press Ctrl+Alt+Shift (Windows) or Command+Option+Shift (Mac OS), and drag a corner handle. When positioned over a corner handle, the pointer becomes a gray arrowhead.

- To warp, click the Switch Between Free Transform And Warp Modes button ⚘ in the options bar. Drag control points to manipulate the shape of the item or choose a warp from the Warp Style pop-up menu in the options bar. After choosing from the Warp Style pop-up menu, you can still drag the control points.

- To change the reference point, click a square on the reference point locator ▦ in the options bar.

- To move an item, enter values for the new location of the reference in the X (horizontal position) and Y (vertical position) text boxes in the options bar. In Photoshop, click the Relative Positioning button △ to specify the new position in relation to the current position.

💡 *To undo the last handle adjustment, choose Edit > Undo.*

4 Do one of the following:

- Press Enter (Windows) or Return (Mac OS), click the Commit button ✔ in the options bar, or double-click inside the transformation marquee.

- To cancel the transformation, press Esc or click the Cancel button ⊘ in the options bar.

Important: When you transform a bitmap image (versus a shape or path), the image becomes slightly less sharp each time you commit a transformation; therefore, performing multiple commands before applying the cumulative transformation is preferable to applying each transformation separately.

The Warp command

The Warp command lets you drag control points to manipulate the shape of images, shapes, or paths, and so on. You can also warp using a shape in the Warp Style pop-up menu in the options bar. Shapes in the Warp Style pop-up menu are also malleable; drag their control points.

When using the control points to distort an item, choosing View > Extras shows or hides the warp mesh and control points.

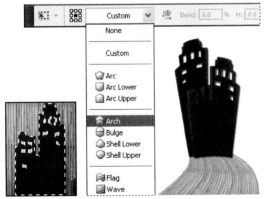

Choosing a warp from the Warp Style pop-up menu in the options bar

To warp an item

1 Select what you want to warp.

2 Do one of the following:

- Choose Edit > Transform > Warp.
- If you chose a different transform command or the Free Transform command, click the Switch Between Free Transform And Warp Modes button 🖳 in the options bar.

3 Do one or more of the following:

- To warp using a specific shape, choose from the Warp Style pop-up menu in the options bar.

Dragging a control point to warp the mesh

- To the manipulate the shape, drag the control points, a segment of the bounding box or mesh, or an area within the mesh. When adjusting a curve, use the control point handles. This is similar to adjusting the handles in the curved segment of a vector graphic.

For information about reshaping a curved segment, see Photoshop Help.

To undo the last handle adjustment, choose Edit > Undo.

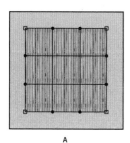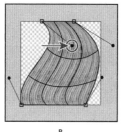

Manipulating the shape of a warp
A. *Original warp mesh* **B.** *Adjusting the handles, mesh segments, and areas within the mesh*

- To change the orientation of the warp, click the Change The Warp Orientation button ⬚ in the options bar.

- To change the reference point, click a square on the Reference point locator ⬚ in the options bar.

- To specify the amount of warp using numeric values, enter the values in the Bend (set bend), X (set horizontal distortion) and Y (set vertical distortion) text boxes in the options bar. You can't enter numeric values if you have chosen None or Custom from the Warp Style pop-up menu.

4 (Optional) To apply the warp using a more detailed algorithm, select High Quality in the options bar.

5 Do one of the following:

- Press Enter (Windows) or Return (Mac OS), click the Commit button ✔ in the options bar, or double-click inside the transformation marquee.

- To cancel the transformation, press Esc or click the Cancel button ⊘ in the options bar.

Important: *When you warp a bitmap image (versus a shape or path), the image becomes slightly less sharp each time you commit a transformation; therefore, performing multiple commands before applying the cumulative transformation is preferable to applying each transformation separately.*

The Liquify filter

The Liquify filter lets you push, pull, rotate, reflect, pucker, and bloat any area of an image. The distortions you create can be subtle or drastic, which makes the Liquify command a powerful tool for retouching images and creating artistic effects. The Liquify filter can be applied to 8-bits-per-channel or 16-bits per-channel images.

For information about using the Liquify filter, see Photoshop Help.

Retouching and repairing images

The Clone Stamp tool

The Clone Stamp tool ⬚ takes a sample of an image, which you can then apply over another image or part of the same image. You can also clone part of one layer over another layer. Each stroke of the tool paints on more of the sample. The Clone Stamp tool is useful for duplicating an object or removing a defect in an image.

When you use the Clone Stamp tool, you set a sampling point on the area you want to apply over another area. By selecting Aligned in the options bar, you can reuse the most current sampling point, no matter how many times you stop and resume painting. When Aligned is deselected, you'll reuse the same sampled pixels each time you paint.

Because you can use any brush tip with the Clone Stamp tool, you have a lot of control over the size of the area you clone. You can also use opacity and flow settings in the options bar to finesse the way you apply the cloned area. You can sample from one image and apply the clone in another image, as long as both images are in the same color mode.

Altering an image with the Clone Stamp tool

To use the Clone Stamp tool

1 Select the Clone Stamp tool ⏺ .

2 Choose a brush tip and set brush options for the blending mode, opacity, and flow in the options bar.

3 Next, determine how you want to align the sampled pixels. Select Aligned in the options bar to sample pixels continuously, without losing the current sampling point, even if you release the mouse button. Deselect Aligned to continue to use the sampled pixels from the initial sampling point each time you stop and resume painting.

4 Select Use All Layers in the options bar to sample data from all visible layers; deselect Use All Layers to sample only from the active layer.

5 Set the sampling point by positioning the pointer in any open image and Alt-clicking (Windows) or Option-clicking (Mac OS).

6 Drag over the area of the image you want to correct.

To use the Pattern Stamp tool

The Pattern Stamp tool lets you paint with a pattern. You can select a pattern from the pattern libraries or create your own patterns.

1 Select the Pattern Stamp tool ⏺ .

2 Choose a brush tip and set brush options (blending mode, opacity, and flow) in the options bar.

3 Select Aligned in the options bar to sample pixels continuously, without losing the current sampling point, even if you release the mouse button. Deselect Aligned to continue to use the sampled pixels from the initial sampling point each time you stop and resume painting.

4 Select a pattern from the Pattern pop-up palette in the options bar.

5 If you'd like to apply the pattern with an impressionistic effect, select Impressionist.

6 Drag in the image to paint with the pattern.

The Healing Brush tool

The Healing Brush tool lets you correct imperfections, causing them to disappear into the surrounding image. Like the cloning tools, you use the Healing Brush tool to paint with sampled pixels from an image or pattern. However, the Healing Brush tool also matches the texture, lighting, transparency, and shading of the sampled pixels to the pixels being healed. As a result, the repaired pixels blend seamlessly into the rest of the image.

Sampled pixels and healed image

To use the Healing Brush tool

1 Select the Healing Brush tool 🖊 .

2 Click the brush sample in the options bar and set brush options in the pop-up palette:

Note: If you're using a pressure-sensitive digitizing tablet, choose an option from the Size menu to vary the size of the healing brush over the course of a stroke. Choose Pen Pressure to base the variation on the pen pressure. Choose Stylus Wheel to base the variation on the position of the pen thumbwheel. Choose Off if you don't want to vary the size.

3 Choose a blending mode from the Mode menu in the options bar. Choose Replace to preserve noise, film grain, and texture at the edges of the brush stroke.

4 Choose a source to use for repairing pixels in the options bar: Sampled to use pixels from the current image, or Pattern to use pixels from a pattern. If you chose Pattern, select a pattern from the Pattern pop-up palette.

5 Select Aligned in the options bar to sample pixels continuously, without losing the current sampling point, even if you release the mouse button. Deselect Aligned to continue to use the sampled pixels from the initial sampling point each time you stop and resume painting.

6 Select Use All Layers in the options bar to sample data from all visible layers. Deselect Use All Layers to sample only from the active layer.

7 For the Healing Brush tool in sampling mode, set the sampling point by positioning the pointer in any open image and Alt-clicking (Windows) or Option-clicking (Mac OS).

Note: If you are sampling from one image and applying to another, both images must be in the same color mode unless one of the images is in Grayscale mode.

8 Drag in the image.

The sampled pixels are melded with the existing pixels each time you release the mouse button. Look in the status bar to view the status of the melding process.

💡 *If there is a strong contrast at the edges of the area you want to heal, make a selection before you use the Healing Brush tool. The selection should be bigger than the area you want to heal but should precisely follow the boundary of contrasting pixels. When you paint with the Healing Brush tool, the selection prevents colors from bleeding in from the outside.*

The Spot Healing Brush tool

The Spot Healing Brush tool quickly removes blemishes and other imperfections in your photos. The Spot Healing Brush works similarly to the Healing Brush: it paints with sampled pixels from an image or pattern and matches the texture, lighting, transparency, and shading of the sampled pixels to the pixels being healed. Unlike the Healing Brush, the Spot Healing Brush doesn't require you to specify a sample spot. The Spot Healing Brush automatically samples from around the retouched area.

Using the Spot Healing Brush to remove a blemish

💡 *If you need to retouch a large area or need more control over the source sampling, you can use the Healing Brush instead of the Spot Healing Brush.*

To use the Spot Healing Brush tool

The Spot Healing Brush quickly removes blemishes and other imperfections in your photos. You can either click once on a blemish, or click and drag to smooth away imperfections in an area.

1 Select the Spot Healing Brush tool from the toolbox. If necessary, click either the Healing Brush tool, Patch tool, or Red Eye tool to show the hidden tools and make your selection.

2 Choose a brush size in the options bar. A brush that is slightly larger than the area you want to fix works best so that you can cover the entire area with one click.

3 (Optional) Choose a blending mode from the Mode menu in the options bar. Choose Replace to preserve noise, film grain, and texture at the edges of the brush stroke.

4 Choose a Type option in the options bar:

Proximity Match Uses the pixels around the edge of the selection to find an image area to use as a patch for the selected area. If this option doesn't provide a satisfactory fix, undo the fix and try the Create Texture option.

Create Texture Uses all the pixels in the selection to create a texture with which to fix the area. If the texture doesn't work, try dragging through the area a second time.

5 Select Use All Layers in the options bar to sample data from all visible layers. Deselect Use All Layers to sample only from the active layer.

6 Click the area you want to fix, or click and drag over a larger area.

The Patch tool

The Patch tool lets you repair a selected area with pixels from another area or a pattern. Like the Healing Brush tool, the Patch tool matches the texture, lighting, and shading of the sampled pixels to the source pixels. You can also use the Patch tool to clone isolated areas of an image.

💡 *When repairing with pixels from the image, select a small area to produce the best result.*

Using the Patch tool to replace pixels

Patched image

To repair an area using sampled pixels

1 Select the Patch tool ⬭ .

2 Do one of the following:

- Drag in the image to select the area you want to repair, and select Source in the options bar.

- Drag in the image to select the area from which you want to sample, and select Destination in the options bar.

Note: You can also make a selection prior to selecting the Patch tool.

3 To adjust the selection, do one of the following:

- Shift-drag in the image to add to the existing selection.

- Alt-drag (Windows) or Option-drag (Mac OS) in the image to subtract from the existing selection.

- Alt+Shift-drag (Windows) or Option+Shift-drag (Mac OS) in the image to select an area intersected by the existing selection.

4 Position the pointer inside the selection, and do one of the following:

- If Source is selected in the options bar, drag the selection border to the area from which you want to sample. When you release the mouse button, the originally selected area is patched with the sampled pixels.

- If Destination is selected in the options bar, drag the selection border to the area you want to patch. When you release the mouse button, the newly selected area is patched with the sampled pixels.

To repair an area using a pattern

1 Select the Patch tool ⬭ .

2 Drag in the image to select the area you want to repair.

Note: You can also make a selection prior to selecting the Patch tool.

3 To adjust the selection, do one of the following:

- Shift-drag in the image to add to the existing selection.

- Alt-drag (Windows) or Option-drag (Mac OS) in the image to subtract from the existing selection.

- Alt-Shift-drag (Windows) or Option-Shift-drag (Mac OS) in the image to select an area intersected by the existing selection.

4 Select a pattern from the Pattern palette in the options bar, and click Use Pattern.

To remove red eye

The Red Eye tool removes red eye in flash photos of people and white or green reflections in flash photos of animals.

1 Select the Red Eye tool .

2 Click in the red eye. If you are not satisfied with the result, undo the correction, set one or more of the following options in the options bar, and click the red eye again:

Pupil Size Sets the size of the pupil (dark center of the eye).

Darken Pupil Sets the darkness of the pupil.

Red eye is caused by a reflection of the camera flash in the subject's retina. You'll see it more often when taking pictures in a darkened room because the subject's iris is wide open. To avoid red eye, use the camera's red eye reduction feature. Or, better yet, use a separate flash unit that you can mount on the camera farther away from the camera's lens.

To use the Color Replacement tool

The Color Replacement tool simplifies replacing specific colors in your image. You can paint over a targeted color with a corrective color. The Color Replacement tool doesn't work in images in Bitmap, Indexed, or Multichannel color modes.

1 Select the Color Replacement tool .

2 Choose a brush tip in the options bar. Generally, you should keep the blending mode set to Color.

3 For the Sampling option, choose one of the following:

Continuous Samples colors continuously as you drag.

Once Replaces the targeted color only in areas containing the color that you first click

Background Swatch Replaces only areas containing the current background color.

4 For the Limits option, select one of the following:

Discontiguous Replaces the sampled color wherever it occurs under the pointer.

Contiguous Replaces colors that are contiguous with the color immediately under the pointer

Find Edges Replaces connected areas containing the sampled color while better preserving the sharpness of shape edges.

5 For tolerance, enter a percentage value (ranging from 0 to 255) or drag the slider. Choose a low percentage to replace colors very similar to the pixel you click, or raise the percentage to replace a broader range of colors.

6 To define a smooth edge in the corrected areas, select Anti-aliased.

7 Choose a foreground color that replaces the unwanted color.

8 Click the color you want to replace in the image.

9 Drag in the image to replace the targeted color.

To use the Smudge tool

The Smudge tool simulates the effect you see when you drag a finger through wet paint. The tool picks up color where the stroke begins and pushes it in the direction you drag.

1 Select the Smudge tool ✎ .

2 Choose a brush tip and options for the blending mode in the options bar.

3 Select Use All Layers in the options bar to smudge using color data from all visible layers. If this is deselected, the Smudge tool uses colors from only the active layer.

4 Select Finger Painting in the options bar to smudge using the foreground color at the beginning of each stroke. If this is deselected, the Smudge tool uses the color under the pointer at the beginning of each stroke.

5 Drag in the image to smudge the pixels.

💡 *In Photoshop, press Alt (Windows) or Option (Mac OS) as you drag with the Smudge tool to use the Finger Painting option.*

To use the Blur tool

The Blur tool softens hard edges or reduces detail in an image.

1 Select the Blur tool ◊ .

2 Do the following in the options bar:

• Choose a brush tip and set options for the blending mode and strength in the options bar.

• Select Use All Layers in the options bar to blur using data from all visible layers. If this is deselected, the tool uses data from only the active layer.

3 Drag over the part of the image you want to blur.

To use the Sharpen tool

The Sharpen tool focuses soft edges to increase clarity or focus.

1 Select the Sharpen tool △ .

2 Do the following in the options bar:

• Choose a brush tip and set options for the blending mode and strength in the options bar.

• Select Use All Layers in the options bar to sharpen using data from all visible layers. If this is deselected, the tool uses data from only the active layer.

3 Drag over the part of the image you want to sharpen.

To use the Dodge tool or the Burn tool

Used to lighten or darken areas of the image, the Dodge tool and the Burn tool are based on a traditional photographer's technique for regulating exposure on specific areas of a print. Photographers hold back light to lighten an area on the print (*dodging*) or increase the exposure to darken areas on a print (*burning*).

1 Select the Dodge tool ✎ or the Burn tool ✋ .

2 Choose a brush tip and set brush options in the options bar.

3 In the options bar, select one of the following:

• Midtones to change the middle range of grays

• Shadows to change the dark areas

• Highlights to change the light areas

4 Specify the exposure for the Dodge tool or the Burn tool.

5 (Photoshop) Click the airbrush button ![airbrush icon] to use the brush as an airbrush. Alternatively, select the Airbrush option in the Brushes palette.

6 Drag over the part of the image you want to lighten or darken.

To use the Sponge tool

The Sponge tool subtly changes the color saturation of an area. In Grayscale mode, the tool increases or decreases contrast by moving gray levels away from or toward the middle gray.

1 Select the Sponge tool ![Sponge tool icon] .

2 Choose a brush tip and set brush options in the options bar.

3 In the options bar, select the way you want to change the color.

- Saturate to intensify the color's saturation

- Desaturate to dilute the color's saturation

4 Specify the flow for the Sponge tool.

5 Drag over the part of the image you want to modify.

Vanishing Point

About Vanishing Point

Vanishing Point is a feature that lets you make perspective-correct edits in images that contain perspective planes—for instance, the sides of a building or any rectangular object. Using Vanishing Point, you specify the planes in an image, and then apply edits such as painting, cloning, copying or pasting, and transforming. All your edits honor the perspective of the plane you're working in. With Vanishing Point, you're no longer retouching an image as if all its contents are on a single flat plane facing you. Instead, you're working dimensionally on the perspective planes in the image. When you use Vanishing Point to retouch, add, or remove content in an image, the results are more realistic because the edits are properly oriented and scaled to the perspective planes.

Making edits on the perspective planes in an image

To use Vanishing Point, you open the Vanishing Point dialog box (choose Filter > Vanishing Point), which contains tools for defining the perspective planes, tools for editing the image, and an image preview that you work in. You first specify the perspective planes in the preview image, and then you can paint, clone, copy, paste, and transform content in the planes. The Vanishing Point tools (Marquee, Stamp, Brush, and others) behave similarly to their counterparts in the main Photoshop toolbox. You can even use the same keyboard shortcuts to set the tool options.

To use Vanishing Point

1 (Optional) Before choosing the Vanishing Point command, you can prepare your image by doing any of the following:

• To put the results of your Vanishing Point work in a separate layer, first create a new layer before choosing the Vanishing Point command.

If you create a new layer each time you use Vanishing Point, the results appear on a separate, editable layer. You can then use such layer features as opacity, layer styles, and blending modes. Putting the Vanishing Point results in a separate layer also preserves your original image.

• If you plan to clone the content in your image beyond the boundaries of the current image size, increase the canvas size to accommodate the

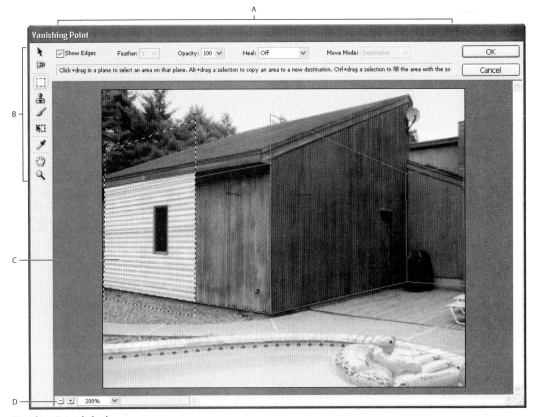

Vanishing Point dialog box
A. *Options* **B.** *Toolbox* **C.** *Preview of vanishing point session* **D.** *Zoom options*

additional content. See also `To change the size of the canvas' on page 251.

- If you plan to paste an item from the Photoshop clipboard into Vanishing Point, copy the item before choosing the Vanishing Point command. The copied item can be from a different Photoshop document. If you're copying type, select the entire text layer and then copy to the clipboard.

- To confine the Vanishing Point results to specific areas of your image, either make a selection or add a mask to your image before choosing the Vanishing Point command. See also `To use the marquee tools' on page 223 and `About masks and alpha channels' on page 243.

Using a selection to confine edits to portions of the perspective planes

2 Choose Filter> Vanishing Point.

3 Select the Create Plane tool 📇 and define the four corner nodes of the plane surface. Try to use a rectangle object in the image as a guide when creating the plane.

After creating the four corner nodes, you can move, scale, or reshape the plane. Keep in mind that your results depend on how accurately the plane lines up with perspective of the image. If there's a problem with the corner node placement, the bounding box and grid turn either red or yellow. Move a corner node until the bounding box and grid are blue, which

indicates that the plane is valid. See also `To define and adjust perspective planes in Vanishing Point' on page 281 and `Bounding box and grid alerts in Vanishing Point' on page 285.

Selecting a corner node

💡 *It's a good idea to adjust the plane or use the Grid Size option to line up the perspective plane and grid with image elements, such as the pattern in the floor, texture on a wall, or frame of a window.*

4 (Optional) Select the Create Plane tool and Ctrl-drag (Windows) or Command-drag (Mac OS) an edge node of the plane to *tear off* a perpendicular plane. You can also tear off a perpendicular plane from the one you just created. All the planes you tear off from each other (as opposed to creating unrelated planes) keep your edits in the proper scale and orientation throughout the image.

Ctrl-drag (Windows) or Command-drag (Mac OS) an edge node to tear off perpendicular planes.

💡 *You can use your first Vanishing Point session for simply creating perspective planes and then clicking OK. The planes appear in subsequent Vanishing Point sessions when you choose Filter > Vanishing Point. This is especially useful if you plan to copy and paste an image into Vanishing Point and need to have a ready-made planes to target.*

5 Do one or more of the following:

• To make a selection, select the Marquee tool ⬚ and drag in a plane. You can set the Marquee tool options (Feather, Opacity, Heal, and Move Mode) at any time, either before or after making the selection. To select an entire plane, double-click the Marquee tool in the plane.

💡 *When you move the Marquee tool, the Stamp tool, or the Brush tool into a plane, the bounding box is highlighted, indicating that the plane is active.*

• To clone a selection, select the Marquee or Transform tool and Alt-drag (Windows) or Option-drag (Mac OS) the selection to tear off a copy. The selection becomes a *floating selection*, which you can scale, move, rotate, or clone again using the Transform tool, or move or clone again using the Marquee tool. You can continue tearing off as many copies as you want. When you move a selection in a plane, the selection conforms to the perspective of the plane.

Tearing off a selection and moving a selection from one perspective plane to another

💡 *Pressing Ctrl+Shift+T (Windows) or Control+Shift+T (Mac OS) duplicates your last duplicating move. This is an easy way to clone content multiple times.*

• To move a selection, select the Marquee or Transform tool and drag the selection. Hold down the Shift key to constrain the move.

• To rotate a selection, select the Transform tool and move the pointer near a node. When the pointer changes to a curved double arrow, drag to rotate the selection. You can also select the Flip option to flip the selection horizontally along the vertical axis of the plane or select the Flop option to flip the selection vertically along the horizontal axis of the plane.

• To scale a selection, select the Transform tool and move the pointer on top of a node. When the pointer changes to a straight double arrow drag to scale the selection.

• To fill a selection with another area of the image, select the Marquee tool, and then Ctrl-drag (Windows) or Command-drag (Mac OS) a selection to the image area you want as the source image. You can also choose Source for the Move Mode and drag the selection to the source image. The filled selection becomes a floating selection that you can scale, rotate, move, or clone using the Transform tool, or move or clone using the Marquee tool.

• To paint with a sample of the image, select the Stamp tool and Alt-click (Windows) or Option-click (Mac OS) a source area in a perspective plane. Now you can paint with the Stamp tool to clone the source anywhere in the image. If you paint in a perspective plane, the Stamp tool paints the cloned area in perspective. For detailed information, see also `To use the Stamp tool in Vanishing Point' on page 286 and `Vanishing Point tools' on page 283.

- To paint with a color, select the Brush tool, set the options for Diameter, Hardness, Opacity, and Heal. Click the Brush Color box to open the Adobe Color Picker to select a color. Drag in the image to paint. When painting in a plane, the brush size and shape scales and orients properly to the plane's perspective. Shift-drag constrains the stroke to a straight line.

For information about creating a brush and setting painting options, see Photoshop Help.

- To transform a floating selection, select the Transform tool ⟦ and scale, rotate, or move the floating selection. You can also select a Transform tool options to flip horizontally or flop vertically the floating selection in relation to the plane orientation.

- To paste an item from the clipboard, press Ctrl+V or Command+V. Move the item into a plane and it conforms to the perspective. For detailed information, see also `To paste an item into Vanishing Point' on page 285.

Note: *If the plane is not the proper size to accommodate your painting, cloning, or transforming, select the Edit Plane tool and drag an edge node of the bounding box to scale the plane.*

Vanishing Point allows multiple undos. Press Ctrl+Z (Windows) or Command+Z (Mac OS) one or more times to undo an operation one or more times. Press Shift+Ctrl+Z (Windows) or Shift+Command+Z (Mac OS) to redo an operation. Press Alt (Windows) or Option (Mac OS) to change the Cancel button to Reset so that you can revert the image to its original state in the Vanishing Point dialog box.

6 Click OK.

To preserve the perspective plane information in an image, save your document in PSD, TIFF, or JPEG format.

To define and adjust perspective planes in Vanishing Point

Vanishing Point lets you define rectangular planes that line up with the perspective in an image. The accuracy of the plane determines whether any edits or adjustments are properly scaled and oriented in your image. After you establish the four corner nodes, you can scale, move, or reshape to fine-tune the perspective plane. Sometimes, lining up the bounding box and grid of the plane with a texture or pattern in your image helps you accurately match the image's perspective.

1 With an image open in Photoshop, choose Filter > Vanishing Point.

2 Select the Create Plane tool ▦ and click in the preview image to add the corner node. Try to use a rectangular object or a plane area in the image as a guide when creating the perspective plane. To help with node placement, hold down the "x" key to zoom into the preview image.

Note: As you add corner nodes, you can delete the last node if it's not correct by pressing the Backspace key (Windows) or Delete key (Mac OS).

3 Select the Edit Plane tool ▶ and do one or more of the following:

• To reshape the perspective plane, drag a corner node.

• To adjust the grid, enter a value in the Grid Size text box or click the down arrow and move the slider. You can also adjust the grid size when the Create Plane tool is selected.

• To move the plane, click inside the plane and drag.

• To scale the plane, drag an edge node in a segment of the bounding box.

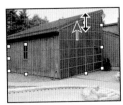

Dragging an edge node to increase the size of a plane to accommodate your edits

Note: The bounding box and grid of a perspective plane is normally blue. If there's a problem with the placement of the corner nodes, the plane is invalid, and the bounding box and grid turn either red (severe problems resolving the plane's aspect ratio) or yellow (problems resolving the vanishing points of the perspective plane). When your plane is invalid, move the corner nodes until the bounding box and grid are blue.

4 (Optional) To tear off a perpendicular plane, select the Create Plane or Edit Plane tool and Ctrl-drag (Windows) or Command-drag (Mac OS) an edge node along the bounding box.

You can create as many planes as you want. To paint, clone, or transform and maintain a consistent scale and orientation, it's best to tear off additional planes rather than create unrelated planes. If a newly created plane does not properly line up with the image, select the Edit Plane tool and move a corner node to adjust the plane. Adjustments made to connected planes are constrained; when you adjust one plane, all the connected planes are affected.

Tearing off multiple planes keeps the planes related to each other so your edits are scaled and oriented in the proper perspective.

💡 *If you have overlapping planes, Ctrl-click (Windows) or Command-click (Mac OS) to cycle through the overlapping planes.*

Overlapping planes

Vanishing Point tools

Vanishing Point tools behave like their counterparts in the main Photoshop toolbox. You can use the same keyboard shortcuts for setting tool options. Selecting a tool changes the available options in the Vanishing Point dialog box.

Edit Plane tool ▶ Selects, edits, moves, and resizes planes.

Create Plane tool Defines the four corner nodes of a plane and also adjusts the size and shape of the plane. Ctrl-drag (Windows) or Command-drag (Mac OS) an edge node to tear off a perpendicular plane.

Marquee tool Makes square or rectangular selections. Drag in the preview image to create a selection. Alt-drag (Windows) or Option-drag (Mac OS) a selection to tear off a copy of the selection. Ctrl-drag (Windows) or Command-drag (Mac OS) a selection to fill the selection with a source image. Specify a value for Feather to blur the edges of the selection. Specifying the Opacity determines to what degree the selection obscures or reveals the image beneath it. Use the Healing menu to choose a blending mode: choose Off so the selection doesn't blend with the colors, shadows, and textures of the surrounding pixels; choose Luminance to blend the selection with the lighting of the surrounding pixels; or choose On to blend the selection with the color, lighting, and shading of surrounding pixels. Use the Move Mode menu to determine the behavior when you move a selection. Select Destination to select the area you move the selection marquee to. Select Source to fill an area with a source image that you move the selection marquee to (same as Ctrl-dragging or Command-dragging a selection). See also `To use the marquee tools' on page 223.

Ctrl-dragging (Windows) or Command-dragging (Mac OS) a selection
A. *Original selection* *B.* *Moving the selection to the source image*
C. *The source image fills the original selection*

💡 *Double-clicking the Marquee tool in a plane selects the entire plane.*

Stamp tool Paints with a sample of the image. Alt-click (Windows) or Option-click (Mac OS) to establish a sampling point and then drag in the image to paint with the Stamp tool. Each stroke paints on more of the sample. You can customize the brush tip by entering values for the brush size (Diameter) and the size of the tool's hard center (Hardness). Specifying the Opacity determines to what degree the selection obscures or reveals the image beneath it. Similar to the Clone Stamp tool, the Vanishing Point Stamp tool lets you paint strokes using blending modes and specifying an Opacity. Use the Healing menu to choose a blending mode: choose Off to prevent the strokes from blending with the colors, shadows, and textures of the surrounding pixels; choose Luminance to blend the strokes with the lighting of the surrounding pixels; or choose On to blend the strokes with the color, lighting, and shading of surrounding pixels. Select the Aligned option to sample pixels continuously without losing the current sampling point, even if you release the mouse. Deselect the Aligned option to continue using the sampled pixels from the initial sampling point each time you stop and resume painting. See also `To use the Stamp tool in Vanishing Point' on page 286 and `To use the Clone Stamp tool' on page 271.

Brush tool Paints a selected color on the image. Double-click the Brush Color swatch to open the Adobe Color Picker and select a color, or select the Eyedropper tool and click in the preview image to specify a brush color. Drag in the image to paint. Shift-drag to constrain the stroke to a straight line. You can customize the brush tip by entering values for the brush size (Diameter) and the size of the tool's hard center (Hardness). Specifying the Opacity determines to what degree the selection obscures or reveals the image beneath it. To paint with a blending mode, use the Healing menu: choose Off to prevent the strokes from blending with the colors, shadows, and textures of the surrounding pixels; choose Luminance to blend the strokes with the lighting of the surrounding pixels; or choose On to blend the strokes with the color, lighting, and shading of surrounding pixels.

💡 *The Brush tool honors marquee selections and can be used to paint a hard line along edge of the selection. For example, if you select an entire plane, you can paint a line along the perimeter of the plane.*

Transform tool Scales, rotates, and moves a *floating selection* by moving the bounding box handles. Its behavior is similar to using the Free

Transform command on a rectangle selection. You can also flip a floating selection horizontally along the vertical axis of the plane or flop a floating selection vertically along the horizontal axis of the plane. Alt-drag (Windows) or Option-drag (Mac OS) a floating selection to tear off a copy of the selection. Ctrl-drag (Windows) or Command-drag (Mac OS) a selection to fill the selection with a source image. See also `To transform freely' on page 267.

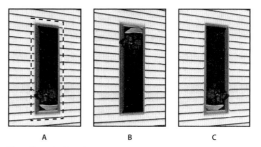

Transform tool options
A. *Original selection* **B.** *Flip* **C.** *Flop*

Eyedropper tool Selects a color for painting when you click in the preview image. Click the Brush Color box to open the Adobe Color Picker.

Zoom tool Magnifies the view of the image in the preview window. Click or click-drag to zoom in. Alt-click/drag (Windows) or Option-click/drag (Mac OS) to reduce the view of the image in the preview window.

Hand tool Moves the image in the preview window. Drag in the window to move the view.

For more information, see `About the Adobe Color Picker' on page 177.

To adjust viewing options in Vanishing Point

❖ Do any of the following:

• To magnify or reduce the preview image, select the Zoom tool 🔍 in the Vanishing Point dialog box, and click or drag in the preview image to zoom in; hold down Alt (Windows) or Option (Mac OS), and click or drag in the preview image to zoom out. You can also specify a magnification level in the Zoom text box at the bottom of the dialog box, or click the Zoom Out 🔍 or the Zoom In 🔍 buttons.

• To move the image in the preview window, select the Hand tool in the Vanishing Point dialog box, and drag in the preview image. Alternatively, hold down the spacebar with any tool selected, and drag in the preview image.

• To show or hide the grid and boundaries of a perspective plane, select or deselect Show Edges.

• To adjust the size of the perspective plane grid, select the Edit Plane ↖ or the Create Plane ▦ tool, and then either enter a pixel value in the Grid Size text box or click the down arrow and move the slider.

• To temporarily zoom into the preview image, hold down the "x" key. This is especially helpful for placing the corner nodes when defining a plane, and for working on details.

Bounding box and grid alerts in Vanishing Point

The bounding box and grid change colors to indicate the plane's current condition. If your plane is invalid, move a corner node until the bounding box and grid are blue.

Blue Indicates a valid plane. Keep in mind that a valid plane doesn't guarantee results with the proper perspective. You must make sure that the bounding box and grid accurately line up with geometric elements or a plane area in the image.

Red Indicates an invalid plane. Vanishing Point cannot calculate the plane's aspect ratio. You won't be able to tear off a perpendicular plane from a red invalid plane. Although it's possible to make edits in a (red) invalid plane, the results will not be oriented properly.

Yellow Indicates an invalid plane. All the vanishing points of the plane cannot be resolved. Although it's possible to tear off a perpendicular plane or make edits in a yellow invalid plane, the results will not be oriented properly.

To paste an item into Vanishing Point

You can paste an item from the clipboard in Vanishing Point. The copied item can be from the same document or a different one. Once pasted into Vanishing Point, the item becomes a floating selection that you can scale, rotate, move or clone. When the floating selection moves into a selected plane, it conforms to the plane's perspective.

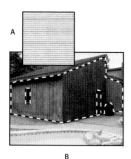

Pasting an item into Vanishing Point
A. Copied pattern from a separate document **B.** *Image with selection to confine results* **C.** *Pasted pattern moved into plane*

💡 *For convenience, it's recommended that you create perspective planes in a previous Vanishing Point session.*

1 Copy an item to the clipboard. The copied item can be from the same or different document. Keep in mind that you can paste only a raster (not vector) item.

Note: *If you're copying type, select the entire text layer and then copy to the clipboard. You'll be pasting a rasterized version of the type into Vanishing Point.*

2 (Optional) Create a new layer.

3 Choose Filter > Vanishing Point.

4 If necessary, create one or more planes in the image.

5 Paste the item. The item is now a floating selection in the preview image. By default, the Marquee tool is selected.

Important: *After pasting the image in Vanishing Point, do not immediately use the Marquee tool to select a perspective plane. This deselects the pasted image so that it's no longer a floating selection.*

To use the Stamp tool in Vanishing Point

In Vanishing Point, the Stamp tool paints with sampled pixels. The cloned image is oriented to the perspective of the plane you're painting in. The Stamp tool is useful for such tasks as blending and retouching image areas, cloning portions of a surface to "paint out" an object, or cloning an image area to duplicate an object or extend a texture or pattern.

1 With an image containing perspective planes open in Vanishing Point, select the Stamp tool 🖈 .

2 In the tool options area, set brush options for Diameter, Hardness, and Opacity.

3 Choose a Healing mode:

- To paint without blending with the color, lighting, and shading of the surrounding pixels, choose Off.

- To paint and blend the strokes with the lighting of the surrounding pixels while retaining the color of the sampled pixels, choose Luminance.

- To paint and maintain the texture of the sampled image while blending with the colors, lighting, and shading of the surrounding pixels, choose On.

4 Select Aligned to sample pixels continuously, without losing the current sampling point even when you release the mouse button. Deselect Aligned to continue using the sampled pixels from the initial sampling point each time you stop and resume painting.

5 Move the pointer into a plane and Alt-click (Windows) or Option-click (Mac OS) to set the sampling point.

6 Drag over the area of the image you want to paint.

Chapter 13: Layers

Layer Basics

About layers

Layers allow you to work on one element of an image without disturbing the others. Think of layers as sheets of acetate stacked one on top of the other. You can see through transparent areas of a layer to the layers below. You can change the composition of an image by changing the order and attributes of layers. In addition, special features such as adjustment layers, fill layers, and layer styles let you create sophisticated effects.

Transparent areas on a layer let you see through to the layers below.

A new image in Photoshop or ImageReady has a single layer. The number of additional layers, layer effects, and layer sets you can add to an image is limited only by your computer's memory.

Layer groups help you organize and manage layers. You can use groups to arrange your layers in a logical order and to reduce clutter in the Layers palette. You can nest groups within other groups. You can also use groups to apply attributes and masks to multiple layers simultaneously.

About the Layers palette

The Layers palette lists all layers, groups, and layer effects in an image. You can use the Layers palette to show and hide layers, create new layers, and work with groups of layers. You can access additional commands and options in the Layers palette menu.

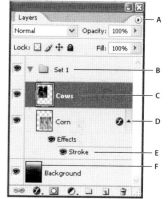

Photoshop Layers palette
A. Layers palette menu B. Group C. Layer D. Expand/Collapse Layer effects E. Layer effect F. Layer thumbnail

- To display the Layers palette, choose Window > Layers.

- To use the Layers palette menu, click the triangle in the upper right corner of the palette. It contains commands for working with layers.

- To change the size of layer thumbnails, choose Palette Options from the Layers palette menu, and select a thumbnail size.

- To change thumbnail contents, choose Palette Options from the Layers palette menu and select Entire Document to display the contents of the entire document. Select Layer Bounds to restrict the thumbnail to the object's pixels on the layer.

  Turn off thumbnails to improve performance and save monitor space.

- To expand and collapse groups (and layer sets in ImageReady), click the triangle to the left of a group folder. See `To view layers and groups within a group' on page 289.

About the background layer

When you create a new image with a white background or a colored background, the bottommost image in the Layers palette is called *Background*. An image can have only one background. You cannot change the stacking order of a background, its blending mode, or its opacity. However, you can convert a background to a regular layer.

When you create a new image with transparent content, the image does not have a background layer. The bottommost layer is not constrained like the background layer; you can move it anywhere in the Layers palette, and change its opacity and blending mode.

To convert a background into a layer

1 Double-click Background in the Layers palette, or choose Layer > New > Layer From Background.

2 Set layer options. (See `To create a new layer or group' on page 288.)

3 Click OK.

To convert a layer into a background

1 Select a layer in the Layers palette.

2 Choose Layer > New > Background From Layer.

Any transparent pixels in the layer are converted to the background color.

Note: You cannot create a background by giving a regular layer the name Background—you must use the Background From Layer command.

To create a new layer or group

A new layer appears either above the selected layer or within the selected group in the Layers palette.

1 Do one of the following:

- To create a new layer or group using default options, click the New Layer button ![icon] or New Group button ![icon] in the Layers palette.

- Choose Layer > New > Layer or choose Layer > New > Group.

- Choose New Layer or New Group from the Layers palette menu.

- Alt-click (Windows) or Option-click (Mac OS) the New Layer button or New Group button in the Layers palette to display the New Layer dialog box and set layer options.

- Ctrl-click (Windows) or Command-click (Mac OS) the New Layer button or New Group button in the Layers palette to add a layer below the currently selected layer.

2 Set layer options, and click OK:

Name Specifies a name for the layer or group.

Use Layer Below To Create Clipping Mask This option is not available for groups. (See `To create a clipping mask' on page 326.)

Color Assigns a color to the layer or group in the Layers palette.

Mode Specifies a blending mode for the layer or group. (See `About blending modes' on page 300.)

Opacity Specifies an opacity level for the layer or group.

(Photoshop) Fill With Mode-Neutral Color Fills the layer with a preset, neutral color.

To create a new layer with the same effects as an existing layer

1 Select the existing layer in the Layers palette.

2 Drag the layer to the New Layer button at the bottom of the Layers palette. The newly created layer contains all the effects of the existing one.

To convert a selection into a new layer

1 Make a selection.

2 Do one of the following:

- Choose Layer > New > Layer Via Copy to copy the selection into a new layer.

- Choose Layer > New > Layer Via Cut to cut the selection and paste it into a new layer.

To show or hide a layer, group, or style

❖ Do one of the following:

- In the Layers palette, click the eye icon next to a layer, group, or layer effect to hide its content in the document window. Click in the column again to redisplay the content.

- Alt-click (Windows) or Option-click (Mac OS) an eye icon to display only the content for that layer or group. Photoshop remembers the visibility states of all layers before hiding them. If you don't change the visibility of any other layer, Alt-clicking (Windows) or Option-clicking (Mac OS) in the eye column again restores the original visibility settings.

- Drag through the eye column to change the visibility of multiple items in the Layers palette.

Note: Only visible layers are printed.

To view layers and groups within a group

1 Click the group in the Layers palette.

2 To open the group, do one of the following:

- Click the triangle to the left of the folder icon.

- Right-click (Windows) or Control-click (Mac OS) the triangle to the left of the folder icon and choose Open This Group.

- Alt-click (Windows) or Option-click (Mac OS) the triangle to open or close a group and the groups nested within it.

To sample from all visible layers

The default behavior of the Magic Wand, Smudge, Blur, Sharpen, Paint Bucket, Clone Stamp, and Healing Brush tools is to sample color only from pixels on the active layer. This means you can smudge or sample in a single layer.

❖ To smudge or sample pixels from all visible layers with these tools, select Use All Layers in the options bar.

To change transparency preferences

1 Do one of the following:

• (Photoshop) In Windows, choose Edit > Preferences > Transparency & Gamut; in Mac OS, choose Photoshop > Preferences > Transparency & Gamut.

• (ImageReady) In Windows, choose Edit > Preference > Transparency; in Mac OS, choose ImageReady > Preferences > Transparency.

2 Choose a size and color for the transparency checkerboard, or choose None for Grid Size to hide the transparency checkerboard.

3 (Photoshop) Select Use Video Alpha to enable Photoshop to send transparency information to your computer's video board. This option requires hardware support—make sure that your computer's video board allows images to be overlaid on top of a live video signal.

4 Click OK.

Unifying layers in animations and rollovers

The unify buttons in the Layers palette determine how the changes you make to a layer in the active rollover state or animation frame apply to the other states in a rollover or frames in an animation. When a unify button is selected, changes apply to all states and frames; when a button is deselected, changes apply to only the active state or frame.

(Photoshop) To display the unify buttons, choose Animation Options from the Layers palette menu and choose an option. Automate (the default) displays the animation controls when the Animation palette is visible.

Selecting, grouping, and linking layers

Selecting layers

You can select one or more layers to work on them. For some activities, such as painting or making color and tone adjustments, you can work on only one layer at a time. A single selected layer is called the *active layer*. The name of the active layer appears in the title bar of the document window (Photoshop).

For other activities, such as moving, aligning, transforming, or applying styles from the Styles palette, you can select and work on multiple layers at a time.

You can select layers in the Layers palette or with the Move tool.

You can also link layers. Unlike multiple layers selected at the same time, linked layers stay linked when you change the selection in the Layers palette. See `To link and unlink layers' on page 292.

If you don't see the desired results when using a tool or applying a command, you may not have the correct layer selected. Check the Layers palette to make sure that you're working on the correct layer.

To select layers in the Layers palette

❖ Do one of the following:

• Click a layer in the Layers palette.

• To select multiple contiguous layers, click the first layer and then Shift-click the last layer.

• To select multiple noncontiguous layers, Ctrl-click (Windows) or Command-click (Mac OS) them in the Layers palette.

• To select all layers, choose Select > All Layers.

• (Photoshop) To select all layers of a similar type (for example all type layers), choose Select > Select Similar Layers.

• To have no layer selected, click in the Layers palette below the background or bottom layer, or choose Select > Deselect Layers.

To select layers in the document window

1 Select the Move tool ⊹.

2 Do one of the following:

• (Photoshop) In the options bar, select Auto Select Layer and click in the document on the layer content you want to select. The topmost layer containing pixels under the cursor is selected.

• (Photoshop) In the options bar, select Auto Select Group and click in the document on the content you want to select. The topmost group containing pixels under the cursor is selected. If you click an ungrouped layer, it becomes selected.

• Right-click (Windows) or Control-click (Mac OS) in the image, and choose a layer from the context menu. The context menu lists all the layers that contain pixels under the current pointer location.

• (ImageReady) In the options bar, select the Layer Select tool ⬆. Click in the document on a single layer to select it, in a group to select the entire group, or in a layer in a set to select only that layer. Note that you can't select locked layers with this tool.

• (ImageReady) In the options bar, select the Direct Select tool ⬆. Click in the document on a layer within a layer set to select the individual layer.

To select a layer in a group

1 Click the group in the Layers palette.

2 To open the group, do one of the following:

• Click the triangle to the left of the folder icon 🗀 .

• Right-click (Windows) or Ctrl-click (Mac OS) the triangle to the left of the folder icon and choose Open This Group from the pop-up menu. (You can choose Open Other Groups to open groups that are not selected.)

3 Click the individual layer in the group.

To group and ungroup layers

1 Select multiple layers in the Layers palette.

2 Do one of the following:

• Choose Layer > Group Layers.

• Alt-drag (Windows) or Option-drag (Mac OS) layers to the folder icon at the bottom of the Layers palette to group the layers.

3 To Ungroup the layers, select the group and choose Layer > Ungroup Layers.

To add layers to a group

❖ Do one of the following:

• Select the group in the Layers palette and click the New Layer button ⬛ .

• Drag a layer to the group folder.

• Drag a group folder into another group folder. The group and all of its layers move.

• Drag an existing group to the New Group button ⬜ .

To link and unlink layers

You can link two or more layers or groups. Unlike multiple layers selected at the same time, linked layers retain their relationship until you unlink them. You can move, apply transformations, and create clipping masks from linked layers.

1 Select the layers or groups in the Layers palette.

2 Do one of the following:

• Click the link icon ⛓ at the bottom of the Layers palette (Photoshop) or next to the layer (ImageReady).

• (ImageReady) Choose Link Layers from the Layers palette menu.

3 To unlink layers do one of the following:

• Select a linked layer and click the link icon.

• (Photoshop) To temporarily disable the linked layer, Shift-click the Link icon for the linked layer. A red X appears. Shift-click the link icon to enable the link again.

• Select the linked layers and click the Link icon. To select all linked layers, select one of the layers and then choose Layer > Select Linked Layers.

Working with groups and sets in ImageReady

Layers you group in Photoshop become layer sets when you open the image in ImageReady. Layer sets you create in ImageReady become groups in Photoshop. The difference between groups and sets in ImageReady is the way that the Layer Select tool responds to a selection in the document window. In a layer set, the Layer Select tool selects individual layers in the set. With a group, the Layer Select tool selects the entire group when you click a layer that is part of the group. To make a layer set into a group, select the layer set, choose Layer > Layer Set Options, and select the Treat Layer Set As Group option.

Moving, copying, and locking layers

To change the order of layers and groups

1 Do one of the following:

- Drag the layer or group up or down in the Layers palette. Release the mouse button when the highlighted line appears where you want to place the layer or group.

- To move a layer into a group, drag a layer to the group folder . If the group is closed, the layer is placed at the bottom of the group.

Note: If a group is expanded so that you can see all the layers within it, adding a layer beneath the expanded group automatically adds the layer to that group. To avoid this, collapse the group before adding the new layer.

- Select a layer or group, choose Layer > Arrange, and choose a command from the submenu. If the selected item is in a group, the command applies to the stacking order within the group. If the selected item is not in a group, the command applies to the stacking order within the Layers palette.

- To reverse the order of selected layers, choose Layer > Arrange > Reverse (Photoshop) or Layer > Reverse Layers (ImageReady). Note that these options appear dimmed if you do not have at least two layers selected.

Note: By definition, the background layer is always at the bottom of the stacking order. Therefore, the Send To Back command places the selected item directly above the background layer.

Manipulating layer content

After you select layers, you can move, transform, align, and distribute them. You can select layers in the Layers palette or directly in the document window.

Showing the boundary or edges of the content in a layer can help you move and align the content. You can also display the transform handles for selected layers and groups so that you can resize or rotate them.

Layer content with edges showing (left) and with transform mode selected (right)

To display the edges of content in a selected layer

❖ Choose View > Show > Layer Edges.

To display transform handles in a selected layer

1 Select the Move tool.

2 Do one of the following:

- (Photoshop) In the options bar, select Show Transform Controls.

- (ImageReady) In the options bar, select Show Transform Box.

You can resize and rotate layer content using the transform handles. See `To transform freely' on page 267.

To move the content of layers

1 In the Layers palette, select the layers containing the objects you want to move.

2 Do one of the following:

• Select the Move tool in the toolbox. In the document window, drag any object on one of the selected layers.

• Press an arrow key on the keyboard to nudge the objects by 1 pixel.

• Hold down Shift and press an arrow key on the keyboard to nudge the objects by 10 pixels.

To align objects on different layers

You can align the content of layers and groups using the Move tool. (See `Moving selections and layers within an image' on page 233.)

1 Do one of the following:

• To align multiple layers, select the layers with the Move tool or in the Layers palette, or select a group.

• To align the content of one or more layers to a selection border, make a selection in the image, and then select the layers in the Layers palette. Use this method to align to any specified point in the image.

2 Choose Layer > Align or Layer > Align Layers To Selection (Photoshop), and choose a command from the submenu. These same commands are available as Alignment buttons in the Move tool options bar.

Top Edges Aligns the top pixel on the selected layers to the topmost pixel on all selected layers, or to the top edge of the selection border.

Vertical Centers Aligns the vertical center pixel on each selected layers to the vertical center pixel of all the selected layers, or to the vertical center of the selection border.

Bottom Edges Aligns the bottom pixel on the selected layers to the bottommost pixel on selected layers, or to the bottom edge of the selection border.

Left Edges Aligns the left pixel on the selected layers to the left pixel on the leftmost layer, or to the left edge of the selection border.

Horizontal Centers Aligns the horizontal center pixel on the selected layers to the horizontal center pixel of all the selected layers, or to the horizontal center of the selection border.

Right Edges Aligns the right pixel on the linked layers to the rightmost pixel on all selected layers, or to the right edge of the selection border.

To evenly distribute layers and groups

1 Select three or more layers.

2 Choose Layer > Distribute and choose a command. Alternatively, select the Move tool and click a distribution button in the options bar.

Top Edges Spaces the layers evenly starting from the top pixel of each layer.

Vertical Centers Spaces the layers evenly starting from the vertical center pixel of each layer.

Bottom Edges ☰ Spaces the layers evenly starting from the bottom pixel of each layer.

Left Edges ⫴ Spaces the layers evenly starting from the left pixel of each layer.

Horizontal Centers ⫴ Spaces the layers evenly starting from the horizontal center of each layer.

Right Edges ⫴ Spaces the layers evenly starting from the right pixel on each layer.

To distribute layers unevenly (ImageReady)

1 Select the Move tool.

2 Select the layers you wish to space.

3 Enter a number in the text box to the right of the Distribution buttons in the options bar. This number equals the number of pixels that will separate the layers. You can choose different numbers for different combinations of layers or groups to create an uneven spacing pattern.

4 Choose the Distribute Layer Vertical Space or Distribute Layer Horizontal Space button to finish the distribution process.

You can specify the space between distributed layers.

To rotate a layer

1 In the Layers palette, select the layer you want to rotate.

2 If anything is currently selected in the image, choose Select > Deselect.

3 Choose Edit > Transform > Rotate. A box defining the boundaries of the layer (called a bounding box) appears.

4 Move the pointer outside of the bounding box (the pointer becomes a curved, two-sided arrow), and then drag. Press Shift to constrain the rotation to 15° increments.

5 When you're satisfied with the results, press Enter (Windows) or Return (Mac OS), or click the check mark in the options bar. To cancel the rotation, press Esc, or click the Cancel Transform icon on the options bar.

To duplicate a layer or group within an image

1 Select a layer or group in the Layers palette.

2 Do one of the following:

- Drag the layer or group to the New Layer button ▣.

- Choose Duplicate Layer or Duplicate Group from the Layers menu or the Layers palette menu. In Photoshop, enter a name for the layer or group, and click OK.

To duplicate a layer or group between images

1 Open the source and destination images.

2 In the Layers palette of the source image, select a layer or group.

3 Do one of the following:

- Drag the layer or group from the Layers palette into the destination image.

- Select the Move tool ▶⊕ , and drag from the source image to the destination image. The duplicate layer or group appears above the active layer in the Layers palette of the destination image. Shift-drag to move the image content to the same location it occupied in the source image (if the source and destination images have the same pixel dimensions) or to the center of the document window (if the source and destination images have different pixel dimensions).

- (Photoshop) Choose Duplicate Layer or Duplicate Group from the Layers menu or the Layers palette menu. Choose the destination document from the Document pop-up menu, and click OK.

- Choose Select > All to select all the pixels on the layer, and choose Edit > Copy. Then choose Edit > Paste in the destination image.

To create a new document from a layer or group

1 Select a layer or group in the Layers palette.

2 Choose Duplicate Layer or Duplicate Group from the Layers menu or the Layers palette menu.

3 Choose New from the document pop-up menu, and click OK.

Locking layers

You can lock layers fully or partially to protect their contents. For instance, you may want to lock a layer fully when you finish with it. You may want to lock a layer partially if it has the correct transparency and styles, but you are still deciding on positioning. When a layer is locked, a lock icon appears to the right of the layer name. The lock icon is solid when the layer is fully locked and hollow when the layer is partially locked.

To lock all properties of a layer or group

1 Select a layer or group.

2 Do one of the following:

- Click the Lock All 🔒 option in the Layers palette.

- (ImageReady) Choose Layer Options from the Layers palette menu, and select the Lock All option.

Note: *When a layer in a locked group has individual lock options applied to it, the lock icon is dimmed* 🔒 .

To partially lock a layer

1 Select a layer.

2 Click one or more lock options in the Layers palette. (In ImageReady, you can also choose Layer Options from the Layers palette menu.) Select one or more lock options:

Lock Transparency ▢ Confines editing to the opaque portions of the layer. This option is equivalent to the Preserve Transparency option in earlier versions of Photoshop.

Lock Image 🖌 Prevents modification of the layer's pixels using the painting tools.

Lock Position ⊹ Prevents the layer's pixels from being moved.

Note: For type layers, Lock Transparency and Lock Image are selected by default and cannot be deselected.

To apply lock options to selected layers or a group

1 Select multiple layers or a group.

2 Choose Lock Layers or Lock All Layers In Group from the Layers menu or the Layers palette menu.

3 Select lock options, and click OK.

Managing layers

To rename a layer or group

As you add layers to an image, it's helpful to give them names that reflect their content. Descriptive names make layers easy to identify in the palette.

❖ Do one of the following:

• Double-click the layer or group name in the Layers palette, and enter a new name.

• Press Alt (Windows) or Option (Mac OS), and double-click the layer (not its name or thumbnail) in the Layers palette. Enter a new name in the Name text box, and click OK.

• (Photoshop) Select a layer or group, and choose Layer Properties or Group Properties from the Layers menu or the Layers palette menu. Enter a new name in the Name text box, and click OK.

• (ImageReady) Select a layer or set, and choose Layer Options or Layer Set Options from the Layers menu or the Layers palette menu. Enter a new name in the Name text box, and click OK.

To assign a color to a layer or group

Color-coding layers and groups helps you locate related layers in the Layers palette.

1 Do one of the following:

• (Photoshop) Select a layer or group, and choose Layer Properties or Group Properties from the Layers menu or the Layers palette menu.

• (ImageReady) Select a layer or layer set, and choose Layer Options or Layer Set Options from the Layers menu or the Layers palette menu.

• For groups, press Alt (Windows) or Option (Mac OS), and double-click the layer (not its name or thumbnail) in the Layers palette.

2 Choose a color from the Color pop-up menu, and click OK.

To rasterize layers

You cannot use the painting tools or filters on layers that contain vector data (such as type layers, shape layers, vector masks, or Smart Objects) and generated data (such as fill layers). However, you can rasterize these layers to convert their contents into a flat, raster image.

❖ Select the layers you want to rasterize, choose Layer > Rasterize, and then choose an option from the submenu:

Type Rasterizes the type on a type layer. Doesn't rasterize any other vector data on the layer.

Shape Rasterizes a shape layer.

Fill Content Rasterizes the fill of a shape layer, leaving the vector mask.

Vector Mask Rasterizes the vector mask of a shape layer, turning it into a layer mask.

Smart Object Converts a Smart Object to a raster layer.

Layer Rasterizes all vector data on the selected layers.

All Layers Rasterizes all layers that contain vector and generated data.

Note: To rasterize linked layers, select a linked layer, choose Layer > Select Linked Layers, and then rasterize the selected layers.

To delete a layer or group

Deleting layers that you no longer need reduces the size of your image file.

1 Select one or more layers or groups in the Layers palette.

2 Do one of the following:

* To delete with a confirmation message, click the Delete icon. Alternatively, choose Layers > Delete > Layer or Delete Layer or Delete Group from the Layers palette menu.

* To delete the layer or group without confirmation, drag it to the Delete icon or Alt-click (Windows) or Option-click (Mac OS) the Delete icon.

* (Photoshop) To delete hidden layers, choose Layers > Delete > Hidden Layers.

(Photoshop) To delete linked layers, select a linked layer, choose Layer > Select Linked Layers, and then delete the layers.

Exporting layers

In Photoshop, you can export all layers or visible layers to separate files. Choose File > Scripts > Export Layers to Files.

In ImageReady, you can export some or all layers of a document as files. You can export layers as Photoshop (PSD), GIF, JPEG, PNG 8, PNG 24, WBMP, or SWF files. See `To export layers as files in ImageReady' on page 354.

Tracking file size

File size depends on the pixel dimensions of an image and the number of layers it contains. Images with more pixels may produce more detail when printed, but they require more disk space to store and may be slower to edit and print. You should keep track of your file sizes to make sure the files are not becoming too large for your purposes. If the file is becoming too large, reduce the number of layers in the image or change the image size.

You can view file size information for an image at the bottom of the application window. For more information, see `To display file information in the document window' on page 14.

Merging and stamping layers

Merging and stamping layers

When you have finalized the content of layers, you can merge them to reduce the size of your image files. When you merge layers, the data on the top layers replaces the overlapped data on the lower layers. The intersection of all transparent areas in the merged layers remains transparent.

Note: You cannot use an adjustment layer or fill layer as the target layer for a merge.

In addition to merging layers, you can stamp them. Stamping allows you to merge the contents of more than one layer into a target layer while leaving the other layers intact. Typically, the selected layer is stamped down to the layer below it.

Note: When you save a merged document, you cannot revert back to the unmerged state; the layers are permanently merged.

To merge two layers or groups

1 Make sure that the layers and groups you want to merge are visible.

2 Select the layers and groups you want to merge.

3 Choose Layer > Merge Layers.

Note: You can merge two adjacent layers or groups by selecting the top item and then choosing Layer > Merge Down or Merge Group. You can merge linked layers by choosing Layer > Select Linked Layers and then merging the selected layers. (In ImageReady you can choose Layer > Merge Linked.)

To merge layers in a clipping mask

1 Hide any layers that you do not want to merge.

2 Select the base layer in the clipping mask.

3 Choose Merge Clipping Mask from the Layers menu or the Layers palette menu.

To merge all visible layers and groups in an image

❖ Choose Merge Visible from the Layers palette or the Layers palette menu.

To stamp multiple layers or linked layers

When you stamp multiple selected layers or linked layers, Photoshop creates a new layer containing the merged content.

1 Select multiple layers.

2 Press Ctrl+Alt+E (Windows) or Command+Option+E (Mac OS).

To stamp all visible layers

❖ Select the layer or group that will contain the merged contents, and press Shift+Ctrl+Alt+E (Windows) or Shift+Command+Option+E (Mac OS).

Alternatively, you can hold down Alt (Windows) or Option (Mac OS), and choose Layer > Merge Visible. The modified Merge command merges all the visible data into the current target layer.

To flatten all layers

Flattening reduces file size by merging all visible layers into the background and discarding hidden layers. Any transparent areas that remain are filled with white.

Note: Converting an image between some color modes flattens the file. Save a copy of your file with all layers intact if you want to edit the original image after the conversion.

1 Make sure that all the layers you want to keep are visible.

2 Choose Layer > Flatten Image, or choose Flatten Image from the Layers palette menu.

Setting opacity and blending options

To specify opacity for a layer or group

A layer's opacity determines to what degree it obscures or reveals the layer beneath it. A layer with 1% opacity appears nearly transparent, whereas one with 100% opacity appears completely opaque.

Note: You cannot change the opacity of a background layer or a locked layer. You can, however, convert a background layer to a regular layer, which does support transparency. See `To convert a background into a layer' on page 288.

1 Select a layer or group in the Layers palette.

2 Do one of the following:

• In the Layers palette, enter a value in the Opacity text box or drag the Opacity pop-up slider.

• Choose Layer > Layer Style > Blending Options. Enter a value in the Opacity text box or drag the Opacity pop-up slider.

• Select the Move tool and type a number indicating the percentage of opacity.

Note: To view blending options for a text layer, choose Layer > Layer Style > Blending Options, or choose Blending Options from the Add A Layer Style button at the bottom of the Layers palette menu.

To specify fill opacity for a layer

In addition to setting opacity, which affects any layer styles and blending modes applied to the layer, you can specify a fill opacity for layers. Fill opacity affects pixels painted in a layer or shapes drawn on a layer without affecting the opacity of any layer effects that have been applied to the layer.

❖ Do one of the following:

• (Photoshop) In the Layers palette, enter a value in the Fill Opacity text box or drag the Fill Opacity pop-up slider.

• Double-click a layer thumbnail, choose Layer > Layer Style > Blending Options.

Note: To view blending options for a text layer, choose Layer > Layer Style > Blending Options, or choose Blending Options from the Add A Layer Style button at the bottom of the Layers palette. Enter a value in the Fill Opacity text box.

About blending modes

A layer's blending mode determines how its pixels blend with underlying pixels in the image. You can create a variety of special effects using blending modes.

By default, the blending mode of a group is Pass Through, which means that the group has no blending properties of its own. When you choose a different blending mode for a group, you effectively change the order in which the image components are put together. All of the layers in the group are put together first. The composite group is then treated as a single image and blended with the rest of the image using the selected blending mode. Thus, if you choose a blending mode other than Pass Through for the group, none of the adjustment layers or layer blending modes inside the group will apply to layers outside the group.

Note: There is no Clear blending mode for layers. In addition, the Color Dodge, Color Burn, Darken, Lighten, Difference, and Exclusion modes are unavailable for Lab images.

To specify a blending mode for a layer or group

1 Select a layer or group in the Layers palette.

2 Choose a blending mode:

- In the Layers palette, choose an option from the Blend Mode pop-up menu.

- Choose Layer > Layer Style > Blending Options, and then choose an option from the Blend Mode pop-up menu.

Filling new layers with a neutral color

You can't apply certain filters (such as the Lighting Effects filter) to layers with no pixels. Selecting Fill With (Mode)-neutral Color in the New Layer dialog box resolves this problem by first filling the layer with a preset, neutral color. This invisible, neutral color is assigned according to the layer's blending mode. If no effect is applied, filling with a neutral color has no effect on the remaining layers. The Fill With Neutral

Color option is not available for layers that use the Normal, Dissolve, Hue, Saturation, Color, or Luminosity modes.

Specifying knockout options

Knockout options let you specify which layers "punch through" to reveal content from other layers. For example, you can use a text layer to knock out a color adjustment layer and reveal a portion of the image using the original colors.

As you plan your knockout effect, you need to decide which layer will create the shape of the knockout, which layers will be punched through, and which layer will be revealed. If you want to reveal a layer other than the Background, you can place the layers you want to use in a group or clipping mask.

Farm logo with shallow knockout to Field layer

To create a knockout

1 Do one of the following in the Layers palette:

- Position the layer that will create the knockout above the layers that will be punched through, and make the layer you want to reveal the Background. (Choose Layer > New > Background From Layer to convert a regular layer to the background.)

- Place the layers you want to use in a group. The top layer in the group will punch through to the bottom layer in the group or the background. If you want to reveal the background, make sure that the blending mode of the group is set to Pass Through (the default setting).

- Place the layers you want to use in a clipping mask. The top layer in the group will punch through to the bottom layer in the group or the Background. (See `To create a clipping mask' on page 326.) If you want to reveal the bottom layer in the group, make sure that the Blend Clipped Layers As Group option is selected for the bottom layer. (See `Grouping blend effects' on page 302.)

2 Select the top layer (the layer that will create the knockout).

3 Double-click a layer thumbnail (Photoshop), choose Layer > Layer Style > Blending Options, or choose Blending Options from the Layers palette menu.

Note: *To view blending options for a text layer, choose Layer > Layer Style > Blending Options, or choose Blending Options from the Add A Layer Style button at the bottom of the Layers palette menu.*

4 Choose an option from the Knockout pop-up menu:

- Select Shallow to knock out to the first possible stopping point, such as the bottom of the group or clipping mask containing the knockout option.

- Select Deep to knock out to the background. If there is no background, Deep knocks out to transparency.

5 Lower the fill opacity or change the blending mode to create the knockout effect.

6 Click OK.

To exclude channels from blending

You can restrict blending effects to a specified channel when you blend a layer or group. By default, all channels are included. When using an RGB image, for example, you can choose to exclude the red channel from blending; in the composite image, only the information in the green and blue channels is affected.

1 Do one of the following:

- Double-click a layer thumbnail.

- Choose Layer > Layer Style > Blending Options.

- Choose Blending Options from the Add A Layer Style button at the bottom of the Layers palette.

Note: *To view blending options for a text layer, choose Layer > Layer Style > Blending Options, or choose Blending Options from the Add A Layer Style button at the bottom of the Layers palette menu.*

2 In the Advanced Blending area of the Layer Style dialog box, deselect any channels you do not want to include when the layer is blended.

Grouping blend effects

By default, layers in a clipping mask are blended with the underlying layers using the blending mode of the bottommost layer in the group. However, you can choose to have the blending mode of the bottommost layer apply only to that layer, allowing you to preserve the original blending appearance of the clipped layers. (See `To create a clipping mask' on page 326.)

You can also apply the blending mode of a layer to layer effects that modify opaque pixels, such as Inner Glow or Color Overlay, without changing layer effects that modify only transparent pixels, such as Outer Glow or Drop Shadow.

To specify the scope of blending options

1 Select the layer that you want to affect.

2 Do one of the following:

- Double-click a layer thumbnail, choose Blending Options from the Layers palette menu (Photoshop), or choose Layer > Layer Style > Blending Options.

Note: *To view blending options for a text layer, choose Layer > Layer Style > Blending Options, or choose Blending Options from the Add A Layer Style button at the bottom of the Layers palette menu.*

3 Specify the scope of blending options:

- Select Blend Interior Effects As Group to apply the blending mode of the layer to layer effects that modify opaque pixels, such as Inner Glow, Satin, Color Overlay, and Gradient Overlay.

- Select Blend Clipped Layers As Group to apply the blending mode of the base layer to all layers in the clipping mask. Deselecting this option, which is always selected by default, maintains the original blending mode and appearance of each layer in the group.

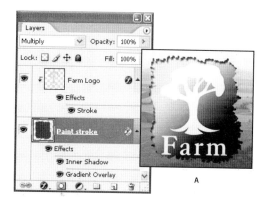

Advanced blending options
A. Farm Logo and Paint Stroke layers each with its own blending mode **B.** *Blend Interior Effects As Group option selected* **C.** *Blend Clipped Layers As Group option selected*

- Select Transparency Shapes Layers to restrict layer effects and knockouts to opaque areas of the layer. Deselecting this option, which is always selected by default, applies these effects throughout the layer.

- Select Layer Mask Hides Effects to restrict layer effects to the area defined by the layer mask.

- Select Vector Mask Hides Effects to restrict layer effects to the area defined by the vector mask.

4 Click OK.

To specify a tonal range for blending layers

The sliders in the Blending Options dialog box control which pixels from the active layer and from the underlying visible layers appear in the final image. For example, you can drop dark pixels out of the active layer or force bright pixels from the underlying layers to show through. You can also define a range of partially blended pixels to produce a smooth transition between blended and unblended areas.

1 Double-click a layer thumbnail, choose Layer > Layer Style > Blending Options, or choose Add A Layer Style > Blending Options from the Layers palette menu.

Note: To view blending options for a text layer, choose Layer > Layer Style > Blending Options, or choose Blending Options from the Add A Layer Style button at the bottom of the Layers palette menu.

2 In the Advanced Blending area of the Layer Style dialog box, choose an option from the Blend If pop-up menu.

- Choose Gray to specify a blending range for all channels.

- Select an individual color channel (for example, red, green, or blue in an RGB image) to specify blending in that channel.

3 Use the This Layer and Underlying Layer sliders to set the brightness range of the blended pixels—measured on a scale from 0 (black) to 255 (white). Drag the white slider to set the high value of the range. Drag the black slider to set the low value of the range.

To define a range of partially blended pixels, hold down Alt (Windows) or Option (Mac OS), and drag one half of a slider triangle. The two values that appear above the divided slider indicate the partial blending range.

Keep the following guidelines in mind when specifying blending ranges:

- Use the This Layer sliders to specify the range of pixels on the active layer that will blend, and therefore appear, in the final image. For example, if you drag the white slider to 235, pixels with brightness values higher than 235 will remain unblended and will be excluded from the final image.

- Use the Underlying Layer sliders to specify the range of pixels in the underlying visible layers that will blend in the final image. Blended pixels are combined with pixels in the active layer to produce composite pixels, whereas unblended pixels show through overlying areas of the active layer. For example, if you drag the black slider to 19, pixels with brightness values lower than 19 will remain unblended and will show through the active layer in the final image.

Layer effects and styles

Layer effects and styles

Photoshop and ImageReady provide a variety of effects—such as shadows, glows, bevels, overlays, and strokes—that let you quickly change the appearance of a layer's contents. Layer effects are linked to the layer contents. When you move or edit the contents of the layer, the effects are modified correspondingly. For example, if you apply a drop shadow effect to a text layer, the shadow changes automatically as you edit the text.

The effects that you apply to a layer become part of the layer's custom *style*. When a layer has a style, an "f" icon  appears to the right of the layer's name in the Layers palette. You can expand the style in the Layers palette to view all the effects that compose the style and edit the effects to change the style.

When you save a custom style, it becomes a preset style. Preset styles appear in the Styles palette and can be applied with a single click. Photoshop and ImageReady provide a variety of preset styles to fill a wide range of uses.

Illustration of a layer with a style

Note: *You cannot apply layer effects and styles to a background, a locked layer, or a group.*

Applying preset styles

You can view and select preset styles from the Styles palette, from the Layer Styles dialog box, or, after you select a pen tool or shape tool, from the Layer Styles

pop-up palette in the options bar. By default, applying a preset style replaces the current layer style. However, you can add the attributes of a second style to those of the current style using a keyboard modifier.

The layer styles that come with Photoshop and ImageReady are grouped into libraries by function. For example, one library contains styles for creating web buttons; another library contains styles adding effects to text.

To display the Styles palette, choose Window > Styles.

To apply a preset style to a layer

❖ Do one of the following:

* Click a style in the Styles palette to apply it to the currently selected layers.

* Drag a style from the Styles palette onto a layer in the Layers palette.

* Drag a style from the Styles palette to the document window, and release the mouse button when the pointer is over the layer content to which you want to apply the style.

Note: *Hold down Shift as you click or drag to add (rather than replace) the style to any existing effects on the destination layer.*

* Choose Layer > Layer Style > Blending Options, and click the word *Styles* in the Layer Styles dialog box (top item in the list on the left side of the dialog box). Click the style you want to apply, and click OK.

* When using a shape tool or pen tool in shape layers mode, select a style from the pop-up palette in the options bar before drawing the shape.

To apply a style from another layer

❖ In the Layers palette, Alt-drag (Windows) or Option-drag (Mac OS) the style from a layer's effect list to another layer.

To change how preset styles are displayed

1 Click the triangle in the Styles palette, Layer Styles dialog box, or Layer Styles pop-up palette in the options bar (Photoshop).

2 Choose a display option from the palette menu:

- (Photoshop) Text Only to view the layer styles as a list.

- Small Thumbnail or Large Thumbnail to view the layer styles as thumbnails.

- Small List or (Photoshop) Large List to view the layer styles as a list, with a thumbnail of the selected layer style displayed.

Custom styles

You can create custom styles using one or more of the following effects:

Drop Shadow Adds a shadow that falls behind the contents on the layer.

Inner Shadow Adds a shadow that falls just inside the edges of the layer's content, giving the layer a recessed appearance.

Outer Glow and Inner Glow Add glows that emanate from the outside or inside edges of the layer's content.

Bevel and Emboss Add various combinations of highlights and shadows to a layer.

Satin Applies interior shading that creates a satiny finish.

Color, Gradient, and Pattern Overlay Fill the layer's content with a color, gradient, or pattern.

Stroke Outlines the object on the current layer using color, a gradient, or a pattern. It is particularly useful on hard-edged shapes such as type.

To apply a custom style to a layer

1 Select a single layer in the Layers palette.

2 Do one of the following:

- Click the Layer Styles button 🎯 at the bottom of the Layers palette and choose an effect from the list.

- Choose an effect from the Layer > Layer Style submenu.

3 Set effect options in the Layer Style dialog box. See 'Layer style options' on page 307.

4 Add other effects to the style, if desired. In the Layer Style dialog box, click the check box to the left of the effect name to add the effect without selecting it.

To hide or show all layer styles in an image

When a layer has a style, an "f" icon 🎯 appears to the right of the layer's name in the Layers palette.

❖ Choose Layer > Layer Style > Hide All Layer Effects or Show All Layer Effects.

To expand or collapse layer styles in the Layers palette

❖ Do one of the following:

- Click the triangle next to the layer styles icon 🎯 to expand the list of layer effects applied to that layer.

- Click the triangle to collapse the layer effects.

- To expand or collapse all of the layer styles applied within a group, hold down Alt (Windows) or Option (Mac OS) and click the triangle or inverted triangle for the group. The layer styles applied to all layers within the group expand or collapse correspondingly.

To edit a layer style

1 Do one of the following:

- In the Layers palette, double-click an effect displayed below the layer name. (Click the triangle next to the "f" icon 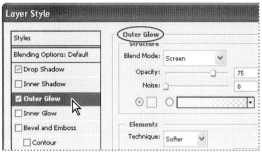 to display the effects contained in the style.)

- Choose Layer > Layer Style and the effect you want to edit.

2 Set one or more options in the Layer Style dialog box. See `Layer style options' on page 307.

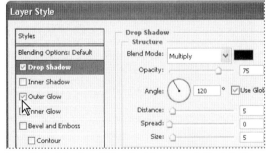

Layer Style dialog box. Click a check box to apply the default settings without displaying the effect's options.

Click an effect name to display the effect's options.

You can edit multiple effects without closing the Layer Style dialog box. Select an effect on the left side of the dialog box to display an effect's options.

Layer style options

Angle Determines the lighting angle at which the effect is applied to the layer. In Photoshop, you can drag in the document window to adjust the angle of a Drop Shadow, Inner Shadow, or Satin effect.

Anti-alias Blends the edge pixels of a contour or gloss contour. This option is most useful on shadows with a small size and complicated contour.

Blend Mode Determines how the layer style blends with the underlying layers, which may or may not include the active layer. For example, an inner shadow blends with the active layer because the effect is drawn on top of that layer, but a drop shadow blends only with the layers beneath the active layer. In most cases, the default mode for each effect produces the best results. See List of blending modes in Photoshop Help.

Choke Shrinks the boundaries of the matte of an Inner Shadow or Inner Glow prior to blurring.

Color Specifies the color of a shadow, glow, or highlight. You can click the color box and choose a color.

Contour With solid-color glows, Contour allows you to create rings of transparency. With gradient-filled glows, Contour allows you to create variations in the repetition of the gradient color and opacity. In beveling and embossing, Contour allows you to sculpt the ridges, valleys, and bumps that are shaded in the embossing process. With shadows, Contour allows you to specify the fade. For more information, see `Modifying layer effects with contours' on page 309.

Distance Specifies the offset distance for a shadow or satin effect. In Photoshop, you can drag in the document window to adjust the offset distance.

Depth Specifies the depth of a bevel. It also specifies the depth of a pattern.

Global Angle Turns on global lighting for the effect. Global lighting applies the same angle to all effects for which the Global Angle option is selected, giving the appearance of a single light source shining on the image. Deselect Global Angle to assign a local angle to Drop Shadow, Inner Shadow, and Bevel effects.

Gloss Contour Creates a glossy, metallic appearance. Gloss Contour is applied after shading a bevel or emboss.

Gradient Specifies the gradient of a layer effect. In Photoshop, click the gradient to display the Gradient Editor or click the inverted arrow and choose a gradient from the pop-up palette. In Photoshop, you can edit a gradient or create a new gradient using the Gradient Editor. In ImageReady, click the inverted arrow next to the gradient sample and select a gradient from the list, or choose a gradient type from the

pop-up list. You can edit the color or opacity in the Gradient Overlay panel the same way you edit them in the Gradient Editor. For some effects, you can specify additional gradient options. Reverse flips the orientation of the gradient, Align With Layer uses the bounding box of the layer to calculate the gradient fill, and Scale scales the application of the gradient. You can also move the center of the gradient by clicking and dragging in the image window. Style specifies the shape of the gradient.

Highlight or Shadow Mode Specifies the blending mode of a bevel or emboss highlight or shadow.

Jitter Varies the application of a gradient's color and opacity.

Layer Knocks Out Drop Shadow Controls the drop shadow's visibility in a semitransparent layer.

Noise Specifies the number of random elements in the opacity of a glow or shadow. Enter a value or drag the slider.

Opacity Sets the opacity of the layer effect. Enter a value or drag the slider.

Pattern Specifies the pattern of a layer effect. In ImageReady, click the inverted arrow next to the pattern sample and choose a pattern from the list. In Photoshop, click the pop-up palette and choose a pattern. Click the New preset button ▣ to create a new preset pattern based on the current settings. Click Snap To Origin to make the origin of the pattern the same as the origin of the document (when Link With Layer is selected), or to place the origin at the upper left corner of the layer (if Link With Layer is deselected). Select Link With Layer if you want the pattern to move along with the layer as the layer moves. Drag the Scale slider or enter a value to specify the size of the pattern. Drag a pattern to position it in the layer; reset the position by using the Snap To Origin button. The Pattern option is not available if no patterns are loaded.

Position Specifies the position of a stroke effect as Outside, Inside, or Center.

Range Controls which portion or range of the glow is targeted for the contour.

Size Specifies the amount of blur or the size of the shadow.

Soften Blurs the results of shading to reduce unwanted artifacts.

Source Specifies the source for an inner glow. Choose Center to apply a glow that emanates from the center of the layer's content, or Edge to apply a glow that emanates from the inside edges of the layer's content.

Spread Expands the boundaries of the matte prior to blurring.

Style Specifies the style of a bevel: Inner Bevel creates a bevel on the inside edges of the layer contents, Outer Bevel creates a bevel on the outside edges of the layer contents, Emboss simulates the effect of embossing the layer contents against the underlying layers, Pillow Emboss simulates the effect of stamping the edges of the layer contents into the underlying layers, and Stroke Emboss confines embossing to the boundaries of a stroke effect applied to the layer. (The Stroke Emboss effect is not visible if no stroke is applied to the layer.)

Technique Applies a technique. For bevel and emboss, Smooth blurs the edges of a matte slightly and is useful for all types of mattes, whether their edges are soft or hard. It does not preserve detailed features at larger sizes. Chisel Hard uses a distance measurement technique and is primarily useful on hard-edged mattes from anti-aliased shapes such as type. It preserves detailed features better than the Smooth technique. Chisel Soft uses a modified distance measurement technique and, although not as accurate as Chisel Hard, is more useful on a larger range of mattes. It preserves features better than the Smooth technique. For glows, Softer applies a blur and is useful on all types of mattes, whether their edges are soft or hard. At larger sizes, Softer does not preserve detailed features. Precise uses a distance measurement technique to create a glow and is primarily useful on hard-edged mattes from anti-aliased shapes such as type. It preserves features better than the Softer technique.

Texture Applies a texture. Use Scale to scale the size of the texture. Select Link With Layer if you want the texture to move along with the layer as the layer moves. Invert inverts the texture. Depth varies the degree and direction (up/down) to which the texturing is applied. Snap To Origin makes the origin of the pattern the same as the origin of the document (if Link With Layer is deselected) or places the origin at the upper left corner of the layer (if Link With Layer is selected). Drag the texture to position it in the layer.

Modifying layer effects with contours

When you create custom layer styles, you can use contours to control the shape of Drop Shadow, Inner Shadow, Inner Glow, Outer Glow, Bevel and Emboss, and Satin effects over a given range. For example, a Linear contour on a Drop Shadow causes the opacity to drop off in a linear transition. Use a Custom contour to create a unique shadow transition. Custom contours created in Photoshop can be used in ImageReady.

You can select, reset, delete, or change the preview of contours in the Contour pop-up palette and Preset Manager.

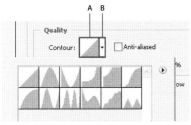

Detail of Layer Style dialog box for Drop Shadow effect
***A.** Click to display the Contour Editor dialog box.* ***B.** Click to display the pop-up palette.*

To create a custom contour

1 Select the Drop Shadow, Inner Shadow, Inner Glow, Outer Glow, Bevel and Emboss, Contour, or Satin effect in the Layer Style dialog box.

2 Click the contour thumbnail in the Layer Style dialog box.

3 Click the contour to add points, and drag to adjust the contour. Or enter values for Input and Output.

4 To create a sharp corner instead of a smooth curve, select a point and click Corner.

5 To save the contour to a file, click Save and name the contour.

6 To store a contour as a preset, choose New.

7 Click OK. New contours are added at the bottom of the pop-up palette.

To load a contour

❖ Click the contour in the Layer Style dialog box, and in the Contour Editor dialog box, choose Load. Go to the folder containing the contour library you want to load and click Open.

To delete a contour

❖ Click the inverted arrow next to the currently selected contour to view the pop-up palette. Press Alt (Windows) or Option (Mac OS), and click the contour you want to delete.

To set a global lighting angle

Using global light gives the appearance of a common light source shining on the image.

❖ To set a global lighting angle for all layers, do one of the following:

• Choose Layer > Layer Style > Global Light. In the Global Light dialog box, enter a value or drag the angle radius to set the angle and altitude, and click OK.

• In the Layer Style dialog box for Drop Shadow, Inner Shadow, or Bevel, select Use Global Light. For Angle, enter a value or drag the slider, and click OK.

The new lighting angle appears as the default for each layer effect that uses the global lighting angle.

To create a new preset style

1 In the Layers palette, select the layer containing the style that you want to save as a preset.

2 Do one of the following:

- Drag the selected layer into the Styles palette or onto the New Item button 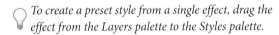 in the Styles palette.

- Click an empty area of the Styles palette.

- Press Alt (Windows) or Option (Mac OS), and click the New Item button at the bottom of the Styles palette.

- Choose New Style from the Styles palette menu.

- Choose Layer > Layer Style > Blending Options, and click New Style in the Layer Style dialog box.

3 Enter a name for the preset style, set style options, and click OK.

To create a preset style from a single effect, drag the effect from the Layers palette to the Styles palette.

To rename a preset style

❖ Do one of the following:

- Double-click a style in the Styles palette. If the Styles palette is set to display styles as thumbnails, enter a new name in the dialog box, and click OK. Otherwise, type a new name directly in the Styles palette, and press Enter (Windows) or Return (Mac OS).

- Select a style in the Styles area of the Layer Styles dialog box. Then choose Rename Style from the pop-up menu, enter a new name, and click OK.

- (Photoshop) When using a shape or pen tool, select a style from the Layer Style pop-up palette in the options bar. Then choose Rename Style from the pop-up palette menu.

To delete a preset style

❖ Do one of the following:

- Drag a style to the Delete icon 🗑 at the bottom of the Styles palette.

- Press Alt (Windows) or Option (Mac OS) and click the layer style in the Styles palette.

- (Photoshop) Select a style in the Styles area of the Layer Styles dialog box. (See `Applying preset styles' on page 305.) Then choose Delete Style from the pop-up menu.

- (Photoshop) When using a shape or pen tool, select a style from the Layer Style pop-up palette in the options bar. Then choose Delete Style from the pop-up palette menu.

To save a set of preset styles as a library

1 Do one of the following:

- Choose Save Styles from the Styles palette menu.

- Select Styles on the left side of the Layer Styles dialog box. Then choose Save Styles from the pop-up menu.

- (Photoshop) When using a shape or pen tool, click the layer style thumbnail in the options bar. Then choose Save Styles from the pop-up palette menu.

2 Choose a location for the style library, enter a file name, and click Save.

You can save the library anywhere. However, if you place the library file in the Presets/Styles folder inside the Photoshop program folder, the library name will appear at the bottom of the Styles palette menu when you restart the application.

Note: You can also use the Preset Manager to rename, delete, and save libraries of preset styles.

To load a library of preset styles

1 Click the triangle in the Styles palette, Layer Style dialog box (Photoshop), or Layer Style pop-up palette in the options bar.

2 Do one of the following:

- Choose Load Styles (Photoshop) or Append Styles (ImageReady) to add a library to the current list. Then select the library file you want to use, and click Load.

- Choose Replace Styles to replace the current list with a different library. Then select the library file you want to use, and click Load.

- Choose a library file (displayed at the bottom of the palette menu). Then click OK to replace the current list, or click Append to append the current list.

3 To return to the default library of preset styles, choose Reset Styles. You can either replace the current list or append the default library to the current list.

Note: You can also use the Preset Manager to load and reset style libraries. See `About the Preset Manager' on page 42.

To copy layer styles between layers

Copying and pasting styles is an easy way to apply the same effects to multiple layers.

1 In the Layers palette, select the layer containing the style you want to copy.

2 Choose Layer > Layer Style > Copy Layer Style.

3 Select the destination layer in the palette, and choose Layer > Layer Style > Paste Layer Style.

The pasted layer style replaces the existing layer style on the destination layer or layers.

To copy layer styles between layers by dragging

❖ Do one of the following:

- In the Layers palette, Alt-drag (Windows) or Option-drag (Mac OS) a single layer effect from one layer to another to duplicate the layer effect, or drag the Effects bar from one layer to another to duplicate the layer style.

- Drag one or more layer effects from the Layers palette to the image to apply the resulting layer style to the highest layer in the Layers palette that contains pixels at the drop point.

To scale a layer effect

A layer style may have been fine-tuned for a target resolution and features of a given size. Using Scale Effects allows you to scale the effects in the layer style without scaling the object to which the layer style is applied.

1 Select the layer in the Layers palette.

2 Choose Layer > Layer Style > Scale Effects.

3 Enter a percentage or drag the slider.

4 Select Preview to preview the changes in the image.

5 Click OK.

To remove an effect from a style

1 In the Layers palette, expand the layer style to see its effects.

2 Do one of the following:

• Drag the effect to the Delete icon.

• (ImageReady) Select the effect, and choose Delete Effect from the Layers palette menu.

To remove a style from a layer

1 In the Layers palette, select the layer containing the style you want to remove.

2 Do one of the following:

• In the Layers palette, drag the Effects bar to the Delete icon.

• Choose Layer > Layer Style > Clear Layer Style.

• Select the layer, and then click the Clear Style button 🚫 at the bottom of the Styles palette.

• (ImageReady) Select an effect in the Layers palette, and choose Delete All Effects from the Layers palette menu.

To convert a layer style to image layers

To customize or fine-tune the appearance of layer styles, you can convert the layer styles to regular image layers. After you convert a layer style to image layers, you can enhance the result by painting or applying commands and filters. However, you can no longer edit the layer style on the original layer, and the layer style no longer updates as you change the original image layer.

Note: The layers produced by this process may not result in artwork that exactly matches the version using layer styles. In Photoshop, you may see an alert when you create the new layers.

1 In the Layers palette, select the layer containing the layer style that you want to convert.

2 Choose Layer > Layer Style > Create Layers.

You can now modify and restack the new layers in the same way as regular layers. Some effects—for example, Inner Glow—convert to layers within a clipping mask.

You can also drag a layer style to the New Layer button at the bottom of the Layers palette to generate a new layer from an existing style.

Adjustment and fill layers

Adjustment layers and fill layers

An adjustment layer applies color and tonal adjustments to your image without permanently changing pixel values. For example, rather than making a Levels or Curves adjustment directly on your image, you can create a Levels or Curves adjustment layer. The color and tone adjustments are stored in the adjustment layer and apply to all the layers below it.

Fill layers let you fill a layer with a solid color, a gradient, or a pattern. Unlike adjustment layers, fill layers do not affect the layers underneath them.

Adjustment layers provide the following advantages:

• Nondestructive edits. You can try different settings and re-edit the adjustment layer at any time. You can also reduce the effect of the adjustment by lowering the opacity of the adjustment layer.

- Reduced loss of image data through combined multiple adjustments. Each time you adjust pixel values directly, you lose some image data. You can use multiple adjustment layers and make small adjustments. Photoshop combines all the adjustments before it applies them to the image.

- Selective editing. Paint on the adjustment layer's image mask to apply an adjustment to part of an image. Later you can control which parts of the image are adjusted by re-editing the layer mask. You can vary the adjustment by painting on the mask with different tones of gray.

- Ability to apply adjustments to multiple images. Copy and paste adjustment layers between images to apply the same color and tone adjustments.

Adjustment layers increase the image's file size, though no more than other layers. If you are working with many layers, you may want to reduce file size by merging the adjustment layers into the pixel content layers. Adjustment layers have many of the same characteristics as other layers. You can adjust their opacity and blending mode, and you can group them to apply the adjustment to specific layers. You can turn their visibility on and off to apply their effect or to preview the effect.

Original (left); adjustment layer applied to barn only (center), which brings out detail in the barn; and adjustment layer applied to entire image (right), which lightens the entire image and pixelates the clouds

Keep in mind that an adjustment layer affects all the layers below it. This means that you can correct multiple layers by making a single adjustment, rather than adjusting each layer separately.

Note: *You can apply and edit adjustment layers only in Photoshop; however, you can view them in ImageReady.*

Creating adjustment layers or fill layers

Adjustment layers and fill layers have the same opacity and blending mode options as image layers. You can rearrange, delete, hide, and duplicate them just as you do image layers. By default, adjustment layers and fill layers have layer masks, as indicated by the mask icon to the left of the layer thumbnail. If a path is active when you create the adjustment or fill layer, a vector mask is created instead of a layer mask.

To confine the effects of an adjustment layer to a group of layers, create a clipping mask consisting of those layers. You can place the adjustment layers in or at the base of the clipping mask. The resulting adjustment is confined to the layers inside the group. (Alternatively, you can create a layer set that uses any blending mode other than Pass Through.)

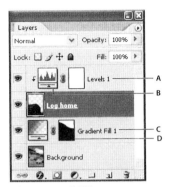

Adjustment and fill layers
A. *Adjustment layer confined to Log Home layer only* **B.** *Layer thumbnail* **C.** *Fill layer* **D.** *Layer mask*

To create an adjustment layer or fill layer

❖ Do one of the following:

- Click the New Adjustment Layer button ⬤ at the bottom of the Layers palette, and choose a layer type.

- Choose Layer > New Fill Layer, and choose an option from the submenu. Then name the layer, set other layer options, and click OK.

- Choose Layer > New Adjustment Layer, and choose an option from the submenu. Then name the layer, set other layer options, and click OK.

Note: *To confine the effects of the adjustment layer or fill layer to a selected area, make a selection, create a closed path and select it, or select an existing closed path. When you use a selection, you create an adjustment layer or fill layer confined by a layer mask. When you use a path, you create an adjustment layer or fill layer confined by a vector mask.*

Adjustment and fill layer types

For complete information on options for each adjustment layer type, search for that adjustment in Photoshop Help.

Solid Color Specify a color.

Gradient Click the gradient to display the Gradient Editor, or click the inverted arrow and choose a gradient from the pop-up palette. Set additional options if desired. Style specifies the shape of the gradient. Angle specifies the angle at which the gradient is applied. Scale changes the size of the gradient. Reverse flips the orientation of the gradient. Dither reduces banding by applying dithering to the gradient. Align With Layer uses the bounding box of the layer to calculate the gradient fill. You can drag in the image window to move the center of the gradient.

Pattern Click the pattern, and choose a pattern from the pop-up palette. Click Scale, and enter a value or drag the slider to scale the pattern. Click Snap To Origin to make the origin of the pattern the same as the origin of the document. Select Link With Layer if you want the pattern to move along with the layer as the layer moves. When Link With Layer is selected, you can drag in the image to position the pattern while the Pattern Fill dialog box is open.

Levels Specify values for the highlights, shadows, and midtones.

Curves Adjust the intensity values of pixels along a 0–255 scale while keeping up to 15 other values constant.

Color Balance Drag a slider toward a color that you want to increase in the image; drag a slider away from a color that you want to decrease.

Brightness/Contrast Specify values for Brightness and Contrast.

Hue/Saturation Choose which colors to edit, and specify values for Hue, Saturation, and Lightness.

Selective Color Choose the color you want to adjust, and drag the sliders to increase or decrease the components in the selected color.

Channel Mixer Modify the color values in a channel by mixing them with other channels.

Gradient Map Choose a gradient and set gradient options.

Photo Filter Make color adjustments by simulating the effect of a filter in front of a camera lens.

Invert Inverted adjustment layers don't have options.

Threshold Specify a threshold level.

Posterize Specify the number of tonal levels for each color channel.

To edit an adjustment or fill layer

You can edit an adjustment or fill layer's settings, or replace it with a different adjustment or fill type.

You can also edit the mask of an adjustment layer or fill layer to control the effect that the layer has on the image. By default, all areas of an adjustment or fill layer are "unmasked" and are therefore visible. (See `Masking layers' on page 321.)

1 Do one of the following:

• Double-click the adjustment or fill layer's thumbnail in the Layers palette.

• Choose Layer > Layer Content Options.

2 Make the desired adjustments, and click OK.

Note: Inverted adjustment layers do not have editable settings.

To change the type of adjustment or fill layer

1 Select the adjustment layer or fill layer that you want to change.

2 Choose Layer > Change Layer Content and select a different fill or adjustment layer from the list.

Merging adjustment layers or fill layers

You can merge an adjustment or fill layer several ways: with the layer below it, with the layers in its own grouped layer, with the layers it is linked to, and with all other visible layers. You cannot, however, use an adjustment layer or fill layer as the target layer for a merge. When you merge an adjustment layer or fill layer with the layer below it, the adjustments are rasterized and become permanently applied within the merged layer. You can also rasterize a fill layer without merging it. (See `To rasterize layers' on page 297.)

Adjustment layers and fill layers whose masks contain only white values do not add significantly to the file size, so it is not necessary to merge these adjustment layers to conserve file space.

Smart Objects

Smart Objects

A Smart Object is a container in which you can embed raster or vector image data, for instance, from another Photoshop or Adobe Illustrator file. The embedded data retains all its original characteristics and remains fully editable. You can create a Smart Object in Photoshop by converting one or more layers. In addition, you can paste or place the data in Photoshop from Illustrator. Smart Objects give you the flexibility to scale, rotate, and warp layers nondestructively in Photoshop.

Once a Smart Object stores source data inside a Photoshop document, you can then work on a composite of that data in the image. When you want to modify the document (for example, scale it), Photoshop re-renders the composite data based on the source data.

A Smart Object is really one file embedded in another. When you create one Smart Object from one or more selected layers, you are really creating a new (child) file that is embedded in the original (parent) document.

Smart Objects are useful because they allow you to do the following:

- Perform nondestructive transforms. For instance, you can scale a layer as much as you want without losing original image data.

- Preserve data that Photoshop doesn't handle natively, such as complex vector artwork from Illustrator. Photoshop automatically transforms the file into something that it recognizes.

- Edit one layer to update multiple instances of the Smart Object.

You can apply transforms (however, some options are unavailable; for example Perspective and Distort), layer styles, opacity, blend modes, and warps to Smart Objects. After you make a change, the layer is updated with the edited content.

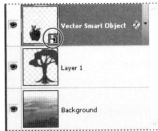

A regular layer and a Smart Object in the Layers palette. The icon in the lower right corner of the thumbnail indicates a Smart Object.

To create and work with Smart Objects

Smart Objects are created through different methods.

❖ Do any of the following:

- Use the Place command to import artwork into the Photoshop document.

- Convert one or more layers into one Smart Object layer. Select one or more layers and choose Layer > Smart Objects > Group Into New Smart Object. The layers are bundled into one layer titled Smart Object.

- Duplicate an existing Smart Object to create two versions that refer to the same source contents. The Smart Objects can be linked so that when you edit one version, the second is updated as well. Or, the Smart Objects can be unlinked so that your edits to one Smart Object do not affect the other. (See `To create a new Smart Object from an existing Smart Object' on page 319.)

- Drag selected PDF or Adobe Illustrator layers or objects into your Photoshop document.

- Copy and paste art from Adobe Illustrator into your Photoshop document. For the greatest flexibility when pasting from Illustrator, make sure that both

PDF and AICB (No Transparency Support) are enabled in the File Handling & Clipboard preferences of Adobe Illustrator.

Note: To find out whether you are looking at a Smart Object thumbnail or a layer thumbnail in the Layers palette, position the cursor over the thumbnail to see the tool tip. You can also look for a small Smart Object icon 🔳 *in the lower right corner of the thumbnail.*

To edit the source contents of a Smart Object

Smart Objects let you edit their source contents. When making edits, the source content file is opened in either Photoshop (if the content is raster data or a camera raw file) or Adobe Illustrator (if the content is vector PDF or EPS data).

Editing Smart Objects in Photoshop works much as it does with Smart Objects in GoLive, and Symbols and Envelopes in Illustrator. When the source content file is updated and saved, the edits appear in all instances of the Smart Object in the Photoshop document.

1 Select the Smart Object from the Layers palette, and do one of the following:

• Choose Layer > Smart Objects > Edit Contents.

• Double-click the Smart Objects thumbnail in the Layers palette.

A dialog box opens, reminding you to save any changes you make to the source content file.

2 Click OK to close the dialog box.

The Smart Object opens with all its associated layers.

3 Make your edits to source content (child) file.

4 Choose File > Save to commit the changes. You can also close the source content file.

5 Return to the main (parent) Photoshop document containing the Smart Object. All instances of the Smart Object have been updated.

To export the contents of a Smart Object

You can export the contents of a Smart Object fully intact to any drive or directory to which you have access permissions.

1 Select the Smart Object from the Layers palette, and choose Layer > Smart Objects > Export Contents. The Save dialog box appears.

2 Navigate to where you want the Smart Object exported and click Save. The Smart Object is saved in PSB format (for raster data) or PDF (for vector data).

To replace the contents of a Smart Object

Using the Replace Contents command lets you update one or multiple instances of a Smart Object at the same time.

1 Select the Smart Object, and choose Layer > Smart Objects > Replace Contents.

2 Navigate to the file you want to use and click Place.

3 Click OK. The new content is placed in the Smart Object. Linked Smart Objects are also updated.

To convert a Smart Object back to a layer

Converting a Smart Object to a regular layer rasterizes the content at the current size.

❖ Select the Smart Object, and choose Layer > Smart Objects > Convert To Layer or Layer > Rasterize > Smart Object.

The Smart Object is converted to a layer again, and the Smart Object thumbnail disappears. If you want to re-create the Smart Object, reselect the layers and start from scratch. However, the new Smart Object won't have the transforms you applied to the original one.

To create a new Smart Object from an existing Smart Object

You can copy a Smart Object along with its full contents. The new instance of the Smart Object can be linked or unlinked to the original, depending on how you create the duplicate.

❖ In the Layers palette, select a Smart Object layer, and do one of the following:

• To create a duplicate Smart Object that is linked to the original, choose Layer > New > Layer Via Copy. You can also drag the Smart Object layer to the Create A New Layer icon at the bottom of the Layers palette. Any edits you make to the copy affect the original Smart Object and vice versa.

• To create a duplicate Smart Object that is not linked to the original, choose Layer > Smart Objects > New Smart Object Via Copy. Any edits you make to the copy do not affect the original Smart Object and vice versa.

A new Smart Object appears on the Layers palette with the same name as the original and "copy" as a suffix. You can rename it.

Layer comps

About layer comps and the Layer Comps palette

Designers often create multiple compositions or *comps* of a page layout to show clients. Using layer comps, you can create, manage, and view multiple versions of a layout in a single Photoshop or ImageReady file. Layer comps are fully inter-changeable between Photoshop and ImageReady if the image color mode is RGB.

A layer comp is a snapshot of a state of the Layers palette. Layer comps record three types of layer options:

• Layer visibility—whether a layer is showing or hidden.

• Layer position in the document.

• Layer appearance—whether a layer style is applied to the layer and the layer's blending mode.

You create a comp by making changes to the layers in your document and *updating* the comp in the Layer Comps palette. You view comps by *applying* them in the document. You can export layer comps to separate files, to a single PDF, or to a web photo gallery.

Choose Window > Layer Comps to show the palette.

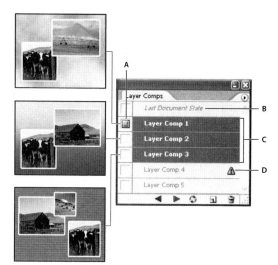

Layer Comps palette
A. Apply Layer Comp icon **B.** *Last Document State* **C.** *Selected comps* **D.** *Layer Comp Cannot Be Fully Restored icon*

To create a layer comp

1 Choose Window > Layer Comps to display the Layer Comp palette. Click the Create New Layer Comp button at the bottom of the Layer Comps palette. The new comp reflects the current state of layers in the Layers palette.

2 In the New Layer Comp dialog box, name the comp, add descriptive comments, and choose options to apply to layers: Visibility, Position, and Appearance.

3 Click OK. Any new comp preserves the options you chose for the previous one, so you don't have to make these choices again if you want the comps to be identical.

💡 *To duplicate a comp, select a comp in the Layer Comps palette and drag the comp to the New Comps button.*

To apply and view layer comps

1 Do any of the following:

• To view a layer comp, you first need to apply it in the document. In the Layer Comp palette, click the Apply Layer Comp icon 🔲 next to a selected comp.

• To cycle through a view of all the layer comps, use the Previous ◀ and Next ▶ buttons at the bottom of the palette.

• To cycle through a view of specific selected comps, select the comps in the Layer Comps palette and then click the Next and Previous buttons at the bottom of the palette. This cycles through only the comps you selected.

• To restore the document to its state before you chose a layer comp, click the Apply Layer Comp icon 🔲 next to Last Document State at the top of the Layer Comp palette.

To change and update a layer comp

If you change the configuration of a layer comp, you need to update it.

1 Select the layer comp in the Layer Comps palette.

2 Make changes to the layer's visibility, position, or style. You may need to change the layer comp's options to record these changes.

3 To change your comp options, select Layer Comp Options from the palette menu and select additional options to record layer position and style.

4 Click the Update Layer Comp button 🔄 at the bottom of the palette.

To clear layer comp warnings

Certain actions create a state where the layer comp can no longer be fully restored. This happens when you delete a layer, merge a layer, convert a layer to a background, or convert a color mode. In such instances, a caution icon ⚠ appears next to the layer comp name.

❖ Do one of the following:

• Ignore the warning, which may result in the loss of one or more layers. Other saved parameters may be preserved.

• Update the comp, which results in the loss of the previously captured parameters but brings the comp up to date.

• Click the caution icon to see the message explaining that the layer comp can't be restored properly. Choose Clear to remove the alert icon and leave the remaining layers unchanged.

• Right-click (Windows) or Control-click (Mac OS) the caution icon to see the pop-up menu that lets you choose either the Clear Layer Comp Warning or the Clear All Layer Comp Warnings command.

To delete a layer comp

❖ Do one of the following:

• Select the layer comp in the Layer Comps palette and click the Delete icon in the palette, or choose Delete Layer Comp from the palette menu.

• Drag it to the Delete icon in the palette.

To export layer comps

You can export layer comps to individual files, to a PDF file containing multiple layer comps, and to a web photo gallery of layer comps.

❖ Choose File > Scripts and then choose one of the following commands:

Layer Comps To Files Exports all layer comps to individual files, one for each comp.

Layer Comps To PDF Exports all layer comps to a PDF file.

Layer Comps To WPG Exports all layer comps to a web photo gallery.

Masking layers

Masking layers

You can use masks to show or hide portions of a layer or protect areas from edits. You can create two types of masks:

• Layer masks are resolution-dependent bitmap images that are created with the painting or selection tools.

• (Photoshop) Vector masks are resolution independent and are created with a pen or shape tool.

In the Layers palette, both the layer and vector masks appear as an additional thumbnail to the right of the layer thumbnail. For the layer mask, this thumbnail represents the grayscale channel that is created when you add the layer mask. The vector mask thumbnail represents a path that clips out the contents of the layer.

Masking layer
A. *Layer mask thumbnail* **B.** *Vector mask thumbnail* **C.** *Vector Mask Link icon* **D.** *New Layer Mask*

You can edit a layer mask to add or subtract from the masked region. A layer mask is a grayscale image, so areas you paint in black are hidden, areas you paint in white are visible, and areas you paint in shades of gray appear in various levels of transparency.

Background painted with black, description card painted with gray, basket painted with white

If you are using a layer mask to hide portions of a layer, you can apply the mask to discard the hidden portions.

A vector mask creates a sharp-edged shape on a layer and is useful anytime you want to add a design element with clean, defined edges. After you create a layer with a vector mask, you can apply one or more layer styles to it, edit them if needed, and instantly have a usable button, panel, or other web-design element.

To add a mask that shows or hides the entire layer

1 Choose Select > Deselect to clear any selection borders in the image.

2 In the Layers palette, select the layer or group.

3 Do one of the following:

- To create a mask that reveals the entire layer, click the New Layer Mask button in the Layers palette, or choose Layer > Layer Mask > Reveal All.

- To create a mask that hides the entire layer, Alt-click (Windows) or Option-click (Mac OS) the New Layer Mask button, or choose Layer > Layer Mask > Hide All.

To add a layer mask that shows or hides part of a layer

1 In the Layers palette, select the layer or group.

2 Select the area in the image, and do one of the following:

- Click the New Layer Mask button in the Layers palette to create a mask that reveals the selection.

- Choose Layer > Layer Mask > Reveal Selection or Hide Selection.

To apply a layer mask from another layer

❖ Do one of the following:

- To move the mask to another layer, drag the mask to the other layer.

- To duplicate the mask, Alt-drag (Windows) or Option-drag (Mac OS) the mask to other layer.

To edit a layer mask

1 Click the layer mask thumbnail in the Layers palette to make it active. A border appears around the mask thumbnail.

2 Select any of the editing or painting tools.

Note: The foreground and background colors assume default grayscale values when the mask is active.

3 Do one of the following:

- To subtract from the mask and reveal the layer, paint the mask with white.

- To make the layer partially visible, paint the mask with gray.

- To add to the mask and hide the layer or group, paint the mask with black.

To edit the layer instead of the layer mask, select it by clicking its thumbnail in the Layers palette. A border appears around the layer thumbnail.

To paste a copied selection into a layer mask, Alt-click (Windows) or Option-click (Mac OS) the layer mask thumbnail in the Layers palette to select and display the mask channel. Choose Edit > Paste, drag the selection in the image to produce the desired masking effect, and choose Select > Deselect. Click the layer thumbnail in the Layers palette to deselect the mask channel.

To select and display the layer mask channel

❖ Do one of the following:

- Alt-click (Windows) or Option-click (Mac OS) the layer mask thumbnail to view only the grayscale mask. To redisplay the layers, Alt-click or Option-click the layer mask thumbnail, or click an eye icon.

- Hold down Alt+Shift (Windows) or Option+Shift (Mac OS), and click the layer mask thumbnail to view the mask on top of the layer in a rubylith masking color. Hold down Alt+Shift or Option+Shift, and click the thumbnail again to turn off the color display.

To disable or enable a layer mask

❖ Do one of the following:

- Shift-click the layer mask thumbnail in the Layers palette.

- Select the layer containing the layer mask you want to disable or enable, and choose Layer > Layer Mask > Disable or Layer > Layer Mask > Enable.

A red X appears over the mask thumbnail in the Layers palette when the mask is disabled, and the layer's content appears without masking effects.

To change the rubylith display for a layer mask

1 Do one of the following:

- Alt-click (Windows) or Option-click (Mac OS) the layer mask thumbnail to select the layer mask channel; then double-click the layer mask thumbnail.

- Double-click the layer mask channel in the Channels palette.

2 To choose a new mask color, in the Layer Mask Display Options dialog box, click the color swatch and choose a new color.

3 To change the opacity, enter a value between 0% and 100%.

Both the color and opacity settings affect only the appearance of the mask and have no effect on how underlying areas are protected. For example, you may want to change these settings to make the mask more easily visible against the colors in the image.

4 Click OK.

To add a vector mask that shows or hides the entire layer

1 In the Layers palette, select the layer to which you want to add a vector mask.

2 Do one of the following:

- To create a vector mask that reveals the entire layer, choose Layer > Vector Mask > Reveal All.

- To create a vector mask that hides the entire layer, choose Layer > Vector Mask > Hide All.

To add a vector mask that shows the contents of a shape

1 In the Layers palette, select the layer to which to add a vector mask.

2 Select a path or use one of the shape or pen tools to draw a work path.

3 Choose Layer > Vector Mask > Current Path.

To edit a vector mask

❖ Click the vector mask thumbnail in the Layers palette or the thumbnail in the Paths palette. Then change the shape using the shape and pen tools.

To remove a vector mask

❖ Do one of the following in the Layers palette:

- Drag the vector mask thumbnail to the Delete icon 🗑 .

- (Photoshop) Select the layer containing the vector mask you want to delete, and choose Layer > Vector Mask > Delete.

To disable or enable a vector mask

❖ Do one of the following:

- Shift-click the vector mask thumbnail in the Layers palette.

- (Photoshop) Select the layer containing the vector mask you want to disable or enable, and choose Layer > Vector Mask > Disable or Layer > Vector Mask > Enable.

A red X appears over the mask thumbnail in the Layers palette when the mask is disabled, and the layer's content appears without masking effects.

To convert a vector mask to a layer mask

❖ Select the layer containing the vector mask you want to convert, and choose Layer > Rasterize > Vector Mask.

Important: After you rasterize a vector mask, you can't change it back into a vector object.

Unlinking layers and masks

By default, a layer or group is linked to its layer mask or vector mask, as indicated by the link icon between the thumbnails in the Layers palette. The layer and its mask move together in the image when you move either one with the Move tool. Unlinking them lets you move them independently and shift the mask's boundaries separately from the layer.

• To unlink a layer from its mask, click the link icon in the Layers palette.

• To reestablish the link between a layer and its mask, click between the layer and mask path thumbnails in the Layers palette.

To apply or delete a layer mask

When you finish creating a layer mask, you can either apply the mask and make the changes permanent or delete the mask without applying changes. Because layer masks are stored as alpha channels, applying and deleting layer masks can help reduce file size.

1 Click the layer mask thumbnail in the Layers palette.

2 To remove the layer mask and make changes permanent, click the Delete icon 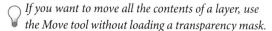 at the bottom of the Layers palette, and then click Apply (Photoshop) or Yes (ImageReady).

3 To remove the layer mask without applying the changes, click the Delete icon at the bottom of the Layers palette, and then click Delete (Photoshop) or No (ImageReady).

You can also apply or delete layer masks using the Layer menu.

To load a layer or layer mask's boundaries as a selection

By loading a layer mask, you can quickly select all the opaque areas on a layer—that is, the areas within the layer boundaries. This is useful when you want to exclude transparent areas from a selection. You can also load the boundaries of a layer mask as a selection.

❖ Do one of the following:

• In the Layers palette, Ctrl-click (Windows) or Command-click (Mac OS) the layer thumbnail or layer mask thumbnail.

• To add the pixels to an existing selection, press Ctrl+Shift (Windows) or Command+Shift (Mac OS), and click the layer thumbnail or layer mask thumbnail in the Layers palette.

• To subtract the pixels from an existing selection, press Ctrl+Alt (Windows) or Command+Option (Mac OS), and click the layer thumbnail or layer mask thumbnail in the Layers palette.

• To load the intersection of the pixels and an existing selection, press Ctrl+Alt+Shift (Windows) or Command+Option+Shift (Mac OS), and click the layer thumbnail or layer mask thumbnail in the Layers palette.

If you want to move all the contents of a layer, use the Move tool without loading a transparency mask.

Clipping masks

You can use the content of a layer to mask the layers above it. The transparent pixels of the bottom or *base layer* mask the content of layers above it that are part of a *clipping mask*. The content of the base layer clips (reveals), the content of the layers above it in the clipping mask.

Clipping mask with Potatoes and Logo layers

You can use multiple layers in a clipping mask, but they must be successive layers. The name of the base layer in the mask is underlined, and the thumbnails for the overlying layers are indented. The overlying layers display a clipping mask icon ⌐ .

The Blend Clipped Layers As Group option in the Layer Style dialog box determines whether the blending mode of the base affects the whole group or just the base. (See `Grouping blend effects' on page 302.)

To create a clipping mask

1 Arrange the layers in the Layers palette so that the base layer with the mask is below the layers that you want to mask.

2 Do one of the following:

- Hold down Alt (Windows) or Option (Mac OS), position the pointer over the line dividing two layers in the Layers palette (the pointer changes to two overlapping circles ⬤), and click.

- Select a layer in the Layers palette, and choose Layer > Create Clipping Mask.

The clipping mask is assigned the opacity and mode attributes of the bottommost layer in the group.

To duplicate a clipping mask to another layer

1 Select the clipping mask.

2 Alt-click (Windows) or Option-click (Mac OS) the mask and drag it to the destination layer. Make sure the destination layer is highlighted before you release the mouse button; otherwise, the layer won't receive the mask properly.

To remove a layer from a clipping mask

❖ Do one of the following:

- Hold down Alt (Windows) or Option (Mac OS), position the pointer over the line separating two grouped layers in the Layers palette (the pointer changes to two overlapping circles ⬤), and click.

- In the Layers palette, select a layer in the clipping mask, and choose Layer > Release Clipping Mask. This command removes the selected layer and any layers above it from the clipping mask.

To release all layers in a clipping mask

1 In the Layers palette, select the base layer in the clipping mask.

2 Choose Layer > Release Clipping Mask.

Chapter 14: Applying filters for special effects

Filters

Using filters

Filters let you change the look of your images, for instance by giving them the appearance of impressionistic paintings or mosaic tiles, or adding unique lighting or distortions. You can also use some filters to clean up or retouch your photos. The filters provided by Adobe appear in the Filter menu. Some filters provided by third-party developers are available as plug-ins. Once installed, these plug-in filters appear at the bottom of the Filter menu.

To use a filter, choose the appropriate submenu command from the Filter menu. These guidelines can help you in choosing filters:

- Filters are applied to the active, visible layer or a selection.

- For 8-bits-per-channel images, most filters can be applied cumulatively through the Filter Gallery. All filters can be applied individually.

- Filters cannot be applied to Bitmap-mode or indexed-color images.

- Some filters work only on RGB images.

- All filters can be applied to 8-bit images.

- (Photoshop only) The following filters can be applied to 16-bit images: Liquify, Average Blur, Bilateral Blur, Blur, Blur More, Box Blur, Gaussian Blur, Lens Blur, Motion Blur, Radial Blur, Sampled Blur, Lens Correction, Add Noise, Despeckle, Dust & Scratches, Median, Reduce Noise, Fibers, Lens Flare, Sharpen, Sharpen Edges, Sharpen More, Smart Sharpen, Unsharp Mask, Emboss, Find Edges, Solarize, De-Interlace, NTSC Colors, Custom, High Pass, Maximum, Minimum, and Offset.

- (Photoshop only) The following filters can be applied to 32-bit images: Average Blur, Bilateral Blur, Box Blur, Gaussian Blur, Motion Blur, Radial Blur, Sampled Blur, Add Noise, Fibers, Lens Flare, Smart Sharpen, Unsharp Mask, De-Interlace, NTSC Colors, High Pass, and Offset.

- Some filters are processed entirely in RAM. If all your available RAM is used to process a filter effect, you may get an error message.

For complete information about using individual filters, and about using the Liquify filter, see Photoshop Help.

Plug-in filters

You can install plug-in filters developed by non-Adobe software developers. Once installed, the plug-in filters appear at the bottom of the Filter menu and work in the same way as built-in filters.

If you are interested in creating plug-in modules, contact Adobe Systems Developer Support.

Note: If you have problems or questions about a third-party plug-in, contact the plug-in's manufacturer for support.

For more information, see 'About plug-in modules' on page 44.

Applying filters

Previewing filters

Applying filters—especially to large images—can be time-consuming. Some filters let you preview the effect before applying it. You can then choose to apply the filter or cancel the operation without wasting time.

If the dialog box contains a preview window, use the following methods to preview the effect:

- Drag in the preview window to center a specific area of the image in the window.

- Use the + or – button under the preview window to zoom into or zoom out of the preview.

- In some preview windows, you can click in the image to center a specific area of the image in the window.

Some filters have dialog boxes that help you customize the filter effect. These filter names are followed by ellipses (…).

To apply a filter

1 Do one of the following:

- To apply a filter to an entire layer, make sure that the layer is active or selected.

- To apply a filter to an area of a layer, select that area.

2 Choose a filter from the submenus in the Filter menu.

If no dialog box appears, the filter effect is applied.

3 If a dialog box appears, enter values or select options, and then click OK.

The Filter Gallery

The Filter Gallery

The Filter Gallery lets you apply filters cumulatively and apply individual filters more than once. You can view thumbnail examples of what each filter does. You can also rearrange filters and change the settings of each filter you've applied to achieve the effect you want. Because it is so flexible, the Filter Gallery is often the best choice for applying filters. However, not all filters listed in the Filters menu are available in the Filter Gallery.

To display the Filter Gallery, choose Filter > Filter Gallery. Clicking a filter category name displays thumbnails of available filter effects.

To change the preview display in the Filter Gallery dialog box

❖ Do one of the following

- Use the + or – button under the preview area to zoom into or zoom out of the image.

- Click the zoom bar (where the zoom percentage appears) to choose a zoom percentage.

- Click the Show/Hide button at the top of the dialog box to hide the filter thumbnails. Hiding the thumbnails expands the preview area.

- Drag in the preview area with the Hand tool to see a different area of the image.

Applying and arranging filter effects

Filter effects are applied in the order you select them. You can rearrange filters after you apply them by dragging a filter name to another position in the list of applied filters. Rearranging filter effects can dramatically change the way your image looks. Click the eye

icon 👁 next to a filter to hide the effect in the preview image. You can also delete applied filters by selecting the filter and clicking the Delete icon 🗑 .

To save time when trying various filters, experiment by selecting a small, representative part of your image.

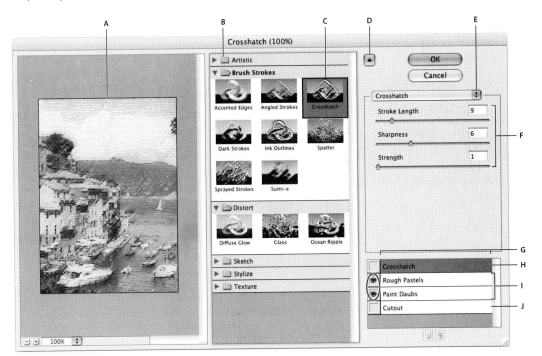

Filter Gallery dialog box.
A. Preview B. Filter category C. Thumbnail of selected filter D. Show/Hide filter thumbnails E. Filters pop-up menu F. Options for selected filter G. List of filter effects to apply or arrange H. Filter effect selected but not applied I. Filter effects applied cumulatively but not selected J. Hidden filter

Applying filters through the Filter Gallery.
A. Original image B. Images each with a single filter applied
C. Three filters applied cumulatively

To apply filters from the Filter Gallery

1 Do one of the following:

- To apply a filter to an entire layer, make sure that the layer is active or selected.

- To apply a filter to an area of a layer, select that area.

2 Choose Filter > Filter Gallery.

3 Click a filter name to add the first filter. You may need to click the inverted triangle next to the filter category to see the complete list of filters. Once added, the filter appears in the applied filter list at the lower right corner of the Filter Gallery dialog box.

4 Enter values or select options for the filter you selected.

5 Do any of the following:

- To apply filters cumulatively, click the New Effect Layer icon 🔲 and choose an additional filter to apply. Repeat this procedure to add more filters.

- To rearrange applied filters, drag the filter to a new position in the applied filter list at the lower right corner of the Filter Gallery dialog box.

- To remove applied filters, select a filter in the applied filter list and click the Delete icon 🗑 .

6 When you're satisfied with the results, click OK.

Blending filter effects and setting options

To blend effects

The Fade command changes the opacity and blending mode of any filter, painting tool, erasing tool, or color adjustment. The Fade command blending modes are a subset of those in the painting and editing tools options (excluding the Behind and Clear modes). Applying the Fade command is similar to applying the filter effect on a separate layer and then using the layer opacity and blending mode controls.

Note: The Fade command can also modify the effects of using the Extract command, Liquify command, and Brush Strokes filters.

1 Apply a filter, painting tool, or color adjustment to an image or selection.

2 Choose Edit > Fade. Select the Preview option to preview the effect.

3 Drag the slider to adjust the opacity, from 0% (transparent) to 100%.

4 Choose a blending mode from the Mode menu.

Note: The Color Dodge, Color Burn, Lighten, Darken, Difference, and Exclusion blending modes do not work on Lab images.

5 Click OK.

For more information, see 'Creating adjustment layers or fill layers' on page 314.

Defining undistorted areas

The Displace, Shear, and Wave filters in the Distort submenu and the Offset filter in the Other submenu let you treat areas undefined (or unprotected) by the filter in the following ways:

Wrap Around Fills the undefined space with content from the opposite edge of the image.

Repeat Edge Pixels Extends the colors of pixels along the edge of the image in the direction specified. Banding may result if the edge pixels are different colors.

Set To Background (Offset filter only) Fills the selected area with the current background color.

To use texture and glass surface controls

The Conté Crayon, Glass, Rough Pastels, Texturizer, and Underpainting filters have texturizing options. These options make images appear as if they were painted onto textures such as canvas and brick or viewed through glass blocks.

1 From the Filter menu, choose Artistic > Rough Pastels, Artistic > Underpainting, Distort > Glass, Sketch > Conté Crayon, or Texture > Texturizer.

2 For Texture, choose a texture type or choose Load Texture to specify a Photoshop file.

3 Drag the Scaling slider to increase or reduce the effect on the image surface.

4 Drag the Relief slider (if available) to adjust the depth of the texture's surface.

5 Select Invert to reverse the light and dark colors on the surface.

6 For Light Direction, indicate the direction from which the light source sheds light on the image.

Tips for creating special effects

Creating edge effects

You can use various techniques to treat the edges of an effect applied to only part of an image. To leave a distinct edge, simply apply the filter. For a soft edge, feather the edge, and then apply the filter. For a transparent effect, apply the filter, and then use the Fade command to adjust the selection's blending mode and opacity.

Applying filters to layers

You can apply filters to individual layers or to several layers in succession to build up an effect. For a filter to affect a layer, the layer must be visible and must contain pixels—for example, a neutral fill color.

Applying filters to individual channels

You can apply a filter to an individual channel, apply a different effect to each color channel, or apply the same filter but with different settings.

Creating backgrounds

By applying effects to solid-color or grayscale shapes, you can generate a variety of backgrounds and textures. You might then blur these textures. Although some filters have little or no visible effect when applied to solid colors (for example, Glass), others produce interesting effects.

Combining multiple effects with masks or duplicate images

Using masks to create selection areas gives you more control over transitions from one effect to another. For example, you can filter the selection created with a mask.

You can also use the History Brush tool to paint a filter effect onto part of the image. First, apply the filter to an entire image. Next, step back in the History palette to the image state before the filter was applied, and set the history brush source to the filtered state. Then paint the image.

Improving image quality and consistency

You can disguise faults, alter or enhance images, or create a relationship among images by applying the same effect to each. Use the Actions palette to record the steps you take to modify one image, and then apply this action to the other images.

For complete information about using the Actions palette, see Photoshop Help.

Chapter 15: Saving and exporting images

Saving images

Saving image files

The saving options vary between Photoshop and ImageReady. The primary focus of ImageReady is producing images for the web. If ImageReady doesn't provide the file format or option you need, you can edit in Photoshop.

To preserve all the Photoshop features in your edited image (layers, effects, masks, styles, and so forth), it's best to save a copy of your image in Photoshop format (PSD). Like most file formats, PSD can support files only up to 2 GB in size. In Photoshop, if you are working with document files larger than 2 GB, you can save your image in the Large Document Format (PSB), Photoshop Raw (flattened image only), and TIFF (up to 4 GB in size only).

You can save 16-bits-per-channel images only in the following formats using the Save As command: Photoshop, Photoshop PDF, Photoshop Raw, Large Document Format (PSB), Cineon, PNG, and TIFF. When using the Save For Web command with a 16-bits-per-channel image, Photoshop automatically converts the image from 16 bits per channel to 8 bits per channel.

You can save 32-bits-per-channel images only in the following formats using the Save As command: Photoshop, OperEXR, Portable Bit Map, Radiance, and TIFF.

You can use the following commands to save images:

Save Saves changes you've made to the current file. In Photoshop, the file is saved in the current format; in ImageReady, the Save command always saves to PSD format.

Save As Saves an image in a different location or under another file name. In Photoshop, the Save As command lets you save an image in a different format and with different options. In ImageReady, the Save As command always saves to PSD format.

Export Original Document (ImageReady) Flattens the layers in a copy of the original image and saves the copy in one of several file formats. Some information (such as slices and optimization settings) is not preserved when an original image is saved to file formats other than Photoshop.

Save A Version (Photoshop) Lets you save different versions of a file and comment on each. This command is available for an image that is managed by a Version Cue Workspace.

💡 *If you're working with a file from an Adobe Version Cue project, the document title bar provides additional information about the status of the file.*

Save For Web (Photoshop), Save Optimized (ImageReady), and Save Optimized As (ImageReady) Save an optimized image for the web.

About file formats

Graphic file formats differ in the way they represent image data (as pixels or as vectors), in compression technique, and in which Photoshop and ImageReady features they support. With a few exceptions, for instance, Large Document Format (PSB), Photoshop Raw, and TIFF, most file formats can't support documents larger than 2 GB.

For information about specific file formats, see Photoshop Help.

To save changes to the current file

❖ Choose File > Save.

To save a file with a different name and location

1 Choose File > Save As.

2 Type a file name, and choose a location for the file.

3 Click Save.

To save a file in a different file format

1 Do one of the following:

- (Photoshop) Choose File > Save As.

- (ImageReady) Choose File > Export > Original Document.

Note: *The Adobe Camera Raw plug-in can save camera raw image files in a different file format, such as Adobe Digital Negative (DNG).*

2 Do one of the following:

- In Photoshop, choose a format from the Format menu.

- In ImageReady, choose from the Save As Type (Windows) or Format (Mac OS) menu.

Note: *In Photoshop, if you choose a format that does not support all features of the document, a warning appears at the bottom of the dialog box. If you see this warning, it's best to save a copy of the file in Photoshop format or in another format that supports all of the image data.*

3 Specify a file name and location.

4 (Photoshop) In the Save As dialog box, select saving options.

5 Click Save.

In both Photoshop and ImageReady, a dialog box appears for choosing options when saving in some image formats.

To copy an image without saving it to your hard disk, use the Duplicate command. To store a temporary version of the image in memory, use the History palette to create a snapshot.

For more information, see 'To save camera raw images in Camera Raw' on page 160.

File saving options

You can set a variety of file saving options in the Save As dialog box. The availability of options depends on the image you are saving and the selected file format. For example, if an image doesn't contain multiple layers, or if the selected file format doesn't support layers, the Layers option is dimmed. If you have Version Cue enabled, additional options are available, such as the ability to save an alternate file and enter version comments.

As A Copy Saves a copy of the file while keeping the current file open on your desktop.

Alpha Channels Saves alpha channel information with the image. Disabling this option removes the alpha channels from the saved image.

Layers Preserves all layers in the image. If this option is disabled or unavailable, all visible layers are flattened or merged (depending on the selected format).

Annotations Saves annotations with the image.

Spot Colors Saves spot channel information with the image. Disabling this option removes spot colors from the saved image.

Use Proof Setup, ICC Profile (Windows), or Embed Color Profile (Mac OS) Creates a color-managed document.

Note: The following image preview and file extension options are available only if Ask When Saving is selected for the Image Previews and Append File Extension options in the File Handling Preferences dialog box.

Thumbnail (Windows) Saves thumbnail data for the file.

Image Previews options (Mac OS) Save thumbnail data for the file. Thumbnails appear in the Open dialog box.

Use Lower Case Makes the file extension lowercase.

File Extension options (Mac OS) Specify the format for file extensions. Select Append to add the format's extension to a file name and Use Lower Case to make the extension lowercase.

For more information, see 'Version Cue managed projects' on page 85.

Image Preview options for Mac OS

The following options are set in the File Handling preferences (Photoshop > Preferences > File Handling).

Icon Displays a file icon on the desktop.

Full Size Saves a 72-ppi version for use in applications that can open only low-resolution Photoshop images.

Macintosh Thumbnail Displays the preview in the Open dialog box.

Windows Thumbnail Saves a preview for display on Windows systems.

Saving large documents

Photoshop supports documents up to 300,000 pixels in either dimension and offers three file formats for saving documents with images having more than 30,000 pixels in either dimension. Keep in mind that most other applications, including older versions of Photoshop, cannot handle files larger than 2 GB or images exceeding 30,000 pixels in either dimension.

To save documents larger than 2 GB

❖ Choose File > Save As and choose one of the following file formats:

Large Document Format (PSB) Supports documents of any pixel size and any file size. All Photoshop features are preserved in PSB files. Currently, PSB files are supported only by Photoshop CS. To save files in PSB format, you must select the Enable Large Document preference (under Preferences > File Handling).

Photoshop Raw Supports documents of any pixel dimension or file size, but does not support layers.

Large documents saved in the Photoshop Raw format are flattened.

TIFF Supports files up to 4 GB in size. Documents larger than 4 GB cannot be saved in TIFF format.

To enable the Large Document Format

1 Choose Edit > Preferences > File Handling (Windows) or Photoshop > Preferences > File Handling (Mac OS).

2 Select the Enable Large Document Format (.psb) option.

Saving PDF files

Saving files in Photoshop PDF format

You can use the Save As command to save RGB, indexed-color, CMYK, grayscale, Bitmap-mode, Lab color, and duotone images in Photoshop PDF format. Because the Photoshop PDF document can preserve Photoshop data, such as layers, alpha channels, spot color, and annotations, you can open the document and edit the images in Photoshop CS2. You can also use the Photoshop PDF format to save multiple images in a multipage document or slide show presentation.

For advanced users, the Photoshop PDF format offers options for making the document PDF/X compliant, which is essential, for example, when you send your document to a large commercial press. PDF/X (Portable Document Format Exchange) is a subset of Adobe PDF that eliminates color, font, and trapping variables that lead to printing problems. You can also specify security options for restricting access to the

PDF document. The 128-bit RC4 (Acrobat 6) encryption has an option for letting users view metadata and thumbnails in a secure PDF document using Adobe Bridge.

You can save your PDF settings as a PDF preset for creating consistent Photoshop PDF files. Adobe PDF presets are shared across Adobe Creative Suite components, including Photoshop, InDesign, Illustrator, GoLive, and Acrobat.

Adobe Creative Suite users can find more information about shared PDF settings for Adobe Creative Suite applications in the PDF Integration Guide on the Creative Suite CD.

For more information, see `Creating a PDF presentation' on page 369 and `To save an Adobe PDF preset' on page 344.

To save a file in Photoshop PDF format

1 Choose File > Save As and choose Photoshop PDF from the Format menu. You can select a Color option if you want to embed a color profile or use the profile specified with the Proof Setup command. You can also include layers, annotations, spot color, or alpha channels. Click Save.

Note: *The first time you save your document as a Photoshop PDF file, you see a dialog box explaining that you can override save options in the Save Adobe PDF dialog box. To prevent the dialog box from being shown again, select the option not to show in future.*

2 In the Save Adobe PDF dialog box, choose an Adobe PDF preset specifying whether the Photoshop PDF file will be printed on a desktop printer or proofer, sent to a commercial printer, distributed by e-mail, displayed on the web, and so on. For details, see `Adobe PDF presets' on page 337.

Choosing a preset is the easiest way to set options for your Photoshop PDF file. After you choose a preset, click Save PDF to generate your Photoshop PDF file. If you want to add security options or fine-tune the saving options for the PDF, follow the remaining steps in this procedure.

3 (Optional) Choose options from the Standard menu and the Compatibility menu to specify the PDF/X compliance and the Acrobat version compatibility for the PDF document. For more information, see `Adobe PDF standards' on page 339 and `Adobe PDF compatibility levels' on page 339.

4 (Optional) Select General in the left pane of the Save Adobe PDF dialog box to set general PDF file saving options. For details of each option, see `General options for Adobe PDF' on page 340.

Note: Users of previous Photoshop versions can open a PDF (containing Photoshop data) as a generic PDF with the layers flattened. Choose File > Open As and then choose Generic PDF from the Files Of Type menu (Windows) or choose File > Open and choose Generic PDF from the Format menu (Mac OS).

5 (Optional) Select Compression in the left pane of the Save Adobe PDF dialog box to specify the compression and downsampling options for the PDF file. For more information, see `Compression and downsampling options for Adobe PDF' on page 341.

6 (Optional) Select Output in the left pane of the Save Adobe PDF dialog box to specify color management and PDF/X options. For more information, see `Color management and PDF/X options for Adobe PDF' on page 342.

7 (Optional) To add security to your PDF document, select Security in the left pane of the Save Adobe PDF dialog box. Specify the password and permissions options for your PDF document. See also `PDF document security options' on page 343.

Note: The Encryption Level depends on the Compatibility setting of your PDF document. Choose a different Compatibility setting to specify a higher or lower Encryption Level.

8 (Optional) Select Summary in the left pane of the Save Adobe PDF dialog box. You can review the options you specified.

9 (Optional) If you want to reuse the PDF save settings, click Save Preset and save your settings as a PDF preset. The new preset appears in the Adobe PDF Preset menu the next time you save a Photoshop PDF file and in the PDF Options dialog box in all Adobe Creative Suite components. See also `To save an Adobe PDF preset' on page 344.

10 Click Save PDF. Photoshop closes the Save Adobe PDF dialog box and creates the PDF document file.

Adobe PDF presets

A PDF preset is a predefined collection of settings that you can use for creating consistent Photoshop PDF files. These settings are designed to balance file size with quality, depending on how the PDF file will be used. You can also create custom presets. Adobe PDF presets are shared across Adobe Creative Suite components, including InDesign, Illustrator, Photoshop, GoLive, and Acrobat.

High Quality Print Creates PDF files that have higher resolution than the Standard job option file. Color and grayscale images with resolutions above 450 ppi are downsampled to 300 ppi, and monochrome images with resolutions above 1800 ppi are downsampled to 1200 ppi. This settings file prints to a higher image resolution and preserves the maximum amount of information about the original document. PDF files created with this settings file can be opened in Acrobat 5.0 and Acrobat Reader 5.0 and later.

PDF/X-1a:2001 Checks incoming PostScript files for PDF/X-1a:2001 compliance and only creates a file that is PDF/X-1a compliant. If the file fails compliance checks, you see a warning message. You can cancel the save or continue by saving a file that is not marked as PDF/X-compliant. PDF/X-1a is an ISO standard for graphic content exchange. PDF/X-1a:2001 requires all fonts to be embedded, the appropriate PDF bounding boxes to be specified, and color to appear as CMYK, spot colors, or both. PDF/X-compliant files must contain information describing the printing condition for which they are prepared. For the PDF/X-1a:2001 settings file, the default output intent profile name is U.S. Web Coated (SWOP). PDF files created with this settings file can be opened in Acrobat 4.0 and Acrobat Reader 4.0 and later.

PDF/X-3:2002 Checks incoming PostScript files for PDF/X-3:2002 compliance and only creates a file that is PDF/X-3:2002 compliant. If the file fails compliance checks, you see a warning message. You can cancel the save or continue by saving a file that is not marked as PDF/X-compliant. Like PDF/X-1a, PDF/X-3 is an ISO standard for graphic content exchange. The main difference is that PDF/X-3 allows the use of color management and device-independent color in addition to CMYK and spot colors. PDF files created with this settings file can be opened in Acrobat 4.0 and Acrobat Reader 4.0 and later.

Press Quality Creates PDF files for high-quality print production (for example, for digital printing or for separations to an imagesetter or platesetter), but does not create files that are PDF/X-compliant. In this case, the quality of the content is the highest consideration. The objective is to maintain all the information in a PDF file that a commercial printer or prepress service needs to print the document correctly. Color and grayscale images with resolutions above 450 ppi are downsampled to 300 ppi, and monochrome images with resolutions above 1800 ppi are downsampled to 1200 ppi. The Press Quality settings file embeds subsets of fonts used in the document (if allowed) and creates a higher-resolution image than the Standard settings file does. When you export a document that uses fonts whose permission bits do not allow embedding, a warning message appears and the fonts are substituted. These PDF files can be opened in Acrobat 5.0 and Acrobat Reader 5.0 and later.

Important: *If you're sending a Photoshop PDF file to a commercial printer or prepress service, find out what the output resolution and other settings should be, or ask for a .joboptions file with the recommended settings. You may need to customize the Adobe PDF settings for a particular provider and then provide a .joboptions file of your own. Adobe PDF settings are saved as .joboptions files.*

Smallest File Size Creates PDF files for display on the web or an intranet, for distribution through an email system for on-screen viewing, or for display on smaller, more portable devices (such as cell phones). This set of options uses compression, downsampling, and a relatively low image resolution. It converts all colors to sRGB and does not embed fonts unless absolutely necessary. It also optimizes files for byte serving. These PDF files can be opened in Acrobat 5.0 and Acrobat Reader 5.0 and later.

Adobe PDF standards

Choose an Adobe PDF standard from the Standards menu at the top of the Adobe PDF Options dialog box. Currently, the most widely used standards for a print publishing workflow are available in two different types of PDF/X formats, PDF/X-1a and PDF/X-3. For more information on PDF/X, see the ISO website and the Adobe website.

None Does not use the PDF/X standard.

PDF/X-1a (2001 and 2003) PDF/X-1a is an ISO standard for graphic content exchange. PDF/X-1a requires all fonts to be embedded, the appropriate PDF bounding boxes to be specified, and color to appear as CMYK, spot colors, or both. PDF/X-compliant files must contain information describing the printing condition for which they are prepared. PDF files created with PDF/X-1a compliance can be opened in Acrobat 4.0 and Acrobat Reader 4.0 and later.

PDF/X-3 (2002 and 2003) Like PDF/X-1a, PDF/X-3 is an ISO standard for graphic content exchange. The main difference is that PDF/X-3 allows the use of color management and device-independent color (CIE Lab, ICC-based color spaces, CalRGB, and CalGray) in addition to CMYK and spot colors. You can use ICC color profiles to specify color data later in the workflow, at the output device. PDF files created with PDF/X-3 compliance can be opened in Acrobat 4.0 and Acrobat Reader 4.0 and later.

Adobe PDF compatibility levels

When you create Photoshop PDF files, you need to decide which PDF version to use. You can change the PDF version by switching to a different preset or choosing a Compatibility option in the Adobe PDF Options dialog box.

Generally speaking, you should use the most recent version (in this case version 1.6) unless there's a specific need for backward compatibility, because the latest version will include all the latest features and functionality. However, if you're creating documents that will be distributed widely, consider choosing Acrobat 4.0 (PDF 1.3) or Acrobat 5.0 (PDF 1.4) to ensure that all users can view and print the document. The following table compares some of the functionality in Adobe PDF files created using the different compatibility settings.

Acrobat 4.0 (PDF 1.3)	Acrobat 5.0 (PDF 1.4)	Acrobat 6.0 (PDF 1.5)	Acrobat 7.0 (PDF 1.6)
PDF files can be opened with Acrobat 3.0 and Acrobat Reader 3.0 and later.	PDF files can be opened with Acrobat 3.0 and Acrobat Reader 3.0 and later. However, features specific to later versions may be lost or not viewable. A warning message appears if the PDF file version exceeds the PDF version supported by the application.	Most PDF files can be opened with Acrobat 4.0 and Acrobat Reader 4.0 and later. However, features specific to later versions may be lost or not viewable. A warning message appears if the PDF file version exceeds the PDF version supported by the application.	Most PDF files can be opened with Acrobat 4.0 and Acrobat Reader 4.0 and later. However, features specific to later versions may be lost or not viewable. A warning message appears if the PDF file version exceeds the PDF version supported by the application.
ICC color management is supported.	ICC color management is supported.	ICC color management is supported.	ICC color management is supported.
Cannot contain artwork that uses live transparency effects. Any transparency must be flattened prior to converting to PDF 1.3.	Supports the use of live transparency in artwork.	Supports the use of live transparency in artwork.	Supports the use of live transparency in artwork.
Layers are not supported.	Layers are not supported.	Preserves layers when creating PDF files from applications that support the generation of layered PDF documents, such as Illustrator CS or InDesign CS.	Preserves layers when creating PDF files from applications that support the generation of layered PDF documents, such as Illustrator CS or InDesign CS.
DeviceN color space with 8 colorants is supported.	DeviceN color space with 8 colorants is supported.	DeviceN color space with up to 31 colorants is supported.	DeviceN color space with up to 31 colorants is supported.
Pages can be up to 45 inches (114.3cm) in either dimension.	Pages can be up to 200 inches (508cm) in either dimension.	Pages can be up to 200 inches (508cm) in either dimension.	Pages can be up to 200 inches (508cm) in either dimension.
Double-byte fonts can be embedded.	Double-byte fonts can be embedded.	Double-byte fonts can be embedded.	Double-byte fonts can be embedded.
40-bit RC4 security supported.	128-bit RC4 security supported.	128-bit RC4 security supported.	128-bit RC4 and 128-bit AES (Advanced Encryption Standard) security supported.

General options for Adobe PDF

You can set the following options in the General section of the Adobe PDF Options dialog box:

Description Displays the description from the selected preset, and provides a place for you to edit the description. You can paste a description from the clipboard. If you edit the description of a preset, the word "(modified)" is added at the end of the preset name. If you change the settings of a preset, "[Based on *<Current Preset Name>*]" is added at the beginning.

Preserve Photoshop Editing Capabilities Preserves Photoshop data in the PDF, such as layers, annotations, alpha channels, and spot colors. Photoshop PDF documents with this option can be opened only in Photoshop CS2.

Embed Page Thumbnails Creates a thumbnail image of artwork. The thumbnail is displayed in the Illustrator Open or Place dialog boxes.

Optimize For Fast Web View Optimizes the PDF file for faster viewing in a web browser.

View PDF After Saving Opens the newly created PDF file in the default PDF viewing application.

Compression and downsampling options for Adobe PDF

When saving artwork in Adobe PDF, you can compress text and line art, and compress and downsample bitmap images. Depending on the settings you choose, compression and downsampling can significantly reduce the size of a PDF file with little or no loss of detail and precision.

The Compression area of the Adobe PDF Options dialog box is divided into three sections. Each section provides the following options for compressing and resampling color, grayscale, or monochrome images in your artwork.

Downsampling If you plan to use the PDF file on the web, use downsampling to allow for higher compression. If you plan to print the PDF file at high resolution, do not use downsampling. Deselect the option to disable all downsampling options.

Downsampling refers to decreasing the number of pixels in an image. To downsample color, grayscale, or monochrome images, choose an *interpolation method*—average downsampling, bicubic downsampling, or subsampling—and enter the desired resolution (in pixels per inch). Then enter a resolution in the For Images Above text box. All images with resolution above this threshold are downsampled.

The interpolation method you choose determines how pixels are deleted:

• **Average Downsampling** Averages the pixels in a sample area and replaces the entire area with the average pixel color at the specified resolution. Average downsampling is the same as Bilinear resampling.

• **Bicubic Downsampling** Uses a weighted average to determine pixel color, which usually yields better results than the simple averaging method of downsampling. Bicubic is the slowest but most precise method, resulting in the smoothest gradations.

• **Subsampling** Chooses a pixel in the center of the sample area and replaces the entire area with that pixel color. Subsampling significantly reduces the conversion time compared with downsampling but results in images that are less smooth and continuous. Subsampling is the same as Nearest Neighbor resampling.

Compression Determines the type of compression that is used. The Automatic option automatically sets the best possible compression and quality for the artwork contained in the file. For most files, this option produces satisfactory results. Use Automatic (JPEG) if you need the greatest compatibility.

• **ZIP compression** Works well on images with large areas of single colors or repeating patterns, and for black-and-white images that contain repeating patterns. ZIP compression can be lossless or lossy, depending on the Quality setting.

• **JPEG compression** Is suitable for grayscale or color images. JPEG compression is *lossy*, which means that it removes image data and may reduce image quality; however, it attempts to reduce file size with a minimal loss of information. Because JPEG compression eliminates data, it can achieve much smaller file sizes than ZIP compression.

• **JPEG2000** Is the new international standard for the compression and packaging of image data. Like JPEG compression, JPEG2000 compression is suitable for grayscale or color images. It also provides additional advantages, such as progressive display.

• **CCITT and Run Length compression** Are available only for monochrome bitmap images. CCITT (Consultative Committee on International Telegraphy and Telephony) compression is appropriate for black-and-white images and any images scanned with an image depth of 1 bit. Group 4 is a general-purpose method that produces good compression for most monochrome images. Group 3, used by most fax machines, compresses monochrome bitmaps one row at a time. Run Length compression produces the best results for images that contain large areas of solid black or solid white.

Image Quality Determines the amount of compression that is applied. The available options depend on the compression method. For JPEG Compression, Photoshop provides Minimum, Low, Medium, High, and Maximum Quality options. For ZIP compression, Photoshop provides 4-bit and 8-bit Quality options. If you use 4-bit ZIP compression with 4-bit images, or 8-bit ZIP compression with 4-bit or 8-bit images, the ZIP method is *lossless*; that is, data is not removed to reduce file size, so image quality is not affected. Using 4-bit ZIP compression with 8-bit data can affect the quality, however, because data is lost.

Tile Size Specifies the size of the tiles used in images with JPEG 2000 compression. When low Image Quality values are used to optimize images smaller than 1024 x 1024 pixels, using the largest tile size produces better results. In general, a tile size of 1024 is best for most images. Lower tile sizes are generally used for images with small dimensions (for viewing on devices such as cell phones).

Convert 16 Bit/Channel Image To 8 Bit/Channel
Converts 16-bits-per-channel images to 8-bits-per-channel images. ZIP is the only compression method available if the Convert 16 Bits option is unselected. If your document's Compatibility setting is Acrobat 5 (PDF 1.4) or earlier, the Convert 16 Bits option is unavailable, and images are automatically converted to 8 bits per channel.

Color management and PDF/X options for Adobe PDF

You can set the following options in the Output section of the Adobe PDF Options dialog box. Interactions between Output options change depending on whether Color Management is on or off and which PDF standard is selected.

Color Conversion Specifies how to represent color information in the Adobe PDF file. When you convert color objects to RGB or CMYK, also select a destination profile from the pop-up menu. All spot color information is preserved during color conversion;

only the process color equivalents convert to the designated color space.

- **No Conversion** Preserves color data as is. This is the default when PDF/X-3 is selected.

- **Convert To Destination** Converts all colors to the profile selected for Destination. Whether the profile is included or not is determined by the Profile Inclusion Policy.

Note: When Convert To Destination is selected, and the Destination doesn't match the document profile, a warning icon appears beside the option.

Destination Describes the gamut of the final RGB or CMYK output device, such as your monitor or a SWOP standard. Using this profile, Photoshop converts the document's color information (defined by the source profile in the Working Spaces section of the Color Settings dialog box) to the color space of the target output device.

Profile Inclusion Policy Determines whether a color profile is included in the file.

Output Intent Profile Name Specifies the characterized printing condition for the document. An output intent profile is required for creating PDF/X-compliant files. This menu is available only if a PDF/X standard (or preset) is selected in the Adobe PDF Options dialog box. The available options depend on whether color management is on or off. For example, if color management is off, the menu lists available printer profiles. If color management is on, the menu lists the same profile selected for Destination Profile (provided it is a CMYK output device), in addition to other predefined printer profiles.

Output Condition Describes the intended printing condition. This entry can be useful for the intended receiver of the PDF document.

Output Condition Identifier A pointer to more information on the intended printing condition. The identifier is automatically entered for printing conditions that are included in the ICC registry.

Registry Name Indicates the web address for more information on the registry. The URL is automatically entered for ICC registry names.

PDF document security options

In the Save Adobe PDF dialog box, you can set security options for your PDF document. These options specify the different access restrictions.

Require A Password To Open The Document Requires the viewer to type a password to view the PDF document. Select this option and type a password in the Document Open Password text box.

Important: If you forget a password, there is no way to recover it from the document. It's a good idea to store passwords in a separate secure location in case you forget them.

Use A Password To Restrict Printing, Editing And Other Tasks Restricts access to the PDF document. If the PDF file is opened in Adobe Acrobat, the user can view the file but must enter the Permissions password to edit, print, or do other tasks with the file. If the file is opened in Photoshop, Illustrator, or InDesign, the user must enter the Permissions password to view, edit, print, or do other tasks with the PDF file. Select this option and type a password in the Permissions Password text box.

Printing Allowed Specifies whether or not the viewer can print the PDF document. You can also choose whether the document can be printed at high or low resolution.

Changes Allowed Specifies whether or not the viewer can make changes to the PDF document. You can specify the extent of the changes allowed.

Enable Copying Of Text, Images And Other Content Lets the viewer access content in the PDF document.

Enable Text Access Of Screen Reader Devices For The Visually Impaired Lets screen readers read the content of the PDF document.

Enable Plaintext Metadata Lets applications access or search for metadata in the PDF document.

To save an Adobe PDF preset

Although the default PDF presets are based on best practices, you may discover that your workflow requires specialized PDF settings that aren't available using any of the built-in presets. In this case, you can create and save your own custom presets for reuse in Photoshop or any product in the Adobe Creative Suite.

In Photoshop, you can save the preset using the Adobe PDF Presets command or clicking the Save Preset button in the Save Adobe PDF dialog box. Adobe PDF presets are saved as files with a .joboptions extension. This is useful, for example, if you want your vendor or printer to send you a .joboptions file with the Adobe PDF presets that work best with their workflow.

1 Do one of the following:

- Choose Edit > Adobe PDF Presets.

- If you're saving a Photoshop PDF document, click the Save Preset button in the Save Adobe PDF

dialog box after you specify your PDF settings. Skip steps 2 and 3.

2 If you chose the Adobe PDF Presets command, do one of the following in the PDF Options Preset dialog box:

- To create a new preset, click the New button in the PDF Options Preset dialog box. In the Edit PDF Preset dialog box, type a name for the preset in the Preset text box and specify your PDF settings.

- To edit an existing custom preset, select the preset and click Edit. (You can't edit the default presets.)

3 Set the PDF options.

4 Save your preset by doing one of the following:

- In the Edit PDF Preset dialog box, click OK. The new preset appears in the Adobe PDF Presets list. Click Done when you finish creating presets.

- In the Save dialog box, type a name for the preset in the File Name text box and click Save.

Adobe PDF presets are stored in Documents and Settings/All Users/Documents/Adobe PDF/Settings (Windows) or Library/Application Support/Adobe PDF/Settings (Mac OS). All the Adobe PDF presets you save in these locations are available in your other Adobe Creative Suite applications.

Note: To save the PDF preset in a location other than the default, do one of the following: In the PDF Options Preset dialog box, click the Save As button and browse to the destination. In the Save dialog box, browse to the destination and click Save.

For more information, see 'To save a file in Photoshop PDF format' on page 336.

To load, edit, or delete Adobe PDF presets

Adobe PDF *presets* (creation settings) are available in Photoshop and other products in the Adobe Creative Suite. From the PDF Options Preset dialog box, you save, load, edit, or delete Adobe PDF presents.

❖ Choose Edit > Adobe PDF Presets and do any of the following:

• To save settings as a new preset, click the New button, specify settings in the Edit PDF Preset dialog box, and click OK.

• To edit an Adobe PDF preset, select the preset in the Preset window, click the Edit button, and change settings in the Edit PDF Preset dialog box.

Note: Although you can't edit the Adobe PDF presets that were installed with Photoshop, you can select one of them and click the New button. In the Edit PDF Preset dialog box, you can modify the settings and save them as a new preset.

• To delete an Adobe PDF preset, select the preset in the Preset window and click the Delete button. You can't delete the Adobe PDF presets that were installed with Photoshop.

• To load an Adobe PDF preset, click the Load button, select the preset file, and click the Load button. The preset is added to the Presets window.

💡 *When you browse for an Adobe PDF preset to load, only files with the .joboptions extension are visible in the Load dialog box.*

• To close the PDF Options Preset dialog box, click the Done button.

• To save a preset in a location other than the default, click the Save As button, give the preset a new name (if necessary), browse to the destination, and click Save.

Saving GIF, JPEG, and PNG files

To save a file in GIF format

You can use the Save As command to save RGB, Indexed Color, Grayscale, or Bitmap mode images directly in CompuServe GIF (known as GIF) format. The image is automatically converted to Indexed Color mode.

1 Choose File > Save As and choose CompuServe GIF from the Format menu.

2 For RGB images, the Indexed Color dialog box appears. Specify conversion options and click OK.

3 Select a row order for the GIF file, and click OK:

Normal Displays the image in a browser only when download is complete.

Interlaced Displays low-resolution versions of the image in a browser as the file downloads. Interlacing makes download time seem shorter, but it also increases file size.

Note: You can also save an image as one or more GIF files using the Save For Web command (Photoshop) or the Save Optimized command (ImageReady).

To save a file in JPEG format

You can use the Save As command to save CMYK, RGB, and grayscale images in JPEG format. JPEG compresses file size by selectively discarding data.

Note: You can also save an image as one or more JPEG files using the Save For Web command (Photoshop) or the Save Optimized command (ImageReady).

1 Choose File > Save As and choose JPEG from the Format menu.

2 In the JPEG Options dialog box, select the options you want, and click OK.

Matte Offers matte color choices to simulate the appearance of background transparency in images that contain transparency.

Image Options Specifies the image quality. Choose an option from the Quality menu, drag the Quality pop-up slider, or enter a value between 0 and 12 in the Quality text box.

Format Options Specifies the format of your JPEG file.

Size Displays the estimated download time after you select a modem speed. (The Size preview is available only when Preview is selected.)

Note: Some applications may not be able to read a CMYK file saved in JPEG format. In addition, if you find that a Java application can't read your JPEG file (in any color mode), try saving the file without a thumbnail preview.

Format options for saving a JPEG file

Baseline ("Standard") Uses a format recognized by most web browsers.

Baseline Optimized Creates a file with optimized color and a slightly smaller file size.

Progressive Displays a series of increasingly detailed versions of the image (you specify how many) as it downloads.

Note: Not all web browsers support optimized and Progressive JPEG images.

To save a file in JPEG 2000 format (optional Photoshop plug-in)

To save files in the JPEG 2000 format, you must get the optional JPEG 2000 plug-in and install it in this location: Adobe Photoshop CS2/Plug-Ins/Adobe Photoshop Only/File Formats. This plug-in is available on the Photoshop CS2 installation CD in Goodies/Optional Plug-Ins/Photoshop Only/File Formats. Extended JPEG 2000 (JPF) format provides an expanded set of options compared to the standard JPEG 2000 (JP2) format. However, you can make files JP2 compatible by selecting the appropriate option in the JPEG 2000 dialog box.

Note: You can't save Duotone, Multichannel, or Bitmap mode images in JPEG 2000 format. To save these files in JPEG 2000 format, first convert them to RGB Color mode.

1 Choose File > Save As, and choose JPEG 2000 from the Format menu.

2 Specify a file name and location, select saving options, and click Save. The JPEG 2000 dialog box opens.

Note: If you want to save a JP2-compatible file, you must select the ICC Profile option (Windows) or the Embed Color Profile option (Mac OS) in the Save As dialog box. Otherwise, the JP2 Compatible option will be unavailable in the JPEG 2000 dialog box. The JP2-

compatible option slightly increases the JPF file size. Keep in mind that JP2 viewers are not required to support ICC profiles and metadata present in JPF files, so color fidelity and other features may not work as expected.

3 (Optional) Enter a value in the File Size text box to set a target size for the saved file. The value in the Quality text box changes to reflect the best quality for the file size you enter.

4 Select any of the following options:

Lossless Compresses the image without losing image quality. Selecting this option creates a larger file. Deselect Lossless to create a smaller file. Then drag the Quality pop-up slider or enter a value in the Quality text box to specify the image quality. A higher value results in better image quality and a larger file size.

If you specify an image quality that conflicts with a target file size you entered previously, Photoshop automatically changes the value in the File Size text box.

Fast Mode Allows faster previewing or encoding of the image. Fast Mode does not support file-size control, progressive optimization, or lossy encoding with an integer wavelet filter.

Include Metadata Includes file information. If your image file contains paths and you wish to store the paths information in the JPEG 2000 file, you must select the Metadata option.

Include Color Settings Includes the color profile embedded in an image.

Deselect the Include Metadata and Include Color Settings options to decrease the size of the image file.

Include Transparency Preserves transparency in the original image. The Include Transparency option is dimmed if the image does not contain transparency.

JP2 Compatible Creates a file that can be displayed in viewing software that supports standard JPEG 2000 (JP2) format but does not support extended JPEG 2000 (JPF) format.

5 Click the Advanced Options button to set the following options:

Compliance Specifies the devices with which the file is compliant. Currently, only general devices (such as web browsers) are supported.

Wavelet Filter Specifies the type of numbers (coefficients) used to encode the file. Float is more accurate but cannot be used for Lossless compression. Selecting the Lossless compression option automatically sets the Wavelet Filter option to Integer.

Choose Float or Integer depending on your image and the result you want. Integer is usually the best option for an overall consistent appearance in the image. Float may sharpen the image but could cause it to lose some quality around the edges.

Tile Size Specifies the size of the tiles used in the image. When you use low quality values to optimize images smaller than 1024 x 1024 pixels, using the largest tile size produces better results.

A tile size of 1024 is best for most images. When creating files with small dimensions (for cell phones, and so forth), use a smaller tile size.

Metadata Format Specifies the metadata formats to include in the image file. JPEG2000 XML is JPEG 2000-specific XML data; this option is available only if the image file contains this data. XMP is File Info data and EXIF is digital camera data.

Color Settings Format Specifies the Color Settings Format to include in the image file. ICC Profile, the default option, includes the full ICC profile specified in the Save As dialog box. The Restricted ICC Profile option is intended for use in portable devices such as cell phones and PDAs. A Restricted ICC Profile must be in a JP2 file.

6 Choose an optimization order from the Order menu:

Growing Thumbnail Presents a sequence of small thumbnail images increasing in size until they reach the image's full size.

Progressive Presents increasingly detailed versions of the entire image as data becomes available (for example, streaming over the web to a browser). Progressive JPEG images have a slightly larger file size, require more RAM for viewing, and are not supported by all applications and JPEG 2000 viewing software.

Color Makes the image appear first as a grayscale image, then as a color image.

Region Of Interest Lets you choose an alpha channel to define a region of interest if your Photoshop document contains one or more alpha channels.

After the alpha channel is loaded as a region of interest, choose an Enhance value to increase or decrease the quality of the region of interest relative to the rest of the image. Note that Enhance does not change the file size of the image, so enhancing the area inside the alpha channel decreases the quality of the area outside the alpha channel (and vice versa).

The Region Of Interest and Enhance options are not available if your Photoshop document does not have an alpha channel.

Note: The channel (alpha, spot, or Quick Mask) used to define the region of interest is discarded in the final saved JPEG 2000 file.

7 To preview how the image will appear in JPEG 2000 viewing software, make sure you chose an optimization order in step 6. The Preview option takes into consideration how the image is optimized and opens the image accordingly. In the Download Preview area of the JPEG 200 dialog box, choose a download rate from the pop-up menu to view the estimated download time of the image, then click the Preview button.

You can use the Set Preview Zoom pop-up menu to zoom in or out of the image for better viewing. You can also use the Zoom tool and the Hand tool to adjust the viewing area of your preview.

8 Click OK to generate the JPEG 2000 image file.

To save a file in PNG format

You can use the Save As command to save RGB, Indexed Color, Grayscale, and Bitmap mode images in PNG format.

Note: You can also save an image as one or more PNG files using the Save For Web command (Photoshop) or the Save Optimized command (ImageReady).

1 Choose File > Save As and choose PNG from the Format menu.

2 Select an Interlace option:

None Displays the image in a browser only when download is complete.

Interlaced Displays low-resolution versions of the image in a browser as the file downloads. Interlacing makes download time seem shorter, but it also increases file size.

3 Click OK.

Saving files in other formats

To save a file in Photoshop EPS format

Virtually all page-layout, word-processing, and graphics applications accept imported or placed EPS (Encapsulated PostScript) files. To print EPS files, you should use a PostScript printer. Non-PostScript printers will print only the screen-resolution preview.

1 Choose File > Save As and choose Photoshop EPS from the Format menu.

2 In the EPS Options dialog box, select the options you want, and click OK:

Preview Creates a low-resolution image to view in the destination application. Choose TIFF to share an EPS file between Windows and Mac OS systems. An 8-bit preview is in color and a 1-bit preview is in black and white with a jagged appearance. An 8-bit preview creates a larger file size than a 1-bit preview. See also `About bit depth' on page 172.

Encoding Determines the way image data is delivered to a PostScript output device.

Include Halftone Screen and Include Transfer Function Control print specifications for high-end commercial print jobs. Consult your printer before selecting these options.

Transparent Whites Displays white areas as transparent. This option is available only for images in Bitmap mode.

PostScript Color Management Converts file data to the printer's color space. Do not select this option if you plan to place the image in another color-managed document.

Note: Only PostScript Level 3 printers support PostScript Color Management for CMYK images. To print a CMYK image using PostScript Color Management on a Level 2 printer, convert the image to Lab mode before saving in EPS format.

Include Vector Data Preserves any vector graphics (such as shapes and type) in the file. However, vector data in EPS and DCS files is available only to other applications; vector data is rasterized if you reopen the file in Photoshop. This option is only available if your file contains vector data.

Image Interpolation Applies anti-aliasing to the printed low-resolution image.

Photoshop EPS encoding options

ASCII or ASCII85 Encodes if you're printing from a Windows system, or if you experience printing errors or other difficulties.

Binary Produces a smaller file and leaves the original data intact. However, some page-layout applications and some commercial print spooling and network printing software may not support binary Photoshop EPS files.

JPEG Compresses the file by discarding some image data. You can choose the amount of JPEG compression from very little (JPEG Maximum Quality) to a lot (JPEG Low Quality). Files with JPEG encoding can be printed only on Level 2 (or later) PostScript printers and may not separate into individual plates.

To save a file in Photoshop DCS format

DCS (Desktop Color Separations) format is a version of EPS that lets you save color separations of CMYK or multichannel files.

1 Choose File > Save As and choose Photoshop DCS 1.0 or Photoshop DCS 2.0 from the Format menu.

2 In the DCS Format dialog box, select the options you want, and click OK.

The dialog box includes all the options available for Photoshop EPS files. Additionally, the DCS menu gives you the option of creating a 72-ppi composite file that can be placed in a page-layout application or used to proof the image:

DCS 1.0 format Creates one file for each color channel in a CMYK image. You can also create a fifth file: a grayscale or color composite. To view the composite file, you must keep all five files in the same folder.

DCS 2.0 format Retains spot color channels in the image. You can save the color channels as multiple files (as for DCS 1.0) or as a single file. The single-file option saves disk space. You can also include a grayscale or color composite.

To save a file in Photoshop Raw format

The Photoshop Raw format is a file format for transferring images between applications and computer platforms.

1 Choose File > Save As and choose Photoshop Raw from the Format menu.

2 In the Photoshop Raw Options dialog box, do the following:

- (Mac OS) Specify values for File Type and File Creator, or accept the default values.

- Specify a Header parameter.

- Select whether to save the channels in an interleaved or noninterleaved order.

Note: *The Photoshop Raw format is not the same as camera raw.*

For more information, see 'Camera raw and Photoshop Raw files' on page 147.

To save a file in BMP format

The BMP format is an image format for the Windows operating system. The images can range from black-and-white (1 byte per pixel) up to 24-bit color (16.7 million colors).

1 Do one of the following:

- (Photoshop) Choose File > Save As and choose BMP from the Format menu.

- (ImageReady) Choose File > Export > Original Document, and choose BMP from the Save As Type (Windows) or Format (Mac OS) menu.

2 Specify a file name and location, and click Save.

3 In the BMP Options dialog box, select a file format, specify the bit depth and, if necessary, select Flip Row Order. For more options, click Advanced Modes and specify the BMP options.

4 Click Save.

To save a 16-bits-per-channel file in Cineon format

RGB images that are 16 bits per channel can be saved in Cineon format for use in the Kodak Cineon Film System.

❖ Choose File > Save As and choose Cineon from the Format menu.

To save files in QuickTime Movie format (ImageReady)

The QuickTime format is used to play back, create, and deliver multimedia. To save in the QuickTime Movie format, you need to install QuickTime on your computer.

1 Choose File > Export > Original Document, and choose QuickTime Movie from the Save As Type (Windows) or Format (Mac OS) menu.

2 Specify a file name and location, and click Save.

3 In the Compression Settings dialog box, choose a compression from the pop-up menu, specify the compression options, and then click OK.

When working in Photoshop, you must jump to ImageReady before saving a document (such as an animation) in QuickTime format.

Saving files in SWF format (ImageReady)

In ImageReady, you can export a document as a SWF file, which can then go directly to the web or be imported into the Macromedia® Flash™ application. In a multilayered PSD file, each layer of the PSD file can be exported as one SWF object, or each layer can be exported as separate SWF files using the Layers As Files command. When the entire PSD file is exported to one SWF file, animation frames are exported as SWF animation frames. URLs in slices and image maps are preserved when exported. Rollovers are ignored. The exported images do not change when you roll over them.

Layers in a PSD file can be preserved when exported from ImageReady and then imported into Macromedia Flash. Use the Layers As Files command to export the individual layers as separate SWF files. When the SWF files are imported in a SWF document, they each appear on separate layers. You can also export individual animation frames as separate SWF files using the Animation As Files command. Again, each SWF file appears on a separate layer when imported into Macromedia Flash.

To export an ImageReady file in SWF format (ImageReady)

1 Do one of the following:

• Choose File > Export > Macromedia Flash SWF.

• Choose File > Export > Original Document. In the Export Original dialog box, choose Macromedia Flash SWF from the Save As Type (Windows) or Format (Mac OS) menu. Enter a name for the SWF file, choose a destination, and click Save.

If you chose File Export > Macromedia Flash SWF, the Macromedia Flash (SWF) Export dialog box opens, letting you select options for exporting to SWF format.

2 Under Export Options, select from the following options:

Preserve Appearance Retains the appearance of the PSD file and may rasterize a text or shape layer if it cannot be exported natively to SWF. If Preserve Appearance is not selected, all effects that cause flattening or rasterization of vectors are dropped, including ones on raster layers.

Generate HTML Generates HTML in addition to the SWF file.

3 Select the Enable Dynamic Text option to map text variables to SWF dynamic text. SWF dynamic text disappears on import into Macromedia® Flash™. Therefore, mapping text variables to SWF dynamic text is useful only if the generated SWF file is going directly to the web.

4 Under Bitmap Options, either leave the Format menu set at Auto Select or choose a file format used for bitmap images. If you choose JPEG, use the JPEG Quality option to specify how much compression to apply.

5 Under Text Options, specify which characters to embed by choosing either None, Full Set, or Partial Set from the Embed Fonts menu.

If you choose Partial Set, click any combination of the Include All Uppercase Characters, Include All Lowercase Characters, Include All Numbers, or Include All Punctuation buttons to specify the characters of the partial set.

You can also enter specific characters to embed in the Extra text box.

Note: Whenever possible, PSD text and vector layers are converted into SWF text and vector objects. If layer effects or blending modes prohibit a native mapping of text and vectors, you can flatten the layers into bitmap objects.

6 Click OK.

💡 *When working in Photoshop, you can jump to ImageReady to save a document (such as an animation) in SWF format.*

7 In the Export As Macromedia SWF dialog box, enter a name for the file, select a destination, and click Save.

To export layers or animation frames as individual SWF files (ImageReady)

1 Do one of the following:

• Choose File > Export > Layers As Files. If you're exporting only specific layers, select the layers in the Layers palette before you choose the Layers As Files command.

• Choose File > Export > Animation As Files. If you're exporting only specific frames, select the frames in the Animation palette before you choose the Animation As Files command.

2 In the Export Layers As Files dialog box, under File Options, click Browse (Windows) or Choose (Mac OS) to select a destination for the exported files.

3 Enter a name in the Base Name text box to specify a common name for the files.

4 Set the Save Options.

5 Choose SWF from the Format menu under Format Options and set the options for your SWF files.

6 Click OK.

For more information, see `To export layers as files in ImageReady' on page 354 and `Exporting animation frames as files' on page 355.

To save a file in Targa format

The Targa (TGA) format supports images of any dimensions with between 1 and 32 bits of color. It is designed for Truevision hardware, but it is also used in other applications.

1 Do one of the following:

- (Photoshop) Choose File > Save As and choose Targa from the Format menu.

- (ImageReady) choose File > Export > Original Document, and choose Targa from the Save As Type (Windows) or Format (Mac OS) menu.

2 Specify a file name and location, and click Save.

3 In the Targa Options dialog box, select a resolution, select the Compress (RLE) option if you want to compress the file, and then click OK.

To save a file in TIFF format using Photoshop

TIFF is a flexible raster (bitmap) image format supported by virtually all paint, image-editing, and page-layout applications.

1 Choose File > Save As, choose TIFF from the Format menu, and click Save.

2 In the TIFF Options dialog box, select the options you want, and click OK.

Image Compression Specifies a method for compressing the composite image data.

Pixel Order Writes the TIFF file with the channels data interleaved or organized by plane. Previously, Photoshop always wrote TIFF files with the channel order interleaved. Theoretically, the Planar order file can be read and written faster, and offers a little better compression. Both channel orders are backward compatible with earlier versions of Photoshop.

Byte Order Selects the platform on which the file can be read. This option is useful when you don't know what program the file may be opened in. Photoshop and most recent applications can read files using either IBM PC or Macintosh byte order.

Save Image Pyramid Preserves multiresolution information. Photoshop does not provide options for opening multiresolution files; the image opens at the highest resolution within the file. However, Adobe InDesign and some image servers provide support for opening multiresolution formats.

Save Transparency Preserves transparency as an additional alpha channel when the file is opened in another application. Transparency is always preserved when the file is reopened in Photoshop or ImageReady.

Layer Compression Specifies a method for compressing data for pixels in layers (as opposed to composite data). Many applications cannot read layer data and skip over it when opening a TIFF file. Photoshop, however, can read layer data in TIFF files. Although files that include layer data are larger than those that don't, saving layer data eliminates the need to save and manage a separate PSD file to hold the layer data. Choose Discard Layers And Save A Copy if you want to flatten the image.

Note: To have Photoshop prompt you before saving an image with multiple layers, select Ask Before Saving Layered TIFF Files in the File Handling area of the Preferences dialog box.

To save a file in TIFF format using ImageReady

1 Choose File > Export > Original Document, and choose TIFF from the Save As Type (Windows) or Format (Mac OS) menu.

2 Specify a file name and location, and click Save.

3 Select a compression method, and click OK.

Exporting layers as files

To export layers to files in Photoshop

In Photoshop, you can export and save layers as individual files using a variety of formats, including PSD, BMP, JPEG, PDF, Targa, and TIFF. You can apply different format settings to individual layers, or one format to all exported layers. Layers are named automatically as they are saved. You can set options to control the generation of names. All format settings are saved with your Photoshop document for convenience when you use this feature again.

1 Choose File > Scripts > Export Layers To Files.

2 In the Export Layers To Files dialog box, under Destination, click Browse to select a destination for the exported files. By default, the generated files are saved in the sample folder as the source file.

3 Enter a name in the File Name Prefix text box to specify a common name for the files.

4 Select the Visible Layers Only option if you want to export only those layers that have visibility enabled in the Layers palette. Use this option if you don't want all the layers exported. Turn off visibility for layers that you don't want exported.

5 Choose a file format from the File Type menu. Set options as necessary.

6 Select the Include ICC Profile option if you want the working space profile embedded in the exported file. This is important for color-managed workflows.

7 Click Run.

To export layers as files in ImageReady

In ImageReady, you can export and save layers as individual files using a variety of formats, including PSD, GIF, JPEG, PNG, WBMP, and SWF. You can apply different format settings to individual layers, or one format to all exported layers. Layers are named automatically as they are saved. You can set options to control the generation of names. All format settings are saved with your ImageReady document for convenience when you use this feature again.

1 Choose File > Export > Layers As Files. If you're exporting only specific layers, select the layers in the Layers palette before you choose the Layers as Files command.

Note: Click a layer in the Layers palette to select it. Shift-click to select a series of layers. Ctrl-click (Windows) or Command-click (Mac OS) to select noncontiguous layers.

2 In the Export Layers As Files dialog box, under File Options, click Choose to select a destination for the exported files.

3 Enter a name in the Base Name text box to specify a common name for the files.

Click the Set button to set up specific options for file naming. Choose elements from the pop-up menus or enter text into the fields to be combined into the default names for all files. Elements include layer name, document name, layer number, file creation date, punctuation, and file extension.

4 Specify how you want to save the files by choosing from the following options:

- For Export, select the layers to be exported by choosing either All Layers, Top Level Layers And Layer Sets, or Selected Layers. The Selected Layers option is available only if you select layers before choosing the Layers As Files command. If your multilayered document has a Background layer, you can select the Include Background option to include it in the export.

- For Layer, choose a layer from the Layer pop-up menu if you are using a separate format for each layer. You can also use the navigation buttons ◀ ▶ to choose the layer.

Note: *Select the Preview option in the Export Layers As Files dialog box to preview the layer you choose.*

- For Apply, choose either One Format For All Layers or Separate Format For Each Layer.

5 Under Format Options, either choose a setting from the Preset pop-up menu or manually set the file format and compression.

If you're using a separate format for each layer, choose another layer and then set the format options. Do this for all the subsequent layers you're exporting.

You can save a custom setting for reuse. Adjust the settings. The Unnamed option is automatically chosen in the Preset menu. Click the Save Current Layer Settings icon ▣ , name the new setting, and save it to the Optimized Settings folder. You can also delete a setting by choosing it from the Preset menu and clicking the Delete icon 🗑 .

6 Click OK.

Exporting animation frames as files

Exporting animation frames as files

You can export and save animation frames as individual files in a variety of formats. In Photoshop, you can export animation frames as files in PSD, BMP, JPEG, PDF, Targa, and TIFF formats. In ImageReady, you can export animation frames as files in GIF, JPEG, PNG, WBMP, and SWF formats.

In ImageReady, you can assign different format settings to individual frames or one format to all exported frames. Frames are named automatically as they are saved. You can set options to control the generation of names. All format settings are saved with your ImageReady document for convenience when using the feature again.

To export animation frames as files in Photoshop

1 In the Animation palette, click the triangle to open the palette menu and choose Flatten Frames Into Layers.

2 In the Layers palette, make sure that only the layers created from animation frames are visible. If necessary, turn off the visibility of the layers that *were not* created from the animation frames. This is important for exporting only the animation frames.

3 Choose File > Scripts > Export Layers To Files.

4 In the Export Layers To Files dialog box, under Destination, click Browse to select a destination for the exported files. By default, the generated files are saved in the same folder as the source file.

5 Enter a name in the File Name Prefix text box to specify a common name for the files.

6 Select the Visible Layers Only option to export layers that have visibility enabled in the Layers palette. Use this option so that only the layers created from the animation frames are exported.

7 Choose a file format from the File Type menu. Set any options if necessary.

8 Select the Include ICC Profile option if you want the working space profile embedded in the exported file. This is important for color-managed workflows.

9 Click Run.

To export animation frames as files in ImageReady

1 Choose File > Export > Animation Frames as Files. If you're exporting only specific frames, select the frames in the Animation palette before you choose the Animation Frames As Files command.

Click a frame in the Animation palette to select it. Shift-click to select a series of frames. Ctrl-click (Windows) or Command-click (Mac OS) to select noncontiguous frames.

2 In the Export Animation Frames As Files dialog box, under File Options, click Choose to select a destination for the exported files.

3 Enter a name in the Base Name text box to specify a common name for the files.

Click the Set button to set up specific options for file naming. Elements include document name, frame number, file creation date, punctuation, and file extension.

4 If you selected frames in the Animation palette before choosing the Animation Frames As Files command, you can enable the Selected Frames Only option to export only the frames you selected. Deselecting this option exports all the frames in your animation regardless of whether you selected them or not.

To preview the exported image for a specific frame, select the Preview option and then use either the Preview menu or navigation buttons to choose the frame to preview.

5 Under Format Options, either choose a setting from the Preset pop-up menu or manually set the file format and compression.

You can save a custom setting for reuse by clicking the Save Current Format Preset icon , naming the new setting, and saving it to the Optimized Settings folder. You can also delete a setting by choosing it from the Preset menu and then clicking the Delete Current Format Preset icon .

6 Click OK.

Exporting images in ZoomView format

Exporting images in ZoomView format

ZoomView is a format for delivering high-resolution images over the web. With the Viewpoint Media Player, users can zoom into or out of an image and pan the image to see its various parts.

When you export an image in ZoomView format, Photoshop creates the following files:

- An MTX file that defines the image to be displayed.

- An HTML file that loads the Viewpoint Media Player and points to the MTX file.

- A folder containing tiles that are used to display the image.

- A folder containing VBS and JavaScript scripts that are used by the HTML file.

To export an image in ZoomView format

1 Choose File > Export > ZoomView.

2 Set the following options, and click OK:

Template Specifies a template for generating the MTX, HTML, and auxiliary files. Choose a template (Plain or With Instructions) from the pop-up menu, or click the Load button to choose a different ZoomView Template (ZVT) file. You can download additional templates from the Viewpoint website.

Output Location Specifies an output location. Click Folder and enter a name in the Base Name text box to specify a common name for the files.

Path to Broadcast License File Specifies a URL for the broadcast license file. The Viewpoint Corporation requires that all publishers of ZoomView content acquire a broadcast license. To apply for a key, click Get License.

Image Tile Options Lets you select a tile size to control how many pixels are in each tile. ZoomView technology uses image tiling to load only the part of a high-resolution image that a user wants see. A tile size of 128 is recommended for small images; a tile size of 256 is recommended for large images. To specify an amount of compression for each tile image, choose an option from the Quality menu, drag the Quality pop-up slider, or enter a value between 0 and 13 in the Quality text box. Select Optimize Tables to create enhanced JPEGs with slightly smaller file sizes. This option is recommended for maximum file compression.

Browser Options Specifies a width and height for the image in the Viewpoint Media Player. Select Preview in Browser to launch your default web browser and load the generated HTML file after you click OK.

Displaying and adding file and image information

About file information

File information—also called *metadata*—is important in all types of publishing. For example, Photoshop supports the information standard developed by the Newspaper Association of America (NAA) and the International Press Telecommunications Council

(IPTC) to identify transmitted text and images. This standard includes entries for descriptions, keywords, categories, credits, and origins.

You can find file information in these sources:

Adobe Bridge Displays metadata and keywords for a selected file.

File Info dialog box Displays camera data (EXIF), file properties, description and keywords, edit history, and copyright and authorship information that has been added to the file. You can also add or modify keywords, a description, and copyright information. You can open the File Info dialog box either in Bridge or in Photoshop.

Status bar Displays information, such as such as the current magnification and file size of the active image, and brief instructions for using the active tool.

Info palette The Info palette displays information about the color values beneath the pointer and, depending on the tool in use, other useful measurements. In Photoshop, the Info palette also displays a hint for using a selected tool, document status information, and can display 8-bit, 16-bit, or 32-bit values.

In addition, Photoshop automatically scans opened images for Digimarc watermarks. If a watermark is detected, a product copyright symbol appears in the image window's title bar along with the information in the Copyright Status, Copyright Notice, and Owner URL sections of the File Info dialog box.

In Windows and Mac OS, you can add file information to files saved in Photoshop, Large Document Format (PSB), TIFF, JPEG, EPS, and PDF formats. In Mac OS, you can also add file information to files in other Photoshop-supported formats except GIF. The information you add is embedded in the file using

XMP (Extensible Metadata Platform). XMP provides Adobe applications and workflow partners with a common XML framework that standardizes the creation, processing, and interchange of document metadata across publishing workflows. When you save files from Photoshop that contain keywords, those keywords are not displayed in Adobe Acrobat's Document Properties dialog box when the file is opened in Acrobat.

Note: It's possible to add metadata in ImageReady using the options in the Optimize palette.

For more information, see `About the Metadata panel in Bridge' on page 68 and `To add metadata using the File Info dialog box' on page 69.

To read a Digimarc watermark

1 Choose Filter > Digimarc > Read Watermark. If the filter finds a watermark, a dialog box displays the creator ID, copyright year (if present), and image attributes.

2 Click OK, or for more information, choose from the following:

• If you have a web browser installed, click Web Lookup to have more information about the owner of the image. This option launches the browser and displays the Digimarc website, where contact details appear for the given creator ID.

• Call the phone number listed in the Watermark Information dialog box to get information faxed back to you.

Annotating images

You can attach note annotations (notes) and audio annotations to an image in Photoshop. This is useful for associating review comments, production notes, or other information with the image. Because Photoshop annotations are compatible with Adobe Acrobat, you can use them to exchange information with Acrobat users as well as Photoshop users.

To circulate a Photoshop document for review in Acrobat, save the document in Portable Document Format (PDF) and ask reviewers to use Acrobat to add notes or audio annotations. Then import the annotations into Photoshop.

Notes and audio annotations appear as small nonprintable icons on the image. They are associated with a location on the image rather than with a layer. You can hide and show annotations, open notes to view or edit their contents, and play audio annotations. You can also add audio annotations to actions, and set them to play during an action or during a pause in an action.

Adding notes and audio annotations

You can add notes and audio annotations anywhere on a Photoshop image canvas. When you create a note, a resizable window appears for typing text. When you record an audio annotation, you must have a microphone plugged into the audio-in port of your computer.

You can also import both kinds of annotations from Photoshop documents saved in PDF or from Acrobat documents saved in PDF or Form Data Format (FDF).

If you need to delete the annotations in your document, select either the Notes or the Audio Annotation tool and click Clear All in the tool options bar. All notes and audio annotations are deleted from your document.

For more information, see 'To delete notes and audio annotations' on page 361.

To create a note

When adding a note to your document, you can use the standard editing commands for your system (Undo, Cut, Copy, Paste, and Select All) to edit the text. (Windows) Right-click the text area and choose the commands from the context menu. (Mac OS) Choose the commands from the Edit and Select menus. You can also use standard keyboard shortcuts for these editing commands.

1 Select the Notes tool .

2 In the options bar, enter or specify the following as needed:

Author Specifies the author's name, which appears in the title bar of the notes window.

Size Chooses the size for the note text.

Color Selects a color for the note icon and the title bar of note windows. Clicking the color box opens the Adobe Color Picker so you can select a color.

3 Click where you want to place the note, or drag to create a custom-sized window.

4 Click inside the window, and type the text. If you type more text than fits in the note window, the scroll bar becomes active. Edit the text as needed:

If you have the required software for different script systems (for example, Roman, Japanese, or Cyrillic) installed on your computer, you can switch between the script systems. Right-click (Windows) or Control-click (Mac OS) to display the context menu, and then choose a script system.

5 To close the note to an icon, click the close box.

To create an audio annotation

1 Make sure that your computer has a built-in microphone, or attach a microphone.

2 Select the Audio Annotation tool 🔊 .

3 In the options bar, enter or specify the following as needed:

Author Specifies the author's name, which appears in the tool tip when you place the pointer over the audio annotation icon in your document.

Color Selects a color for the audio annotation icon. Clicking the color box opens the Adobe Color Picker, from which you select a color.

4 Click where you want to place the annotation icon.

5 Click Start and then speak into the microphone. When you finish, click Stop.

To import annotations

1 Choose File > Import > Annotations.

2 Select a PDF or FDF file that contains annotations, and then click Load. The annotations appear in the locations where they were saved in the source document.

Opening and editing annotations

A note or audio annotation icon marks the location of an annotation on an image. When you move the pointer over an annotation icon and pause, a message displays the author name. You use the icons to open notes or play audio annotations. You can show, hide, or move the icons and edit the contents of notes.

Note: Resizing an image does not resize the annotation icons and note windows. The icons and note windows keep their locations relative to the image. Cropping an image removes any annotations in the cropped area; you can recover the annotations by undoing the Crop command.

To open a note or play an audio annotation

❖ Double-click the icon:

• If you are opening a note, a window appears, displaying the note text.

• If you are playing an audio annotation and have a sound card installed, the audio file begins to play.

To show or hide annotation icons

❖ Do one of the following:

• Choose View > Show > Annotations.

• Choose View > Extras. This command also shows or hides grids, guides, selection edges, target paths, and slices.

To edit annotations

❖ Do any of the following:

• To move an annotation icon, move the pointer over the icon until it turns into an arrow, and then drag the icon. You can do this with any tool selected. Moving a note icon does not move its note window.

• To move a note window, drag it by the title bar.

• To edit the contents of a note, open the note, change any options, and add, delete, or change the text. You can use the same editing commands that you use when creating a note.

To delete notes and audio annotations

❖ Do any of the following:

• To delete a note or audio annotation, select either the Notes or the Audio Annotation tool, right-click (Windows) or Control-click (Mac OS) the Note or Audio Annotation icon in the image, and choose Delete Note or Delete Audio Annotation, or press the Delete key.

• To delete all notes or audio annotations, select either the Notes or the Audio Annotation tool and click Clear All in the tool options bar. You can also select either the Notes or the Audio Annotation tool, right-click (Windows) or Control-click (Mac OS) the Note or Audio Annotation icon in the image, and choose Delete All Notes or Delete All Annotations from the context menu.

Adding and viewing digital copyright information

Adding digital copyright information

You can add copyright information to Photoshop images and notify users that an image is copyright-protected via a digital watermark that uses Digimarc ImageBridge technology. The watermark—a digital code added as noise to the image—is virtually imperceptible to the human eye. The Digimarc watermark is durable in both digital and printed forms, surviving typical image edits and file format conversions.

Embedding a digital watermark in an image lets viewers obtain information about the creator of the image. This feature is particularly valuable to image creators who license their work to others. Copying an image with an embedded watermark also copies the watermark and any information associated with it.

For more detailed information on embedding Digimarc digital watermarks, refer to the Digimarc website at www.digimarc.com.

Before adding a digital watermark

Keep in mind the following considerations before embedding a digital watermark in your image.

Color variation The image must contain some degree of variation or randomness in color to embed the digital watermark effectively and imperceptibly. The image cannot consist mostly or entirely of a single flat color.

Pixel dimensions The Digimarc technology requires a minimum number of pixels to work. Digimarc recommends the following minimum pixel dimensions for the image to be watermarked:

- 100 pixels by 100 pixels if you don't expect the image to be modified or compressed prior to its actual use.

- 256 pixels by 256 pixels if you expect the image to be cropped, rotated, compressed, or otherwise modified after watermarking.

- 750 pixels by 750 pixels if you expect the image to appear ultimately in printed form at 300 dpi or greater.

There is no upper limit on pixel dimensions for watermarking.

File compression In general, a Digimarc watermark will survive lossy compression methods such as JPEG, though it is advisable to favor image quality over file size (a JPEG compression setting of 4 or higher works best). In addition, the higher the Watermark Durability setting you choose when embedding the watermark, the better the chances that the digital watermark will survive compression.

Workflow Digital watermarking should be one of the very last tasks you perform on an image, except for file compression.

Use the following recommended workflow:

- Make all necessary modifications to your image until you are satisfied with its final appearance (this includes resizing and color correction).

- Embed the Digimarc watermark.

- If needed, compress the image by saving it in JPEG or GIF format.

- If the image is intended for printed output, perform the color separation.

- Read the watermark and use the signal strength meter to verify that the image contains a watermark of sufficient strength for your purposes.

- Publish the digital watermarked image.

To embed a watermark

To embed a digital watermark, you must first register with Digimarc Corporation—which maintains a database of artists, designers, and photographers and their contact information—to get a unique Digimarc ID. You can then embed the Digimarc ID in your images, along with information such as the copyright year or a restricted-use identifier.

1 Open the image that you want to watermark. You can embed only one digital watermark per image. The Embed Watermark filter won't work on an image that has been previously watermarked.

If you're working with a layered image, you should flatten the image before watermarking it; otherwise, the watermark will affect the active layer only.

Note: You can add a digital watermark to an indexed-color image by first converting the image to RGB mode, embedding the watermark, and then converting the image back to Indexed Color mode. However, the results may be inconsistent. To make sure that the watermark was embedded, run the Read Watermark filter.

2 Choose Filter > Digimarc > Embed Watermark.

3 If you are using the filter for the first time, click the Personalize button. Get a Digimarc ID by clicking Info to launch your web browser and visit the Digimarc website at www.digimarc.com, or by contacting

Digimarc at the telephone number listed in the dialog box. Enter your PIN and ID number in the Digimarc ID text box, and click OK.

After you enter a Digimarc ID, the Personalize button becomes a Change button, allowing you to enter a new Digimarc ID.

4 Enter a copyright year, transaction ID, or image ID for the image.

5 Select any of the following image attributes:

Restricted Use Limits the use of the image.

Do Not Copy Specifies that the image should not be copied.

Adult Content Labels the image contents as suitable for adults only. (Within Photoshop, this option does not limit access to adult-only images, but future versions of other applications may limit their display.)

6 For Target Output, specify whether the image is intended for monitor, web, or print display.

7 For Watermark Durability, drag the slider or enter a value, as described in the next section.

8 Select Verify to automatically assess the watermark's durability after it is embedded.

9 Click OK.

Using the Watermark Durability setting

The default Watermark Durability setting is designed to strike a balance between watermark durability and visibility in most images. However, you can adjust the Watermark Durability setting yourself to suit the needs of your images. Low values are less visible in an image but less durable, and may be damaged by applying filters or by performing some image-editing,

printing, and scanning operations. High values are more durable but may display some visible noise in the image.

Your setting should depend on the intended use of the image and on the goals you've set for your watermarks. For example, it may be quite acceptable to use a higher Watermark Durability setting with JPEG images posted on a website. The higher durability helps to ensure the persistence of the watermark, and the increased visibility often is not noticeable with medium-resolution JPEG images. Digimarc recommends experimenting with various settings as part of your testing process to determine which setting works best for the majority of your images.

Using the signal strength meter

The signal strength meter helps you determine whether a watermark is durable enough to survive the intended use of the image. The signal strength meter is available only for images containing digital watermarks that you yourself have embedded.

Digimarc recommends that you check the signal strength meter before publishing your images. For example, if you often compress watermarked images for inclusion in a website, check the meter before posting the images. You can also use the signal strength meter to gauge the effectiveness of different Watermark Durability settings that you are experimenting with.

To check the signal strength meter

❖ Choose Filter > Digimarc > Read Watermark. The signal strength meter appears at the bottom of the dialog box.

You can also display the meter automatically by selecting Verify while embedding the watermark.

Preferences for saving files

To set file saving preferences

1 Do one of the following:

- (Windows) Choose Edit > Preferences > File Handling.

- (Mac OS) Choose Photoshop > Preferences > File Handling.

2 Set the following options:

Image Previews Choose an option for saving image previews: Never Save to save files without previews, Always Save to save files with specified previews, or Ask When Saving to assign previews on a file-by-file basis. In Mac OS, you can select one or more preview types.

File Extension (Windows) Choose an option for the three-character file extensions that indicate a file's format: Use Upper Case to append file extensions using uppercase characters, or Use Lower Case to append file extensions using lowercase characters.

Append File Extension (Mac OS) File extensions are necessary for files that you want to use on or transfer to a Windows system. Choose an option for appending extensions to file names: Never to save files without file extensions, Always to append file extensions to file names, or Ask When Saving to append file extensions on a file-by-file basis. Select Use Lower Case to append file extensions using lowercase characters.

To toggle the Append File Extension option for a single file, hold down Option when you choose a file format in the Save As dialog box.

Mac OS image preview options

In Mac OS, you can select one or more of the following preview types (to speed the saving of files and minimize file size, select only the previews you need).

Icon Uses the preview as a file icon on the desktop.

Full Size Saves a 72-ppi version of the file for use in applications that can open only low-resolution Photoshop images. For non-EPS files, this is a PICT preview.

Macintosh Thumbnail Displays the preview in the Open dialog box.

Windows Thumbnail Saves a preview that Windows systems can display.

To set the History Log preferences

By default, history log data about each session is saved as metadata embedded in the image file. You can specify where the history log data is saved and the level of detail contained in the history log.

1 Choose Edit > Preferences > General (Windows) or Photoshop > Preferences > General (Mac OS).

2 Specify where to save the history log data:

Metadata Saves the history log as metadata embedded in the file.

Text File Saves the history log to a text file. Select Text File. In the Save dialog box, browse to the destination, give the text file a name, and click Save.

Both Saves the history log as metadata and in a text file. Select Both. In the Save dialog box, browse to the destination, give the text file a name and click the Save button.

3 Choose from the Edit Log Items menu to specify the level of detail in the history log:

Sessions Only Records the start time and date of every editing session. Does not include any information about edits made to the file.

Concise Records every editing session on the file (both start and end times), and also includes edits recorded in the History palette.

Detailed Records the same information as the Concise option, plus such information as the path of the file and an account of every edit made to the file (including detailed edits not recorded in the History palette, such as preference changes).

For more information, see`About file information' on page 357 and `To add metadata using the File Info dialog box' on page 69.

Creating multiple-image layouts

Creating contact sheets

Contact sheets let you easily preview and catalog groups of images by displaying a series of thumbnails on a single page. You can automatically create and place thumbnails on a page using the Contact Sheet II command.

A contact sheet

To create a contact sheet

1 Do one of the following:

- (Photoshop) Choose File > Automate > Contact Sheet II.

- (Bridge) Select a folder of images or specific image files. From the Bridge menu, choose Tools > Photoshop > Contact Sheet II. Unless you select specific images, the contact sheet will include all the images currently displayed in Adobe Bridge. You can select a different image folder or select other currently open images after the Contact Sheet II dialog box opens.

Note: Click to select an image in Bridge. Shift-click to select a series of images. Ctrl-click (Windows) or Command-click (Mac OS) to select noncontiguous images.

2 In the Contact Sheet II dialog box, specify the images to use by choosing one of the following from the Use menu in the Source Images area:

Current Open Documents Uses any image that is currently open in Photoshop.

Folder Lets you click Browse (Windows) or Choose (Mac OS) to specify the folder containing the images you want to use. Select Include All Subfolders to include images inside any subfolders.

Selected Images From Bridge Uses images displayed in Bridge. All images in Bridge are used unless you select specific images before choosing the Contact Sheet II command. Images in subfolders are not included.

3 In the Document area, specify the dimensions, resolution, and color mode for the contact sheet. Select Flatten All Layers to create a contact sheet with all images and text on a single layer. Deselect Flatten All Layers to create a contact sheet in which each image is on a separate layer and each caption is on a separate text layer.

4 In the Thumbnails area, specify layout options for the thumbnail previews.

* For Place, choose whether to arrange thumbnails across first (from left to right, then top to bottom) or down first (from top to bottom, then left to right).

* Enter the number of columns and rows that you want per contact sheet. The maximum dimensions for each thumbnail are displayed to the right, along with a visual preview of the specified layout.

* Select Use Auto-Spacing to let Photoshop automatically space the thumbnails in the contact sheet. If you deselect Use Auto-Spacing, you can specify the vertical and horizontal space around the thumbnails. The contact sheet preview in the dialog box is automatically updated as you specify the spacing.

* Select Rotate For Best Fit to rotate the images, regardless of their orientation, so they fit efficiently on a contact sheet.

When Rotate For Best Fit is deselected, thumbnails appear in their correct orientation (left). When it is selected, the pictures are rotated to achieve the best fit (right).

5 Select Use Filename As Caption to label the thumbnails using their source image file names. Use the menu to specify a caption font and font size.

6 Click OK.

Creating picture packages

With the Picture Package command, you can place multiple copies of a source image on a single page, much as portrait studios do with school photos and other photo packages. You also have the option of placing different images on the same page. You can choose from a variety of size and placement options to customize your package layout.

A picture package layout

To put multiple photos into a picture package

1 Do one of the following:

- (Photoshop) Choose File > Automate > Picture Package. If you have multiple images open, Picture Package uses the frontmost image.

- (Bridge) Choose Tools > Photoshop > Picture Package. The Picture Package command uses the first image listed in Bridge unless you select a specific image before giving the Picture Package command.

If you're using only the frontmost image or a selected image from Bridge, skip to step 3.

2 Add one or more images to the layout by doing one of the following:

- In the Source Images area of the Picture Package dialog box, choose either File or Folder from the

Use menu and click Browse (Windows) or Choose (Mac OS). If you choose Folder, you can select Include All Subfolders to include images inside any subfolders.

- Click a placeholder in the preview layout and browse to select an image.

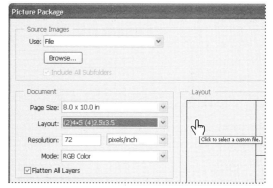

Click a placeholder in the Picture Package preview layout, then browse to select an image.

- Drag an image from the desktop or a folder into a placeholder.

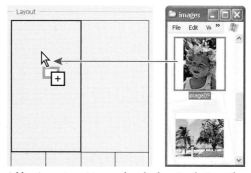

Add an image to a picture package by dragging the image from the desktop into a placeholder.

You can change any image in the layout by clicking a placeholder and browsing to select an image.

3 In the Document area of the Picture Package dialog box, select page size, layout, resolution, and color mode. A thumbnail of the chosen layout appears on the right side of the dialog box. You can also create your own custom layouts.

4 Select Flatten All Layers to create a picture package with all images and label text on a single layer. Deselect Flatten All Layers to create a picture package with separate image layers and text layers (for labels). If you place each image and label on a separate layer, you can update your picture package after it's been saved. However, the layers increase the file size of your picture package.

5 In the Label area, choose the source for label text from the Content menu or choose None. If you choose Custom Text, enter the text for the label in the Custom Text field.

6 Specify font, font size, color, opacity, position, and rotation for the labels.

7 Click OK.

To customize a picture package layout

You can modify existing layouts or create new layouts using the Picture Package Edit Layout feature. Your custom layouts are saved as text files and stored in the Layouts folder inside the Presets folder. You can then reuse your saved layouts. The Picture Package Edit Layout feature uses a graphic interface that eliminates the need to write text files to create or modify layouts.

1 Do one of the following:

• (Photoshop) Choose File > Automate > Picture Package.

• (Bridge) Choose Tools > Photoshop > Picture Package.

2 In the Picture Package dialog box, choose a layout from the Layout menu if you're creating a layout or customizing an existing one.

3 Click the Edit Layout button.

4 In the Picture Package Edit Layout dialog box, enter a name for the custom layout in the Name text box.

5 (Optional) In the Layout area of the Picture Package Edit Layout dialog box, choose a size from the Page Size menu or enter values in the Width and Height text boxes. You can use the Units menu to specify inches, centimeters, pixels, or millimeters.

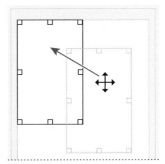

Dragging a placeholder to a new location in the Picture Package layout

6 In the Grid area of the Picture Package Edit Layout dialog box, select the Snap To option to display a grid to help you position the elements in the custom layout. Enter a value in the Size text box to change the appearance of the grid.

7 To add or delete a placeholder, do one of the following:

- Click Add Zone to add a placeholder to the layout.

- Select a placeholder and click Delete Zone to delete it from the layout.

8 To modify a placeholder, select a placeholder and do one of the following:

- Enter values in the Width and Height text boxes to resize a placeholder.

- Click and drag a handle to resize a placeholder. If you resize a rectangle placeholder with an image in it, Picture Package will snap the image within the vertical or horizontal placeholder, depending on the way the zone is being resized.

- Enter values in the X and Y text boxes to move a placeholder.

- Enter values in the Position and Size text boxes to position and size a placeholder.

- Click and drag a placeholder to the location you want in the layout.

9 Click Save.

Creating a PDF presentation

Creating a PDF presentation

The PDF Presentation command lets you use a variety of images to create a multipage document or slide show presentation. You can set options to maintain image quality in the PDF, specify security settings, and set the document to open automatically as a slide show.

PDF presentation as a slide show
*A. First slide **B.** Wipe Left transition **C.** Second slide*

To create a PDF presentation

1 Do one of the following:

- (Photoshop) Choose File > Automate > PDF Presentation.

- (Bridge) Select the images you want to use and Choose Tools > Photoshop > PDF Presentation. If you don't select the images you want to use, the presentation will contain all the images currently displayed in Bridge.

Note: *Click a file to select it. Shift-click to select a series of files. Ctrl-click (Windows) or Command-click (Mac OS) to select noncontiguous files.*

2 In the PDF Presentation dialog box, click Browse and navigate to add files to the PDF presentation. Select the Add Open Files option to add files already open in Photoshop.

You can remove any unwanted file by selecting it in the Source Files window and clicking the Remove button.

The files in the Source Files window are used to generate the pages in the PDF presentation, starting with the topmost file for the first page and progressing down the list for subsequent pages. To change the sequence, select the file and drag it to a new position Source Files window.

Note: If you want a file to appear more than once in your PDF presentation, select the file and click the Duplicate button. You can then drag the duplicate file to the desired location in the Source Files window.

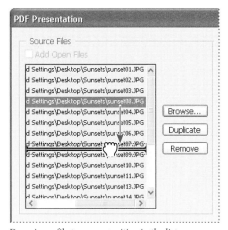

Dragging a file to a new position in the list

3 In the Output Options area of the PDF Presentation dialog box, select from the following options:

Multi-Page Document Creates a PDF document with the images on separate pages.

Presentation Creates a PDF slide show presentation.

4 If you selected Presentation as the Output Option, in the Presentation Options area, you can specify the following options:

Advance Every [5] Seconds Specifies how long each image is displayed before the presentation advances to the next image. The default duration is 5 seconds.

Loop After Last Page Specifies that the presentation automatically starts over after reaching the end. Deselect this option to stop the presentation after the final image is displayed.

Transition Specifies the transition when moving from one image to the next. Choose an transition from the Transition menu.

5 Click Save.

6 In the Save dialog box, enter a name for the PDF presentation, select a destination for the saved file, and then click Save.

7 In the Save Adobe PDF dialog box, choose an Adobe PDF preset or specify save options for the PDF document.

8 Click Save PDF. Photoshop closes the Save Adobe PDF dialog box and creates the PDF presentation. A dialog box appears telling you whether the PDF presentation was successfully created.

For information about file compression or saving a file in Photoshop PDF format, see Photoshop Help.

Placing Photoshop images in other applications

Placing Photoshop images in other applications

Photoshop provides a number of features to help you use images in other applications. Because of the tight integration between Adobe products, many Adobe applications can directly import Photoshop (PSD) format files and use Photoshop features like layers, layer styles, masks, transparency, and effects. Additionally, programs such as Adobe GoLive can use variables set in ImageReady and Photoshop (topmost text layer only) when creating multiple iterations of an image.

To prepare images for page-layout programs

How you prepare an image for a page-layout program depends upon the file formats the program recognizes:

- Adobe InDesign 2.0 and later can place Photoshop PSD files. You do not need to save or export your Photoshop image to a different file format. Transparent areas are displayed and printed as expected.

- Most other page-layout programs require you to save the image as a TIFF or EPS file. However, if the image contains fully transparent areas, you must first define those areas using a clipping path. Check the documentation for your page-layout program to determine the best format for importing Photoshop images.

If the page-layout program cannot place Photoshop PSD files, follow these steps:

1 If your image contains a transparent background or areas that you want to be transparent, create a clipping path around the opaque areas of the image. Even if you have deleted the background around the image, you must define the area with a clipping path before converting the file to TIFF or EPS format. Otherwise, areas that are transparent may appear as white in the page-layout program.

2 Choose File > Save As.

3 In the Save As dialog box, choose the appropriate format from the Format menu. The format you choose depends upon the final output for the document. For printing to non-PostScript printers, choose TIFF. For printing to PostScript printers, choose Photoshop EPS. Then click Save.

4 In the TIFF Options or EPS Options dialog box, set the following options. Leave any remaining options at their default setting, and click OK.

- TIFF Options dialog box: set Image Compression to None.

- EPS Options dialog box (Windows): set Preview to TIFF (8 bits/pixel) and Encoding to ASCII85.

- EPS Options dialog box (Mac OS): set Preview to Mac (8 bits/pixel) and Encoding to ASCII85.

If the layout program displays transparent areas as white, try printing the document. Some layout programs do not display clipping paths properly but print them as expected.

To use Photoshop artwork in Adobe Illustrator

Adobe Illustrator can both open or place Photoshop files; you do not need to save or export your Photoshop image to a different file format. If you place an image into an open Illustrator file, you can incorporate the image as if it were any other element in the artwork, or you can maintain a link to the original file. Although you can't edit a linked image within Illustrator, you can jump back to Photoshop, using the Edit Original command, to revise it. Once saved, any changes you make are reflected in the version in Illustrator.

1 If the image file is open in Photoshop, save it as a Photoshop (PSD) file, and close the file.

2 In Adobe Illustrator, do one of the following:

• To open the file directly in Illustrator, choose File > Open. Locate the image in the Open File dialog box, and click OK.

• To incorporate the image into an existing Illustrator file, choose File > Place. Locate the file in the Place dialog box, make sure the Link option is not selected, and click OK.

• To place the image into a file but maintain a link to the original, choose File > Place. In the Place dialog box, locate the file, select the Link option, and click OK. Illustrator centers the image in the open illustration. A red X through the image indicates it is linked and not editable.

3 If you opened or placed the image without linking, the Photoshop Import dialog box appears. Choose the appropriate option as follows, and click OK:

• Convert Photoshop Layers To Objects to convert the layers to Illustrator objects. This option

preserves masks, blending modes, transparency, and (optionally) slices and image maps. However, it does not support Photoshop adjustment layers and layer effects.

• Flatten Photoshop Layers To A Single Image to merge all the layers into a single layer. This option preserves the look of the image, but you can no longer edit individual layers.

Using image clipping paths to create transparency

You can use image clipping paths to define transparent areas in images you place in page-layout applications. In addition, Mac OS users can embed Photoshop images in many word-processor files.

For assistance with image clipping paths, choose Help > Export Transparent Image. This interactive wizard helps you prepare images with transparency for export to a page-layout application.

You may want to use only part of a Photoshop image when printing it or placing it in another application. For example, you may want to use a foreground object and exclude the background. An *image clipping path* lets you isolate the foreground object and make everything else transparent when the image is printed or placed in another application.

Image imported into Illustrator or InDesign without image clipping path (left), and with image clipping path (right)

To save a path as an image clipping path

1 Draw a work path that defines the area of the image you want to show.

Note: Paths are vector-based; therefore, they have hard edges. You cannot preserve the softness of a feathered edge, such as in a shadow, when creating an image clipping path.

2 In the Paths palette, save the work path as a path.

3 Choose Clipping Path from the Paths palette menu, set the following options, and click OK:

• For Path, choose the path you want to save.

• For Flatness, leave the flatness value blank to print the image using the printer's default value. If you experience printing errors, enter a flatness value to determine how the PostScript interpreter approximates the curve. The lower the flatness value, the greater the number of straight lines used to draw the curve and the more accurate the curve. Values can range from 0.2 to 100. In general, a flatness setting from 8 to 10 is recommended for high-resolution printing (1200 dpi to 2400 dpi), and a setting from 1 to 3 for low-resolution printing (300 dpi to 600 dpi).

4 If you plan to print the file using process colors, convert the file to CMYK mode.

5 Save the file by doing one of the following:

• To print the file using a PostScript printer, save in Photoshop EPS, DCS, or PDF format.

• To print the file using a non-PostScript printer, save in TIFF format and export to Adobe InDesign, or to Adobe PageMaker® 5.0 or later.

For more information, see 'To prepare images for page-layout programs' on page 371 and 'Converting an image to another mode' on page 174.

Printing image clipping paths

Sometimes an imagesetter cannot interpret image clipping paths, or an image clipping path is too complex for a printer, resulting in a Limitcheck error or a general PostScript error. Sometimes you can print a complex path on a low-resolution printer without difficulty but run into problems when printing the same path on a high-resolution printer. This is because the lower-resolution printer simplifies the path, using fewer line segments to describe curves than the high-resolution printer does.

You can simplify an image clipping path in the following ways:

• Manually reduce the number of anchor points on the path.

• Increase the tolerance setting used to create the path. To do this, load the existing path as a selection, choose Make Work Path from the Paths palette menu, and increase the tolerance setting (4 to 6 pixels is a good starting value). Then re-create the image clipping path.

To export paths to Adobe Illustrator

The Paths To Illustrator command lets you export Photoshop paths as Adobe Illustrator files. Exporting paths in this way simplifies the task of combining Photoshop and Illustrator artwork or using Photoshop features with Illustrator artwork. For example, you may want to export a pen tool path and stroke it to use as a trap with a Photoshop clipping path you are printing in Illustrator. You can also use this feature to align Illustrator text or objects with Photoshop paths.

1 Draw and save a path or convert an existing selection into a path.

2 Choose File > Export > Paths To Illustrator.

3 Choose a location for the exported path, and enter a file name. Make sure Work Path is chosen in the Write menu to export the path.

4 Click Save.

5 Open the file in Adobe Illustrator. You can manipulate the path or use the path to align Illustrator objects that you add to the file.

Note that the crop marks in Adobe Illustrator reflect the dimensions of the Photoshop image. The position of the path within the Photoshop image is maintained, provided you don't change the crop marks or move the path.

Object linking and embedding (OLE) (Windows only)

Photoshop is an OLE 2.0 server, which means it supports embedding or linking an image in an OLE container application (usually a word-processing or page-layout program). For example, you can insert Photoshop files and selections into other OLE applications such as Adobe PageMaker, Adobe FrameMaker, and Microsoft Word using copy and paste or other methods.

- Linking lets you place a link in the OLE container file that refers to the Photoshop file on the hard drive.

- Embedding lets you insert the Photoshop file into the OLE container file.

After the image is in the container application, you can double-click it for editing in Photoshop. When you close the image in Photoshop, it is updated in the container application.

To link or embed a selection or image in an OLE application

❖ Do one of the following:

- Copy a selection in Photoshop, and insert it in your OLE container application using the application's Paste Special command. Refer to your word-processing or page-layout application documentation for more instructions. Pasted selections can only be embedded, not linked.

- Use your OLE container application's Insert Object command to insert a new Photoshop image or existing Photoshop file as an OLE-embedded or OLE-linked object. Refer to your word-processing or page-layout application documentation for instructions.

To insert an unlinked screen-resolution bitmap into an OLE application

❖ With the Move tool ▶⊕ , drag a selection to the OLE container application. When you drop the object, it appears as a 72-ppi bitmap, which cannot be automatically updated in Photoshop.

To modify and update a linked or embedded image in an OLE application

1 Double-click the linked or embedded image in your word-processing or page-layout application to start Photoshop (if it is not already running), and open the image for editing.

2 Modify the image as desired.

3 Do one of the following:

• For embedded images, close the file, or choose File > Update or File > Close & Return to *[application name]*.

• For linked images, save and close the file.

Note: You can also modify linked files without first opening the container document. The linked image is updated the next time you open the document in its OLE container application.

Saving images for use in video and motion graphics

Saving images for use in video

In addition to supporting square pixel images, Photoshop supports nonsquare pixel images, allowing you to create documents that are displayed properly on devices such as video monitors. Use the preset file sizes in the Preset menu of the New file dialog box to create images at a size and pixel aspect ratio that compensates for scaling when the images are incorporated into video. The presets also create a document with nonprinting guides that delineate the action-safe and title-safe areas of the image. Using the preset file sizes, you can produce images for specific video systems—NTSC, PAL, or HDTV.

To help you create images for video, Photoshop has a Pixel Aspect Ratio Correction viewing mode that displays your image at a specific aspect ratio. For more accurate previews, Photoshop also has a Video Preview command that lets you immediately preview your document on a display device, such as a video monitor. To use this feature, you must have the device connected to your computer via FireWire. See also `To preview your document on a video monitor' on page 379.

When using a computer to create a document for video, keep in mind that an image on a computer monitor is made up of pixels that are essentially square. Video monitors display analog images, which do not not involve pixel shape. Nonsquare pixels are most commonly used by encoding devices for video. When importing an image created by a square-pixel graphics program into a video-editing program like Adobe Premiere, the square pixels are scaled to the nonsquare pixels for video encoding. This scaling results in a distorted image.

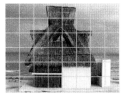

A

B

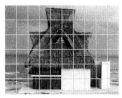

C

Pixel aspect ratio scaling
A. *Square pixel image viewed on a computer monitor* **B.** *Square pixel image viewed on a video monitor* **C.** *Same image with the correct pixel aspect ratio viewed on a video monitor*

Also keep these considerations in mind when creating images for use in video:

- Video-editing applications, such as Adobe Premiere, do not support 16-bits-per-channel images.

- Some video-editing applications can import an individual layer from a multilayer Photoshop (PSD) file.

- If your Photoshop image file has transparency, some video applications, such as Adobe Premiere, preserve it.

- If your file uses a layer mask or multiple layers, you might not have to flatten the layers, but you might want to include a flattened copy of the PSD file in the PSD format to maximize backward compatibility. In this way, you will be able to import your Photoshop file successfully into video-editing applications such as Adobe Premiere.

Photoshop provides actions that are useful for creating images for video. The actions automate tasks such as constraining the luminance range and saturation levels in an image to comply with broadcast standards, resizing and converting an image to nonsquare pixels for used in DVD slide shows (NTSC and PAL, standard and widescreen aspect ratios), creating an alpha channel from all currently visible layers, adjusting image areas that are likely to cause interlace flicker, and generating a title-safe overlay.

To create images for use in video

1 Create a new document.

2 In the New dialog box, choose the appropriate preset from the Preset menu for the video system on which the image will be shown.

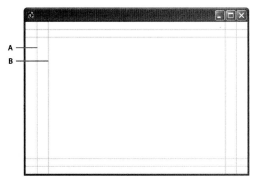

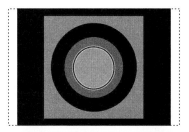

Video preset file size guides
A. *Action safe area (outer rectangle)* **B.** *Title safe area (inner rectangle)*

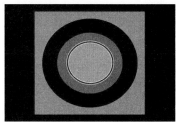

A circle in a NTSC DV 720 x 480 document viewed on a (square pixel) computer monitor with Pixel Aspect Ratio Correction turned on (top) and Pixel Aspect Ratio Correction turned off (bottom)

For more options, click the Advanced button ⌄ to specify a color profile and specific pixel aspect ratio.

Important: *By default, nonsquare pixel documents open with Pixel Aspect Ratio Correction enabled. This scales the image as it would look on the nonsquare-pixel output device (usually a video monitor).*

3 (Optional) Choose View > Pixel Aspect Ratio Correction to turn off the scaling correction and view the image as it displays on a computer (square pixel) monitor.

💡 *You can simultaneously view an image with the Pixel Aspect Ratio Correction turned on and turned off. With the nonsquare pixel image open and Pixel Aspect Ratio Correction enabled, choose Window > Arrange > New Window for [name of document]. With the new window active, choose View > Pixel Aspect Ratio Correction to turn the correction off.*

4 If you have a display device, such as a video monitor, connected to your computer via FireWire, do one of the following to preview your document on the device:

• To set output options before viewing your image on the device, choose File > Export > Video Preview.

• To view your image immediately on the device without setting any output options, choose File > Export > Send Video Preview To Device.

For more information, see 'To preview your document on a video monitor' on page 379.

To add images to a nonsquare pixel document

❖ Do one of the following:

• Copy and paste an image.

• Drag an image from another document window.

• Choose File > Place, select the file you want to place, and click the Place button.

Photoshop automatically converts and scales the image to the pixel aspect ratio of the nonsquare pixel document. Images brought in from Adobe Illustrator are also properly scaled.

For more information, see 'To create a new image' on page 136.

To assign a pixel aspect ratio value to an existing document

❖ With the square pixel document open, choose Image > Pixel Aspect Ratio and select a pixel aspect ratio.

To create a custom pixel aspect ratio

1 With a document open, choose Image > Pixel Aspect Ratio > Custom Pixel Aspect Ratio.

2 In the Save Pixel Aspect Ratio dialog box, enter a value in the Factor text box, name the custom pixel aspect ratio, and click OK.

The new custom pixel aspect ratio will appear in the both the Pixel Aspect Ratio menu of the New dialog box and in the Pixel Aspect Ratio submenu of the Image menu.

To delete a pixel aspect ratio

1 With a document open, choose Image > Pixel Aspect Ratio > Delete Pixel Aspect Ratio.

2 In the Delete Pixel Aspect Ratio dialog box, choose the option you want to delete from the Pixel Aspect Ratio menu and click Delete.

To reset the pixel aspect ratios

1 With a document open, choose Image > Pixel Aspect Ratio > Reset Pixel Aspect Ratios.

2 In the dialog box, choose one of the following:

Append Replaces the current pixel aspect ratios with the default values plus any custom pixel aspect ratios. This option is useful if you deleted a default value and want to restore it to the menu but also want to retain any custom values.

Cancel Cancels the command.

OK Replaces the current pixel aspect ratios with the default values. Custom pixel aspect ratios are discarded.

Saving images for use in motion graphics

You can save images in Photoshop for use in motion graphics software such as Adobe After Effects. A Photoshop (PSD) file can be imported directly into an After Effects project with the option of preserving individual layers, layer styles, transparent areas and layer masks, and adjustment layers. Importing layers makes it easy to prepare still images for animation.

You can reduce the rendering times and problems in After Effects by doing the following:

• Organize and name layers. If you change a layer name or delete a layer in a Photoshop document after you have imported it into After Effects, After Effects will not be able to find the renamed or deleted layer. The After Effects Project window lists that layer as missing.

• Make sure that each layer has a unique name, because After Effects manages layers by their names. Duplicate layer names can cause problems when you update footage.

• If you want to import a composited version of a layered Photoshop file along with a layered version, choose Always for Maximize PSD File Compatibility in the File Handling Preferences dialog box.

If you are creating a Photoshop file for export to After Effects for use in a video project, use one of the file size presets for video in the New File dialog box.

To preview your document on a video monitor

The Video Preview plug-in lets you preview your Photoshop document through FireWire on a display device, such as a video monitor. You can also adjust the aspect ratio for proper display of images. The Video Preview plug-in supports RGB, grayscale, and indexed images, either 8 or 16 bits per channel. (The plug-in converts 16-bits-per-channel images to 8-bits-per-channel images.) The Video Preview plug-in does not support alpha channels. Transparency is displayed as black.

Note: The Video Preview plug-in does not lock the display device. When Photoshop goes into the background on your computer and another application is brought into the foreground, the preview turns off and the device is unlocked so other applications can use it for preview purposes.

1 Connect a display device, such as a video monitor, to your computer via FireWire.

2 With a document open in Photoshop, do one of the following:

• If you don't want to set output options for viewing your document on a device, choose File > Export > Send Video Preview To Device. You can skip the rest of the steps in this procedure.

• To set output options before viewing your document on the device, choose File > Export > Video Preview.

The Video Preview dialog box opens. You see an alert if your document's pixel aspect ratio doesn't match the aspect ratio settings of the display device.

Note: The Send Video Preview To Device command uses the previous settings in the Video Preview dialog box.

3 Under Device Settings, specify options for the device that will display the image:

• (Mac OS only) To specify an output mode, select NTSC or PAL. If the output mode and the device do not match (for example, specifying NTSC for the output mode and connecting to a device in PAL mode), black patches appear on previewing.

- To specify the aspect ratio of the display device, choose either Standard (4:3) or Widescreen (16:9) from the Aspect Ratio menu.

Note: The Aspect Ratio setting determines which Placement options are available.

4 Under Image Options, choose a Placement Option to determine how the image appears in the display device:

Center Places the center of the image at the center of the screen, cropping the portions that fall outside the display edges of the video preview device.

Pillarbox Displays a 4:3 image on a 16:9 display with the center of the image at the center of the screen and gray bands on the left and right sides of the image. This option is available only if you chose Widescreen (16:9) for the device aspect ratio.

Crop to 4:3 Displays a 16:9 image on a 4:3 display with the center of the image at the center of the screen and without distortion by cropping the left and right edges of the frame that fall outside the display edges of the video preview device. This option is available only if you chose Standard (4:3) for the device aspect ratio.

Letterbox Scales a 16:9 image to fit on a 4:3 display. Gray bands appear on the top and bottom of the image due the difference in aspect ratio between the 16:9 image and the 4:3 display. This maintains the display aspect ratio without cropping or distorting the image. This option is available only if you chose Standard (4:3) for the device aspect ratio.

Crop To 14:9/Letterbox Displays a widescreen image cropped to a 14:9 aspect ratio with black bands on the top and bottom of the image. This maintains the display aspect ratio without distorting the image. This

option is available only if you chose Standard (4:3) for the device aspect ratio.

5 Choose an option from the Image Size menu to control whether the document pixels are scaled to the device display:

Do Not Scale Applies no vertical scaling to the image. The image is cropped if its height is greater than that of the video display.

Scale To Fit Within Frame Increases or decreases the image height and width proportionally to fit in the video frame. With this option, a 16:9 image appears on a 4:3 display as letterbox, and a 4:3 image appears on a 16:9 display as pillarbox.

6 Select the Apply Pixel Aspect Ratio To Preview check box to display the image using the document's (nonsquare) pixel aspect ratio. Deselect this option to display the image as it appears on your computer (square pixel) monitor.

By default, the Apply Pixel Aspect Ratio To Preview check box is selected to maintain the image's pixel aspect ratio. In general, you would deselect this option if the document's pixel aspect ratio is assumed to be square and you want to view the image as it would appear on a computer (square pixel) monitor.

7 Click OK to export the document to the device display.

Chapter 16: Printing

Printing from Photoshop

About printing

Printing is the process of sending your image to an output device. You can print on paper or film (positive or negative), to a printing plate, or directly to a digital printing press. Whether you are printing an image on your desktop printer or sending it to a prepress facility, knowing a few basics about printing makes the print job go more smoothly and helps ensure that the finished image appears as intended.

For information about preparing images for press, trapping, and printing duotones, see Photoshop Help.

Types of printing For many Photoshop users, printing a file means sending the image to an inkjet printer. Photoshop can send your image to a variety of devices to be printed directly onto paper or converted to a positive or negative image on film. In the latter case, you can use the film to create a master plate for printing by a mechanical press.

Types of images The simplest images, such as line art, use only one color in one level of gray. A more complex image, such as a photograph, has varying color tones. This type of image is known as a *continuous-tone image*.

Halftoning To create the illusion of continuous tones in images, printers break images down into dots. For photos printed on a printing press, this process is called *halftoning*. Varying the sizes of the dots in a halftone screen creates the optical illusion of variations of gray or continuous color in the image.

Note: Although inkjet printers also use dots to create the illusion of continuous tones, those dots are of uniform size and much smaller than the dots used by most printing presses.

Color separation Artwork intended for commercial reproduction and containing more than one color must be printed on separate master plates, one for each color. This process, called *color separation*, generally calls for the use of cyan, yellow, magenta, and black (CMYK) inks. In Photoshop, you can adjust how the various plates are generated.

Quality of detail The detail in a printed image depends on its resolution and screen frequency. The higher the resolution of an output device, the finer (higher) a screen ruling (lines per inch) you can use. Many inkjet printer drivers offer simplified print settings for higher quality printing.

About desktop printing

Unless you work in a commercial printing company or service bureau, you probably print images on a desktop printer, such as an inkjet, dye sublimation, or laser printer, and not to an imagesetter. Photoshop lets you control how your image is printed.

Monitors display images using light, whereas desktop printers reproduce images using inks, dyes, or pigments. For this reason, a desktop printer can't reproduce all the colors displayed on a monitor. However, by incorporating certain procedures (such as a color management system) into your workflow, you can achieve predictable results when printing your images on a desktop printer. Keep these considerations in mind when working with an image that you intend to print:

- If your image is in RGB mode, do not convert the document to CMYK mode when printing to a desktop printer. Work entirely in RGB mode. As a rule, desktop printers are configured to accept RGB data and use internal software to convert to CMYK. If you send CMYK data, most desktop printers apply a conversion anyway, with unpredictable results.

- If you want to preview an image as printed on any device for which you have a profile, use the Proof Colors command.

- To reproduce screen colors accurately on the printed page, you must incorporate color management into your workflow. Work with a monitor that is calibrated and characterized. You should also create a custom profile specifically for your printer and the paper you print on. Using the profile supplied with your printer (although better than using no profile at all) yields only mediocre results.

For more information, see 'Soft-proofing colors' on page 197 and 'About color profiles' on page 201.

Printing images

Photoshop provides the following printing commands:

Page Setup and Print Display options specific to your printer, printer drivers, and operating system.

Print With Preview Displays Photoshop's printing, output, and color management options.

Print Online Allows you to send your print file directly to an online service that will do the printing for you.

Print One Copy Prints one copy of a file without displaying a dialog box.

Note: You cannot print images directly from ImageReady. If you have an image open in ImageReady and need to print it, use the Edit In Photoshop command to open the image in Photoshop. Keep in mind that ImageReady images open at screen resolution (72 ppi); this resolution may not be high enough to produce a high-quality print.

To print an image with current options

❖ Do one of the following:

- Choose File > Print, and click Print or OK.

- To print one copy of a file without displaying a dialog box, choose File > Print One Copy.

Note: If you get a warning that your image is larger than the paper's printable area, click Cancel, choose File > Print With Preview, and select the Scale To Fit Media box. Click Page Setup to make any changes to your paper size and layout, and attempt to print the file again.

To set printer and page setup options

1 Choose File > Page Setup, or File > Print.

2 Select a printer from the pop-up menu.

3 Set additional options, such as paper size and layout, as desired. The available options depend on your printer, printer drivers, and operating system.

If you plan to scale the printed image, choose Print With Preview and use the scaling options in the Print dialog box rather than the Page Setup dialog box. The Print dialog box is more helpful because it shows you a preview of the scaled image. Also, you don't want to set the scaling options in both the Page Setup and Print dialog boxes. This applies scaling twice, and the resulting image may not be printed at the intended size.

To set Photoshop print options

1 Choose File > Print With Preview.

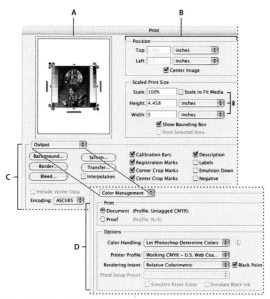

Print With Preview dialog box
*A. Preview print **B**. Position and scale image **C**. Specify options to prepare a file for prepress **D**. Specify the document's working space and choose a color management profile for printing on a desktop printer*

2 Make sure that More Options is selected (if it is, the Fewer Options button is displayed). Then do one or more of the following:

- Adjust the position and scale of the image in relation to the selected paper size and orientation.

- Set Output and Color Management options from the pop-up menu.

3 Do one of the following:

- Click Print to print the image.

- Click Cancel to close the dialog box without saving the options.

- Click Done to preserve the options and close the dialog box.

- Hold down Alt (Windows) or Option (Mac OS) and click Print One to print one copy of the image.

- Hold down Alt (Windows) or Option (Mac OS) and click Reset to reset the print options.

- Hold down Alt (Windows) or Option (Mac OS) and click Remember to save the print options without closing the dialog box.

Note: If you get a warning that your image is larger than the paper's printable area, click Cancel, choose File > Print With Preview, and select the Scale To Fit Media box. Click Page Setup to make any changes to your paper size and layout, and attempt to print the file again.

To preview the current image position and options

- Position the pointer over the file information box (at the bottom of the application window in Windows or the document window in Mac OS) and hold down the mouse button.

Positioning and scaling images

You can adjust the position and scale of an image and preview how the image will be printed on the selected paper using the Print With Preview command. The shaded border at the edge of the paper represents the margins of the selected paper; the printable area is white.

The base output size of an image is determined by the document size settings in the Image Size dialog box. Scaling an image in the Print With Preview dialog box changes the size and resolution of the printed image only. For example, if you scale a 72-ppi image to 50% in the Print With Preview dialog box, the image will print at 144 ppi; however, the document size settings in the Image Size dialog box will not change.

Many printer drivers, such as AdobePS and LaserWriter, provide a scaling option in the Page Setup dialog box. This scaling affects everything on the page, including the size of all page marks such as crop marks and captions, whereas the scaling percentage provided by the Print With Preview command affects only the size of the printed image (and not the size of page marks).

Note: The Print With Preview command may not reflect accurate values for Scale, Height, and Width if you set a scaling percentage in the Page Setup dialog box. To avoid inaccurate scaling, specify scaling using the Print With Preview command rather than the Page Setup command; do not enter a scaling percentage in both dialog boxes.

For more information, see`Adjusting image size and resolution' on page 129.

To reposition an image on the paper

1 Choose File > Print With Preview, and do one of the following:

- Select Center Image to center the image in the printable area.

- Deselect Center Image and then enter values for Top and Left to position the image numerically.

- Deselect Center Image, and drag the image in the preview area.

To scale the print size of an image

1 Choose File > Print With Preview, and do one of the following:

- Click Scale To Fit Media to fit the image within the printable area of the selected paper.

- With Scale To Fit Media deselected, enter values for Height and Width to rescale the image numerically.

- Select Show Bounding Box, and drag a bounding box handle in the preview area to achieve the desired scale.

To print part of an image

1 Use the Rectangle Marquee tool to select the part of an image you want to print.

2 Choose File > Print With Preview, select Print Selected Area, and click Print.

Note: If you get a warning that your image is larger than the paper's printable area, click Cancel, choose File > Print With Preview, and select the Scale To Fit Media box. Click Page Setup to make any changes to your paper size and layout, and attempt to print the file again.

To print vector data

If an image includes vector graphics, such as shapes and type, Photoshop can send the vector data to a PostScript printer. When you choose to include vector data, Photoshop sends the printer a separate image for each type layer and each vector shape layer. These additional images are printed on top of the base image, and clipped using their vector outline. Consequently, the edges of vector graphics print at the printer's full resolution, even though the content of each layer is limited to the resolution of your image file.

1 Choose File > Print With Preview.

2 Make sure that More Options is selected (if it is, Fewer Options is displayed), and choose Output from the pop-up menu.

3 Select the Include Vector Data option. If necessary, you can select an encoding algorithm (ASCII, ASCII85, Binary, or JPEG) from the Encoding pop-up menu. This allows you to choose the way the data is saved and how much disk space it requires. If Include Vector Data is dimmed, your image doesn't contain vector data.

4 Click Print.

Note: If you get a warning that your image is larger than the paper's printable area, click Cancel, choose File > Print With Preview, and select the Scale To Fit Media box. Click Page Setup to make any changes to your paper size and layout, and attempt to print the file again.

Printing with color management

To have your printer manage colors when printing

If you don't have a custom profile for your printer and paper type, you can let the printer driver handle the color conversion. See `Letting the printer determine colors when printing' on page 200.

1 Choose File > Print With Preview.

2 Make sure that More Options is selected (if it is, the Fewer Options button is displayed), and that Color Management is selected in the pop-up menu.

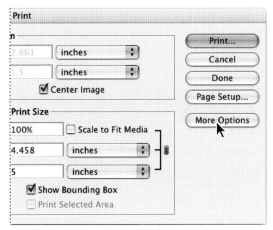

Click the More Options button to display options for prepress and color management

3 In the Print area, select Document. The profile is displayed in parentheses on the same line.

4 In the Options area, for Color Handling, choose Let Printer Determine Colors.

5 (Optional) Choose a rendering intent for converting colors to the destination color space. Most non-PostScript printer drivers ignore this option and use the Perceptual rendering intent. (For more information, see `About rendering intents' on page 210.)

6 Access the color management options for the printer driver from the second print dialog box, which automatically appears after you click Print. In Windows, click the Properties button to access the printer driver options. In Mac OS, use the pop-up menu from the second Print dialog box to access the printer driver options.

For inkjet printer drivers, color management options are usually labeled ColorSync (Mac OS) or ICM (Windows).

7 Specify the color management settings to let your printer driver handle the color management during printing.

Every printer driver has different color management options. If it's not clear how to turn on color management, consult your printer documentation.

8 Click Print.

Note: If you get a warning that your image is larger than the paper's printable area, click Cancel, choose File > Print With Preview, and select the Scale To Fit Media box. Click Page Setup to make any changes to your paper size and layout, and attempt to print the file again.

For more information, see `Printing with color management' on page 199.

To have Photoshop manage colors when printing

If you have a custom color profile for a specific printer, ink, and paper combination, letting Photoshop manage colors may produce better results than letting the printer manage colors. See `Letting the application determine colors when printing' on page 200.

1 Choose File > Print With Preview.

2 Make sure that More Options is selected (if it is, the Fewer Options button is displayed) and that Color Management is selected in the pop-up menu.

3 In the Options area, for Color Handling, choose Let Photoshop Determine Colors.

4 For Printer Profile, select the profile for your output device.

The more accurately the profile describes the behavior of the output device and printing conditions (such as paper type), the more accurately the color management system can translate the numeric values of the actual colors in a document. (See `Obtaining custom profiles for desktop printers' on page 200.)

5 (Optional) Set any of the following options. In most cases, it is best to use the default settings.

Rendering Intent Specifies how Photoshop converts colors to the destination color space. (See `About rendering intents' on page 210.)

Black Point Compensation Preserves the shadow detail in the image by simulating the full dynamic range of the output device.

6 Access the color management options for the printer driver from the second print dialog box, which automatically appears after you click Print. In Windows, click the Properties button to access the printer driver options. In Mac OS, use the pop-up menu from the second Print dialog box to access the printer driver options.

💡 *For inkjet printer drivers, color management options are usually labeled ColorSync (Mac OS) or ICM (Windows).*

7 Turn off color management for the printer so that the printer profile settings don't override your profile settings.

Every printer driver has different color management options. If it's not clear how to turn off color management, consult your printer documentation.

8 Click Print.

Note: If you get a warning that your image is larger than the paper's printable area, click Cancel, choose File > Print With Preview, and select the Scale To Fit Media box. Click Page Setup to make any changes to your paper size and layout, and attempt to print the file again.

For more information, see 'Printing with color management' on page 199.

To print a hard proof

A *hard proof* (sometimes called a *proof print* or *match print*) is a printed simulation of what your final output on a printing press will look like. A hard proof is produced on an output device that's less expensive than a printing press. Some inkjet printers have the resolution necessary to produce inexpensive prints that can be used as hard proofs.

1 Choose View > Proof Setup, and select the output conditions you want to simulate. You can do this using a preset or by creating a custom proof setup. (See 'To soft-proof colors' on page 197.)

The view changes automatically according to the proof you chose, unless you chose Custom. In this case, the Customize Proof Condition dialog box appears. You must save custom proof settings for them to appear in the Proof Setup Preset menu of the Print With Preview dialog box. Follow the instructions to customize a proof.

2 After you select a proof, choose File > Print With Preview.

3 Make sure that More Options is selected (if it is, the Fewer Options button is displayed) and that Color Management is selected in the pop-up menu.

4 In the Print area, select Proof. The profile that appears in parentheses, should match the proof setup you selected earlier.

5 In the Options area, for Color Handling, choose Let Photoshop Determine Colors.

6 For Printer Profile, select the profile for your output device.

7 (Optional) Set any of the following options. In most cases, it is best to use the default settings.

Rendering Intent Specifies how Photoshop converts colors to the destination color space. When printing a hard proof, you should choose either Absolute Colorimetric or Relative Colorimetric. (See 'About rendering intents' on page 210.)

Proof Setup Preset This option is available if you select Proof from the Print area. From the pop-up menu, choose any customized proofs that exist locally on your hard drive.

Simulate Paper Color Simulates what colors look like on the paper of the simulated device. Using this option produces the most accurate proof, but it is not available for all profiles.

Simulate Black Ink Simulates the brightness of dark colors of the simulated device. Using this option results in more accurate proofs of dark colors, but it is not available for all profiles.

8 Access the color management options for the printer driver from the second print dialog box, which automatically appears after you click Print. In Windows, click the Properties button to access the printer driver options. In Mac OS, use the pop-up menu from the second Print dialog box to access the printer driver options.

Ω *For inkjet printer drivers, color management options are usually labeled ColorSync (Mac OS) or ICM (Windows).*

9 Turn off color management for the printer so that the printer profile settings don't override your profile settings.

Every printer driver has different color management options. If it's not clear how to turn off color management, consult your printer documentation.

10 Click Print.

Note: If you get a warning that your image is larger than the paper's printable area, click Cancel, choose File > Print With Preview, and select the Scale To Fit Media box. Click Page Setup to make any changes to your paper size and layout, and attempt to print the file again.

To print targets for creating custom profiles

A *target* is a document you use when creating a custom profile. Generally, a target document with swatches is supplied as part of a third-party color management software package. You print this document with all color management turned off in both Photoshop and the printer driver. The third-party measuring instrument reads or scans the printed target to create the custom profile.

1 Open the color target document in Photoshop.

2 Choose File > Print With Preview.

3 Make sure that More Options is selected (if it is, the Fewer Options button is displayed) and that Color Management is selected in the pop-up menu that appears below.

4 In the Print area, select Document. The profile is displayed in parentheses on the same line.

5 In the Options area, from the Color Handling pop-up menu, choose No Color Management. When this option is selected, Photoshop sends the RGB numbers in the file to the printer without conversion.

6 Access the color management options for the printer driver from the second print dialog box, which automatically appears after you click Print. In Windows, click the Properties button to access the printer driver options. In Mac OS, use the pop-up menu from the second Print dialog box to access the printer driver options.

Ω *For inkjet printer drivers, color management options are usually labeled ColorSync (Mac OS) or ICM (Windows).*

7 Turn off color management for the printer so that the printer profile settings don't override your profile settings.

Every printer driver has different color management options. If it's not clear how to turn off color management, consult your printer documentation.

8 Click Print.

Note: *If you get a warning that your image is larger than the paper's printable area, click Cancel, choose File > Print With Preview, and select the Scale To Fit Media box. Click Page Setup to make any changes to your paper size and layout, and attempt to print the file again.*

Index